FIFTH EDITION

Focus on Grammar 5

Jay Maurer

Focus on Grammar 5: An Integrated Skills Approach, Fifth Edition

Pearson Education, 221 River Street, Hoboken, NJ 07030

Staff credits: The people who made up the *Focus on Grammar 5, Fifth Edition* team, representing content creation, design, manufacturing, marketing, multimedia, project management, publishing, rights management, and testing, are Pietro Alongi, Rhea Banker, Elizabeth Barker, Stephanie Bullard, Jennifer Castro, Tracey Cataldo, Aerin Csigay, Mindy DePalma, Dave Dickey, Warren Fischbach, Pam Fishman, Nancy Flaggman, Lester Holmes, Gosia Jaros-White, Leslie Johnson, Barry Katzen, Amy McCormick, Julie Molnar, Brian Panker, Stuart Radcliffe, Jennifer Raspiller, Lindsay Richman, Robert Ruvo, Alexandra Suarez, Paula Van Ells, and Joseph Vella.

Text design and layout: Don Williams
Composition: Page Designs International
Project supervision: Bernard Seal
Contributing editors: Julie Schmidt and Bernard Seal

Cover image: Andy Roberts / Getty Images

Library of Congress Cataloging-in-Publication Data

A catalog record for the print edition is available from the Library of Congress.

Printed in the United States of America

ISBN 10: 0-13-413339-0
ISBN 13: 978-0-13-413339-3

12 2019

Contents

Contents (continued)

WELCOME TO
FOCUS ON GRAMMAR
FIFTH EDITION

BUILDING ON THE SUCCESS of previous editions, *Focus on Grammar* continues to provide an integrated-skills approach to engage students and help them understand, practice, and use English grammar. Centered on thematic instruction, *Focus on Grammar* combines comprehensive grammar coverage with abundant practice, critical thinking skills, and ongoing assessment, helping students accomplish their goals of communicating confidently, accurately, and fluently in everyday situations.

New in the Fifth Edition

New and Updated Content

Focus on Grammar continues to offer engaging and motivating content that appeals to learners from various cultural backgrounds. Many readings and activities have been replaced or updated to include topics that are of high interest to today's learners.

Updated Charts and Redesigned Notes

Clear, corpus-informed grammar presentations reflect real and natural language usage and allow students to grasp the most important aspects of the grammar. Clear signposting draws attention to common usage, the difference between written and spoken registers, and common errors.

Additional Communicative Activities

The new edition of *Focus on Grammar* has been expanded with additional communicative activities that encourage collaboration and the application of the target grammar in a variety of settings.

Expanded Writing Practice

Each unit in *Focus on Grammar* now ends with a structured "From Grammar to Writing" section. Supported by pre-writing and editing tasks, students engage in activities that allow them to apply the target grammar in writing.

New Assessment Program

The new edition of *Focus on Grammar* features a variety of new assessment tools, including course diagnostic tests, formative and summative assessments, and a flexible gradebook. The assessments are closely aligned with unit learning outcomes to inform instruction and measure student progress.

Revised MyEnglishLab

The updated MyEnglishLab offers students engaging practice and video grammar presentations anywhere, anytime. Immediate feedback and remediation tasks offer additional opportunities for successful mastery of content and help promote accuracy. Instructors receive instant access to digital content and diagnostic tools that allow them to customize the learning environment to meet the needs of their students.

The *Focus on Grammar* Approach

At the heart of the *Focus on Grammar* series is its unique and successful four-step approach that lets learners move from comprehension to communication within a clear and consistent structure. The books provide an abundance of scaffolded exercises to bridge the gap between identifying grammatical structures and using them with confidence and accuracy. The integration of the four skills allows students to learn grammar holistically, which in turn prepares them to understand and use English more effectively.

STEP 1: Grammar in Context integrates grammar and vocabulary in natural contexts such as articles, stories, dialogues, and blog posts. Students engage with the unit reading and theme and get exposure to grammar as it is used in real life.

STEP 2: Grammar Presentation presents the structures in clear and accessible grammar charts and notes with multiple examples of form and meaning. Corpus-informed explanations and examples reflect natural usage of the target forms, differentiate between written and conversational registers whenever appropriate, and highlight common errors to help students avoid typical pitfalls in both speaking and writing.

STEP 3: Focused Practice provides numerous and varied contextualized exercises for both the form and meaning of the new structures. Controlled practice ensures students' understanding of the target grammar and leads to mastery of form, meaning, and use.

STEP 4: Communication Practice provides practice with the structures in listening exercises as well as in communicative, open-ended speaking activities. These engaging activities provide ample opportunities for personalization and build students' confidence in using English. Students also develop their critical thinking skills through problem-solving activities and discussions.

Each unit now culminates with the **From Grammar to Writing** section. Students learn about common errors in writing and how to recognize them in their own work. Engaging and motivating writing activities encourage students to apply grammar in writing through structured tasks from pre-writing to editing.

Recycling

Underpinning the scope and sequence of the *Focus on Grammar* series is practice that allows students to use target structures and vocabulary many times, in different contexts. New grammar and vocabulary are recycled throughout the book. Students have maximum exposure, leading them to become confident in using the language in speech and in writing.

Assessment

Extensive testing informs instruction and allows teachers and students to measure progress.

- **Unit Reviews** at the end of every unit assess students' understanding of the grammar and allow students to monitor their own progress.

- **Diagnostic Tests** provide teachers with a valid and reliable means to determine how well students know the material they are going to study and to target instruction based on students' needs.

- **Unit Review Tests, Mid- and End-of-Term Review Tests, and Final Exams** measure students' ability to demonstrate mastery of skills taught in the course.

- The **Placement Test** is designed to help teachers place students into one of the five levels of the *Focus on Grammar* course.

The Importance of Context

A key element of *Focus on Grammar* is presenting important grammatical structures in context. The contexts selected are most relevant to the grammatical forms being introduced. Contextualized grammar practice also plays a key role in improving fluent use of grammar in communicative contexts. It helps learners to develop consistent and correct usage of target structures during all productive practice.

The Role of Corpus

The most important goal of *Focus on Grammar* has always been to present grammar structures using natural language. To that end, *Focus on Grammar* has incorporated the findings of corpus linguistics,* while never losing sight of what is pedagogically sound and useful. By taking this approach, *Focus on Grammar* ensures that:

- the language presented reflects real, natural usage
- themes and topics provide a good fit with the grammar point and elicit the target grammar naturally
- findings of the corpus research are reflected in the syllabus, readings, charts, grammar notes, and practice activities
- examples illustrate differences between spoken and written registers, and formal and informal language
- students are exposed to common errors in usage and learn how to recognize and avoid errors in their own speech and writing

Focus on Grammar Efficacy

The fifth edition of *Focus on Grammar* reflects an important efficacy initiative for Pearson courses—to be able to demonstrate that all teaching materials have a positive impact on student learning. To support this, *Focus on Grammar* has been updated and aligned to the **Global Scale of English** and the **Common European Framework** (CEFR) to provide granular insight into the objectives of the course, the progression of learning, and the expected outcomes a learner will be able to demonstrate upon successful completion.

To learn more about the Global Scale of English, visit www.English.com.

Components

Student Books with Essential Online Resources include access codes to the course audio, video, and self-assessment.

Student Books with MyEnglishLab offer a blended approach with integration of print and online content.

Workbooks contain additional contextualized practice in print format.

Digital Teacher's Resources include printable teaching notes, GSE mapping documents, answer keys, audio scripts, and downloadable tests. Access to the digital copy of the student books allows teachers to project the pages for whole-class instruction.

FOG Go app allows users to access the student book audio on their mobile devices.

---

* A principal resource has been Douglas Biber et al, *Longman Grammar of Spoken and Written English*, Harlow: Pearson Education Ltd., 1999.

The *Focus on Grammar* Unit

Focus on Grammar introduces grammar structures in the context of unified themes. All units follow a four-step approach, taking learners from grammar in context to communicative practice. Thematic units add a layer to learning so that by the end of the unit students will be able to discuss the content using the grammar points they have just studied.

STEP 1   GRAMMAR IN CONTEXT

Before You Read activities create interest and elicit students' knowledge about the topic.

Vocabulary exercises help students improve their command of English.

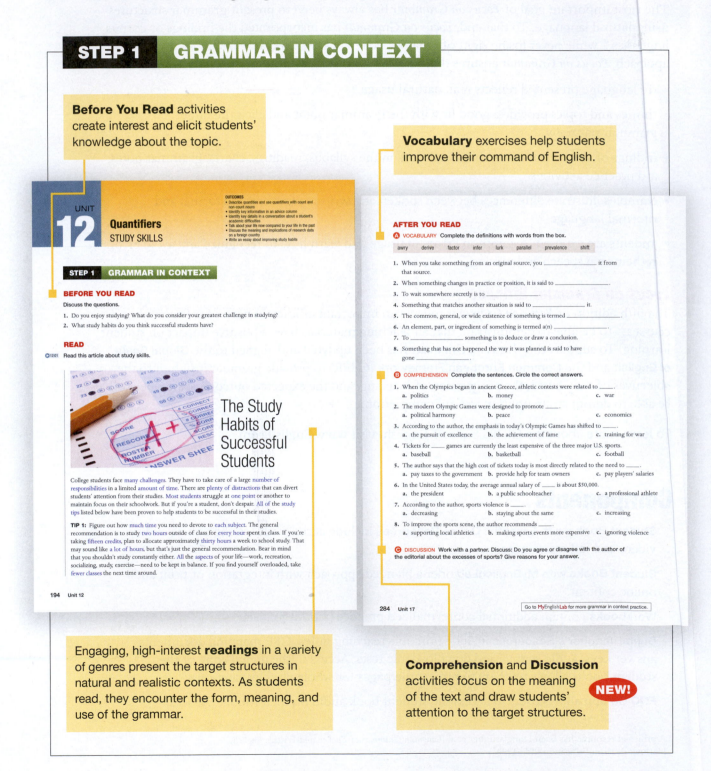

Engaging, high-interest **readings** in a variety of genres present the target structures in natural and realistic contexts. As students read, they encounter the form, meaning, and use of the grammar.

Comprehension and **Discussion** activities focus on the meaning of the text and draw students' attention to the target structures.

NEW!

Grammar Charts present the structures in a clear, easy-to-read format.

NEW!

The newly designed **Grammar Notes** highlight the main point of each note, making navigation and review easier. Simple corpus-informed **explanations** and **examples** ensure students' understanding.

STEP 2   GRAMMAR PRESENTATION

INFINITIVES

Infinitive as Subject

Infinitive (Subject)	Verb	Object
To procrastinate	causes	a lot of problems.
Not to go ahead	proved	a mistake.

Infinitive as Object

Subject	Verb	Infinitive (Object)
Not everyone	wants	to procrastinate.
He	decided	not to go ahead.

Infinitive as Subject Complement

Subject	Verb	Infinitive (Subject Complement)
His job	is	to motivate people.
Their real intention	is	not to succeed.

It + Be + Adjective + Infinitive

It	Be	Adjective	(For / Of + Noun / Pronoun)	Infinitive
It	is	foolish	(for Alice / her)	to procrastinate.
It	was	wrong	(of Hal / him)	not to go ahead.

Verbs Followed by Infinitives

	Verb	(Noun / Pronoun)	Infinitive
They	decided	Ø*	
	convinced	Steve / him	to call.
	expected	(Steve / him)	

* Ø = When *decide* is used with an infinitive, it cannot be followed by a noun or object pronoun.

Adjectives Followed by Infinitives

	Adjective	Infinitive	
Hal is	reluctant	to complete	his work on time.
He's	careful	not to make	mistakes.
They're	happy	to hear	the test has been postponed.

Nouns Followed by Infinitives

	Noun	Infinitive	
He can always think of	reasons	to put off	studying.
It seems like	the thing	to do.	
She always shows	reluctance	to finish	a job.

Infinitives   **143**

GRAMMAR NOTES

1 Passive Voice vs. Active Voice

A sentence in the passive voice has a corresponding sentence in the active voice. In an **active** sentence, the **subject** acts upon the **object** of the sentence. In a **passive** sentence, the **subject** is acted upon by the agent.

- active

  SUBJECT   OBJECT
  The police **catch** *some criminals*.

- passive

  SUBJECT   AGENT
  Some criminals **are caught** by the police.

The **subject** of the active sentence **becomes the agent** (preceded by the preposition *by*) in the passive sentence, or disappears.

AGENT
Some criminals are caught **by the police**.
Some criminals are caught.

Transitive verbs are followed by an **object**. **Intransitive** verbs are not followed by an object. Many verbs can be used both transitively and intransitively.

They **returned** *the clothes* to the store. *(transitive)*
They **returned** home late in the evening. *(intransitive)*

BE CAREFUL! Only **transitive** verbs can be made **passive**. **Intransitive** verbs **cannot** be made passive.

Several people **died** in the accident.
NOT Several people ~~were~~ died in the accident.

2 Forms of the Passive

To form **passive** sentences, use *be* + past participle or *get* + past participle. They occur in **present**, **past**, and **future** forms, as well as in the **progressive**.

- **present**

  Police officers **are** well **trained**. They **get tested** on the job almost daily.

- **past**

  The suspect **was arrested** yesterday. He **got caught** committing a crime.

- **future**

  He **will be held** in the local jail. He'll **get charged** soon.

To make a **negative** passive sentence, place *not* after the first verb.

Cooper **has** *not* **been caught**.
The man **did** *not* **get killed** in the robbery.

To form **progressive** passive sentences, use *being* + past participle.

The prisoner **is** currently **being questioned**.
The suspect **is being held** in prison.

USAGE NOTE Use the **present progressive** and **past progressive** passives to describe actions **in progress** (= not finished) at a certain time.

The robbery occurred while the money **was being taken** to a bank.

90   Unit 6

NEW!

Clear signposting provides corpus-informed notes about common usage, differences between spoken and written registers, and common errors.

Pronunciation Notes are now included with the grammar presentation to highlight relevant pronunciation aspects of the target structures and to help students understand authentic spoken English.

NEW!

PRONUNCIATION NOTE

Reducing *of* in Quantifiers

Quantifiers containing the preposition *of* are often reduced in rapid speech and in conversation. The word *of* is often reduced to "a." This reduction often happens when the word following *of* begins with a consonant. When the word following *of* begins with a vowel, full forms are generally used.

a couple of	→	"a couple a"	We met **"a couple a"** new people at the party.
a lot of	→	"a lotta"	I had **"a lotta"** work to do tonight.
lots of	→	"lotsa"	There are **"lotsa"** great movies playing.
plenty of	→	"plentya"	There's **"plentya"** time to get there.
a number of	→	"a numbera"	I had **"a numbera"** problems with the homework.
amount of	→	"amounta"	The **"amounta"** traffic today was incredible.
a bit of	→	"a bitta"	He had **"a bitta"** trouble hearing the lecture.
most of	→	"mosta"	I was able to solve **"mosta"** the problems.

IN WRITING The forms *couple a, lotta, lotsa, plentya, a numbera, amounta, bitta,* and *mosta* are **not used** in writing.

We have **a lot** of work left to do.
There's **plenty** of food for everyone.
We had **lots** of fun at the amusement park.
The **amount** of money she earns is amazing.

The *Focus on Grammar* Unit   **ix**

STEP 3   FOCUSED PRACTICE

Discover the Grammar activities develop students' recognition and understanding of the target structures before they are asked to produce them.

Controlled practice activities lead students to master form, meaning, and use of the target grammar.

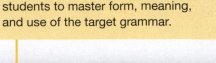

STEP 3   FOCUSED PRACTICE

EXERCISE 1   DISCOVER THE GRAMMAR

A | GRAMMAR NOTES 1–6   Read the sentences based on the reading. Underline the verbs showing future time and label the ways they show future time.

1. So you're visiting some new countries this year?   _present progressive_
2. You leave in exactly four weeks.
3. A month from now, you'll be relaxing in the sunshine.
4. I'm going to give you suggestions in five areas.
5. The suggestions will help you with your trip.
6. You'll have been flying for eight to ten hours.
7. When you land, it will probably be late morning.
8. By then, you'll have acquired nice memories.

B | GRAMMAR NOTES 1, 3–4, 6   Look at the underlined verbs in the sentences based on the reading. Check (✓) *Present Time* or *Future Time*.

	Present Time	Future Time
1. So you're <u>visiting</u> some new countries this year?	☐	☑
2. You already <u>have</u> your tickets.	☐	☐
3. You <u>leave</u> in exactly four weeks.	☐	☐
4. When you <u>land</u>, it will probably be late morning.	☐	☐
5. You can get package deals that <u>include</u> accommodations.	☐	☐
6. Airbnb <u>links</u> owners with renters.	☐	☐
7. Find out about the countries where you're <u>going</u>.	☐	☐
8. You'll have learned a lot by the time you <u>arrive</u>.	☐	☐
9. Put yourself in the shoes of the people who <u>live</u> there.	☐	☐
10. So there you <u>have</u> it.	☐	☐

40   Unit 3

EXERCISE 2   SENTENCE ADVERBS

GRAMMAR NOTE 1   Combine each pair of statements into one statement containing a sentence adverb. Use the adverb form of the word in parentheses. Vary your sentences so that the sentence adverb appears in different positions in the sentences: beginning, middle, and end.

1. National service is beneficial. (obvious)
   National service is obviously beneficial.
2. Military service can be dangerous. (unfortunate)
3. I'm against the death penalty because I consider it cruel. (essential)
4. There's a lot more violence in movies than in the past. (certain)
5. Nuclear weapons can be eliminated. (hopeful)
6. A vaccine against AIDS can be developed. (possible)
7. The prime minister's position is wrong. (clear)

EXERCISE 3   FOCUS ADVERBS

GRAMMAR NOTE 2   Complete the sentences. Circle the correct answers.

1. Bill believes that women should not fight. He feels _____ in noncombat roles.
   (a.) they should only serve   b. only they should serve
2. Carrie thinks women can do most jobs men can do, but she feels _____ in combat.
   a. men should serve only   b. only men should serve
3. Samantha is against gambling, but _____ the benefits of lotteries.
   a. even she can recognize   b. she can even recognize
4. I'm in favor of higher taxes. _____ taxing food and medicine.
   a. Even I'm in favor of   b. I'm even in favor of
5. My husband has some good reasons for supporting nuclear power. However, I _____.
   a. don't just agree   b. just don't agree
6. My father _____ the military draft; he's a military recruiter.
   a. doesn't just support   b. just doesn't support
7. My friend and I _____ $100 for the tickets, but the concert was worth the money.
   a. almost paid   b. paid almost

Adverbs: Sentence, Focus, and Negative   **273**

A variety of exercise types engage students and guide them from recognition and understanding to accurate production of the grammar structures.

Editing exercises allow students to identify and correct typical mistakes.

EXERCISE 7   EDITING

GRAMMAR NOTES 1–5   Read the email from Elena Gutierrez to her sister Rosa in Colombia. There are eight mistakes in the use of adjective clauses and phrases. The first mistake is already corrected. Find and correct seven more. Delete verbs, change pronouns, or add words where necessary. Do not change punctuation.

TO: Rosa111@yoohoo.com
FROM: ElenaGut@gomail.com
RE: Life in L.A.

Hi Rosa,

I'm writing this in English because I think we both need the practice. How are you doing? Please say "hi" to everyone back there, ~~included~~ *including* all our friends in the neighborhood.

I'm still having a hard time here in Los Angeles, but things are a little better than they were. I'm not quite as lonely as before because I've met some people in my neighborhood, many of which are friendly, but so far I don't know anyone really well. I do have some friends who from my classes at the university, most whom are very interesting. I'm looking forward to getting to know them better as time goes on. The hardest thing is the food, most of it I just don't like very much. It's difficult to find quality food that's not too expensive.

I did do one really fun thing recently. One of my friends from school and I went to Universal

Listenings in a variety of genres allow students to hear the grammar in natural contexts.

EXERCISE 9
LISTENING

A Listen to the radio call-in show. Overall, what does the caller think about human nature?

_____

_____

B Read each statement. Then listen to the talk show again. Check (✓) *True* or *False*.

	True	False
1. Capital punishment is used in every state in the United States.	☐	☑
2. The host of the radio show says that there clearly seems to be a worldwide movement to abolish capital punishment.	☐	☐
3. The caller is in favor of capital punishment, overall.	☐	☐
4. Capital punishment is apparently used in China.	☐	☐
5. Generally, the caller feels that people have gotten more civilized.	☐	☐
6. The caller believes that robbery is clearly a capital crime.	☐	☐
7. According to the caller, rehabilitation is clearly impossible for all criminals.	☐	☐
8. The caller hopes that the death penalty will not be abolished worldwide.	☐	☐

C Work with a partner. Discuss the questions. Give reasons for your answers.

1. Do you basically agree or disagree with the viewpoint of the caller in the Listening?
2. Do you believe that, overall, people have become more or less civilized than they were in ancient times?
3. Do you believe that, generally, criminals are capable of rehabilitation?

EXERCISE 10 **HOW DO YOU FEEL ABOUT . . . ?**

A SURVEY Work in a group. Ask your classmates for their opinions on the controversial issues in the chart on page 279. Then add up your group's responses, noting the number of students supporting and opposing each viewpoint.

EXAMPLE: A: How do you feel about making all schools coeducational?
  B: I'm absolutely in favor of it. Boys and girls should go to school together.
  C: I'm against it, overall. Coeducational schools are fine, generally, but some students do better in single-sex schools.

278 Unit 16

Engaging **communicative activities** (conversations, discussions, presentations, surveys, and games) help students synthesize the grammar, develop fluency, and build their problem-solving skills.

EXERCISE 10 **THE NOUN GAME**

A GAME Divide into two teams. First, work with your own team. Look at the words in the word box. Match them with their definitions in the chart.

advice	a space	baldness	fast food	people	talk	work
a criterion	a talk	cancer	film	rice	the police	
a film	a tan	cholesterol	lightning	space	thunder	
a people	a work	criteria	news	sunblock	traffic	

a. an art form that involves moving pictures on a screen	f. a brownish color that the sun gives to the skin	k. a cream used on the skin to protect it from burning by the sun	p. a sudden electrical discharge in the atmosphere	u. a movie
b. *advice* an opinion about what could or should be done about a situation	g. movement of people or vehicles along routes of transportation	l. a substance found in the human body and in various foods	q. people who are responsible for capturing criminals, etc.	v. a booming sound that occurs with an electrical discharge in the air
c. conversation	h. a disease involving the abnormal growth of cells in the body	m. standards, rules, or tests on which judgments can be made	r. a grain that many people eat, grown in warm climates	w. a particular ethnic group
d. a condition that involves the loss of hair on the head	i. a blank or empty area	n. hamburgers, fries, and fried chicken, for example	s. your job or activities that you do regularly to earn money	x. the area beyond the atmosphere of the earth
e. a painting, book, play, or piece of music, for example	j. *a criterion* a standard, rule, or test on which judgments can be made	o. information about events that have happened recently	t. human beings	y. a formal discussion

B Work with the other team. Take turns asking and answering *what* questions about each word or phrase in the word box. Then check your answers on page 435. Which team got the most answers correct?

EXAMPLE: TEAM A: What is *advice*?
  TEAM B: *Advice* is an opinion about what could or should be done about a situation.
  TEAM B: What is *a criterion*?
  TEAM A: *A criterion* is a standard, rule, or test on which judgments can be made.

Go to **MyEnglishLab** for more communication practice.

Count and Non-Count Nouns 175

In the **listening activities**, students practice a range of listening skills. A **new step** has been added in which partners complete an activity that relates to the listening and uses the target grammar.

FROM GRAMMAR TO WRITING

A **From Grammar to Writing** section, now in every unit, helps students to confidently apply the unit's grammar to their own writing. **NEW!**

FROM GRAMMAR TO WRITING

A BEFORE YOU WRITE Consider the personality categories that have been mentioned in this unit and choose the one that fits you best. Write a few sentences about why you believe you fit into this particular category.

B WRITE Using your ideas in A, write a five-paragraph essay about the personality type that best fits you. Remember to use identifying and nonidentifying adjective clauses. Try to avoid the common mistakes shown in the chart. Use the example below to help you begin your essay.

EXAMPLE: No single personality type applies perfectly to a person, but for me one comes closer than all the others. The personality category that fits me most closely is Type B. First, Type Bs are social people who are basically extroverts. I've always enjoyed my friends, which is why I think this category fits me quite well. . . .

Common Mistakes in Using Adjective Clauses

Use *who*, not *which*, to refer to **people**.	The neighbor **who** is the nicest is Mrs. Lopez. **NOT** The neighbor which is the nicest is Mrs. Lopez.
Don't use a **double subject** in an adjective clause.	I'm impressed by people **who** are kind and helpful. **NOT** I'm impressed by people who they are kind and helpful.
Don't enclose identifying adjective clauses with **commas**.	People who put others before themselves are admirable. **NOT** People, who put others before themselves, are admirable.
Don't use *that* to introduce a **nonidentifying** adjective clause. Use *who*, *whom*, or *which*.	Hussein, **who** is my best friend, was born in Tanzania. **NOT** Hussein, that is my best friend, was born in Tanzania.

C CHECK YOUR WORK Look at your essay. Underline adjective clauses. Use the Editing Checklist to check your work.

Editing Checklist

Did you . . . ?
- [ ] use *who* or *whom* to refer to people and *which* to refer to things
- [ ] avoid using a double subject in adjective clauses
- [ ] enclose nonidentifying clauses with commas
- [ ] avoid using *that* to introduce a nonidentifying adjective clause

D REVISE YOUR WORK Read your essay again. Can you improve your writing? Make changes if necessary.

Go to **MyEnglishLab** for more writing practice.

Adjective Clauses: Introduction **245**

The **Before You Write** task helps students generate ideas for their writing assignment.

In the **Write** task, students are given a writing assignment and guided to use the target grammar and avoid common errors.

Check Your Work includes an Editing Checklist that allows students to proofread and edit their writing.

In **Revise Your Work**, students are given a final opportunity to improve their writing.

UNIT **REVIEW**

Unit Reviews give students the opportunity to check their understanding of the target structures. Students can check their answers against the Answer Key at the end of the book. They can also complete the Review on MyEnglishLab.

UNIT 15 **REVIEW**

Test yourself on the grammar of the unit.

A Complete the sentences. Circle the correct answers.

1. Dr. Brand and Dr. Wang, neither of whom / which I've met yet, are well-known professors.
2. Professor Meemook, which / whose classes I enjoy, is originally from Thailand.
3. My two roommates, both of who / whom are from Nigeria, are experiencing culture shock.
4. Hamburgers and hot dogs, neither of them / which I like, are not popular in my country.
5. Rashid and Hussein, who / whom are both newcomers to this country, work in a grocery store.
6. Anyone interested / interesting in culture shock should attend the lecture.
7. Pelé, born / was born in Brazil, used to be a great soccer player.
8. You can do several things to get over culture shock, includes / including befriending local people and learning more about their culture.

B Complete the sentences with words from the box. You will use some words more than once.

that	which	who	whom	whose

1. I've met five new colleagues, all of _____ I like.
2. I'm taking three new courses, none of _____ are very interesting.
3. I made two friends, both of _____ are teachers, this week.
4. I've lived in several countries, examples of _____ are Chile and Mexico.
5. Two famous authors, both of _____ books I've read, are here today.
6. I read a novel about a young man _____ is caught in a dead-end job.
7. The country _____ Emiko moved to is very different from Japan.

C Find and correct five mistakes.

MyEnglishLab

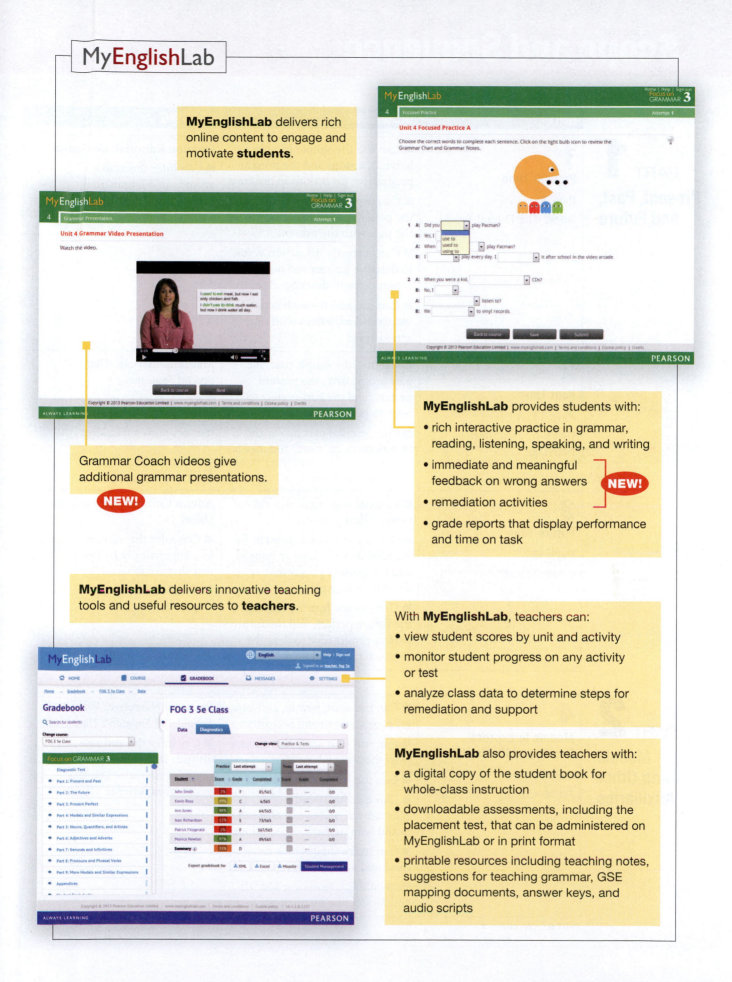

MyEnglishLab delivers rich online content to engage and motivate **students**.

Grammar Coach videos give additional grammar presentations.

NEW!

MyEnglishLab delivers innovative teaching tools and useful resources to **teachers**.

MyEnglishLab provides students with:

- rich interactive practice in grammar, reading, listening, speaking, and writing
- immediate and meaningful feedback on wrong answers **NEW!**
- remediation activities
- grade reports that display performance and time on task

With **MyEnglishLab**, teachers can:

- view student scores by unit and activity
- monitor student progress on any activity or test
- analyze class data to determine steps for remediation and support

MyEnglishLab also provides teachers with:

- a digital copy of the student book for whole-class instruction
- downloadable assessments, including the placement test, that can be administered on MyEnglishLab or in print format
- printable resources including teaching notes, suggestions for teaching grammar, GSE mapping documents, answer keys, and audio scripts

Scope and Sequence

UNIT	GRAMMAR	READING
PART 1 **Present, Past, and Future** **1** **Present Time** Page 4 THEME The Digital World	■ Can use the simple present for habitual actions and the present progressive for actions in progress ■ Can use the present perfect and the perfect progressive to connect the past with the present ■ Can correctly use action verbs to describe actions and non-action verbs to describe states ■ Can use adverbs with action words and adjectives with non-action verbs	**Opinion Editorial:** *Connected!* ■ Can infer the author's attitude in a linguistically complex text that contains the author's opinions
2 **Past Time** Page 18 THEME Intercultural Marriage	■ Can use the simple past, the past progressive, the present perfect, and the past perfect to refer to past events ■ Can describe past habits and situations using *would* and *used to*	**Magazine Article:** *That Special Someone* ■ Can infer the author's attitude in a linguistically complex text that contains a narrative
3 **Future Time** Page 35 THEME Travel	■ Can use *be going to* and *will* to refer to future events ■ Can use the simple present for scheduled events, and *be going to* and the present progressive to describe future plans ■ Can use the future progressive, the future perfect, and the future perfect progressive to describe future actions or states	**Advice Column:** *Get the Most Out of It* ■ Can infer the author's attitude in a linguistically complex text that contains advice or suggestions
PART 2 **Modals and Other Auxiliaries** **4** **Modals to Express Degrees of Necessity** Page 52 THEME Cultural Differences	■ Can use *must, have to,* and *have got to* to show strong necessity ■ Can use *must not* and *don't have to* to show prohibition ■ Can use *had better* for warnings ■ Can use *should* and *ought to* to offer advice, and use *be supposed to* and *be to* to show expectations ■ Can make suggestions using *could* and *might (have)* PRONUNCIATION Reducing Modals and Modal-like Auxiliaries	**Personal Narrative:** *What We Should and Shouldn't Have Done* ■ Can infer the author's attitude in a linguistically complex narrative about a personal experience

PART **2** CONTINUES ▼

LISTENING	SPEAKING	WRITING	VOCABULARY
A conversation about identity theft ■ Can follow a group discussion on a complex topic such as identity theft	■ Can contribute fluently and naturally to a conversation about common uses of technology	■ Can write a detailed essay that highlights the benefits of an electronic device	access **AWL** associate (with) do without downside exposure **AWL** origin put things in perspective **AWL** undeniably **AWL**
A news broadcast ■ Can recognize important details in a news broadcast or interview about complex, unfamiliar topics	■ Can clearly and precisely offer opinions about past events or goals, agreeing or disagreeing with others' opinions	■ Can write a linguistically complex discursive essay about a past experience	acknowledge **AWL** ethnic **AWL** eventually **AWL** furthermore **AWL** priority **AWL** rely **AWL** sustain **AWL** unique **AWL**
A conversation about travel plans ■ Can recognize details in a fast-paced conversation about a schedule or itinerary	■ Can speculate and make predictions about future plans or events	■ Can write a linguistically complex discursive essay about future goals and aspirations	acquire **AWL** chart your own course excruciatingly hectic inevitable **AWL** maximize **AWL** minimize **AWL** out of whack
A conversation about suggestions ■ Can identify the suggestions that are being made in a fast-paced conversation between fluent speakers	■ Can discuss do's and don'ts in different cultures, using linguistically complex language	■ Can write a linguistically complex discursive essay, offering regrets, opinions, and/or advice about a past situation	albeit **AWL** colleague **AWL** etiquette gracious occur **AWL** odd **AWL** overall **AWL** reciprocate

AWL = Academic Word List item

UNIT	GRAMMAR	READING

LISTENING	SPEAKING	WRITING	VOCABULARY
An academic discussion ■ Can follow a group discussion on an academic topic	■ Can clarify own points and ideas about an ambiguous event, using linguistically sophisticated language	■ Can write a complex essay about a mystery, using modals to speculate about clues and possibilities	cohort debris hypothesize AWL nonetheless AWL potential AWL specification AWL stem from theory AWL
An interview about a crime ■ Can identify key details in a fast-paced interview conducted by native speakers	■ Can critically evaluate evidence presented in an article to discuss and speculate about a crime	■ Can write a linguistically complex essay about a crime, using the passive voice to illustrate actions	diminish AWL equip (with) AWL inadvertently notwithstanding AWL presumably AWL proceed (to) AWL recover AWL reveal AWL
A news bulletin about a natural disaster ■ Can follow chronological sequences in extended informal speech at natural speed	■ Can contribute fluently and naturally to a conversation about an academic topic	■ Can write a linguistically complex discursive essay about a legend or myth from one's culture	devote (to) AWL focal obtain AWL participation AWL practitioner AWL predominate AWL repulsive ritual
A telephone conversation between friends ■ Can identify key details in a telephone conversation between native speakers, spoken at a normal rate	■ Can contribute to group discussions about personal topics, even when speech is fast-paced and colloquial	■ Can write a well-developed, grammatically varied essay about a personal experience	abandon AWL coincide AWL compatible AWL context AWL likewise AWL naive seek AWL vulnerable
A news bulletin about a prison escape ■ Can recognize key information in a news bulletin spoken by a native speaker and containing reported speech	■ Can contribute fluently and naturally to a personal interview, alternating between answering and asking questions	■ Can write a well-developed, grammatically varied essay about a personal experience	connotation illustrate AWL motivate AWL scenario AWL straightforward AWL syndrome widespread AWL

AWL = Academic Word List item

LISTENING	SPEAKING	WRITING	VOCABULARY
A conversation about health issues ■ Can identify important details from a fast-paced conversation	■ Can orally convey information from different sources, reconstructing arguments to present the overall result	■ Can write a well-developed, grammatically varied essay about personal attributes	advocate (v) `AWL` authority `AWL` category `AWL` deviate `AWL` hence `AWL` imperative (adj) in moderation offset `AWL`
A conversation about a controversial topic ■ Can follow a fast-paced conversation between fluent speakers well enough to form one's own opinion about the topics discussed	■ Can contribute to a group discussion about a controversial topic, using linguistically complex language	■ Can write a linguistically complex discursive essay about a topic of environmental or social importance	considerable `AWL` crucial `AWL` diversity `AWL` institute (v) `AWL` nevertheless `AWL` restrict `AWL` strategy `AWL` vanish
A conversation between a professor and a student ■ Can follow a fast-paced conversation held by fluent speakers	■ Can consult a variety of sources, using one's findings give a linguistically complex presentation about a country	■ Can write a well-developed essay that clearly states one's opinion about how to improve study habits	allocate `AWL` approximate (adj) `AWL` aspect `AWL` despair (v) orientation `AWL` precise `AWL` refine `AWL` ultimately `AWL`
A conversation about performance ■ Can follow a fast-paced conversation well enough to recognize key details	■ Can contribute fluently and naturally to a literary analysis of a short story or poem	■ Can write a discursive essay that discusses people's expectations about major life events in detail	contrary `AWL` emerge `AWL` ensure `AWL` intense `AWL` outcome `AWL` persist `AWL` rave (about) thereby `AWL`

`AWL` = Academic Word List item

LISTENING	SPEAKING	WRITING	VOCABULARY
A conversation about university life ■ Can follow a fast-paced conversation about life in a university setting	■ Can summarize findings appropriately in an oral report about a famous person	■ Can write a linguistically complex essay that supports an opinion with a multitude of ideas, facts, or references	conflict (n) AWL data AWL discount (v) enable AWL gravitate insight AWL moreover secure (adj) AWL
A conversation between a student and a guidance counselor ■ Can follow a fast-paced conversation between native speakers	■ Can use a complex graphic to describe their own cultural experiences, using linguistically complex language	■ Can write a grammatically rich, discursive essay that describes a cultural experience in detail	adjustment AWL attain AWL convert (v) AWL disorientation dwarf (v) flexible AWL maturity AWL whereas AWL
An excerpt from a radio call-in show ■ Can follow a fast-paced conversation about a controversial topic, identifying the speakers' opinions	■ Can contribute fluently and naturally to a group debate about a controversial topic	■ Can write a well-developed, grammatically varied essay that states and explains one's opinion on a controversial topic	compulsory controversial AWL fundamentally AWL inherent interfere (with) promote AWL stereotype (n) voluntary AWL
An interview with an athlete ■ Can follow a fast-paced interview given by a fluent speaker well enough to recall detailed information	■ Can offer, defend, and elicit an opinion that's derived from a quotation	■ Can write a well-developed, grammatically varied essay that discusses the pros and cons of sports	awry derive AWL factor (n) AWL infer AWL lurk parallel AWL prevalence shift (v) AWL

AWL = Academic Word List item

UNIT	GRAMMAR	READING

LISTENING	SPEAKING	WRITING	VOCABULARY
A news broadcast about world affairs ■ Can infer opinions in a linguistically complex news broadcast	■ Can contribute to a fast-paced group discussion about experiences that were witnessed in the past	■ Can write a complex discursive essay about a situation that was witnessed or experienced in the past	civility confrontation dawn (on) decrepit elude media ooze (v) status AWL
An excerpt from a workshop ■ Can identify a speaker's point of view in a linguistically complex presentation	■ Can give one's opinion in response to a literary quote and comment on the opinions of others	■ Can write a detailed discursive essay about a memorable experience from the past	core AWL deteriorate enhance AWL highlight AWL induce AWL mitigate recollect vivid
A conversation about a child's problems ■ Can follow a fast-paced conversation between a family therapist and the parents of a troubled child	■ Can elicit and participate in a conversation that is based on data from a survey or questionnaire	■ Can apply an academic theory to one's personal life in a well-developed, grammatically varied essay	compelling (adj) configuration conscientious enterprise innovator AWL niche (n) sole (adj) AWL temperament
An interview about communication techniques ■ Can identify the main ideas and opinions in a fast-paced interview with an expert in her field	■ Can discuss communication techniques in a group setting, using linguistically complex language	■ Can write a complex essay that uses direct and indirect speech to provide a detailed account of an event witnessed in the past	address (v) arbitrary AWL distressed (adj) duration AWL inhibit AWL rancor rigid AWL self-righteous

AWL = Academic Word List item

UNIT	GRAMMAR	READING
PART 9 **Conditionals and the Subjunctive**		
22 **Conditionals; Other Ways to Express Unreality** Page 374 THEME Achievements and Inventions	■ Can use real conditionals to refer to general truths, facts, habits, and repeated events ■ Can use present and past unreal conditionals to refer to hypothetical (counterfactual) past results of a previous action or situation ■ Can use *wish* and *if only* to express sadness or a desire for a different situation	**Scientific Article:** *How Would Our World Be Different?* ■ Can extract information, ideas, and opinions from a linguistically complex text
23 **More Conditions; The Subjunctive** Page 392 THEME Advice	■ Can use implied and inverted conditions ■ Can use the subjunctive as a verb form to express unreal conditions, wishes, and possibilities ■ Can use the subjunctive with the base form of the verb in noun clauses following verbs and adjectives of advice, necessity, and urgency	**Advice Column:** *Ask Rosa* ■ Can extract information, ideas, and opinions from a complex text that offers advice or suggestions

LISTENING	SPEAKING	WRITING	VOCABULARY
A classroom discussion ■ Can follow a fast-paced classroom discussion about a technological concept	■ Can use real and unreal conditionals to discuss actual and hypothetical situations	■ Can write a linguistically complex, highly detailed essay about the impact of a technological development or invention	attribute (to) **AWL** e.g. evolve **AWL** formulate **AWL** i.e. mutually **AWL** ubiquitous utilize **AWL**
A conversation about advice ■ Can follow a fast-paced conversation held by fluent speakers	■ Can give a formal presentation to a group of peers, advising them to choose specific actions or outcomes	■ Can write a linguistically complex discursive essay that uses the subjunctive to describe past experiences related to following advice	capable **AWL** manipulate **AWL** mediate **AWL** overbearing semblance slob resistant violate **AWL**

AWL = Academic Word List item

About the Author

Jay Maurer has taught English in binational centers, colleges, and universities in Spain, Portugal, Mexico, the Somali Republic, and the United States; and intensive English at Columbia University's American Language Program. In addition, he has been a teacher of college composition, literature, technical writing, speech, and drama at Santa Fe Community College and Northern New Mexico Community College. Since 1997, he has conducted his own business as an individual English-language coach. He is the co-author with Penny LaPorte of the three-level *Structure Practice in Context* series; co-author with Irene Schoenberg of the five-level *True Colors* series and the *True Voices* video series; co-author with Irene Schoenberg of *Focus on Grammar 1*; and author of *Focus on Grammar 5*, editions 1 through 5. Mr. Maurer holds an M.A. and an M.Ed. in applied linguistics and a Ph.D. in the teaching of English, all from Columbia University. Currently he lives and writes in Arizona and Washington State. *Focus on Grammar 5*, Fifth Edition, has grown out of the author's experiences as a practicing teacher of both ESL and college writing.

Acknowledgments

Writing the fifth edition of *Focus on Grammar 5* has been just as interesting, challenging, and rewarding as writing the first four editions. I'm indebted to many people who helped me in different ways. Specifically, though, I want to express my appreciation to:

- My students over the years.

- **Marjorie Fuchs** and **Irene Schoenberg**—the other members of the FOG author team—for their support and encouragement.

- **Gosia Jaros-White**, the Publisher for *Focus on Grammar*, 5th edition. Gosia has been a perceptive, strong, and effective leader of the project.

- **Don Williams**, the series designer and compositor. Don has an excellent eye for the appearance of text and art on the page.

- **Bernard Seal**, for his vision, dedication, and careful attention to the task. Bernard has been an excellent editorial manager. Thank you greatly.

Above all, I am grateful to:

- **Julie Schmidt**, my editor, for her dedication, her excellent eye for detail and logic, and her focus on quality. Julie has been instrumental in making this a better book. Many thanks.

- My wife, **Priscilla**, for her love, wonderful support, and assistance with the manuscript.

- My best friend.

Reviewers

We are grateful to the following reviewers for their many helpful comments.

Susanna Aramyan, Glendale Community College, Glendale, CA; **Homeretta Ayala**, Baltimore Co. Schools, Baltimore, MD; **Barbara Barrett**, University of Miami, Miami, FL; **Rebecca Beck**, Irvine Valley College, Irvine, CA; **Crystal Bock Thiessen**, University of Nebraska-PIESL, Lincoln, NE; **Janna Brink**, Mt. San Antonio College, Walnut, CA; **Erin Butler**, University of California, Riverside, CA; **Joice Cain**, Fullerton College, Fullerton, CA; **Shannonine M. Caruana**, Hudson County Community College, Jersey City, NJ; **Tonya Cobb**, Cypress College, Cypress, CA; **David Cooke**, Mt. San Antonio College, Walnut, CA; **Lindsay Donigan**, Fullerton College, Fullerton, CA; **Mila Dragushanskya**, ASA College, New York, NY; **Jill Fox**, University of Nebraska, Lincoln, NE; **Katalin Gyurindak**, Mt. San Antonio College, Walnut, CA; **Karen Hamilton**, Glendale Community College, Glendale, CA; **Electra Jablons**, International English Language Institute, Hunter College, New York, NY; **Eva Kozlenko**, Hudson County Community College, Jersey City, NJ; **Esther Lee**, American Language Program, California State University, Fullerton, CA; **Yenlan Li**, American Language Program, California State University, Fullerton, CA; **Shirley Lundblade**, Mt. San Antonio College, Walnut, CA; **Thi Thi Ma**, Los Angeles City College, Los Angeles, CA; **Marilyn Martin**, Mt. San Antonio College, Walnut, CA; **Eve Mazereeuw**, University of Guelph English Language Programs, Guelph, Ontario, Canada; **Robert Mott**, Glendale Community College, Glendale, CA; **Wanda Murtha**, Glendale Community College, Glendale, CA; **Susan Niemeyer**, Los Angeles City College, Los Angeles, CA; **Wayne Pate**, Tarrant County College, Fort Worth, TX; **Genevieve Patthey-Chavez**, Los Angeles City College, Los Angeles, CA; **Robin Persiani**, Sierra College, Rocklin, CA; **Denise Phillips**, Hudson County Community College, Jersey City, NJ; **Anna Powell**, American Language Program, California State University, Fullerton, CA; **JoAnna Prado**, Sacramento City Community College, Sacramento, CA; **Mark Rau**, American River College, Sacramento, CA; **Madeleine Schamehorn**, University of California, Riverside, CA; **Richard Skinner**, Hudson County Community College, Jersey City, NJ; **Heather Snavely**, American Language Program, California State University, Fullerton, CA; **Gordana Sokic**, Douglas College, Westminster, British Columbia, Canada; **Lee Spencer**, International English Language Institute, Hunter College, New York, NY; **Heather Stern**, Irvine Valley College, Irvine, CA; **Susan Stern**, Irvine Valley College, Irvine, CA; **Andrea Sunnaa**, Mt. San Antonio College, Walnut, CA; **Margaret Teske**, Mt. San Antonio College, Walnut, CA; **Johanna Van Gendt**, Hudson County Community College, Jersey City, NJ; **Daniela C. Wagner-Loera**, University of Maryland, College Park, MD; **Tamara Williams**, University of Guelph, English Language Programs, Guelph, Ontario, Canada; **Saliha Yagoubi**, Hudson County Community College, Jersey City, NJ; **Pat Zayas**, Glendale Community College, Glendale, CA

Credits

Present, Past, and Future

PART 1

OUTCOMES

- Describe events, states, and situations in the present
- Recognize an author's attitude in an article about technology
- Identify main points in a conversation about identity theft
- Participate in discussions about technology, expressing opinions, agreeing and disagreeing
- Write a five-paragraph essay about the benefits of an electronic device

OUTCOMES

- Describe events, states, and situations in the past
- Describe past habits and situations with *would* and *used to*
- Identify past events in an article and a news broadcast
- Discuss past events, goals, and life changes, expressing opinions and giving examples
- Write an essay about a past experience

OUTCOMES

- Discuss future actions, plans, events, and predictions
- Identify main points in an article about travel
- Identify main points in a conversation about travel plans
- Speculate about future events
- Make predictions about the future
- Write an essay about future goals and aspirations

Present Time
THE DIGITAL WORLD

OUTCOMES
- Describe events, states, and situations in the present
- Recognize an author's attitude in an article about technology
- Identify main points in a conversation about identity theft
- Participate in discussions about technology, expressing opinions, agreeing and disagreeing
- Write a five-paragraph essay about the benefits of an electronic device

STEP 1   GRAMMAR IN CONTEXT

BEFORE YOU READ

Discuss the questions.

1. What electronic devices do you use for communication with others? How often do you use them?

2. Do you think digital advances have changed our world for the better or for the worse?

READ

▶ 01|01   Read this article about staying in close connection with other people.

Connected!

Most of us hardly go anywhere today without a cell phone, an iPad, or a laptop—or so it seems. We're trying to communicate with each other 24/7. We want to be "connected." How do we accomplish this? We access the Internet to contact friends on Facebook or Twitter. We send and receive emails, write and read blogs, call others and text them on our cell phones. We're "available" most of the time. Is this constant communication good? I think it's positive overall, though there are some downsides to living digitally.

My 17-year-old daughter, Allison, is an excellent example. She has joined the social networking sites Facebook and Twitter. Facebook has been around since 2005 and Twitter since 2006. This evening, Allison is sitting in front of her computer. She's reading posts from her friends and writing responses. At the moment, she's laughing, probably at a picture or amusing comment. She's having a great time, but she still hasn't done her homework, and she probably won't finish it until very late tonight.

Then there's my 15-year-old son, Nick. It seems that he just can't do without his cell phone, which he's had since his birthday four months ago. Right now, Nick is texting friends. He's been doing that for the last half hour and shows no signs of stopping. I'm afraid that Nick spends far too much time on his phone, and that it's affecting his powers of concentration. Nick's teachers say he isn't doing well in the classroom. They've been having difficulty getting his attention.

Then there's my wife Elena, who loves email. After dinner every night, Elena gets out her laptop, logs on to the Internet, and reads and answers her messages. These days, she's getting hundreds of email messages a week, and she's having trouble staying on top of them. This makes her feel stressed out.

And then there's yours truly.[1] I go to the office three days a week and telecommute the other two. When I'm working at home, I write a blog. (By the way, do you know the origin of the word "blog"? It's a contraction of "web log," which is a type of website.) On my blog, I write regular entries and comment on what others say. I really enjoy doing this, but it takes up a lot of my time. In addition, I start to feel anxious if I don't update it frequently.

Staying in near-constant communication with others often leads to stress. It tends to prevent us from spending quiet time alone, from reading, from enjoying nature. It can be addictive. It can have undeniably negative effects on our ability to work or study efficiently.

There are a few downsides to living digitally. Does that mean we should limit our exposure to the digital world? As with so many other things in our lives, we need to put things in perspective. Most people realize that there are many advantages associated with frequent communication with others. Through texting and the Internet, my family and I find out important news almost immediately, and we stay in touch with friends we seldom see. So would we give it all up? Not on your life!

---

1 *yours truly:* me, myself

AFTER YOU READ

A **VOCABULARY** Match the words in **bold** with their meanings.

_____	**1.** We **access** the Internet to contact friends.	**a.** see things clearly
_____	**2.** Should we limit our **exposure to** the digital world?	**b.** disadvantages
_____	**3.** There are a few **downsides** to living digitally.	**c.** live without
_____	**4.** There are advantages **associated with** frequent communication.	**d.** clearly
_____	**5.** We need to **put things in perspective**.	**e.** starting point
_____	**6.** It can have **undeniably** negative effects.	**f.** experience of
_____	**7.** Do you know the **origin** of the word "blog"?	**g.** use
_____	**8.** It seems that he just can't **do without** his cell phone.	**h.** connected to

B COMPREHENSION Read the statements. Check (✓) *True* or *False*.

	True	False
1. Most people today want to be in frequent communication with others.	☐	☐
2. The author thinks digital living is positive overall.	☐	☐
3. Facebook and Twitter are computer search engines.	☐	☐
4. People have been using Twitter longer than Facebook.	☐	☐
5. The author's daughter is not having a good time tonight.	☐	☐
6. The author's son has had his cell phone for over a year.	☐	☐
7. The author and his wife think that digital living is sometimes stressful.	☐	☐
8. The author seems to think it's good to spend quiet time alone.	☐	☐

C DISCUSSION Work with a partner. Compare your answers in Exercise B. Give reasons for your answers.

> Go to MyEnglishLab for more grammar in context practice.

STEP 2 GRAMMAR PRESENTATION

PRESENT TIME

Present Time: In General or Now

Simple Present
Simple Present Verb
Today, we **spend** a lot of money on electronic devices.

Present Progressive
Be + Base Form + *-ing*
Jack **is looking** for a new iPad.

Present Time: From a Time in the Past Until Now

Present Perfect
Have + Past Participle
We **have had** email for fifteen years.

Present Perfect Progressive
Have been + Base Form + *-ing*
He**'s been texting** his friends for the last half hour.

Action + Non-Action Uses

Action Verbs	
Simple Form	Progressive Form
They normally **drive** to work.	Today, they**'re taking** the bus.

Most Non-Action Verbs
Simple Form
Teachers **know** he is a good student. They **want** to understand his problem.

Some Verbs: Action + Non-Action Uses

Simple Form (Non-Action Use)	Progressive Form (Action Use)
I **have** a new iPhone.	I'**m having** problems with it.
I **think** I **need** a better computer.	I'**m thinking** about getting one this week.
Our laptop **is** a great computer.	It'**s being** difficult today, though.

Action Verbs

+ Adverb
She **works constantly**. He'**s doing badly** in class.

Some Non-Action Verbs

+ Adjective (Non-Action Use)	+ Adverb (Action Use)
Your car **looks good**. She **feels bad** about what she said. The soup **tastes delicious**.	He **looks** at his iPhone **constantly**. **Feel** the surface **carefully**; it might still be hot. **Taste** the soup **quickly** before it gets cold.

GRAMMAR NOTES

1 Simple Present

Use the **simple present** to show actions or states that are true in general or habitual, and for events in a sequence.

• **general truths** • **habitual actions** • **events in a sequence**	We **use** the Internet to stay in touch with friends. After dinner every night, Elena **gets out** her laptop. Elena **logs** on to the Internet, **reads** her email, and **starts** responding.

2 Present Progressive

Use the **present progressive** to show actions **in progress right now** (not finished).	Allison **is sitting** in front of the computer. At the moment, she'**s laughing**.
You can also use the present progressive to show actions that are **in progress** but are **not happening right now**.	He'**s spending** a lot of time on the Internet these days. *(He isn't on the Internet right now.)*
BE CAREFUL! We generally don't use the progressive with **non-action** verbs, especially in more formal English.	We **need** to put things in perspective. **NOT** We're ~~needing~~ to put things in perspective.

3 Present Perfect and Present Perfect Progressive

The **present perfect** and the **present perfect progressive** connect the past with the present. Use them to show actions and states that **began in the past** and **continue until now**.

• present perfect	I**'ve had** my iPad for six months.
• present perfect progressive	He**'s been writing** a blog for eight years.

We often use the present perfect and the present perfect progressive with *for* + a length of time and *since* + a starting point.	Mary **has worked** at her company *for six years*. Mary **has been working** at her company *since 2011*.

BE CAREFUL! Use the **present perfect**, not the present perfect progressive, to describe **completed actions** with a connection to the present.	I**'ve bought** four cell phones in the last two years. **NOT** I've ~~been buying~~ four cell phones in the last two years.

4 Action Verbs

Action verbs (also called **active** or **dynamic** verbs) describe **actions**. Action verbs carry the suggestion that the subject is in control of the action.

Use **simple** verb forms (without *-ing*) to describe all of an action—the **action in general**.	I **write** articles for a psychology magazine. Computers **perform** tasks quickly.

Use **progressive** verb forms (with *-ing*) to describe part of an action—**in progress at a specific time**.	Right now, I**'m writing** my blog. Today, my computer **is performing** well.

5 Non-Action Verbs

Non-action verbs describe **states** such as appearance, emotions, mental states, perceptions, possession, and wants. We most often use non-action verbs in the **simple** form and not in the progressive.

• appearance	You **look** stressed.
• emotions	Elena **loves** email.
• mental states	I **know** the answer to that question.
• perceptions	We **hear** that all the time.
• possession	They **own** four computers.
• wants and preferences	I **need** a new phone.

USAGE NOTE We sometimes use **non-action verbs** in the **progressive** when they describe **states that can be changed**. They can also **describe actions** when the performer of the action has a choice.	We **have** a new laptop. *(possession)* We**'re having** trouble with it. *(experiencing trouble)* He **is** a nice fellow. *(a state)* Today, he**'s not being** nice. *(a choice—not behaving nicely)*

6 Adverbs and Adjectives

We normally use **adverbs** with **action** verbs and **adjectives** with **non-action** verbs.

• **Action verbs + adverbs**	She always **listens** *carefully*. He **works** *quickly* at his job.
• **Non-action verbs + adjectives**	You **sound** really *excited*! You **look** *beautiful*.
BE CAREFUL! Use **non-action** verbs with **adverbs**, not adjectives, to **show actions**.	I don't **hear** *well* when others are talking. **NOT** I don't hear ~~good~~ when others are talking. The fire alarm **sounded** a warning *loudly*. **NOT** The fire alarm sounded a warning ~~loud~~.

REFERENCE NOTES

For definitions and examples of **grammar terms**, see the Glossary on page 423.

For a list of **non-action verbs**, see Appendix 2 on page 413.

For a list of **non-action verbs sometimes used in the progressive**, see Appendix 3 on page 413.

Go to MyEnglishLab to watch the grammar presentation.

STEP 3   FOCUSED PRACTICE

EXERCISE 1 DISCOVER THE GRAMMAR

Ⓐ **GRAMMAR NOTES 1–2** Look at the underlined verbs in the sentences based on the reading. Check (✓) *Habitual Action*, *Action in Progress*, or *Action in Progress, But Not Happening Right Now*.

	Habitual Action	Action in Progress	Action in Progress, But Not Happening Right Now
1. Most of us hardly <u>go</u> anywhere today without an electronic device.	✓	☐	☐
2. We're <u>trying</u> to stay in touch with people all the time.	☐	☐	☐
3. We <u>access</u> the Internet to contact friends.	☐	☐	☐
4. Allison <u>is sitting</u> in front of the computer.	☐	☐	☐
5. At the moment, she's <u>laughing</u>.	☐	☐	☐
6. Nick's teachers say he <u>isn't doing</u> well at school.	☐	☐	☐
7. Elena <u>is having</u> trouble staying on top of her email.	☐	☐	☐
8. I'm <u>working</u> at home these days.	☐	☐	☐
9. I <u>write</u> a blog.	☐	☐	☐
10. Through the Internet, I <u>stay</u> in touch with friends.	☐	☐	☐

B GRAMMAR NOTES 4–5 Read the sentences based on the reading. Circle the verbs that describe actions. Underline the verbs that describe states.

1. People (use) their electronic devices constantly these days.

2. At least, it seems that way.

3. We want to be connected 24/7.

4. We text people on our cell phones.

5. Nick appears to be addicted to his cell phone.

6. On Facebook, you develop your own page.

7. Do you know the origin of the word "blog"?

8. Elena loves her email.

9. I telecommute two days a week.

10. We need to put things in perspective.

EXERCISE 2 SIMPLE PRESENT AND PRESENT PROGRESSIVE

GRAMMAR NOTES 1–2 Complete the account of a day in the life of James Marx, magazine writer and Internet blogger. Circle the correct answers.

Today is Monday, one of the two days a week that (I telecommute)/ I'm telecommuting. On
                                                                    1.
these days, I walk / I'm walking about 50 steps to my home office, turn on / am turning on
              2.   **3.**
the computer, and start / am starting writing. For some reason, my computer printer
                     4.
gives / is giving me problems today, so at the moment, I try / I'm trying to fix it. Ah, here we go.
     5.   **6.**
It works / It's working again.
   7.
    This week, I write / I'm writing on my blog about the dangers of text messaging. Currently,
                  8.
our state legislature considers / is considering a law that would prohibit texting while driving or
                              9.
operating machinery. I think / I'm thinking it would be a good idea to pass the law.
                     10.
    It's now 12:30 p.m., time for lunch. On these days I spend / I'm spending at home,
                                                     11.
I make / I'm making my own lunch. On the other three days, I have / I'm having lunch in the
    12.   **13.**
company cafeteria.

    It's 3:30 p.m. I finished my blog an hour ago, and now I do / I'm doing some Internet
                                                          14.
research for an article I'm going to write in a few days. I love / I'm loving these quiet days
                                                          15.
at home.

EXERCISE 3 PRESENT PERFECT AND PRESENT PERFECT PROGRESSIVE

GRAMMAR NOTE 3 Complete the paragraph with present perfect or present perfect progressive forms of the verbs in parentheses. Use the progressive form where possible. Do not use contractions.

James and Elena Marx _____*have known*_____ each other for twenty years, and they
1. (know)
_____ married for eighteen years. They _____ in their
2. (be)   **3.** (live)
current house for three years. James _____ a writer for ten years. He
4. (be)
_____ for *In Touch Magazine* for the past eight years, and he
5. (work)
_____ an Internet blog for the past six years. He _____
6. (write)   **7.** (also write)
four books on popular culture.

Elena _____ a high school English teacher for the last twelve years.
8. (be)
During that time, she _____ at six different schools. She
9. (teach)
_____ at her current school for five years now.
10. (teach)

The Marxes are a "wired" family. They _____ at least one desktop
11. (have)
computer for fifteen years. Over the years, they _____ six different
12. (own)
computers. James, Elena, Allison, and Nick _____ with friends and relatives
13. (communicate)
online for almost as long as they can remember.

EXERCISE 4 VERBS AND ADJECTIVES OR ADVERBS

GRAMMAR NOTES 4–6 Complete each statement with the correct forms of the words in parentheses. Change the adjective to an adverb if necessary.

1. Your new iPhone _____*looks similar*_____ to mine.
   (look / similar)

2. My old computer crashed, but my new one _____.
   (work / good)

3. If your day _____, you are having a bad day.
   (go / bad)

4. Cell phone use _____; today, more people are using cell phones than
   (grow / rapid)
   land lines.

5. People who _____ should do something fun to cheer themselves up.
   (feel / sad)

6. I was fine yesterday, but today I _____.
   (feel / sick)

7. When a person _____, that person is using his or her brain.
   (think / clear)

8. I think that new proposal _____.
   (sound / terrible)

9. Usually, Molly _____ to her classmates.
   (be / kind)

10. Today, however, she _____.
    (be / obnoxious)

EXERCISE 5 EDITING

GRAMMAR NOTES 1–6 Read this student essay. There are eleven mistakes in the use of present time verbs, adjectives, and adverbs. The first mistake is already corrected. Find and correct ten more.

No Cell Phone Restrictions!

It seems
~~It's seeming~~ that I constantly hear the same thing: "Cell phones are dangerous. We're needing to restrict them. People are dying because of cell phones." Well, I'm thinking cell phones themselves aren't the problem. I'm completely opposed to restrictions on them, and here's why:

First, people say cell phones are being dangerous to health. Supporters of this idea say that cell phones produce harmful radiation, and they can even cause cancer. They say that many studies have been proving this. I think this is nonsense. There hasn't been any real proof. All those studies aren't meaning anything.

Second, teachers don't allow cell phones in classes because they're a distraction. I feel pretty angrily about this. Cell phones can save lives. Here's an example: Two weeks ago in my history class, a student had his cell phone on. He always keeps it on because his mother isn't speaking English, and sometimes she needs his help. His mother did call that day, and she had an emergency. He had to call someone to help her. What if the phone hadn't been on?

Third, people argue that using a cell phone while driving is dangerous. This idea is sounding crazy to me. It isn't more dangerous than turning on the car radio or eating a sandwich. People are allowed to do those things when they drive. The law says you have to have one hand on the steering wheel at all times. It's possible to use a cell phone correctly with one hand. If you know how to drive good, you can do this easily.

This has always been being a free country. I hope it stays that way.

Go to **MyEnglishLab** for more focused practice.

EXERCISE 6 LISTENING

▶ 01|02 **A** Listen to the conversation. Check (✓) the topic that is *not* mentioned.

☐ credit cards   ☐ cell phones

☐ identity theft   ☐ the Internet

▶ 01|02 **B** Read the questions. Then listen to the conversation again and answer the questions.
Use complete sentences.

1. What is Jim doing?

   He is checking out action figures on the Internet.

2. What does Jim want to do?

   _____

3. What do criminals sometimes do on insecure websites?

   _____

4. Who has been a victim of identity theft?

   _____

5. What has Uncle Jerry been doing for a long time?

   _____

6. How much money has someone charged on Uncle Jerry's credit card?

   _____

7. Does Uncle Jerry have to pay back the money?

   _____

8. When are people supposed to report problems like thefts?

   _____

9. What does Mary think we need to be careful about?

   _____

10. According to Mary, what is the problem with the Internet?

    _____

C Work with a partner. Discuss these questions. Then report your conclusions to the class.

1. Is identity theft a serious problem in the digital world?

2. Have you ever had problems like the one described in the Listening, or do you know
anyone who has?

3. What have people and companies been doing to deal with these problems? Do they need
to do more?

EXERCISE 7 ELECTRONIC DEVICES IN YOUR LIFE

A QUESTIONNAIRE What part do electronic devices play in your life? Fill out the chart with information about yourself. Check (✓) the appropriate boxes. Add another electronic device at the end of the chart.

Electronic Device	Have It	Don't Have It	Works Well	Often Use It	Seldom or Never Use It	Comments
Desktop computer	✓		✓	✓		*I spend several hours a day on it. I use it for writing, homework, and entertainment. I am addicted to it.*
Laptop computer						
Cell phone / smartphone						
Tablet						

B Work with a partner. Discuss your answers to the questionnaire. Talk about which electronic devices are important in your life and which are not.

EXAMPLE: **A:** I have a desktop computer, and I love using it. I spend several hours a day on it. Actually, I'm addicted to it.
B: Do you think you spend too much time on the computer?
A: Well . . .

EXERCISE 8 THEN AND NOW

DISCUSSION Work with a partner. Choose an electronic device that you own from the chart in Exercise 7. Discuss these questions. Then report your conclusions to the class.

1. How long have you had this device?

2. How many of these devices have you bought in the last ten years?

3. What do you use this device for? How long have you been using it for this purpose or these purposes?

4. How has this device changed since it was first invented?

5. Is the latest version of this device better in every way than the older versions, or are there any advantages to some of the older devices?

EXERCISE 9 WHAT DO YOU THINK?

Ⓐ CRITICAL THINKING You are going to discuss how to solve the problem of distracted driving. First, read this article.

Every day in the United States, at least nine people are killed and more than 1,100 injured in accidents possibly caused by distracted driving. The CDC identifies three main ways in which drivers become distracted and lose focus:

- **Visually:** Drivers take their eyes off the road.
- **Manually:** Drivers take their hands off the steering wheel.
- **Cognitively:** Drivers take their minds off driving.

Distracted driving usually involves eating, using a cell phone, and/or texting.

Recent surveys have confirmed this information. In one survey, 31 percent of U.S. drivers admitted that they sometimes read, text, or send emails while they are driving. In Europe, the percentage ranges from 21 percent in the United Kingdom to 59 percent in Portugal.

Nearly 50 percent of U.S. high school students sixteen or older say that they text or email while driving. Younger drivers—those under twenty—have the highest percentage of fatal accidents caused by distracted driving.

All but four states now have laws that prohibit texting while driving.

Source: Centers for Disease Control and Prevention

Ⓑ Work in a group. Discuss the following questions.

1. In all but four U.S. states today, texting while driving is illegal. Why is it illegal?

2. Do you agree that distracted driving has been causing a lot of accidents?

3. Do you believe that the problem of texting while driving is most serious among younger drivers?

4. What is the best way to solve this problem? Make several suggestions.

Go to MyEnglishLab for more communication practice.

FROM GRAMMAR TO WRITING

A **BEFORE YOU WRITE** Write a few sentences on the benefits of one of the following electronic devices:

- cell phone / smartphone
- desktop computer
- tablet

B **WRITE** Using your ideas in A, write a five-paragraph essay on the device you have selected. Remember to use the simple present, present progressive, present perfect, and present perfect progressive. Try to avoid the common mistakes in the chart. Use the example below to help you begin your essay.

EXAMPLE: My smartphone is very important to me. I've had it for three years now. I use it several times a day. Actually, I've been using it since one o'clock this afternoon.

There are several reasons why my smartphone is so essential to me. It has many benefits. For example, . . .

Common Mistakes in Using Present Time Verbs

Don't use most non-action verbs in the present progressive. Be sure to use **non-action verbs in the simple present** unless they are being used in an active sense.	We **need** to buy a new computer. **NOT** We're needing to buy a new computer.
Don't confuse the present perfect and the present perfect progressive. Be sure to use the **present perfect for completed actions**.	Robert **has** already **taken** twenty courses for his degree. **NOT** Robert has already been taking twenty courses for his degree.
Don't use adverbs with sense verbs. Make sure to use **adjectives with sense verbs**.	The soup **tastes good**. **NOT** The soup tastes well.

C **CHECK YOUR WORK** Look at your essay. Underline the present time verbs. Use the Editing Checklist to check your work.

Editing Checklist

Did you . . . ?

- ☐ use the simple present for habitual actions
- ☐ use the present progressive for actions that are in progress
- ☐ use the simple present with most non-action verbs
- ☐ use the present perfect for completed actions
- ☐ use adjectives with sense verbs and adverbs with action verbs

D **REVISE YOUR WORK** Read your essay again. Can you improve your writing? Make changes if necessary.

Go to **MyEnglishLab** for more writing practice.

UNIT 1 REVIEW

Test yourself on the grammar of the unit.

(A) Complete the email. Circle the correct answers.

Hi Amy,

Just a note to tell you how we do / we're doing here in Phoenix. Tim loves / is loving
                        1.   **2.**
his new job. Our house is on a bus line, so he takes / he's taking the bus to work every day.
                                              3.
I get / I'm getting to know our neighbors. They seem / They're seeming friendly. Nancy
4.   **5.**
attends / is attending the local high school, and she makes / she's making a lot of new
6.   **7.**
friends there. But she texts / she's texting her old friends in Boston all the time! I think she
                          8.
misses them.

Love,

Martha

(B) Complete the paragraph with the correct forms of the verbs in parentheses. Use the
present perfect progressive where possible. Do not use contractions.

Doug and Lisa Cho _____ in Los Angeles since last March.
                          1. (live)
Doug is a film director. He _____ five movies in his career, and
                                2. (direct)
he _____ on a sixth since they moved to Los Angeles. Doug
        3. (work)
and Lisa _____ their own house for six months. They
              4. (own)
_____ it since they bought it. Lisa works in advertising, and she
    5. (remodel)
_____ her own advertising business for the last three months.
        6. (run)

(C) Find and correct six mistakes.

My neighbor Jeff is a teacher. His job is going good in general, and he likes it. But

sometimes he sounds angrily when he talks about it. He feels frustratedly because a few

students in his class behave bad. They pretend to listen to him, and they look quietly and

innocent in class. But they don't take their studies serious. Instead, they surf the Internet and

text each other during class.

Now check your answers on page 427.

Go to MyEnglishLab to complete the review online.

Past Time
INTERCULTURAL MARRIAGE

OUTCOMES
* Describe events, states, and situations in the past
* Describe past habits and situations with *would* and *used to*
* Identify past events in an article and a news broadcast
* Discuss past events, goals, and life changes, expressing opinions and giving examples
* Write an essay about a past experience

STEP 1   GRAMMAR IN CONTEXT

BEFORE YOU READ

Discuss the questions.

1. What do you understand by the term "intercultural marriage"?

2. What are some basic challenges that individuals who marry someone from a different culture might face?

READ

02|01   Read this article about intercultural marriage.

That Special Someone

Intercultural marriage is on the rise, not only in North America but in other parts of the world as well. An intercultural couple consists of two people who have different cultural backgrounds. They may come from different countries or from different regions in the same country. They may have different religions, or they may come from different ethnic groups. These couples may have found true love, but they often face difficult and unique challenges. The divorce rate among partners in intercultural marriages seems high, but such marriages can work under the right circumstances, as we will see by examining the case of one intercultural couple.

Both Hector Garcia and Jessica Chapman were born in the United States, but their backgrounds are 180 degrees apart. Hector's parents came to the United States from Mexico decades ago. They settled in California, and by the time Hector was born, they had earned their American citizenship. Hector had

to work to be able to afford college. Jessica, in contrast, grew up in a wealthy Caucasian family in New England. Her parents paid for her college expenses, so she didn't have to work. Hector and Jessica met in biology lab in their senior year of college, and it was a case of love at first sight. After they graduated, Hector asked Jessica to marry him. Hector says, "I used to think I would marry a Hispanic woman whose background was similar to mine. But the minute I met Jessica, I knew she was the one for me." Jessica felt the same and accepted Hector's proposal, and for a while everything went smoothly.

Pretty soon, though, problems arose. Jessica explains: "I thought our relationship was going to stay the same as it had always been. I didn't think we would ever argue about anything. But Hector wanted to buy a house, and he refused to accept any help from my parents. He was working long hours, and I didn't think he was paying enough attention to me. It occurred to me that work had become his top priority. Furthermore, I didn't feel comfortable with Hector's family. We would go to gatherings at his family's house most weekends. Everyone would be talking at once, and I would feel shut out. Eventually, I got so frustrated that I was ready to leave him. Fortunately, I had a heart-to-heart talk with a close friend who was also in an intercultural marriage. She advised me to think about what motivated Hector and to try to understand the culture and values of his extended family. I realized that because he had grown up in a family without much money and had married a woman from a wealthier background, it was important for Hector to do things on his own. That's why he didn't want to rely on help from my father. I realized that I'd been wrong about several things. His family weren't trying to shut me out at their gatherings; they were just a typical Mexican family who liked to talk! I also realized I hadn't been giving Hector's family a fair chance. Since then, his mother and I have become really good friends, and Hector's and my relationship has improved greatly."

This is a case of an intercultural marriage that has worked. One key point emerges[1] from Hector and Jessica's story: Partners in an intercultural marriage should try to understand and acknowledge the cultural values of their spouses and their extended families. If they do, they may well be able to sustain their relationship with that special someone.

---

1 *emerges:* becomes known or apparent

AFTER YOU READ

A VOCABULARY Match the words in **bold** with their meanings.

_____ 1. They may come from different **ethnic** groups.

_____ 2. They often face difficult and **unique** challenges.

_____ 3. **Eventually**, I got so frustrated I was ready to leave him.

_____ 4. **Furthermore**, I didn't feel comfortable with Hector's family.

_____ 5. Hector didn't want to **rely** on Jessica's father.

_____ 6. It seemed that work had become his top **priority**.

_____ 7. They must **acknowledge** the cultural values of their spouses.

_____ 8. They may **sustain** their relationship with that special someone.

a. in addition

b. depend

c. continue

d. main goal

e. the only one of its kind

f. recognize as valuable

g. racial or national

h. at a later time

B COMPREHENSION Read the statements. Check (✓) *True* or *False*. Correct the false statements.

	True	False
1. Hector and Jessica had similar backgrounds.	☐	☐
2. Jessica had to pay for college herself.	☐	☐
3. Jessica didn't expect that she and Hector would have arguments.	☐	☐
4. Hector thought he would marry a woman of his own background.	☐	☐
5. Hector came from a wealthy family.	☐	☐
6. Jessica and her mother-in-law now have a friendly relationship.	☐	☐

C DISCUSSION Work with a partner. What kinds of problems did Hector and Jessica have with their marriage? What do you think caused the problems, and how did they solve them?

Go to MyEnglishLab for more grammar in context practice.

STEP 2   GRAMMAR PRESENTATION

PAST TIME

Past Time: General or Specific (Definite)

Simple Past
Simple Past Verb
Hector's parents **settled** in California.
Jessica's parents **paid** for her college expenses.

Past Progressive
Was/Were + Base Form + *-ing*
Hector **was working** long hours.

Past Time: Not Specific (Indefinite)

Present Perfect
Has/Have + Past Participle
Hector's mother and I **have become** good friends.
This is an intercultural marriage that **has worked**.

Past Time: Habitual or Repeated

Used to + Base Form
I **used to think** I would marry a Hispanic woman.

Would + Base Form
We **would go** to family gatherings every weekend.

Past Time: Before a Time in the Past

Past Perfect
Had + Past Participle
By the time Hector was born, they **had earned** their American citizenship.

Past Perfect Progressive
Had been + Base Form + *-ing*
I realized I **hadn't been giving** Hector's family a fair chance.

Future in the Past

Was/Were going to + Base Form
I thought our relationship **was going to stay** the same.

Would + Base Form
I didn't think we **would** ever **argue** about anything.

GRAMMAR NOTES

1 Simple Past

Use the **simple past** to express an action or state occurring at a general or specific time in the past.	
• **a general time**	Jessica **wanted** to find the right person to marry.
• **a specific time**	Hector **met** his future wife during his senior year in college.

2 Past Progressive

Use the **past progressive** to express an action that was **in progress** (not finished) at a time in the past.	Hector **wasn't paying** enough attention to me.

3 Present Perfect

Use the **present perfect** to express an action or state occurring at an indefinite time in the past.	
• **present perfect** for **indefinite** past	Jessica **has learned** a great deal about Hector's family.
• **simple past** for **definite** past	After they **graduated**, Hector **asked** Jessica to marry him.
You can also use the **present perfect** to connect the **past** and the **present**. (See Unit 1.)	Hector and Jessica **have been** married for five years.
BE CAREFUL! Don't use the **present perfect** with a **past time expression**.	Hector and Jessica **got** married five years ago. *(at a definite time in the past)* **NOT** Hector and Jessica ~~have gotten~~ married five years ago.

4 Used to and Would

You can use *used to* and *would* + base form to express habitual past actions or states.

We use *used to* to show a **habitual past action** or state that was true in the past but is **no longer true**. *Used to* is generally not used with past-time expressions.	I **used to be** quite lonely. *(I'm not lonely anymore.)*
We use *would* to express actions or states that **occurred regularly** during a period in the past.	When I was single, I **would get up** early every morning. *(I did it every morning.)*
USAGE NOTE We often use *would* with **past time expressions**.	When I was single, I **would** get up early **every morning**.
USAGE NOTE *Used to* and *would* are similar in meaning when they express past actions. However, only *used to* can express past location, state of being, or possession.	Jessica **used to live** in New England. *(location)* **NOT** Jessica ~~would~~ live in New England. Mia **used to be** a nurse. *(state of being)* **NOT** Mia ~~would~~ be a nurse. We **used to have** a summer home. *(possession)* **NOT** We ~~would~~ have a summer home.
BE CAREFUL! In more formal English, we drop the "d" in *used to* in questions and negatives.	Didn't you **use to** date a lot? **NOT** Didn't you use~~d~~ to date a lot? Mary didn't **use to** attend many parties. **NOT** Mary didn't use~~d~~ to attend many parties.

5 Past Perfect

Use the **past perfect** with the **simple past** to show which of two actions or states happened **first**.	Hector and Jessica **had known** each other for a year when they *got* married. By the time our wedding day *arrived*, Jessica's family **had prepared** everything.
USAGE NOTE We don't often use the past perfect in sentences containing *before* or *after*. Use the **simple past** to describe both events.	Hector and Jessica **left** on their honeymoon the day after they **got** married.

6 Past Perfect Progressive

Use the **past perfect progressive** to express an action that was **in progress before** another past action.	Jessica **had been attending** college for three years when she and Hector met.

7 Future in the Past

Future in the past means that an action was planned or expected at a time in the past (before now). Use *was/were going to* or *would* + base form to describe future in the past actions or states.

• *was/were going to* + base form	Hector and Jessica knew that they **were going to get** married on July 15, 2015.
• *would* + base form	They knew where the wedding **would take** place. However, they didn't know where they **would go** on their honeymoon.
USAGE NOTE *Would* can have two different meanings in past time sentences:	
• **habitual past action**	When I was single, I **would go out** every Saturday night with my buddies.
• **future in the past**	I didn't realize that **would change** after I got married.

REFERENCE NOTE

For a list of **irregular verbs**, see Appendix 1 on page 411.

Go to MyEnglishLab to watch the grammar presentation.

STEP 3   FOCUSED PRACTICE

EXERCISE 1 DISCOVER THE GRAMMAR

Ⓐ GRAMMAR NOTES 1, 4–7 Read the sentences based on the reading. Write the earlier-occurring action or state on the first line and the later-occurring action or state on the second.

1. By the time Hector was born, they had earned their American citizenship.

   earlier-occurring <u>*they had earned their American citizenship*</u>

   later-occurring <u>*By the time Hector was born*</u>

2. I thought our relationship was going to stay the same.

   earlier-occurring _____

   later-occurring _____

3. I realized I hadn't been giving Hector's family a fair chance.

   earlier-occurring _____

   later-occurring _____

4. I used to think I would marry a Hispanic woman.

   earlier-occurring _____

   later-occurring _____

5. I didn't think we would ever argue about anything.

earlier-occurring _____

later-occurring _____

6. It occurred to me that work had become his top priority.

earlier-occurring _____

later-occurring _____

7. I realized the importance of the fact that Hector had grown up without much money.

earlier-occurring _____

later-occurring _____

8. I realized that I'd been wrong about several things.

earlier-occurring _____

later-occurring _____

B GRAMMAR NOTES 4, 7 Read the sentences based on the reading. Check (✓) *Future in the Past* or *Habitual Action in the Past*.

	Future in the Past	Habitual Action in the Past
1. I used to only date women from my own cultural background.	☐	☑
2. I thought our relationship would stay the same.	☐	☐
3. I didn't think we would ever argue about anything.	☐	☐
4. We would go to family gatherings most weekends.	☐	☐
5. Everyone would speak at once.	☐	☐
6. I would feel shut out.	☐	☐

EXERCISE 2 SIMPLE PAST AND PRESENT PERFECT

GRAMMAR NOTES 1, 3 Complete the story. Circle the correct answers.

Carmen Peralta and Josh Smith (got married) / have gotten married five years
ago. Their marriage almost didn't happen / hasn't happened, though. They
met / have met at a restaurant when Josh was studying in Spain. Carmen's
friend Ramón invited / has invited her and her girlfriend Alicia to go with him
and Josh. Carmen says, "That night, I thought / I've thought, 'He's the most
opinionated man I ever met / I've ever met.' Then, a couple of weeks
afterwards, Josh called / has called me and asked / has asked
me out. I wanted / I've wanted to say no, but something

made / has made me accept. After that, one thing led / has led to another."
    10.   **11.**

For his part, Josh says, "Carmen is unique. I never knew / I've never known

                                         12.

anyone even remotely like her." Carmen says, "At first glance, you

might have trouble seeing how Josh and I could be married. In certain

ways, we're as different as night and day. I was born in Spain; he was

born in the United States. I'm an early bird; he's a night owl. He's

conservative; I'm liberal. He always loved / has always loved sports, and

                                   13.

I was never able / I've never been able to stand them. I guess you might say,

                 14.

ultimately, that we're a case of opposites being attracted to each other."

EXERCISE 3   PAST PROGRESSIVE AND PAST PERFECT PROGRESSIVE

GRAMMAR NOTES 2, 6   Complete the sentences about two intercultural couples and how they met. Use the past progressive or past perfect progressive forms of the verbs in parentheses. Use contractions where possible.

1. Abimbola _____*had been living*_____ in New York for two years when he first met his
                     (live)

   wife, Linda.

2. In July 2010, Abimbola _____ in a restaurant in Queens.
                               (work)

3. He _____ much money until he started working at the restaurant.
         (not / make)

4. Linda, on the other hand, _____ college for three years when she
                             (attend)

   took a job as a hostess at the restaurant.

5. Two of her friends _____ at the restaurant, and they introduced
                          (work)

   her to Abimbola.

6. One night, Abimbola and Linda _____ work at the same time, and
                             (leave)

   they decided to go to a movie together. That's when they fell in love.

7. Ali _____ a taxi in Chicago in the fall of 2014.
          (drive)

8. He _____ landscape work before he was hired by the
          (do)

   taxi company.

9. One day, Mei-Ling _____ a taxi home from work, and she started
                    (take)

   talking to the driver. That driver was Ali.

10. When Mei-Ling met Ali, she _____ about moving away from
                            (think)

    Chicago for almost a year. But after she met Ali, she changed her mind and decided to stay.

EXERCISE 4 *USED TO* AND *WOULD*

GRAMMAR NOTE 4 Safiya Abbott and Carmen Peralta, who both got married fairly recently, now live in the same city in the United States. Complete their conversation with the correct forms of *used to* or *would* and the verbs in parentheses. Use *would* and contractions where possible.

SAFIYA: Carmen, how do you feel about life in the United States? How does it compare with living in Spain?

CARMEN: Well, it was really hard at first, but I'm feeling better about it now.

SAFIYA: How so? What's changed?

CARMEN: Well, I guess the first thing I'd say is that _____*my life used to be*_____ a lot more
                                                                  1. (my life / be)
spontaneous. Everything wasn't as planned out as it is here. Like on Friday nights, for

example, if my friends and I felt like having a get-together, _____
                                                                2. (we / organize)
one on the spot. _____ to find a bunch of people who wanted to
                  3. (We / always manage)
go dancing or something. Here everything has to be scheduled and written on your

calendar. But I've more or less gotten accustomed to that. And one really positive thing is

that I've made different kinds of friends. The friends _____ in
                                                        4. (I / have)
Spain were all my age. Now I know people of all different ages.

SAFIYA: Good. So what else has changed for the better?

CARMEN: Well, my job is a lot more interesting now. In Spain, _____ a
                                                                  5. (I / be)
bank teller. _____ to work every morning just to earn a
             6. (I / go)
paycheck. It wasn't very exciting. Now I'm a Spanish teacher, and that's a challenge.

Anyway, what about you? How's your life?

SAFIYA: Good overall. Until recently, I'd never had to work. _____ with
                                                                7. (I / live)
my parents, and they supported me. Then I met Peter, and he supported me. But when

we left Lebanon and moved to the United States, I started working. Now I'm working for

a company downtown, and I really like it. It's fun to see people every day, and I've made a

lot of new friends. I realize now that _____ kind of boring. The
                                        8. (my life / be)
other thing that's changed is where we live. _____ the house
                                              9. (I / love)
where I lived with lots of people from my family before I married Peter. Now it's just the

two of us in a small apartment. At first, I missed the big house and my family, but now I

like our apartment.

CARMEN: So how do you feel about being married?

SAFIYA: I love it.

CARMEN: Me, too. I wouldn't really change a thing. You know how everyone says how great it is to

be single? _____ so, too. But not now.
            10. (I / think)

EXERCISE 5
SIMPLE PAST AND PAST PERFECT

GRAMMAR NOTES 1, 5

Years ago, Samantha Yang emigrated to Canada from China. Use the simple past and past perfect to complete the story of how Samantha and Darrell Hammer met and decided to get married. Combine each pair of sentences into one sentence. Put the word(s) in parentheses in the logical place in each sentence. Do not use contractions.

1. Samantha Yang attended high school in Canada for a year. Then she met Darrell Hammer. (when)

   Samantha Yang had attended high school in Canada for a year when she met Darrell Hammer.

2. Darrell liked Samantha right away. He never met such an interesting girl before. (because)

   _____

   _____

3. Samantha was nervous about dating Darrell. Her mother told her not to date Canadian men. (because)

   _____

   _____

4. Darrell asked Samantha out. Samantha already decided she couldn't disobey her mother. (by the time)

   _____

   _____

5. They graduated from high school. Samantha still did not agree to go out with Darrell. (by the time)

   _____

   _____

6. They both returned to their hometown four years later. Darrell completed military service, and Samantha graduated from college. (by the time)

   _____

   _____

7. Samantha and her mother went to the hospital one morning. Samantha's mother woke up with chest pains. (because)

_____

_____

8. Darrell was at the hospital, too. He got a job there. (because)

_____

_____

9. Darrell was very kind and helpful to Samantha's mother. He didn't forget Samantha. (because)

_____

_____

10. Samantha's mother apologized to Darrell. She made a mistake in forbidding Samantha to go out with him. (because)

_____

_____

11. A week passed. Darrell asked Samantha out on a date . . . again. (when)

_____

_____

12. Darrell and Samantha dated for six months. They got married . . . with her mother's blessing! (when)

_____

_____

EXERCISE 6 PAST TIME QUESTIONS

GRAMMAR NOTES 1–7 Answer the questions about your past experiences. Write complete sentences. Use the grammatical structures in parentheses.

1. How long ago did you start school? (simple past)

I started school ten years ago.

2. Which countries have you visited? (present perfect)

3. Where were you living one year ago? (past progressive)

4. Had you already met any of your classmates when you started this class? (past perfect)

5. How long had you been studying English when you started this class? (past perfect progressive)

6. What did you use to do when you lived in the country you were born in? (habitual past action with *used to*)

7. What would you do regularly when you first moved to the United States? (habitual past action with *would*)

8. What did you think you were going to be when you were a child? (future in the past with *be going to*)

9. What didn't happen recently that you thought would happen? (future in the past with *would*)

EXERCISE 7 EDITING

GRAMMAR NOTES 1–7 Read Lynne Kim's journal entry. There are ten mistakes in the use of past tense verbs. The first mistake is already corrected. Find and correct nine more.

ve had
I'd had a tiring day today, but I just had to write. It's our three-year anniversary. Sejun

and I are married three years as of today. So maybe this is the time for me to take stock

of my situation. The obvious question is whether I'm happy I got married. The answer is,

"Absolutely." When I remember what my life has been like before we were married, I realize

now how lonely I've been before. I use to have some problems with his family, but now I

really gotten to know them. I love spending time with them! I've even learn some Korean!

And Sejun is a wonderful guy. When we were dating, I didn't know how he will behave after

we got married. I thought I'll have to do all the housework. But I wasn't having any reason

to worry. Today, we split everything 50/50. The only complaint I have is that Sejun snores at

night! I guess I'm pretty lucky!

Go to MyEnglishLab for more focused practice.

EXERCISE 8 LISTENING

02|02 **A** Listen to the news broadcast. What is the topic of the broadcast?

_____

_____

02|02 **B** Read the questions. Listen again to the news broadcast. Answer each question in a complete sentence.

1. What did Tracy Chadwick and Sunil Kapoor hire Reverend Martinez to do?

   They hired him to marry them while they were jumping from a plane.

2. How long have they been members of the jumping group?

   _____

3. To date, how many jumps have Tracy and Sunil each made?

   _____

4. How were they originally going to get married?

   _____

5. Why did they decide not to do this? (first reason)

   _____

6. Why did they decide not to do this? (second reason)

   _____

7. Had Reverend Martinez ever done this kind of wedding before?

   _____

8. Where did Reverend Martinez use to be a pastor?

   _____

C Work with a partner. Discuss these questions. Report interesting examples to the class.

1. Have you ever done anything as unusual as the wedding described in the Listening, or have you known anyone who did? What did you or this person do?

2. Why did you or the person you know do this unusual thing?

EXERCISE 9 WHAT'S THE STORY?

INFORMATION GAP Work with a partner. Student A will follow the instructions below. Student B will follow the instructions on page 437.

STUDENT A

- The story below is missing some information. Your partner has the same story that contains your missing information. Ask your partner questions to find the missing information.

  EXAMPLE: **A:** What kind of company did he use to work for?
  B: He used to work for a company that...

- Your partner's story is missing some information. Answer your partner's questions so that your partner can fill in his or her missing information.

  EXAMPLE: **B:** How long would he stay on the road?
  A: He would stay on the road for...

Jack Strait's life is quite different now from the way it used to be. He used to work for a company that _____. His job required him to do a lot of traveling. He would stay on the road for two or three weeks at a time. It was always the same: As soon as he pulled into a town, he would look for _____.

The next morning, he'd leave his business card at a lot of different establishments, hoping that someone would agree to see him. If he'd been lucky enough to arrange an appointment in advance, he'd show them _____. Occasionally they would order a carpet or some linoleum; most often they wouldn't.

Jack's marriage began to suffer. His wife, Ivana, had come to the United States from Russia to marry him. She didn't know anyone in their town, and her family was back in Russia. She was lonely. He missed Ivana a lot, but there wasn't much he could do about the situation. And when he was on the road, he hardly ever saw his children. He would try to _____ if he had a spare moment. Usually, however, it was so late that they had already gone to bed. The children were growing up without him.

Finally, Ivana laid down the law, saying, "Why should we even be married if we're never going to see each other? I didn't come to this country to be a job widow." Jack decided she was right. He took a risk. He quit his job and started his own business. Things were difficult at first, but at least the family was together.

That was five years ago. Things have changed a lot since then. Jack and his family used to live in a small apartment. Now they own a house. Life is good.

EXERCISE 10 CHANGES IN YOUR LIFE

DISCUSSION Work in a group. Talk about a significant change in each person's life.
Discuss one of the topics in the box or choose your own topic. Ask the questions below.
Then report back to the class.

| a move to another place | education plans | marriage | career plans |

EXAMPLE: My career plans have changed. I wasn't going to attend college. I was going to . . .
Now I've decided to . . .

1. What are some things in your life that have changed significantly in recent years?
2. What were you going to do before that you've decided not to do now?
3. What did you think that you would never do?
4. What did you use to think that you don't think now?
5. What are you now planning to do that you hadn't considered before?

EXERCISE 11 TIMES HAVE CHANGED

DISCUSSION Work in a group. Discuss differences
between marriages sixty years ago and today. Report
your opinions to the class.

1. Were intercultural marriages common sixty years
ago? What kinds of people would usually marry
each other sixty years ago? What kinds of people
often marry each other now? Were there fewer
opportunities for people of different ethnicities and
races to interact in the past than there are today?

2. Sixty years ago, what problems did intercultural
couples use to face? Do you think people were
more racist in the past than today?

3. Do you believe that people sixty years ago thought
that relationships between different ethnic groups
would change? How have they changed, in your
opinion? Are they still changing today?

Go to MyEnglishLab for more communication practice.

FROM GRAMMAR TO WRITING

A **BEFORE YOU WRITE** Think about an experience you've had that turned out differently from what you expected. Write a few sentences on each of the following topics:

- What you thought would happen
- What actually happened
- What you've learned

B **WRITE** Using your ideas in A, write a five-paragraph essay on your experience. Remember to use past time verb constructions. Try to avoid the common mistakes in the chart. Use the example below to help you begin your essay.

EXAMPLE: I've been happily married to my wife, Kate, for years now. But the first time Kate and I met in China, I never dreamed that we would end up husband and wife. In fact, I didn't understand a word Kate was saying because she spoke only English, and I spoke Chinese. . . .

Common Mistakes in Using Past Time Verbs

Don't confuse the present perfect and the simple past. Make sure to use the **present perfect for the indefinite past** and the **simple past for the definite past**.	I **have visited** Nigeria twice. I **was** there last fall. **NOT** I ~~visited~~ Nigeria twice. I ~~'ve been~~ there last fall.
Don't confuse *will* and *would*. Use **would** to express the **future in the past**.	Don't worry. Hussein said he **would be** here by five. **NOT** Hussein said he ~~will be~~ here by five.
Don't confuse *used to* and *would*. Remember to use **used to** for **past location**, **state of being**, and **possession**.	I **used to have** a motorcycle, but I don't anymore. **NOT** I ~~would have~~ a motorcycle, but I don't anymore.
Used to is sometimes misspelled in formal English. **Drop the "d"** in questions and negatives.	Didn't you **use to live** in Accra? **NOT** Didn't you ~~used to live~~ in Accra?

C **CHECK YOUR WORK** Look at your essay. Underline the past time verbs. Use the Editing Checklist to check your work.

Editing Checklist

Did you . . . ?

- ☐ use the present perfect for the indefinite past
- ☐ use the simple past for the definite past
- ☐ use the past perfect to show actions or states before a time in the past
- ☐ use *was going to* or *would* to describe future-in-the-past situations
- ☐ use *used to* for habitual past actions or states that are no long true

D **REVISE YOUR WORK** Read your essay again. Can you improve your writing? Make changes if necessary.

Go to MyEnglishLab for more writing practice.

UNIT 2 REVIEW

Test yourself on the grammar of the unit.

A Complete the paragraph with simple past or present perfect forms of the verbs in parentheses.

Ever since Bob Maynard and Victoria Kwanza _____ married, they
1. (get)
_____ a lot of traveling. They _____ to six
2. (do) **3. (be)**
countries, and they plan to tour another two this summer. So far, their favorite is South

Africa, which they _____ twice. The first time _____
4. (visit) **5. (be)**
in 2009. They _____ again last year. Victoria says, "When I was a girl, I
6. (go)
always _____ to marry a man who would travel with me all over the
7. (want)
world. Bob is that man. I _____ anyone so adventurous."
8. (never know)

B Complete the paragraph with simple past or past perfect forms of the verbs from the box.

be	come	learn	live	meet	not / know	not / speak

Julio Sanchez and Liv Carlsson have an intercultural marriage. Liv is Swedish, and she

_____ to the United States to work. She and Julio _____ at a party.
1. **2.**
Liv _____ many people at the party, and neither did Julio. He is from Colombia,
3.
and he _____ English very well at that time. Luckily, before she got the job in the
4.
United States, Liv _____ in Spain for several years, and she _____
5. **6.**
to speak Spanish very well. So it _____ easy for Liv and Julio to talk to each other
7.
at the party . . . and the rest is history!

C Find and correct five mistakes.

Solange grew up in Brazil, and she misses it. When she was a teenager, she didn't used

to study very hard at school. Instead, she will go to the beach every day and have fun with

her friends. Solange has been being married to Ty, who is American, for ten years. Solange

and Ty have two children, Ava and Jacob. Solange wants to show her homeland to her family.

They would go to Brazil last year, but unfortunately, they had to call off the trip, though they

been planning it for months. Solange hopes that they can go next year instead.

Now check your answers on page 427.

Go to MyEnglishLab to complete the review online.

Future Time

TRAVEL

OUTCOMES
- Discuss future actions, plans, events, and predictions
- Identify main points in an article about travel
- Identify main points in a conversation about travel plans
- Speculate about future events
- Make predictions about the future
- Write an essay about future goals and aspirations

STEP 1	**GRAMMAR IN CONTEXT**

BEFORE YOU READ

Discuss the questions.

1. What problem are the travelers in the cartoon having?
2. What can people do to try to prevent this problem?
3. Do you like to travel to distant places, or would you rather stay close to home?

READ

 03|01 Read this article about getting the most out of a trip.

Get the Most Out of It

So you're visiting some new countries this year? You already have your tickets, and you leave in exactly four weeks. A month from now, you'll be relaxing in the sunshine or touring famous landmarks. But are you prepared to maximize the enjoyment of your experience? In my capacity as *Times* travel editor, I've been journeying abroad since 2007, so I've learned a few things. In this week's column, I'm going to give you suggestions in five areas that will help you get the most out of your trip.

FIRST TIP: Jetlag. If you've ever flown a significant distance away from your home time zone, you know lack of sleep is a problem. By the time you arrive, you'll have been flying for eight to ten hours and won't be able to keep your eyes open. Then your entire body will be out of whack for days. Some effects of jetlag are inevitable, but here's my suggestion for minimizing them: Take a late afternoon or evening flight, and make every effort to sleep on the plane, even if it's only for an hour or so. When you land, it will probably be late morning or early afternoon. Stay up until evening! Don't take a nap, no matter how excruciatingly tired and sleepy you feel. That way, you'll fall into a new rhythm as naturally as possible. Your body will adjust much more quickly.

SECOND TIP: Tours. If you've been abroad before, I'd say go ahead and chart your own course. If you haven't, join a tour group. You can get excellent package deals that include accommodations and tours that hit the high points. Good tour leaders will show you the things you want to see. You'll make new friends and learn a lot. Yes, it's true that tours can be hectic and intense. They're worth it, though.

THIRD TIP: Accommodations. Consider using Airbnb, a website that started in 2008. It's an online marketplace that links people who have property to rent with visitors who are looking for a place to stay. If you want to use Airbnb, you'll need to go to their website and create an account. Then you'll be able to find all kinds of lodging situations—everything from an air mattress in the corner of someone's living room to an entire home or apartment. You can stay in boats, castles, and even igloos and tree houses. You'll certainly meet interesting people, too.

FOURTH TIP: Money and valuables. Resist the temptation to carry your money, passport, or other valuables in a purse or wallet. Keep them in a money belt instead. Potential thieves will be out in force everywhere you go. They'll have a lot more difficulty stealing from a money belt worn around your waist under your clothes.

FIFTH TIP: Language and culture. Few things will please the inhabitants of the countries where you're going more than if you make an effort to learn something about them. Buy a phrasebook and start acquiring some of the basics of the language. Begin now, and you'll have learned enough to accomplish some basic communication by the time you arrive. Discover a bit of the history. Try to step out of your own mindset and put yourself into the shoes of the people who live there.

So there you have it. Take my advice. By the time you get home, you'll have acquired some wonderful memories for your mental scrapbook. Make it the trip of a lifetime.

AFTER YOU READ

A VOCABULARY   Choose the word or phrase that is closest in meaning to the word in **bold**.

1. Are you prepared to **maximize** the enjoyment of your experience?
   a. make easy   **b.** decrease   **c.** complicate   **d.** increase

2. Your entire body will be **out of whack** for days.
   a. not working well   **b.** ill   **c.** wounded   **d.** in good shape

3. You'll have **acquired** some wonderful memories.
   a. lost   **b.** gained   **c.** understood   **d.** treasured

4. Some effects of jetlag are **inevitable**.
   a. discouraging   **b.** amazing   **c.** unavoidable   **d.** stressful

5. Here's my suggestion for **minimizing** them.
   a. understanding   **b.** increasing   **c.** avoiding   **d.** decreasing

6. Don't take a nap, no matter how **excruciatingly** tired and sleepy you feel.
   a. pleasantly   **b.** terribly   **c.** interestingly   **d.** boringly

7. Go ahead and **chart your own course**.
   a. take a cruise   **b.** hire a tour guide   **c.** make your own plans   **d.** ask for help

8. Tours can be **hectic** and intense.
   a. stressful   **b.** pleasurable   **c.** dangerous   **d.** expensive

B COMPREHENSION   Complete the statements from the reading.

1. Jetlag is strongly related to _____ of sleep.

2. To avoid jetlag, you should stay up until the _____ of the day you arrive.

3. The author recommends taking _____ if you haven't been abroad before.

4. Airbnb is an online _____ that links owners and renters.

5. You may be victimized by _____ if you carry valuables in a wallet or purse.

6. The author suggests keeping valuables in a _____.

7. To please the residents of countries you visit, you should buy and study a _____.

8. You'll understand the local people better if you put _____ in their shoes.

C DISCUSSION   Work with a partner. Compare your answers in B. Give reasons for your answers. Then discuss: What do you do when you travel to get the most out of your trip? Have you tried any of the tips in the article, and if so, were they helpful?

Go to MyEnglishLab for more grammar in context practice.

FUTURE TIME

Simple Future

Will/Be going to + Base Form

You**'ll like** the hotel.
You**'re going to like** the hotel.

Future Progressive

Will be/Be going to + *Be* + Base Form + *-ing*

A week from now, you**'ll be relaxing** in the sun.
A week from now, you**'re going to be relaxing** in the sun.

Simple Present

Simple Present Verb

The tour **starts** tomorrow at 4:00 p.m.

Present Progressive

Be + Base Form + *-ing*

We**'re visiting** our friends later this summer.

Two Actions in the Future

Will/Be going to + Simple Present

I**'ll call** you as soon as we **land**.
We**'re going to visit** Florence after we **tour** Rome.

Future Perfect

Will have + Past Participle

We**'ll have arrived** by 4:00 p.m.

Future Perfect Progressive

Will have been + Base Form + *-ing*

We **will have been flying** for hours by then.

GRAMMAR NOTES

1 *Be Going to* and *Will*

Use *be going to* or *will* to say what you think will happen in the future.

- *be going to*
- *will*

I think I**'m going to enjoy** the trip.
I think I**'ll enjoy** the trip.

We most often use *be going to* to talk about a future situation that is **planned** or already developing.

We**'re going to take** our vacation in June this year.
Look at that sky! It**'s going to rain** for sure!

BE CAREFUL! Use *will*, not *be going to*, to express a future action **decided** on at the moment of speaking.

Oh, no! I can't go to my dentist appointment this afternoon. I**'ll call** and **change** it.
NOT ~~I'm going to~~ call and change it.

2 Actions in Progress in the Future

Use the **future progressive** (*will be* or *be going to be* + base form + *-ing*) to describe an action that will be **in progress at a certain time** in the future.

• *will be*	We**'ll be visiting** Florence on our Italy trip.
• *be going to be*	We**'re going to be spending** time in Rome, too.
We often use the future progressive informally to talk about a **future intention**.	Next week at this time, we**'ll be climbing** Mount Kilimanjaro.

3 Future Scheduled Events

You can use the **simple present** to talk about a future action or state that is part of a **schedule**.	We **leave** on Saturday at 8:00 p.m. The plane **arrives** in Rome at 8:30 a.m.

4 Future Plans

You can use the **present progressive** to talk about a future action or state that is not just an intention but is **already arranged**.	We**'re traveling** to Japan in August. *(We already have our tickets.)* Our friend Cosimo **is arriving** tonight from Venice. *(He just called with the information.)*

5 Two Separate Actions in the Future

To talk about two separate actions or states in the future, use *will* or *be going to* in the **independent clause** and the **simple present** in the **dependent clause**.

• *will*	INDEPENDENT CLAUSE DEPENDENT CLAUSE We**'ll rent** a car when we **get** to Italy.
• *be going to*	DEPENDENT CLAUSE INDEPENDENT CLAUSE When we**'re** in Hawaii, we**'re going to surf**.
BE CAREFUL! The verb in the **dependent** clause is in the **simple present**, but its **meaning is future**. Don't use *will* or *be going to* in the dependent clause.	We'll leave as soon as the taxi **gets** here. **NOT** We'll leave as soon as the taxi ~~will get~~ here.

6 Actions Before a Time in the Future

Use the **future perfect** to refer to an action or state that will **happen before a certain time** in the future. Use the **future perfect progressive** to refer to an action or state that **will be happening before a certain time** in the future.

• future perfect	By the end of our trip, we**'ll have seen** a lot.
• future perfect progressive	By June 1st, we**'ll have been traveling** for two weeks.
USAGE NOTE We often use the **future perfect** with *by* and *by the time*.	*By the time* we finish our trip, we**'ll have visited** ten countries.

Go to MyEnglishLab to watch the grammar presentation.

EXERCISE 1   DISCOVER THE GRAMMAR

A GRAMMAR NOTES 1–6   Read the sentences based on the reading. Underline the verbs showing future time and label the ways they show future time.

1. So you're visiting some new countries this year?   *present progressive*

2. You leave in exactly four weeks.   _____

3. A month from now, you'll be relaxing in the sunshine.   _____

4. I'm going to give you suggestions in five areas.   _____

5. The suggestions will help you with your trip.   _____

6. You'll have been flying for eight to ten hours.   _____

7. When you land, it will probably be late morning.   _____

_____

8. By then, you'll have acquired nice memories.   _____

B GRAMMAR NOTES 1, 3–4, 6   Look at the underlined verbs in the sentences based on the reading. Check (✓) *Present Time* or *Future Time*.

	Present Time	Future Time
1. So you're visiting some new countries this year?	☐	✓
2. You already have your tickets.	☐	☐
3. You leave in exactly four weeks.	☐	☐
4. When you land, it will probably be late morning.	☐	☐
5. You can get package deals that include accommodations.	☐	☐
6. Airbnb links owners with renters.	☐	☐
7. Find out about the countries where you're going.	☐	☐
8. You'll have learned a lot by the time you arrive.	☐	☐
9. Put yourself in the shoes of the people who live there.	☐	☐
10. So there you have it.	☐	☐

EXERCISE 2 PRESENT PROGRESSIVE FOR THE FUTURE

GRAMMAR NOTES 1, 3–4 Nancy Osborne is traveling in Europe. Complete her email to her friend Evelyn with the correct future forms of the verbs in the box. Use the present progressive where possible.

arrive	leave	move		see	take
go	mind	not be able to use		~~shine~~	write

To: evelyn111@cmail.com
From: NancyOsb@yoohoo.com
Re: London

Hi Evelyn,

Well, I've been in London for three days now, and it hasn't stopped raining. Fortunately, I read online that the sun _____*is going to shine*_____ tomorrow.
1.
Hallelujah! I went to the British Museum yesterday and had such a good time that I _____ again this
2.
morning. In the afternoon, I _____ a tour of
3.
the Tower of London.

I've been staying at a bed and breakfast that's really nice, but it's also pretty expensive, so I _____ to a hostel tonight. I don't think I
4.
_____ staying there, since I don't need luxury.
5.

I've met some really nice people at the B and B, including a lady who gave me a theater ticket she _____. So I _____ a play at a West End
6.   7.
theater on Friday night. On Saturday, I _____ for France at 6 p.m. via
8.
the Chunnel train. I _____ in Paris at 8:30 p.m. Can you believe that?
9.

That's it for now. Hope things are OK with you. I _____ again soon.
10.

Best,
Nancy

EXERCISE 3 TWO SEPARATE ACTIONS IN THE FUTURE

GRAMMAR NOTE 5 Complete the sentences about the rest of Nancy's trip to Europe. Describe two actions or events in the future in each sentence. Use the correct forms of the verbs in parentheses. Use contractions where possible.

1. As soon as _____*Nancy arrives*_____ in Paris,
   (Nancy / arrive)
   _____*she'll find*_____ an inexpensive place
   (she / find)
   to stay.

2. _____ her friend Carolyn
   (She / meet)
   the day after _____.
   (she / arrive)

3. _____ the Eiffel Tower, the
   (Nancy and Carolyn / visit)
   Louvre, and the Palace of Versailles before
   _____ Paris.
   (they / leave)

4. When _____ touring Paris,
   (they / finish)
   _____ a train to Rome.
   (they / take)

5. _____ Florence and Venice
   (They / visit)
   after _____ Rome.
   (they / tour)

6. Before _____ back to the
   (they / fly)
   United States, _____
   (they / buy)
   souvenirs.

Eiffel Tower

EXERCISE 4 FUTURE TIME VERBS

GRAMMAR NOTES 1–6 Answer the questions. Write complete sentences based on your own experience.

1. What do you think your career will be?
   I think I will be a nurse.

2. Where do you think you'll be living in five years?

3. What are you going to do this evening after dinner?

4. Where are you going on your next vacation?

5. What are you going to do as soon as you leave English class today?

6. What time does your next English class begin?

7. By what date will you have finished your studies?

8. In a year's time, how long will you have been studying English?

EXERCISE 5 EDITING

GRAMMAR NOTES 1–6 Read the blog. There are 11 mistakes in the use of future verbs. The first mistake is already corrected. Find and correct 10 more.

August 20

I am writing these words in English because I need the practice. At this moment, I am waiting to get on an airplane. I'm on my way to a year of study at Columbia University in the United States. It's a ten-hour flight, so I hope I will have gotten some sleep by the time we ~~will~~ land. I am looking forward to being there, but I am also a little afraid. What do I find when I will get to America? Will the Americans be arrogant and unfriendly? Will I make any friends? Am I happy? My best friend back home in Nigeria said, "You don't make any real friends when you'll be there." I am not so sure. I guess I find out.

September 20

I have been here in New York for a month now, and I have found that things are a lot different from what I expected. The majority of people here are friendly. They go out of their way to help you if you need it, and my American friends invite me to go places. Soon, I go hiking with a group from my dormitory.

Two of the ideas I had about the United States, however, seem to be true. One is that Americans pay more attention to rules than people do in Nigeria. For example, American drivers will seem to obey traffic laws more often than Nigerian drivers do. The other idea is about the American family. In Nigeria, the family is very important, but some Nigerian people think the family means nothing in the United States. I think it might be true, since my American friends almost never mention their parents or their brothers and sisters. Anyway, I am going to have a chance to see a real American family. I go with my roommate Susan to spend Thanksgiving break with her family in Pennsylvania. When I see her family, maybe I'm going to understand more.

Go to MyEnglishLab for more focused practice.

EXERCISE 6　LISTENING

▶03|02　**A**　The Fosters are traveling in Canada. Listen to their conversation. What are they going to do today?

_____

▶03|02　**B**　Listen again. Read the sentences. Check (✓) *True* or *False*.

	True	False
1. Tim is still in bed.	✓	☐
2. The Fosters are going to the mall this morning.	☐	☐
3. Amy and Tim want to go to the museum.	☐	☐
4. Dad thinks the children will learn something at the museum.	☐	☐
5. Tim thinks it's always important to learn new things.	☐	☐
6. The Fosters are on the tour bus now.	☐	☐
7. The Fosters will miss the bus if they don't hurry.	☐	☐
8. Tim and Amy like tours.	☐	☐
9. Amy and Tim don't want to go on a tour.	☐	☐
10. The Fosters are going to the mall before they go on the tour.	☐	☐
11. The tour will end after 12:30.	☐	☐
12. Amy and Tim are happy that they are going to go ice-skating.	☐	☐

C　Work with a partner. Look at the following list of events or activities that will take place in the city on the following day. Which events do you think the parents will want to attend? The children? Both parents and children? Share your predictions with the class.

EXAMPLE:　The parents will want to attend the guided tour of the downtown section . . .

- Guided tour of the downtown section of the city
- Disco roller-skating
- *Broadway Across Canada*—a Broadway musical
- Indiana Jones and the Adventures of Archaeology
- GPS Adventures Canada—interactive maze combining technology, nature, and hidden treasure
- Wildlife Photographer of the Year competition
- Emerging artists—exhibition of new student art works
- Valley Zoo excursion
- Kids' indoor tennis practice
- Walk Alberta—guided trail walk through Wolf Willow

EXERCISE 7 WHAT WILL HAPPEN?

A QUESTIONNAIRE You are going to discuss the future. First, answer the questions about things that might happen in the next twenty-five years. If you think the event will happen, write *yes* in the chart. If you don't think it will happen, write *no*. Add your own question in the last row. Then ask your partner the questions and record his or her responses.

Event	You	Partner
Will we take vacations at the bottom of the sea?		
Will we travel to other planets in the solar system?		
Will we end poverty?		
Will we stop climate change?		

B Report your findings to the class. Discuss.

EXAMPLE: **A:** Pablo and I think we'll have stopped climate change within twenty-five years.
B: Really? Ming and I don't think we will. We're still going to have problems with flooding and storms caused by climate change . . .

EXERCISE 8 WHERE IN THE WORLD ARE WE?

GAME Form two teams. With your team, use the prompts to construct eight travel statements about the future. Then create two statements of your own. Present each statement to the other team. They guess what place is being referred to, choosing from the words in the box. Take turns. To check answers, see page 435.

EXAMPLE: **Prompt:** be landing / largest country in the world / an hour

      TEAM A: We'll be landing in the largest country in the world in an hour.

      TEAM B: You'll be landing in Russia in an hour.

Brazil	Cairo	China	Mount Kilimanjaro	New York	Rome	the Volga	Toronto

Team A's Prompts:

1. be landing / capital of Egypt / half an hour

2. going to arrive / largest country in South America / three hours

3. arriving / largest city in Canada / an hour

4. going to cross / longest river in Europe / two hours

5. leave for / largest city in the United States / 8 p.m. tonight

6. be / world's most populous country / tomorrow

7. see / Africa's highest mountain / when we land

8. arriving / The Eternal City / forty-five minutes

9. _____

10. _____

Angel Falls	Australia	Canada	Johannesburg	Mumbai	Paris	Tehran	the Nile

Team B's Prompts:

1. be landing / capital of Iran / forty-five minutes

2. going to arrive / largest country in North America / an hour and twenty minutes

3. arriving / largest city in India / an hour and a half

4. going to cross / longest river in Africa / four hours

5. leave for / largest city in South Africa / tomorrow night

6. be / the world's smallest continent / tomorrow morning

7. see / highest waterfall in the world / when we land

8. arriving / the City of Love / ninety minutes

9. _____

10. _____

Flying cars

Personal jet-pack

Magnetic levitation train

EXERCISE 9 HOW WILL WE GET AROUND IN THE FUTURE?

A PRESENTATION Work in a group. You are going to make a presentation about travel in the future. Choose one of the types of transportation in the pictures above, or choose another type. Search for information about it on the Internet. Take notes, and try to find pictures.

B Write your presentation together. Find the answers to these questions, and include them in your presentation.

1. What power sources will this new type of transportation be using?
2. How expensive is it going to be to fund this new type of transportation?
3. Who will be paying for it?
4. How expensive will it be for citizens to use it?
5. By approximately when will this new type of transportation be ready to use?
6. What will its potential downsides be?
7. Do you think people will want to use this type of transportation instead of their own cars?

C Make your presentation to the class. Listen to their presentations. Then discuss: Which type of transportation do you think will be most common in the future? Give reasons for your answer.

Go to MyEnglishLab for more communication practice.

FROM GRAMMAR TO WRITING

A BEFORE YOU WRITE Think about a goal you would like to accomplish in the next ten years of your life. Write a few sentences on each of the following aspects of that goal:

- what your goal is
- how and when you expect to achieve it
- what difficulties you think you will encounter

B WRITE Using your ideas in A, write a five-paragraph essay on the goal you want to achieve. Remember to use future time verb constructions. Try to avoid the common mistakes in the chart. Use the example below to help you begin your essay.

EXAMPLE: For most of my life, one of my goals has been to visit China. This dream is finally going to come true. I leave next Friday for a two-week trip to China with a group from work. We're going to visit Beijing, Shanghai, and the Great Wall. We're even going to . . .

Common Mistakes in Using Future Time Verbs

Don't use *will* and *be going to* interchangeably. Use *will* for **actions decided on at the moment of speaking**. Use *be going to* for actions that are **already planned**.	Oh, no! It's raining. I**'ll get** my umbrella. **NOT** Oh, no! It's raining. I'm going to get my umbrella. We**'re going to see** a movie. Do you want to come? **NOT** We'll see a movie. Do you want to come?
Use the **simple present** for the future **only with schedules and timetables**.	I**'ll call** her soon. **or** I**'m going to call** her soon. **NOT** I call her soon.
In sentences describing two future actions or events, use the **simple present** in **dependent clauses**.	We'll call you as soon as we **arrive**. **NOT** We'll call you as soon as we will arrive.

C CHECK YOUR WORK Look at your essay. Underline the future time constructions. Use the Editing Checklist to check your work.

Editing Checklist

Did you . . . ?

- [ ] use *will* for actions decided at the moment of speaking
- [ ] use *be going to* for planned actions
- [ ] use the simple present for future schedules and timetables
- [ ] use the simple present in dependent clauses in sentences with two actions in the future

D REVISE YOUR WORK Read your essay again. Can you improve your writing? Make changes if necessary.

Go to MyEnglishLab for more writing practice.

UNIT 3 REVIEW

Test yourself on the grammar of the unit.

A Complete the telephone message with the correct forms of the verbs in the box.

| be | call | come | have to | let | stop by |

Hi, Mary. This is Bill. I _____ work late tonight, so I _____
             1.   **2.**

late for dinner. I _____ you as soon as my boss _____ me
                   3.   **4.**

leave. I _____ the store and pick up dessert before I _____
         5.   **6.**

home. Bye. Love you.

B Complete the email with the correct forms of the words in parentheses. More than one answer is possible in some items. Use contractions where possible.

Hi Andy,

_____ our vacation in Australia this year!
    1. (Sam and I / take)

_____ tonight and arrives in Tokyo tomorrow. Then there's a ten-hour
    2. (Our flight / leave)

flight to Sydney. By the time _____ there,
                                                   3. (we / get)

_____ for over twenty-four hours. _____
    4. (we / fly)   **5. (We / be)**

exhausted, but it will certainly be worth it. _____ two and a half weeks
                                                            6. (We / spend)

in Australia. _____ you a postcard as soon as
                       7. (We / send)

_____ settled in our bed and breakfast in Sydney. Stay tuned!
    8. (we / be)

Martha

C Find and correct six mistakes.

A: Hey, Cheryl! How are you doing?

B: Good! I've been traveling all over the country for work. By the time the summer is over, I'll

    have visiting ten cities, and I'll have been traveled for three months straight!

A: Wow! That's a lot! Do you come to New York, too?

B: Yes! Actually, I'll come to New York next week! Can we get together?

A: Sure! Call me when you're getting to town. It'll be great to see you!

B: I call you as soon as I arrive at my hotel!

Now check your answers on page 427.

Go to MyEnglishLab to complete the review online.

Modals and Other Auxiliaries

PART **2**

OUTCOMES

- Express necessity or lack of necessity
- Recognize an author's attitude in an article about cultural differences
- Identify suggestions made in a conversation
- Discuss cultural differences and correct behavior in different cultures
- Write an essay about a past situation that should have been handled differently

OUTCOMES

- Make statements with varying degrees of certainty
- Identify an author's attitude in an academic article
- Identify main ideas and supporting details in an academic discussion
- Discuss possible explanations for various mysterious events
- Write an essay about a mystery

Modals to Express Degrees of Necessity
CULTURAL DIFFERENCES

OUTCOMES
• Express necessity or lack of necessity
• Recognize an author's attitude in an article about cultural differences
• Identify suggestions made in a conversation
• Discuss cultural differences and correct behavior in different cultures
• Write an essay about a past situation that should have been handled differently

STEP 1   GRAMMAR IN CONTEXT

BEFORE YOU READ

Look at the photos on pages 52 and 53 and discuss the questions.

1. What are the people in the pictures doing? Do people do these things in your culture?

2. What are some things that should and shouldn't be done in your culture? Make a short list.

READ

04|01 Read this article about cultural differences.

What We Should and Shouldn't Have Done

A few months ago, my company sent me to work at our branch office in Japan. My colleague Masayuki and Yukiko, his wife, invited my wife Helen and me out to dinner one night. Although they were very polite and friendly, we didn't feel that the evening went all that smoothly. In fact, we had the impression that we'd made some mistakes in etiquette. I asked my friend Junichi about our experience. He's lived in Japan and the United States, so he knows the cultural differences. He gave me several pointers, so now we know what we should and shouldn't have done at the dinner.

Junichi's first tip was about shoes and sitting down. Some Japanese restaurants have Western-style furniture, but our restaurant had pillows you sit down on. We knew you're supposed to take your shoes off in a Japanese home. It never occurred to us, though, that we should take them off when we sat down on the pillows. Junichi said we definitely ought to have done that.

His second pointer was all about chopsticks. We'd both used them a couple of times at Asian restaurants in the United States, albeit not very skillfully, and we thought we knew the rules for using them. However, I saw Masayuki grimace[1] a bit when I used a chopstick to spear a piece of meat from a bowl and pass it to Helen. He grimaced again when Helen used one of her chopsticks to point at a bowl of food she thought was tasty. Junichi chuckled. "One thing you absolutely mustn't do is use a chopstick to spear food and pass it to someone

---

1 *grimace:* reaction on his face to express disapproval

else. That reminds Japanese people of the custom of passing cremated bones at a funeral. And you must never point with a chopstick."

We continued to make a few more blunders.[2] I took a bottle of soy sauce on the table and poured it all over my rice. Yukiko seemed a bit shocked when she saw what I was doing. Junichi chuckled again. "You shouldn't ever pour soy sauce directly onto your food. What you have to do is pour soy into a little dish next to your plate and then dip your food into it. And you've also got to be careful not to waste the soy; just pour a small amount of it into the dish."

Then I remembered another point of etiquette. "Do you have to finish everything on your plate?" I asked Junichi. "Towards the end of the meal, Helen still had some food left. But then our waiter brought her some more."

"If you've finished everything, that basically means you're satisfied with the meal and don't want any more. If you still have food on your plate, you're signaling that you want another helping," replied Junichi.

The next pointer was about not using your handkerchief. I'd been suffering from allergies for a week or so, and suddenly I felt I had to blow my nose. I got out my handkerchief and did so. Both Masayuki and Yukiko again looked somewhat surprised. "What did I do wrong?" I asked.

Junichi responded, "You're not supposed to blow your nose in public. It's not considered appropriate."

"What should I have done? I was desperate."

"Well, you could have gotten up and gone to the toilet. Or you could have sniffled.[3]"

I thought that sounded odd. "Sniffled?"

"Yes, it's considered acceptable to sniffle—to avoid blowing your nose."

Finally, the dinner was over. As we got up to leave, I asked Masayuki if we could split the bill with him. He looked troubled and said, "No, no." He and Yukiko walked ahead of us to pay. I said to Helen, "Well, hadn't we better leave a tip?" She nodded, so I left some cash on the table. Just as we were putting our coats on at the restaurant entrance, our waiter came running up to us and handed me back the money. When I asked Junichi about it, he said, "You're not supposed to leave tips in Japan. It's not common at all."

I asked what we might do to express our appreciation to Masayuki and Yukiko. "Shall we reciprocate by inviting Masayuki and Yukiko out?"

"Yes, I think you ought to do that."

Junichi had given me good advice, I thought. What really struck me is how much we all have to learn about other cultures.

---

2 *blunders:* mistakes caused by confusion or ignorance
3 *sniffled:* breathed so others could hear him because his nose was runny or congested

AFTER YOU READ

A **VOCABULARY** Complete the sentences with the correct words from the box.

albeit	etiquette	occurred	overall
colleagues	gracious	odd	reciprocate

1. To be _____ is to be polite, kind, and pleasant.

2. Something true _____ is something true in general.

3. A person's _____ are people that he or she works with.

4. Something that seems _____ is something strange or peculiar.

5. If something hasn't _____ to you, you haven't realized it.

6. To _____ is to do or give something because something similar has been done or given to you.

7. When you behave politely, you follow the rules of _____.

8. If you say "clear _____ cold weather," you mean weather that is clear although cold.

B **COMPREHENSION** Complete the sentences. Circle the correct answers.

1. The author and his wife knew / didn't know they should remove their shoes when they sat down on the pillows.

2. In Japan, it's unacceptable / all right to use a chopstick to spear food and pass it to someone.

3. At a meal in Japan, one should pour soy sauce directly on rice / into a small dish.

4. At a meal in Japan, it's quite all right / not acceptable to use one's handkerchief at the dining table.

5. The author and his wife thought / didn't think it was necessary to leave a tip.

6. According to their Japanese friend, the author and his wife should invite Masayuki and Yukiko to their home / a restaurant for dinner.

C **DISCUSSION** Work with a partner. Discuss these questions: Which of the Japanese customs mentioned in the reading are similar to customs in your country, and which are different?

Go to MyEnglishLab for more grammar in context practice.

MODALS TO EXPRESS DEGREES OF NECESSITY

Necessity 100%

Obligation (Necessity)

You	must have to have got to	call	them.		You	must not can't are not allowed to	call	them.
You	had to	call	them.		You	weren't allowed to	call	them.

Advice

You	had better should ought to	leave	early.		You	had better not shouldn't	leave	early.
You	should have ought to have	left	early.		You	shouldn't have	left	early.

Expectation

You	are supposed to are to	take	a gift.		You	are not supposed to are not to	do	this.
You	were supposed to were to	take	a gift.		You	were not supposed to were not to	do	this.

Suggestion

You	could might	give	roses.
You	could have might have	given	roses.

No Obligation (No Necessity)

You	don't have to	call	them.
You	didn't have to	call	them.

0%

GRAMMAR NOTES

1 Definition of Modals

Modals are auxiliary verbs that show speakers' attitudes toward the actions they are describing. Modals are used to talk about **obligations**, **advice**, **expectations**, and **suggestions**.

The modals include *can*, *could*, *shall*, *should*, *will*, *would*, *may*, *might*, *must*, and *had better*. Each modal has only one form for all persons.	I **could take** them some flowers. We **should get** them a gift. You **might invite** them out for dinner.
Use **simple modals** (modal + base form) to show **degrees of necessity** in the **present** and the **future**.	We **should invite** Jim to the party tonight.
Use **perfect modals** (modal + *have* + past participle) to show **degrees of necessity** in the **past**.	We **should have invited** Jim to last week's party.

2 Modal-like Expressions

Modal-like expressions are similar in meaning to modals.

Have to and *have got to* are similar in meaning to *must*.	You **have to** eat everything on your plate.
	   (You **must** eat everything on your plate.)
	You **have got to** go to bed.
	   (You **must** go to bed.)

Ought to and *be supposed to* are similar in meaning to *should*.	You **ought to** take a gift.
	   (You **should** take a gift.)
	You**'re supposed to** take off your shoes.
	   (You **should** take off your shoes.)

Be allowed to is similar in meaning to *may* and *can*.	Children **are allowed to** play here. (Children **can** play here.)

3 Strong Necessity

Use *must*, *have to*, and *have got to* to show **strong necessity**. They are similar in meaning.

Use *must* in **more formal** English to show a very strong obligation that can't be escaped.	You **must eat** everything they offer you.
Use *have to* in all situations.	We **have to arrive** on time.
Use *have got to* in **conversation** and **informal** writing.	We**'ve got to leave** now.
Use *will have to* to show **future necessity**.	We**'ll have to invite** them over.
BE CAREFUL! Use *had to* + base form to show **past necessity**. Don't use *must have* + past participle.	We **had to leave**. **NOT** We ~~must have left~~.
BE CAREFUL! *Have got to* is rarely used in the negative. Use *don't have to* instead.	We **don't have to leave** yet. **NOT** We ~~haven't got to~~ leave yet.

4 Prohibition and Lack of Necessity

Use *must not* + base form to say that it is **necessary not** to do something—i.e., that it is prohibited. Use *don't/doesn't have to* + base form to say that something is **not necessary** to do.

• *must not* + base form	You **must not smoke** here. (It is prohibited to smoke here.)
• *don't/doesn't have to* + base form	You **don't have to eat** all the food. (It's not necessary to eat all the food.)
In past time, use *didn't have to* + base form to say that something **was not necessary**.	You **didn't have to bring** a gift.
BE CAREFUL! Although *must* and *have to* have equivalent meanings, *must not* and *don't have to* have very **different meanings**.	**A:** Is it OK if we miss the flight? **B:** No! We **mustn't miss** the flight. **NOT** We ~~don't have to~~ miss the flight.

5 Advice

Use *should* and *ought to* to offer **advice**. Both these modals mean "It would be a good idea if..." or "It's the right thing to do."

• *should*	You **should decline** gently.
• *ought to*	We **ought to give** them flowers.

We normally use *should*, not *ought to*, in **questions** and **negatives**.	A: **Should** we **offer** to help pay the bill? B: No, you **shouldn't**.

Use *should have/ought to have* + past participle to express **advice** about **past situations**. *Should have* and *ought to have* suggest that an action didn't happen. *Shouldn't have* and *ought not to have* suggest that it did.	You **should have done** that the first time. *(but you didn't)* You **ought not to have mentioned** your gift. *(but you did)*

USAGE NOTE We often use *shall* in **questions** to ask for advice or direction. In this meaning, *shall* is used only with *I* or *we*. When it is used with *we*, it is often followed by a sentence with *let's* + base form. In this meaning, *shall* is similar to *should*.	A: **Shall** we **get** them some flowers? B: Yes, **let's do** that.

6 Warnings

Use *had better* to give a **warning** that something bad or negative will happen if a suggestion or piece of advice is not followed.

Had better is similar to *should* and *ought to*, but **stronger**.	We**'d better go**, or we'll be late for work.

In **questions**, we usually use *had better* in the **negative**.	**Hadn't** you **better avoid** talking about politics during dinner? *(You'll probably offend our hosts if you do.)*

7 Expectations

Use *be supposed to* and *be to* to show **expectations**.

• *be supposed to*	You**'re supposed to take off** your shoes when you enter a Japanese home.
• *be to*	All employees **are to attend** the company office party.

Use *be supposed to* only in the **present** and the **past**. In the past, the affirmative suggests that an action didn't happen. The negative suggests that it did.	We **were supposed to take** flowers. *(but we didn't)* We **weren't supposed to mention** the gift we'd brought. *(but we did)*

Use *be to* in more **formal** English to express a strong expectation.	You**'re not to ask** any personal questions at the meeting.

Use *could* and *might* to make polite, not-too-strong **suggestions**. *Could* is much more common than *might* in this function.

Use *could* or *might* + base form to make **polite suggestions** about the **present** or **future**.	You **could take** them some chocolates. You **might send** a thank-you note.
Use *could have*/*might have* + past participle to make **polite suggestions** about a **past** opportunity. In this meaning, *could have* and *might have* mean that the action didn't happen. However, you can also use *could have* and *might have* to speculate about the past. (See Unit 5.)	You **could have taken** them some flowers. You **might have offered** to help clean up.

PRONUNCIATION NOTE

▶ 04|02 **Reducing Modals and Modal-like Auxiliaries**

Modals and modal-like auxiliaries are often **reduced** in rapid speech and in conversation. Note that the full forms are also acceptable.

have to → "hafta"	We **hafta** leave now.
has to → "hasta"	She **hasta** work today.
should have → "should've" (before a vowel)	I **should've eaten** a bigger lunch.
should have → "shoulda" (before a consonant)	You **shoulda called** sooner.
could have → "could've" (before a vowel)	They **could've** *invited* us to the party.
could have → "coulda" (before a consonant)	You **coulda** *brought* some flowers.
might have → "might've" (before a vowel)	He **might've** *advised* me to do that.
might have → "mighta" (before a consonant)	You **mighta told** me about that.
supposed to → "sposta"	You're not **sposta** do that.
had better → "better"	We **better** get going.
ought to → "oughta"	Bob **oughta** study harder.
got to → "gotta"	We've **gotta** leave now.

IN WRITING Don't use the forms *hafta, hasta, sposta, oughta,* and *gotta* in writing. You can use the forms *should've, could've, might've,* and *'d better* in written dialogue and less formal English, but don't use them in formal English.	I **have to** fly to Buenos Aires tonight. We **ought to** have them over for a card game. We**'d better** give her a call. People aren't **supposed to** smoke here.

Go to **MyEnglishLab** to watch the grammar presentation.

EXERCISE 1 DISCOVER THE GRAMMAR

GRAMMAR NOTES 1–8 Read the sentences based on the reading. Circle the choice that best explains the meaning of each sentence.

1. We knew that you're supposed to take off your shoes when you enter a Japanese home.
    a. Japanese people expect guests to remove their shoes.
    b. It doesn't matter whether or not you wear your shoes in a Japanese home.

2. Junichi told us we ought to have removed our shoes.
    a. We removed our shoes, and that was the right thing to do.
    b. We didn't remove our shoes, and that was a cultural mistake in Japan.

3. You have to pour soy sauce into a little dish next to your plate.
    a. You must do this. It's necessary.
    b. You should do this, but it's not really necessary.

4. I felt I had to blow my nose.
    a. It wasn't necessary for me to blow my nose.
    b. It was necessary for me to blow my nose.

5. You are not to blow your nose in public.
    a. It's not acceptable to do this.
    b. It's acceptable to do this.

6. You could have sniffled.
    a. You did sniffle.
    b. You didn't sniffle.

7. Hadn't we better leave a tip?
    a. Shouldn't we leave a tip?
    b. Does it matter whether or not we leave a tip?

8. You're not supposed to leave tips in Japan.
    a. Tips are not expected.
    b. Tips are expected.

9. Yes, I think you ought to do that.
    a. I don't think it matters whether or not you do that.
    b. That would be the right thing to do.

10. Shall we invite Masayuki and Yukiko out for dinner?
    a. Do you think they will go out to dinner with us?
    b. Do you think we should ask them to go out for dinner with us?

EXERCISE 2 MODALS

GRAMMAR NOTES 3–5, 7–8 Read the conversation between Manuela, a visiting exchange student, and her American friend Jane. Complete the conversation with phrases from the box.

~~are you supposed to leave~~	don't have to do	ought to have given	should you leave
could have left	don't have to leave	should we have left	were supposed to leave
could leave	had to worry	should you do	you're supposed to do

JANE: Hi, Manuela. How are things going?

MANUELA: Really well. But I need some pointers about something.

JANE: Sure. What?

MANUELA: Tipping. I don't really understand it. ____Are you supposed to leave____ a tip everywhere
1.
you eat? This is kind of bothering me. I've never _____ about
2.
this before. We don't tip very much in Brazil.

JANE: You don't?

MANUELA: No. Generally you _____ that. If the service is really great,
3.
you _____ something, or round your bill up.
4.

JANE: Tell me more. Have you had a problem with this?

MANUELA: Yeah. Last week a Chinese friend of mine and I had dinner at a restaurant. We knew we
_____ a tip, but we didn't know how much.
5.

JANE: How much did you leave?

MANUELA: About 25 percent. _____ more?
6.

JANE: Wow! Twenty-five percent. That's quite a bit. The service must have been really good.

MANUELA: Actually, it wasn't. The waiter was pretty rude . . . and slow.

JANE: If you're not satisfied with the service, you _____ anything.
7.

MANUELA: So what _____ if you're satisfied?
8.

JANE: You should tip the waiter between 15 and 20 percent. Fifteen is the usual.

MANUELA: Hmmm. OK. Now here's another question. I'm confused about what
_____ if you're sitting at a lunch counter instead of at a
9.
table. _____ anything for the person behind the counter?
10.

JANE: It's a nice gesture. Why do you ask?

MANUELA: Yesterday, I had lunch at a cafeteria counter. The waitress was really nice and polite. I felt
like I _____ her something.
11.

JANE: Did you?

MANUELA: No.

JANE: Well, you _____ something. Maybe 5 to 10 percent.
12.

MANUELA: Oh. OK. Next time I will.

EXERCISE 3 MUST, HAVE TO, SHOULD, AND BE SUPPOSED TO

A GRAMMAR NOTES 3–5, 7 Read this short essay about the treatment of babies in two different cultures.

An American woman was spending a month teaching on the Indonesian island of Bali. She was staying at the home of a Balinese family. Late one afternoon, the woman of the house needed to leave home for a time. When she came back, her eight-month-old son was lying on a large bed, crying loudly. "What is happening with my son?" asked the Balinese woman. "Oh," said the American teacher, "I don't think there's anything wrong with him. I just thought it would be good for him to crawl on the floor for a bit. I put him down to let him crawl, but he didn't seem to like it, and he started crying. I thought maybe it would be a good idea if he just cried to let his frustration out."

A discussion followed. The Balinese woman told the American that in Bali it is not considered a good thing to let babies cry. Since Balinese culture is characterized by the strength of the extended family, there is almost always someone available to pick children up if they start crying and carry them around. In fact, there is even a "putting down" ceremony that occurs when the child is ready to walk and may be put down on the ground for the first time. Furthermore, the Balinese mother said, their children are not expected to crawl because that activity is seen as too much like what animals do.

The American was fascinated with what her Balinese host had told her. She pointed out that in the United States, the extended family is not nearly as prevalent as in Bali, so there is often no one around to help with children. In many families, both mother and father work, so at the end of the day both are too tired to carry children around for long periods. Many also feel that it doesn't hurt babies to allow them to cry for a time. As for crawling, said the American woman, most American parents are delighted when their children learn to crawl, feeling that it is essential for them to develop that skill in order to gain muscular strength and prepare for walking.

Both women learned a great deal that day about the other's culture.

B GRAMMAR NOTES 3–5, 7 Complete the sentences about the article in A. Use *must*, *have to*, *should*, and *be supposed to*. Use negative or past forms if necessary.

1. The incident happened because the Balinese woman _____*had to*_____ leave home for a time.

2. The American woman thought the baby _____ crawl around a bit on the floor.

3. In Bali, parents believe that babies _____ be picked up and held most of the time, especially if they are crying.

4. The Balinese mother no doubt felt that her American guest _____ put the baby down.

5. In Bali, children _____ crawl since that is too much like what animals do.

6. Most American parents believe that their children _____ crawl because if they don't, they won't develop muscular strength and learn to walk.

EXERCISE 4 *SHOULD HAVE* AND *COULD HAVE*

GRAMMAR NOTES 5, 8 Read the example sentences. Then think about past situations you have experienced. Write five sentences about things you should or shouldn't have done. Then write five additional sentences about things you could have done.

I should have studied more for my English test.
I shouldn't have spent so much money on my new computer.
I could have given my sister a better present for her birthday.

EXERCISE 5 REDUCING MODALS AND MODAL-LIKE AUXILIARIES

▶04|03 **A** PRONUNCIATION NOTE Listen to each sentence. How is the modal or modal-like auxiliary pronounced? Check (✓) *Full Form* or *Reduced Form*.

	Full Form	Reduced Form
1. We have to take a gift to the party.	☐	☑
2. We should have had them over for dinner.	☐	☐
3. We're supposed to have dinner at their house on Monday.	☐	☐
4. You could have declined their offer to have a drink.	☐	☐
5. We had better leave now.	☐	☐
6. You might have gotten them some flowers.	☐	☐
7. He wasn't supposed to be here until Monday.	☐	☐
8. The gift has to be wrapped.	☐	☐
9. We ought to go to a movie tonight.	☐	☐
10. You should have eaten your vegetables.	☐	☐
11. We've got to get going soon.	☐	☐
12. You might have asked me if I wanted to go.	☐	☐
13. She could have accepted the job offer.	☐	☐
14. You'd better not mention politics at the dinner table.	☐	☐

▶04|03 **B** Listen again. Repeat the sentences.

EXERCISE 6 EDITING

GRAMMAR NOTES 1–8 Read the email from Tong-Li, an international exchange student in Australia, to her friend Indira in Singapore. There are nine mistakes in the use of modals or modal-like expressions. The first mistake is already corrected. Find and correct eight more.

To: indira444@cmail.com
From: TongLi5@cmail.com
Re: Australia

Dear Indira,

Sorry it's taken me so long to email. I ~~should to~~ *should* have gotten to this weeks ago, but I've been so busy. I'm really looking forward to seeing all you guys again. School is tough but really interesting, and I'm sure I should be studying even more than I have been. Part of the problem is that I'm taking too many classes. You're only suppose to take five a term, but I'm taking six.

Anyway, I've gotten to know a lot of new people. I have this one really good friend, a girl named Jane. She invited me to her house last week for a party. Actually, it was my birthday, but I didn't know she knew that. I figured I better take some kind of gift, but I couldn't decide what it should be. Finally, I came up with the idea of a bouquet of flowers. As soon as I got to the party, I gave it to Jane. But then the funniest thing happened. I guess I ought to expect something was up from the mysterious way Jane was acting, but I didn't. This was a surprise party—for me! As soon as I sat down, a lot of people jumped up from places where they'd been hiding and shouted, "Surprise! Happy birthday!" I was embarrassed, but I must not have been because everyone was really friendly, and pretty soon I forgot about my embarrassment. Then they gave me presents. I was about to put them away, but Jane said, "Aren't you going to open them?" I didn't know what to do. In Singapore, you shouldn't have opened gifts right when you get them, but apparently you are supposed to in Australia. So I opened them. The nicest gift was a new blouse from Jane. She told me I must have gone and try it on immediately, so I did. It's beautiful. Anyway, what a party! I thought I knew all about Australian culture, but the custom of opening up presents in front of the gift giver is a strange one to me.

The weather is kind of chilly. How is it back in Singapore? Nice and warm? I shall bring you something special from Australia when I come?

Well, Indira, I got to sign off now. Write soon.

Love,
Tong-Li

Go to MyEnglishLab for more focused practice.

EXERCISE 7 LISTENING

▶ 04|04 **A** Listen to the telephone conversation. Where are Dad and Ray, and why are they there?

_____

▶ 04|04 **B** Read the questions. Then listen again. Write complete answers.

1. Why should Dad and Ray get home as soon as possible?

   Mom's surprise party is supposed to start in half an hour.

2. Why does Bev think Dad has to get Mom's present today?

   _____

3. What should Dad have done last week?

   _____

4. Why doesn't Dad think they should buy a camera?

   _____

5. Why can't Dad buy Mom a dress?

   _____

6. How does Dad respond when Bev says he could get Mom a blouse?

   _____

7. What does Bev think Dad should get?

   _____

8. What does Mom think is supposed to happen this afternoon?

   _____

C Work with a partner. Discuss these questions. Then share your conclusions with the class.

1. When you attend a birthday party in your culture, are you supposed to take a gift?

2. Are gifts supposed to be wrapped?

3. What types of gifts should you *not* take to a birthday party?

EXERCISE 8 THE KINDNESS OF STRANGERS

INFORMATION GAP Work with a partner. Student A will follow the instructions below. Student B will follow the instructions on page 438.

- The story below is missing some information. Your partner has the same story that contains your missing information. Ask your partner questions to find the missing information.

  EXAMPLE: **A:** Where were the married couple supposed to stay?
  B: They were supposed to stay at . . .

- Your partner's story is missing different information. Answer your partner's questions so that he or she can fill in the missing information.

  EXAMPLE: **B:** What should the married couple have gotten?
  A: They should have gotten . . .

A married couple was traveling in Europe and had just entered a new country. They had been having a wonderful time, but now everything was going wrong. The first problem was finding accommodations. They were supposed to stay at _____, but when they got to the hotel, there was no record of their reservation. The wife said they should have gotten a confirmation number. They hadn't, unfortunately, so they had to spend the night _____. The next day, they finally found a room at a hotel far from the center of town. There were two rooms available: a large one and a tiny one. Since they were on a tight budget, they decided they had better take the tiny one.

The second problem was communication. They were starving after spending hours looking for accommodations, so they went into a restaurant. A waiter brought them a menu, but they couldn't understand it. The husband said they should have _____. They hadn't done that, though, so they didn't know what to order.

Time passed. Other people were being served, but they weren't. Frustrated, they decided they had to do something. But what? They noticed that a boy about eleven years old seemed to be listening to their conversation. Soon, the boy came over to their table. "Excuse me," he said. "You have to _____. Then they'll take your order." The husband and wife were both astonished but grateful. The wife said, "You speak our language very well. Did you study it somewhere?" The boy said, "I lived in Australia for three years. I learned English there." He asked, "Shall I help you order? I can translate the menu."

When the couple got back home, their friends asked them what they had liked best about the trip. The wife said, "Well, the best part was visiting that country where everything went wrong, and that boy helped us. He could have ignored us, but he didn't. It's wonderful when strangers help you. It's made me realize that we should all _____ when the need arises."

EXERCISE 9 DO'S AND DON'TS

A QUESTIONNAIRE Decide whether each of the behaviors in the chart is required, advised, allowed, or unimportant in your culture or another culture you are familiar with. Check (✓) the appropriate boxes.

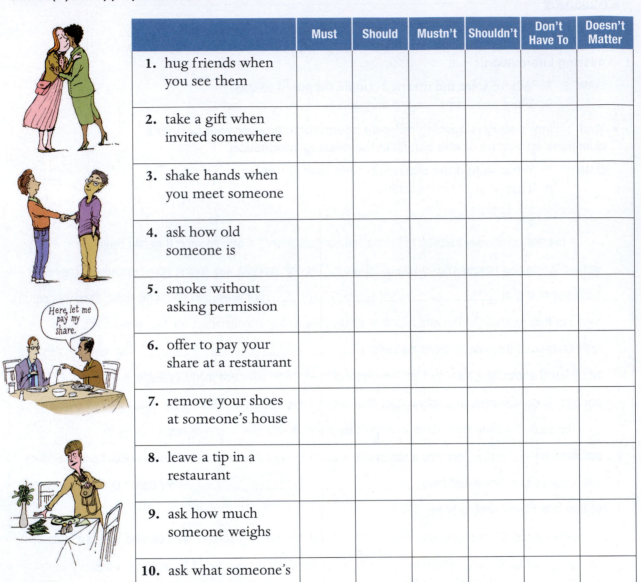

	Must	Should	Mustn't	Shouldn't	Don't Have To	Doesn't Matter
1. hug friends when you see them						
2. take a gift when invited somewhere						
3. shake hands when you meet someone						
4. ask how old someone is						
5. smoke without asking permission						
6. offer to pay your share at a restaurant						
7. remove your shoes at someone's house						
8. leave a tip in a restaurant						
9. ask how much someone weighs						
10. ask what someone's occupation is						
11. call people by their first name						

Here, let me pay my share.

John, come over here, please.

B Work in a group. Share your answers in A. Then report your opinions to the rest of the class.

EXAMPLE: **A:** When you're invited to dinner in your culture, are you supposed to take a gift?
        B: Absolutely. You must take a gift. And it has to be wrapped. What about in your culture?
        A: You can if you want to. You should take a gift if it's a birthday party, but . . .

Go to MyEnglishLab for more communication practice.

FROM GRAMMAR TO WRITING

A **BEFORE YOU WRITE** Think of a past situation that you feel you and other people could and should have handled differently. Write a few sentences on the following points:

- How you handled the situation
- What people must, have to, or should do in these types of situations
- What you could and should have done instead

B **WRITE** Using your ideas in A, write a five-paragraph essay about your situation. Remember to use modals of necessity. Try to avoid the common mistakes in the chart. Use the example below to help you begin your essay.

EXAMPLE: Two years ago, my friend and I were traveling on a train in Europe. It was the middle of the night, and we were both asleep. Suddenly, our compartment door was opened and several young people came in. They began talking very loudly. I told them, "You really have to be quiet. We're trying to sleep here." But they didn't pay attention to me.

There were several things that everyone in the situation could and should have done. We should have known that there would be a problem because we weren't in a private compartment. We could have gotten a private compartment. But we weren't the only ones at fault. People ought to be quiet when they enter a train late at night. The young people should have talked a lot more quietly . . .

Common Mistakes in Using Modals of Necessity

Don't confuse *must not* and *do not have to*. **Must not** means that an action is **prohibited**. **Do not have to** means an action is **not necessary**.	We **mustn't forget** our passports. We won't be able to travel if we do. **NOT** We ~~don't have to~~ forget our passports.
Don't use *had* instead of *have* in past modals. Be sure to use **have + past participle** after *could*, **should**, **may**, and **might**.	You **should have let** me know you couldn't come. **NOT** You should ~~had~~ let me know you couldn't come.
Be careful not to omit the **to** after *ought*.	You **ought to give** her a call soon. **NOT** You ~~ought give~~ her a call soon.

C **CHECK YOUR WORK** Look at your essay. Underline the modals of necessity. Use the Editing Checklist to check your work.

Editing Checklist

Did you . . . ?

- [ ] use *must not* for actions that are prohibited
- [ ] use *do not have to* for actions that are not necessary
- [ ] use *have* in past constructions with *should*, *could*, and *might*
- [ ] include *to* after *ought*

D **REVISE YOUR WORK** Read your essay again. Can you improve your writing? Make changes if necessary.

Go to MyEnglishLab for more writing practice.

UNIT 4 REVIEW

Test yourself on the grammar of the unit.

A Complete the sentences. Circle the correct answers.

1. You <u>weren't supposed to / were supposed to</u> mention the gift. Now it won't be a surprise!

2. She <u>had to / didn't have to</u> bring food. We have a lot left over from the party.

3. Bill <u>might not have / shouldn't have</u> told Ai about it! Now everyone will know.

4. You <u>could / should</u> take some flowers. Or a box of chocolates would be good.

5. <u>We shouldn't / We'd better not</u> discuss anything political. Sam loses his temper easily.

6. You <u>must have / should have</u> your passport with you. You'll be deported if you don't.

7. <u>Chie should / Chie's got to</u> pay her rent by Saturday. She'll be evicted if she doesn't.

8. You <u>aren't allowed to / don't have to</u> go into a Japanese kitchen. It's just not done.

9. Sami <u>should have / could have</u> given them a CD. They like flowers, too.

10. <u>Hadn't we better / Must we</u> get going? The play starts in thirty minutes.

B Look at the underlined phrase in each sentence. Write a modal that has a similar meaning to the phrase.

1. You <u>have to</u> be there by 10 a.m. sharp.   _____

2. We <u>ought to</u> invite Hana over for dinner.   _____

3. We <u>aren't allowed to</u> smoke in the office.   _____

4. Ken <u>has got to</u> study harder.   _____

5. <u>Are</u> you <u>supposed to</u> leave a tip here?   _____

C Find and correct five mistakes.

A: Did you see the email? All employees is to attend the good-bye party for our CEO, Brent Chang.

B: Yes, I did see it. His wife was invited too, but she must decline because she is going on a trip.

A: Since it's a good-bye party, we don't have to forget to buy him a present. We had better to get him something nice. We ought buy him something useful, too.

B: I agree.

Now check your answers on page 427.

Go to MyEnglishLab to complete the review online.

Modals to Express Degrees of Certainty

MYSTERIES

| STEP 1 | GRAMMAR IN CONTEXT |

BEFORE YOU READ

Discuss the questions.

1. When people say, "Columbus discovered the New World," what do they mean?

2. What theories have you heard regarding who might have "discovered" the New World?

READ

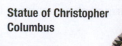 Read this article about the discovery of America.

Who *Really* Discovered America?

A well-known school rhyme goes like this: "In fourteen hundred and ninety-two, Columbus sailed the ocean blue"—and then discovered America. However, Columbus may not have been the first non-Native American to visit the Western Hemisphere. So many other potential discoverers have been nominated[1] that the question might almost be rephrased as "Who didn't discover America?" What does history show? Who really discovered the New World? Those suggested include the Vikings, the Japanese, the Chinese, the Egyptians, the Hebrews, the Portuguese, and some Irish monks.

The Vikings are the best-known contenders. Evidence suggests that Leif Erickson and cohorts visited the New World about the year 1000, almost 500 years before Columbus. Viking records and New World artifacts[2] indicate they arrived at a place they named "Vinland the Good"—the land of grapes. Scholars originally hypothesized that Vinland must have been Newfoundland. Today, however, it is believed that Vinland couldn't have been that island since it is too far north for grapes to grow. Could the climate have been warmer in Erickson's day? Perhaps. However, current thought is that Vinland may have been the New England coast.

The Japanese are more recent candidates. Pottery fragments discovered in 1956 on the coast of Ecuador date back about 5,000 years. These fragments resemble Japanese pottery of the same era, and it has been

---

1 *nominated:* proposed, suggested
2 *artifacts:* manmade objects

Statue of Christopher Columbus

established that there was no native pottery in Ecuador in 3000 B.C.E. Could the Japanese have introduced it? Smithsonian Institute scholars conclude that individuals may have sailed from Japan across the Pacific to Ecuador, or Japanese fishermen might have been swept out to sea and carried 10,000 miles across the ocean. This theory may sound unlikely and may eventually be disproved. Nonetheless, the pottery evidence must mean something.

One interesting theory stems from the story of St. Brendan, a sixth-century Irish monk who made many voyages to establish monasteries. A sixth-century document suggests that Brendan made a journey far out into the Atlantic, reports of which may have influenced Columbus to believe that there really was a New World. Brendan and his fellow monks saw "sea monsters," "crystals rising up into the sky," and "a rain of bad-smelling rocks." In 1976, British navigation scholar Tim Severin decided to see if Brendan and his companions could really have accomplished this voyage. Using the specifications described in the St. Brendan text, they built a curragh, an Irish leather boat, and attempted the journey. On the way, they passed Greenland and wintered in Iceland, where they saw whales, a volcano, and icebergs. They theorized that Brendan's sea monsters might have been whales, the ice crystals icebergs, and the bad-smelling rocks volcanic debris. Severin's group did eventually get to Newfoundland, proving that a curragh could have made the journey to North America. Religious artifacts and stone carvings bearing vocabulary and grammatical constructions from Old Irish have been found in Virginia. This suggests that other missionaries[3] could have gone to the New World after Brendan's return. Thus the story may be true.

But back to the original question: Who really "discovered" the New World? Future research should get us closer to an answer. Columbus and the others mentioned above did not, of course, really discover America. The real finders were the Native Americans who migrated across the Bering Strait more than 10,000 years ago. In any case, even if Columbus did not discover the New World, no one disputes that he started two-way communication between the Old World and the New. In that sense, his reputation is still safe.

---

3 *missionaries:* persons sent to distant places to teach and spread religion

AFTER YOU READ

A VOCABULARY Match the words in **bold** with their meanings.

_____ **1.** Many other **potential** discoverers have been nominated.

_____ **2.** Leif Erickson and **cohorts** arrived about the year 1000.

_____ **3.** Scholars **hypothesized** that Vinland was Newfoundland.

_____ **4.** **Nonetheless**, the pottery evidence must mean something.

_____ **5.** Severin used the **specifications** described by St. Brendan.

_____ **6.** This idea **stems from** the story of St. Brendan.

_____ **7.** This **theory** seems unlikely.

_____ **8.** The bad-smelling rocks may have been volcanic **debris**.

a. is from

b. remains of an explosion

c. companions

d. descriptions or directions

e. proposed as an explanation

f. however

g. possible

h. proposed explanation

B **COMPREHENSION** Read the statements. Check (✓) *True* or *False*.

		True	False
1.	Schoolchildren are often taught that Columbus discovered America.	☐	☐
2.	Scholars originally theorized that Vinland was probably Newfoundland.	☐	☐
3.	Vinland could have been Newfoundland because grapes grow there.	☐	☐
4.	Pottery fragments found in Ecuador date from the year 5000 B.C.E.	☐	☐
5.	The story of St. Brendan definitely convinced Columbus that there was a New World.	☐	☐
6.	St. Brendan and his companions could have gotten to America in a curragh.	☐	☐
7.	The ice crystals seen by Brendan and his companions must have been icebergs.	☐	☐
8.	Columbus opened up communication between the Old World and the New.	☐	☐

C **DISCUSSION** Work with a partner. Compare your answers in A. Then discuss: Which theory in the article do you think is the most convincing? Who do *you* think discovered America?

Go to MyEnglishLab for more grammar in context practice.

STEP 2   GRAMMAR PRESENTATION

MODALS TO EXPRESS DEGREES OF CERTAINTY

Speculations about the Present

It	must has (got) to	be	true.	It	can't/couldn't must not	be	true.
It	may/might could	be	true.	It	may not might not	be	true.

Speculations about the Past

It	must have had to have	been	true.	It	can't have couldn't have must not have	been	true.
It	may have might have could have	been	true.	It	may not have might not have	been	true.

Speculations about the Future

We	should ought to	solve	it soon.				
We	may might could	solve	it soon.	We	may not might not	solve	it soon.

GRAMMAR NOTES

1 Different Degrees of Certainty

We use **modals** and **modal-like expressions** to express different **degrees of certainty**. We use them to speculate based on logic and facts.

• Approximately **90% certain**	The story **must be** true.
• Approximately **50% certain**	The story **might be** true.
We use modals with **progressive** as well as **simple** forms.	He **may be planning** another trip.
When we want to state a fact we are absolutely, 100% **sure** of, we **don't use modals**.	That story **is** true. He **was planning** another trip.

2 Almost Certain about the Present

Use *must / have to / have got to*, *can't / couldn't*, and *must not* + base form to speculate about the **present** when you are **almost certain**.

• *must*	The evidence **must mean** something.
• *have to*	That **has to be** the answer to the question.
• *have got to*	He**'s got to be** wrong about what he's saying.
• *can't*	That theory **can't be** right.
• *couldn't*	That **couldn't be** the correct explanation.
• *must not*	It **must not be** correct.
In **questions**, use *could / might* + base form.	**Could** that **be** the case? **Couldn't** that **be** the explanation?
BE CAREFUL! We normally **don't contract** *must not* with this meaning of *must*.	The explorer **must not be** famous. **NOT** The explorer ~~mustn't~~ be famous.

3 Less Certain about the Present

Use *may / might / could* and *may not / might not* + base form to speculate about the **present** when you are **less certain**.

• *may*	We **may know** the answer soon.
• *might*	That **might be** the solution to the problem.
• *could*	That **could be** the reason for the confusion.
• *may not*	They **may not have** any evidence.
• *might not*	It **might not rain** today after all.
In **questions**, use *could / might* + base form.	**Could** that theory **be** correct? **Might** that **be** the real answer?
BE CAREFUL! We usually **do not contract** *might not*, and we **never contract** *may not*.	They **may not** have any evidence. **NOT** They ~~mayn't~~ have any evidence.

4 Almost Certain about the Past

Use *must have/had to have/must not have* + past participle when you are speculating about the **past** and are **almost certain**.

• *must have*	They **must have visited** America.
• *had to have*	They **had to have experienced** many difficulties.
• *must not have*	He **must not have made** the voyage.

In the **negative**, use *can't have/couldn't have* + past participle to suggest impossibility.	That **can't have happened**. That **couldn't have been** the reason.

In **questions**, use *can have/could have* + past participle.	**Can** that really **have taken** place? **Could** that **have been** the solution?

5 Less Certain about the Past

Use *may have/might have/could have* + past participle when you are speculating about the **past** and are **less certain** (about 50%).

• *may have*	They **may have reached** the New World.
• *might have*	Japanese sailors **might have arrived** in America.
• *could have*	They **could have encountered** whales on the trip.

In the **negative**, use *may not have/might not have* + past participle.	They **may not have found** it. They **might not have understood** it.

In **questions**, use *might have/could have* + past participle.	**Might** they **have had** trouble? **Could** they **have reached** the New World?

USAGE NOTE *Could have* + past participle has two meanings:	
• **possibility**; a degree of certainty	He **could have gone**; I don't know for sure.
• **missed opportunity**	He **could have gone**, but he didn't.

6 Almost Certain about the Future

Use *should/ought to* + base form when you are **almost certain** about a **future** action or event.	Continued research **should help**. We **ought to have** a solution soon.

7 Less Certain about the Future

Use *may/might/could* + base form when you are **less certain** (about 50%) about a **future** action or event.

• *may*	We **may know** the answer soon.
• *might*	She **might win** the election.
• *could*	This plan **could be** successful.

In the **negative**, use *may/might* + *not/never* + base form.	However, we **may never know** the answer. We **might not be able to solve** the problem.

Go to MyEnglishLab to watch the grammar presentation.

EXERCISE 1 DISCOVER THE GRAMMAR

GRAMMAR NOTES 1–7 Read each sentence based on the reading. Circle the choice that is closer in meaning to the sentence.

1. Columbus may not have been the first to visit the Western Hemisphere.
   (a.) He might not have been the first.
   b. He could not have been the first.

2. It must have been about the year 1000 when Leif Erickson visited the New World.
   a. I'm almost certain it was about the year 1000.
   b. I think maybe it was about the year 1000.

3. Vinland couldn't have been Newfoundland.
   a. It must not have been Newfoundland.
   b. It can't have been Newfoundland.

4. How could the voyage have happened?
   a. I'd like an explanation of how the voyage was impossible.
   b. I'd like an explanation of how the voyage was possible.

5. Individuals may have sailed from Japan to Ecuador.
   a. It's possible they did it.
   b. It's almost certain they did it.

6. The pottery evidence must mean something.
   a. I'm almost sure it means something.
   b. I strongly doubt it means something.

7. Other missionaries could have gone to the New World after Brendan's return.
   a. It's possible that they went.
   b. They had the opportunity to go, but they didn't.

8. Continued research should get us closer to an answer.
   a. It's possible that it will.
   b. It's almost certain that it will.

EXERCISE 2 AFFIRMATIVE MODALS

GRAMMAR NOTES 1–6 Read the conversation. Complete it with the words from the box.

could be working	may have had to	might be meeting	must have been visiting
~~could have gotten~~	might be	must have	should be

BLAKE: I wonder what's keeping Harry. He's usually on time for office parties. I suppose he

_____*could have gotten*_____ stuck in traffic.
                          1.

SAMANTHA: Yeah, that's a possibility. Or he _____ work late. I've
                                                        2.

never known him to be late for a party.

BLAKE: You know, I've always felt there's something a little puzzling—or even mysterious—about Harry.

SAMANTHA: What makes you say that?

BLAKE: Well, he never says much about his past. He's an interesting guy, but I don't know much about him. For all I know, he _____ an international spy
3.
who works with mysterious cohorts.

SAMANTHA: I think I know what you mean. Or he _____ as a
4.
government agent.

BLAKE: This is potentially a case of *cherchez la femme*.

SAMANTHA: What does that mean?

BLAKE: It means "look for the woman." I figure he _____ a
5.
girlfriend that he doesn't want us to know about.

SAMANTHA: Yeah, maybe so. You know, now that I think of it, he always leaves work early on Friday afternoons. I see him go to the parking garage about 4:00, and it always seems like he's trying not to be seen. He _____ his secret love.
6.

(The doorbell rings.)

BLAKE: Oh, wait a minute. There's the doorbell. Everyone else is here. That _____ him.
7.

HARRY: Hi, folks. Sorry I'm late. Had some business to take care of.

SAMANTHA: Business, huh. You mean romantic business?

HARRY: Romantic business? What are you talking about?

BLAKE: We figure you _____ your lady love. After all, we see you
8.
leave early every Friday afternoon.

HARRY: Pretty funny. Well, there is a lady, and I love her. But it's not what you think.

SAMANTHA: What is it, then?

HARRY: My mother. She's 88 years old, and she lives in a retirement home. I go to see her every Friday.

EXERCISE 3 PRESENT AND PAST MODALS

GRAMMAR NOTES 2–5 Read the article about past cultures. Complete the sentences with past and present modal or modal-like verbs, using the words in parentheses.

WORLD REVIEW

Have you ever heard of the Anasazi and the Mayans? Both were once great civilizations, but they no longer exist today. Why? There are a number of possible explanations.

First, let's consider the ancient Pueblo people of the U.S. Southwest, called the Anasazi or "ancient ones" by the Navajo. Scholars think that these people _____may have settled_____
1. (may / settle)
in about 100 B.C.E. in the Four Corners area, where today the states of Arizona, Utah, Colorado, and New Mexico come together. We know from the evidence of artifacts and ruins that the Anasazi developed agriculture and built impressive cities and cliff dwellings. About the year 1300, though, something happened. The Anasazi abandoned their dwellings and deserted the region. What _____ this? Drought? Warfare? No one knows for sure.
2. (could / cause)
However, these people _____ completely. Anthropologists believe that
3. (could / not / disappear)
they _____ to the Rio Grande Valley in New Mexico and the White
4. (had to / migrate)
Mountains in Arizona. They assume that today's Pueblo peoples in the Southwest
_____ their descendants. This means that descendants of the
5. (must / be)
Anasazi _____ the earth. Even if they are, we still don't know what
6. (might / still / walk)
_____ an end to the Anasazi's flourishing culture.
7. (might / bring)

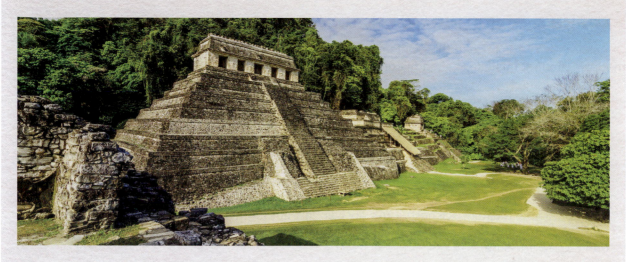

Thousands of years ago, the Mayan people dominated large parts of Mexico and Central America. Their culture was technologically advanced, and they built huge cities with elaborate stone palaces and pyramids. Then suddenly, around the year 900 C.E., most of the Mayans abandoned their cities, and the great Mayan civilization collapsed. Nobody knows the reason for this mysterious decline, though scholars have developed several competing theories. One theory holds that by the ninth century, the Mayan population _____ so large
8. (must / grow)
that it could no longer be supported by agriculture. In other words, the Mayans _____ their cities because they ran out of food. Another idea is that
9. (may / leave)
Mayan society _____ because the different Mayan city-states were
10. (might / collapse)
constantly warring with each other. In addition, some scholars claim that an environmental disaster, such as a drought, _____ . Mayan cities _____
11. (could / occur)   12. (had to / be)
dependent on rain for their water supply, and without it, they _____
13. (must / struggle)
to survive . . . and eventually lost the struggle. And finally, other experts believe that all three of these factors _____ a part in the Mayan downfall.
14. (may / play)

EXERCISE 4 DEGREES OF CERTAINTY ABOUT THE FUTURE

GRAMMAR NOTES 6–7 Write ten sentences about things you might accomplish in the next ten years. Write two sentences each with *should*, *ought to*, *may*, *might*, and *could*.

I should finish my college education by 2022.
I ought to speak very good English in ten years.
I might get married within ten years.

EXERCISE 5 EDITING

GRAMMAR NOTES 1–7 Read this student essay. There are eight mistakes in the use of modals. The first mistake is already corrected. Find and correct seven more.

Why We Itch

Why do we itch? You ~~must~~ *might* think that scientists have found the answer to this very simple question. Unfortunately, scientists can't answer this question with any certainty. They simply don't know for sure.

There are some clear cases involving itching. If a patient goes to her doctor and complains of terrible itching, the doctor will look for some kind of rash. If he finds a rash, the doctor will probably say that she must eat something she was allergic to, or that an insect must not have stung or bitten her. Scientists can easily explain this kind of case. Most itching, however, does not have an obvious cause.

Here's what scientists do know: Right under the surface of the skin, there are sensory receptors. These receptors detect pain and let the brain know about it. If there is a lot of stimulation to the body, the sensory receptors might carried a message of pain to the brain. If there isn't much stimulation, the sensors might be report it as itchiness.

There has been a lot of speculation about the function of itching. Some researchers think the function of itching may to warn the body that it is about to have a painful experience. Others theorize that early humans might developed itching as a way of knowing they needed to take insects out of their hair. Still others believe that itching could be a symptom of serious diseases such as diabetes and Hodgkin's disease.

One of the most interesting aspects of itching is that it may have be less tolerable than pain. Research has shown, in fact, that most of us tolerate pain better than itching. Many people are willing to injure their skin just so they can get rid of an itch.

Go to MyEnglishLab for more focused practice.

EXERCISE 6   LISTENING

05|02   **A** Listen to a discussion in a biology class. What is the main idea of the listening? Circle the correct answer.

a. The way we hear our own voices is different from the way other people hear them.

b. The way we hear our own voices is the same as the way other people hear them.

c. The way we hear our own voices is more accurate than the way other people hear them.

05|02   **B** Now listen to statements made during the discussion. For each statement, circle the sentence that gives the same information.

1. **a.** It's almost impossible that it was me.
   b. It's possible that it was me.

2. **a.** There must be some mistake.
   b. There's possibly some mistake.

3. **a.** It's possible that all of you have had this experience before.
   b. It's almost certain that all of you have had this experience before.

4. **a.** You have probably figured out the answer.
   b. You will probably be able to figure out the answer.

5. **a.** It's got to be because we hear the sound in a different way.
   b. It's possibly because we hear the sound in a different way.

6. **a.** It's possibly because the sound travels through different substances.
   b. It's almost certainly because the sound travels through different substances.

7. **a.** That must affect the way we hear our own voices.
   b. That may affect the way we hear our own voices.

8. **a.** It's almost certain they're not as accurate as they're supposed to be.
   b. It's possible they're not as accurate as they're supposed to be.

9. **a.** It's almost certain it's the opposite.
   b. It's possible it's the opposite.

10. **a.** It's almost certain that's why you don't like it.
    b. It's possible that's why you don't like it.

C Work with a partner. Continue the last part of the discussion in the listening about why many people may not like their own voices. Discuss these questions:

1. Do you think it is true that many people don't like their own voices? Why do you think this might be the case?

2. Have you heard a recording of your own voice? If so, how did you feel about it? What do you think could be the reason for your reaction?

EXERCISE 7 DETECTIVE WORK

A PUZZLE Work with a partner. Solve the puzzles. Suggest several possible solutions to each puzzle. Write them down—from most likely to least likely—and label them accordingly.

1. On November 22, 1978, an eighteen-year-old thief broke into a lady's house and demanded all her money. She gave him all she had: $11.50. The thief was so angry that he demanded she write him a check for $50. Two hours later, the police caught the thief. How?

   The lady must have called the police and told them about the check. (most likely)

   Someone might have seen the thief when he ran away from the lady's house. (less likely)

2. A dog owner put some food in a bowl for her cat. Then, because she didn't want her dog to eat the cat's food, she tied a six-foot rope around his neck. Then she left. When she came back, she discovered that the dog had eaten the cat's food. What happened?

3. Two monks decided to ride their bicycles from their monastery to another monastery in a town 6 miles away. They rode for a while and then reached a crossroads where they had to change direction. They discovered that the sign with arrows pointing to different towns in the area had blown down. They didn't know which road was the right one. Nevertheless, they were able to figure out which road to take. What do you think they did?

4. Roy Sullivan, a forest ranger in Virginia, had several experiences in his life in which he was struck by a powerful force. Two times his hair was set on fire. He had burns on his eyebrows, shoulder, stomach, chest, and ankle. Once he was driving when he was hit and was knocked 10 feet out of his car. What do you think happened to him?

B Report your answers to the class.

EXAMPLE: We think that the most likely explanation for the first puzzle is that the lady must have called the police and told them about the check. Then the thief must have tried to cash the check at a bank.

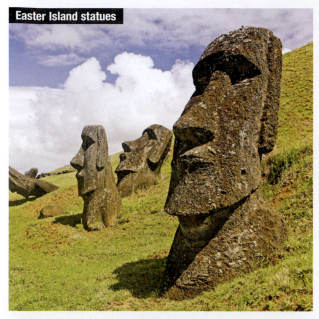
Easter Island statues

Nazca lines or geoglyphs

Crop circles

Stonehenge

EXERCISE 9 FAMOUS WORLD MYSTERIES

A PROJECT Work with a partner. Look at the photos above of famous world mysteries. Choose one of the mysteries and research it on the Internet. Find the answers to these questions:

1. Who must have made this?
2. How could they have made it?
3. Why might they have made it?
4. What might people have used this place for?

B Present the information you have discovered to the class. If possible, make a poster, and include visuals in your presentation. Then, as a class, vote on your favorite mystery.

Go to MyEnglishLab for more communication practice.

FROM GRAMMAR TO WRITING

A BEFORE YOU WRITE Think of an interesting world mystery that you have heard about. Take notes on at least three reasons why you think it is interesting, focusing on unanswered questions about the mystery.

B WRITE Using your ideas in A, write a five-paragraph essay about the mystery you have chosen. Remember to use modals of certainty. Try to avoid the common mistakes shown in the chart. Use the example below to help you begin your essay.

EXAMPLE: I have visited Stonehenge twice. I think it's a fascinating place, but I still have many questions about it. For example, how might the builders have moved the gigantic stones? Even if there was a quarry close by, how could people have transported them even a short distance?
       Then there's the question of why Stonehenge was built. Some scholars have said people might have built Stonehenge for religious purposes. Others think it must have been a kind of astronomical observatory. . . .

Common Mistakes in Using Modals of Certainty

Don't use *mustn't* in speculations about the present or past. Use **must not**.	You **must not have understood** what I meant. **NOT** You ~~mustn't~~ have understood what I meant.
Don't use *had* in past modals. Use **have + past participle** after *could*, *should*, *may*, and *might*.	You **should have told** me you couldn't come. **NOT** You should ~~had~~ told me you couldn't come.
Don't omit **to** after the modal **ought**.	We **ought to know** the answer soon. **NOT** We ~~ought know~~ the answer soon.

C CHECK YOUR WORK Look at your essay. Underline the modals of certainty. Use the Editing Checklist to check your work.

Editing Checklist

Did you . . . ?

☐ avoid contracting *must* and *not* when speculating about the present or past

☐ use *have* in past modal constructions

☐ use *to* after the modal *ought*

D REVISE YOUR WORK Read your essay again. Can you improve your writing? Make changes if necessary.

Go to MyEnglishLab for more writing practice.

UNIT 5 REVIEW

Test yourself on the grammar of the unit.

A Complete the sentences. Circle the correct answers.

1. That <u>must / may</u> be the answer to the mystery. All evidence points to it.
2. Ellen <u>might / will</u> be here later, but I don't know for sure.
3. A monk <u>must / might</u> have made the trip, but the evidence isn't conclusive.
4. It <u>couldn't / shouldn't</u> have been Newfoundland, which is too far north.
5. We <u>should / can't</u> find out what really happened later today. Louis says he knows.
6. You <u>may / ought not to</u> have trouble solving the problem—you're good at math.
7. They <u>had to / might</u> have been home—I heard their music.
8. She <u>might be / has got to be</u> the one who took it. No one else had access to it.
9. They <u>had to be / must have been</u> away last week. Their car was gone.
10. There <u>must / might</u> be a key around here somewhere. Dad said he had one.

B Look at the underlined phrase in each sentence. Write a phrase with a modal that is similar in meaning to the underlined phrase.

1. It's possible that Jeremy had to work late.   _____
2. It's very likely that Mari missed her flight.   _____
3. It's impossible that they heard the news.   _____
4. It's likely that we'll know the answer soon.   _____
5. You had the opportunity to get a scholarship.   _____

C Find and correct five mistakes.

A: Hi, Jack. I'm glad you finally made it to the party! But where's Gina? Do you think she

  might have forgotten about the party, or could she had to work late?

B: I think Gina must to be sick. She didn't look good earlier today.

A: That's too bad. What about Al and Lisa?

B: Al told me that he couldn't get here by 7:00, but he should to make it by 8:00. I don't know

  about Lisa. I suppose she could be work late, but she didn't say anything to me about it.

A: I guess she might been on her way here right now. I hope so!

Now check your answers on page 428.

Go to MyEnglishLab to complete the review online.   Modals to Express Degrees of Certainty   **83**

Passive Voice

PART 3

OUTCOMES

- Use the passive in the past, present, and future
- Use the passive causative to talk about services or activities that people arrange for others to do
- Identify main ideas and details in a narrative
- Identify key details in an interview
- Discuss crime stories and speculate about possible solutions
- Write an essay about a crime

OUTCOMES

- Describe situations or states, and report ideas, beliefs, and opinions with the passive
- Identify the meaning of key concepts in an academic article
- Identify events in a news broadcast
- Participate in discussions on academic topics, expressing and supporting opinions with details
- Write an essay about a legend or myth

UNIT

6

Passives: Part 1
CRIME

OUTCOMES
- Use the passive in the past, present, and future
- Use the passive causative to talk about services or activities that people arrange for others to do
- Identify main ideas and details in a narrative
- Identify key details in an interview
- Discuss crime stories and speculate about possible solutions
- Write an essay about a crime

STEP 1   **GRAMMAR IN CONTEXT**

BEFORE YOU READ

Discuss the questions.

1. Many people find crimes fascinating. Do you enjoy hearing about them? If so, why?

2. Do you know of any unsolved crimes?

3. Why do people sometimes sympathize with criminals and want them to get away with their crimes?

READ

06|01   Read this news article about an unsolved crime.

Did He Get Away With It?

Have you ever heard of Dan Cooper? He was the central figure in a crime that happened decades ago and still hasn't been solved. Late in November of 1971, on a short flight between Portland, Oregon, and Seattle, Washington, a flight attendant was handed a note by a mysterious middle-aged man dressed in a dark suit. Leaning close to her, he said, "Miss, you'd better look at that note. I have a bomb." He then opened his briefcase so that she could see several red cylinders and a lot of wires. The man, who used the alias "Dan Cooper," was demanding $200,000 (worth about $1,160,000 in 2015 dollars), four parachutes, and a plane to fly him to Mexico.

The plane proceeded to Seattle with none of the other passengers even aware it was being hijacked. The passengers got off the plane, and "Cooper" got what he was demanding: $200,000, all in $20 bills that had been photocopied by FBI agents so they could easily be identified. Then the plane was refueled and took off for Mexico with only Cooper and five crew members on board.

Once the flight was under way, Cooper ordered the flight attendant to go to the cockpit and stay there. As she was leaving, she noticed him trying to tie something around his waist—presumably the bag of money. Then he opened the plane's rear stairway and jumped out of the plane. The crew felt pressure bumps that were probably caused by Cooper's jump. The air temperature was seven degrees below zero. Cooper was not equipped with any survival gear and was wearing only light, casual shoes.

Cooper has not been seen or heard from since that night. Who was he? Did he get away with his plan? Or was he killed trying to commit the perfect crime?

Authorities speculate that Cooper landed near Ariel, a small town near the Columbia River north of Portland. Only one real clue has been discovered. In 1980, an eight-year-old boy inadvertently dug up $5,880 of Cooper's money near a riverbank. It was only a few inches below the surface of the earth, but it had decayed so much that only the picture and the serial numbers on the bills were visible. Rotting[1] rubber bands were found along with the money, indicating that the cash had to have been deposited there before the bands fell apart. Since then, the area has been searched thoroughly, but no trace of Cooper has been found.

What really happened? Many investigators believe that Cooper must have been killed by the combination of the weather conditions and the impact of his fall, but if so, why have none of his remains ever been discovered? Is more information known than has been revealed? Is Cooper's body in some remote part of the wilderness area into which he jumped, or is he living a luxurious life under an alias somewhere? Did he have the $5,880 buried by an accomplice to throw the authorities off the track? Or did he bury it himself? After all these years, one can legitimately ask why this case hasn't been solved.

Cooper has become a legend. His story has been told in books and articles and even in the movie *The Pursuit of D. B. Cooper*. In Ariel, the hijacking is still celebrated every year. Notwithstanding the FBI's claims that Cooper could not have survived the jump, some believe that he did. Local bar owner Dona Elliot says, "He did get away with it . . . so far." Others don't think so. Jerry Thomas, a retired soldier who has been working independently on the case, thinks that Cooper didn't survive the fall and his body will eventually be found. "I know there is something out here," he says. "There has to be."

Will this case ever get solved? Who knows? As of July 2016, none of the missing money had been recovered. Although the case has been officially closed by the FBI, interest in the case of Dan Cooper has not diminished, and it remains the only unsolved air piracy case in American aviation.

Police Sketch of Dan Cooper

1 *rotting:* decaying

AFTER YOU READ

A VOCABULARY Choose the word or phrase that is closest in meaning to the word in **bold**.

1. The plane **proceeded to** Seattle with none of the passengers even aware it was being hijacked.
   a. arrived in   b. continued to   c. stopped in   d. avoided

2. He was tying something around his waist, **presumably** the bag of money.
   a. definitely   b. definitely not   c. most likely   d. probably not

3. Cooper was not **equipped with** any survival gear.
   a. provided with   b. thinking about   c. impressed with   d. interested in

4. An eight-year-old boy **inadvertently** dug up $5,880 of Cooper's money.
   a. eagerly   b. with help   c. with great effort   d. by accident

5. Is more information known than has been **revealed**?
   a. rejected   b. made known   c. manufactured   d. suggested

6. **Notwithstanding** the claims that Cooper couldn't have survived, many believe he did.
   a. In spite of   b. Involving   c. Because of   d. Along with

7. As of 2016, none of the missing money had been **recovered**.
   a. destroyed   b. known about   c. seen   d. gotten back

8. Interest in the case of Dan Cooper has not **diminished**.
   a. lessened   b. increased   c. continued   d. been proved

B COMPREHENSION Read the statements. Check (✓) *True* or *False*. Correct the false statements.

	True	False
1. The flight Cooper hijacked originated in Seattle.	☐	☐
2. Dan Cooper claimed to have a bomb.	☐	☐
3. The money Cooper received was in bills of different denominations.	☐	☐
4. The passengers were aware of what Cooper was doing.	☐	☐
5. A portion of Cooper's money was discovered by authorities.	☐	☐
6. Cooper was definitely killed when he fell from the plane.	☐	☐
7. Cooper may have buried the money that the boy dug up.	☐	☐
8. Almost everyone thinks Cooper got away with the crime.	☐	☐

C DISCUSSION Work with a partner. Based on what you have read so far, do you think Cooper was killed in the jump or survived? Give reasons for your opinion.

Go to **MyEnglishLab** for more grammar in context practice.

PASSIVES: PART 1

Active Sentences

Subject	Verb	Object
Cooper	**hijacked**	the plane.
Someone	**found**	the bills.
Authorities	**never solve**	some crimes.

Passive Sentences

Subject	*Be/Get* + Past Participle	(*By* + Agent)
The plane	**was hijacked**	by Cooper.
The bills	**were found**.	
Some crimes	**never get solved**	(by authorities).

Passive Verb Forms

		Be (not)	Past Participle	
Simple Present		**is (not)**		
Present Progressive		**is (not) being**		
Simple Past		**was (not)**		
Past Progressive		**was (not) being**		
Future	The crime	**will (not) be** **is (not) going to be**	**investigated**	(by the new team).
Present Perfect		**has (not) been**		
Past Perfect		**had (not) been**		
Future Perfect		**will (not) have been**		

The Passive with Modals

	Modals	*Be/Have been*	Past Participle	
The case	**can (not)** **may (not)** **might (not)** **should (not)** **ought (not) to** **must (not)** **had better (not)**	**be**	**reopened**	in the future.
	could (not) **might (not)** **must (not)** **should (not)** **ought (not) to**	**have been**		years ago.

The Passive Causative

Subject	*Have/Get*	Object	Past Participle	(*By* + Agent)
We	**had**	the evidence	**checked**	by experts.
She	**has had**	the note	**analyzed**.	
They	**got**	the report	**printed**	by professionals.
He	**is going to get**	a copy	**made**.	

GRAMMAR NOTES

1 Passive Voice vs. Active Voice

A sentence in the passive voice has a corresponding sentence in the active voice. In an **active** sentence, the **subject acts upon the object** of the sentence. In a **passive** sentence, the **subject is acted upon by the agent**.

• **active**	SUBJECT OBJECT The police **catch** *some criminals*.
• **passive**	SUBJECT AGENT *Some criminals* **are caught** by the police.

The **subject** of the active sentence **becomes the agent** (preceded by the preposition *by*) in the passive sentence, or disappears.

AGENT
Some criminals are caught **by the police**.
Some criminals are caught.

Transitive verbs are followed by an **object**. **Intransitive** verbs are not followed by an object. Many verbs can be used both transitively and intransitively.

They **returned** *the clothes* to the store. *(transitive)*
They **returned** home late in the evening. *(intransitive)*

BE CAREFUL! Only **transitive** verbs can be made **passive**. **Intransitive** verbs **cannot** be made **passive**.

Several people **died** in the accident.
NOT Several people ~~were~~ died in the accident.

2 Forms of the Passive

To form **passive** sentences, use *be* + past participle or *get* + past participle. They occur in **present**, **past**, and **future** forms, as well as in the **progressive**.

• **present**	Police officers **are** well **trained**. They **get tested** on the job almost daily.
• **past**	The suspect **was arrested** yesterday. He **got caught** committing a crime.
• **future**	He **will be held** in the local jail. He**'ll get charged** soon.

To make a **negative** passive sentence, place *not* after the first verb.

Cooper **has** *not* **been caught**.
The man **did** *not* **get killed** in the robbery.

To form **progressive passive** sentences, use *being* + past participle.

The prisoner **is** currently **being questioned**.
The suspect **is being held** in prison.

USAGE NOTE Use the **present progressive** and **past progressive** passives to describe actions **in progress** (= not finished) at a certain time.

The robbery occurred while the money **was being taken** to a bank.

3 Uses of the Passive

You can use the **passive** in the following situations:

• when you **don't know who** performed the action or it is **not important to say** who performed it	The money **was stolen**. The plane **was refueled**.
• when you want to **avoid mentioning** who performed the action	Information is known that **hasn't been released**. *(We don't want to say who hasn't released it.)* I **was given** some bad advice. *(We don't want to say who gave the advice.)*
• when you want to **focus on the receiver** or the **result** of an action instead of on the agent	**RECEIVER** **RESULT** **AGENT** The **thief** **was caught**. *Emma* **was written** by Jane Austen. *(focus on the title of the novel)*

4 The Passive with a *By* Phrase

You can use a *by* phrase in the following situations:

• when you introduce **new information** about the agent	The money was stolen **by a person who has a criminal record**.
• when you want to **credit** or **identify** someone who did something	The bills were photocopied **by FBI agents**.
• when the agent is **surprising**	The money was found **by a little boy**.
Remember, you can **omit the** *by* **phrase** in a passive sentence if you feel it is **unnecessary** or **undesirable** to mention the agent.	Why **hasn't** this crime **been solved**?

5 Direct and Indirect Objects as Passive Subjects

Most commonly, **direct objects** of active sentences become subjects of their corresponding passive sentences. However, **indirect objects** can also be subjects of passive sentences.

• **direct object → subject**	DIRECT OBJECT The police **arrested** *the suspect*. SUBJECT *The suspect* **was arrested** by the police.
• **indirect object → subject**	INDIRECT OBJECT The FBI **gave** the money to *Cooper*. SUBJECT *Cooper* **was given** the money by the FBI.

6 Passives with Modals

We often use **modals** and **modal-like auxiliaries** in the passive.

To form the **present passive** with a **modal**, use the modal + *be* + past participle.	The criminal **should be arrested**.
To form the **past passive** with a **modal**, use the modal + *have been* + past participle.	He **could have been arrested** before this.
Use *have (got) to*, *had better*, *had to*, *must*, *should*, and *ought to* in passive sentences to express obligation, necessity, and advisability.	The charges **had to be dropped**. Criminal suspects **must be charged**.
Use *can* and *could* to express **present** and **past ability**.	Suspects **can't be kept** in jail. The thief **could have been caught**.
Use *will* and *be going to* to talk about **future** events.	This prisoner **will be tried**. The suspects **are going to be released**.
Use *can't*, *could*, *may*, and *might* to talk about **future possibility** and impossibility.	The mystery **may never be solved**. He **can't be released** from jail this year.

7 *Get*-passive vs. *Be*-passive

The *get*-passive gives a sense of a process someone or something goes through; that is, it shows change. The *be*-passive often shows the result of a process.

USAGE NOTE We often use the *get*-passive in conversation. It is rare in more formal writing.	The prisoners **get fed** every evening. Right now, the Blue Team **is getting beaten** in the soccer game.
BE CAREFUL! Although you can use the *be*-passive both with action and non-action verbs, use *get*-passive only with **active** verbs.	More research **is needed** about the causes of crime. NOT More research ~~gets~~ needed about the causes of crime.

8 Forms of the Passive Causative

Use *have* and *get* to form the **passive causative** in the past, present, future, and with modals. There is usually little difference in meaning between the causative with *have* and with *get*.

• *have* + past participle	You should **have** your car **serviced**.
• *get* + past participle	I just **got** my best suit **dry-cleaned**.
• **past** causative	We **had** the windows **washed**.
• **present** causative	I **get** my car **tuned up** twice a year.
• **future** causative	She**'s going to get** her hair **cut**.
• **modal** causative	We **should have** our house **remodeled**.

Use the **passive causative** to talk about services or activities that people **arrange for someone else to do**.

The passive causative can occur with a *by phrase*, but this phrase is often omitted.	The detective **had** the evidence **analyzed**. Sometimes criminals **get** their hair **dyed**. I **got** my photos **developed** at the drugstore.
Use the *by* phrase only when it is necessary to mention the **agent**.	We **had** our house **inspected** *by Jim*.

Note that the passive causative has a **different meaning** from the expression *to get something done*, which means *to finish something*.	I **got** the work **done** by a mechanic.
	    (passive causative)
	 I **got** the work **done** by noon.
	    (I finished the work myself by 12 p.m.)

BE CAREFUL! Don't confuse the simple past causative with the past perfect.	**SIMPLE PAST CAUSATIVE**
	 They **had** the grass **cut**.
	    (Someone else cut the grass)
	 PAST PERFECT
	 They **had cut** the grass.
	    (They had done this before a specific time in the past.)

REFERENCE NOTE

For more information on **modals**, see Unit 4 on page 55 and Unit 5 on page 71.

EXERCISE 1   DISCOVER THE GRAMMAR

GRAMMAR NOTES 1–9   Read the sentences based on the reading. Underline the passive construction in each sentence. Then write *a*, *b*, or *c* to show why the writer chose to use the passive.

> **a** = The writer doesn't know who performed the action, or it is not important to say.
> **b** = The writer is identifying who performed the action because that information is important.
> **c** = The writer knows who performed the action, but does not want to identify them.

_a_   **1.** Some crimes never get solved.

_____   **2.** A flight attendant was handed a note by a mysterious middle-aged man.

_____   **3.** None of the other passengers were even aware the plane was being hijacked.

_____   **4.** The bills were found by an eight-year-old boy.

_____   **5.** Only one real clue has been discovered.

_____   **6.** Rotting rubber bands were found along with the money.

_____   **7.** Many investigators believe Cooper must have been killed in the jump.

_____   **8.** It makes me suspicious that so many questions have not yet been answered.

_____   **9.** Did he have the $5,880 buried by an accomplice?

_____   **10.** It is embarrassing that this case hasn't been solved yet.

EXERCISE 2   TRANSITIVE AND INTRANSITIVE

GRAMMAR NOTES 1–2   Complete the sentences with the active or passive present time form of the verb in parentheses. Then check (✓) *Transitive* or *Intransitive* to identify how each verb is used in the sentence.

	Transitive	Intransitive
1. Criminals often ____return____ to the scene of a crime. (return)	☐	☑
2. Usually, when they are not careful, they _____ by the authorities. (catch)	☐	☐
3. Smart criminals _____ entirely. (disappear)	☐	☐
4. They never _____ back to the scene of the crime. (go)	☐	☐
5. Usually a smart criminal _____ by accomplices. (help)	☐	☐
6. The accomplices _____ by the criminal. (reward)	☐	☐
7. Some criminals _____ they have left evidence at the scene. (not / realize)	☐	☐
8. Crime scenes _____ very closely by the police. (examine)	☐	☐

EXERCISE 3 PROGRESSIVE PASSIVES

GRAMMAR NOTE 2 Complete the TV news bulletin with the present progressive and past progressive passive forms of the verbs in parentheses.

Here is breaking news from KKBO Channel 6. Two suspects _____*are being held*_____

1. (hold)

in the county jail, where they _____ about their role

2. (question)

in a bank robbery. The robbery took place this morning at the downtown branch of First

International Bank. As the bank's doors _____ at 9 a.m.,

3. (open)

the suspects, wearing masks and carrying guns, burst in and demanded that an undisclosed

amount of money be placed in a paper bag. They escaped with the funds but were later caught.

A customer who _____ at the time of the robbery

4. (serve)

noticed the license plate number of the vehicle the suspects were driving, and she notified the

police. The identities of the two suspects _____ while

5. (not / reveal)

the investigation _____. Other bank customers

6. (complete)

_____ for additional information. This is Ron Mason

7. (currently / interview)

for KKBO News Channel 6. Stay tuned for further updates.

GRAMMAR NOTES 2, 6 Complete the article with passive constructions with *be* and the
correct forms of the verbs in parentheses.

An Unsolved Crime Continues to Fascinate

The pages of history are full of crimes that
_____have not been solved_____. Consider, for
1. (not / solve)
example, the case of the ship *Mary Celeste*. It had left

New York for Italy in November of 1872. About a month

later, it _____ floating east of
2. (discover)
the Azores. No one _____ on
3. (find)
board, though everything _____ to be in order, and there was no
4. (determine)
indication why the *Mary Celeste* _____. Apparently, in fact, tables
5. (abandon)
_____ for afternoon tea. However, the lifeboat and most of the ship's
6. (even / set)
papers were missing. One theory speculates that the ship _____ by an
7. (might / threaten)
explosion that _____ by fumes from its cargo of alcohol. That theory,
8. (cause)
however, _____. It doesn't seem an entirely satisfactory explanation,
9. (never / prove)
especially since no real evidence of an explosion was apparent. Over the decades, other scenarios

_____, many involving charges of foul play. One theory states that the
10. (propose)
Mary Celeste _____ by its own crew. Another holds that the ship's
11. (take over)
personnel _____ by pirates. Still another proposes that the ship's
12. (overcome)
personnel _____ as part of an insurance fraud scheme.
13. (kidnap)

The story of the *Mary Celeste* _____ in movies, novels, and plays, so
14. (dramatize)
much so that it is a challenge to separate fact from fiction. For the time being, at least, the fate of

the *Mary Celeste* will have to remain a mystery.

EXERCISE 5 PASSIVE CAUSATIVE

GRAMMAR NOTES 7–9 Read each sentence. Then circle the choice that is closest in meaning to the sentence.

Last week, the private detective Mitch Hanson had an extremely busy schedule.

1. On Monday morning, he had a tooth pulled before going to work.
   a. He pulled the tooth himself.   (b.) He arranged for someone to pull the tooth.

2. When he got to work, he had some facts checked for accuracy.
   a. He checked them himself.   b. Someone else checked them.

3. In the afternoon, he had to review a report. He had finished it by 6:00 p.m.
   a. He finished it himself.   b. Someone else finished it.

4. On Tuesday and Wednesday, he had to take photographs of a suspect in a case he had been working on. He got it done by the end of the day on Wednesday.
   a. He did it himself.   b. Someone else did it.

5. On Thursday, Mitch got some photos scanned.
   a. He scanned them himself.   b. Someone else scanned them.

6. On Friday, he worked until 5:30 p.m. and then went to an appointment. He'd had his income taxes done, and he needed to go over them.
   a. He did the taxes himself.   b. Someone else did the taxes.

EXERCISE 6 PASSIVE CAUSATIVE VS. PAST PERFECT

GRAMMAR NOTES 1–3, 8–9 Complete the paragraph with the passive causative or active past perfect forms of the verbs in parentheses. Use progressive forms of the verbs where necessary.

Yesterday was a typically unpredictable day in the life of Detective Anita Mendoza. Since Anita hadn't been able to eat at home, she _____*got breakfast delivered*_____ to her office
1. (get / breakfast / deliver)

as soon as she arrived. After breakfast, she emailed some photos of a crime scene to the lab to

_____. She spent two hours going over files. Then she left for
2. (have / them / enlarge)

the garage. While she _____, the mechanic said that she should
3. (get / her car / tune up)

also _____. Anita agreed and arranged to pick the car up later.
4. (have / a taillight / replace)

At lunchtime, she met with the members of her team. Time was short, so one of Anita's

colleagues _____ from a restaurant. The team studied evidence
5. (have / order / pizza)

that they _____ by the crime lab. By 2:00, they
6. (have / get / analyze)

_____. After the meeting, Anita and her team arrested a suspect
7. (have / complete / the work)

in a robbery case. Anita _____ by one of her colleagues. When
8. (have / the suspect / interview)

the interview was over, she _____ back to his jail cell. Then she
9. (have / the suspect / take)

discussed the interview with her team. At 5:30, she left the station, picked up her car, and met

her husband for dinner at a restaurant. They _____ and
10. (have / their kitchen / remodel)

couldn't do any cooking. At 9:00 p.m., they got home. It's good that Anita loves her work

because it was another long, tiring, but interesting day.

EXERCISE 7 EDITING

GRAMMAR NOTES 1–9 Read this student essay about the disappearance of Judge Joseph Crater. There are nine mistakes in the use of the passive voice. The first one is already corrected. Find and correct eight more.

The Legend of Judge Crater

On the evening of August 6, 1930, Judge Joseph Force Crater, a wealthy, successful, and good-looking New Yorker, disappeared without a trace. Earlier in the evening, he had ^been^ seen with friends at a Manhattan restaurant. At 9:10 p.m., he walked out the door of the restaurant and got into a taxi. The taxi drove away . . . and Judge Crater was never saw or heard from again. It was ten days before he even reported missing. On August 16, his wife, who had been vacationing in Maine, called the courthouse, asked where he was, and learned that he had probably get

called away on political business. This news reassured Mrs. Crater for a time. But when the judge still hadn't turned up by August 26, an investigation was started a group of his fellow judges. A grand jury was formed, but its members could not decide what had happened to Judge Crater. They theorized that the judge might have gotten amnesia or run away voluntarily. He might also have been the victim of a crime. His wife disagreed with the first two possibilities. She believed the judge been murdered by someone in the Tammany Hall organization, the political machine that controlled New York City at the time. The mystery still unsolved today. Crater could have been kill by a Tammany Hall agent, murdered by a girlfriend, or kidnapped by an organized crime group. He might actually have suffered from amnesia, or he might have planned his own disappearance. Sightings of Judge Crater have been reported over the past several decades, and various solutions to the mystery have been proposed, but none of them have being proved authentic.

Go to **MyEnglishLab** for more focused practice.

EXERCISE 8 LISTENING

06|02 **A** Listen to the interview. What has been stolen?

_____

06|02 **B** Listen again. Circle the sentence in each pair that gives correct information about what happened.

1. **a.** The janitor found the keeper.
   b. The keeper found the janitor.

2. **a.** First, the animals eat. Then the food preparation area is cleaned.
   b. First, the food preparation area is cleaned. Then the animals eat.

3. **a.** Akimura examined the keeper.
   b. A physician examined the keeper.

4. **a.** The keeper had apparently been drugged.
   b. The keeper had apparently taken drugs.

5. **a.** Two sea turtles were taken away for two weeks.
   b. Two sea turtles were taken two weeks ago.

6. **a.** The police were notified quickly about the first robbery.
   b. The police were not notified at all about the first robbery.

7. **a.** The zoo expansion has been completed.
   b. The zoo expansion has not been completed.

8. **a.** Voters have not yet approved the zoo expansion.
   b. Voters have already approved the zoo expansion.

9. **a.** Detective Sadler will check the janitor's references himself.
   b. Detective Sadler will arrange for someone to check the janitor's references.

C Work with a partner. Discuss these questions. Report your answers to the class.

1. Have you heard of other cases in which animals have been stolen? Describe them.

2. Do you think that people who steal animals should be punished severely?

3. Should taxpayer money be spent to solve crimes like the one in the Listening?

EXERCISE 9 WHO STOLE THE PAINTING?

INFORMATION GAP Work with a partner. Student A will follow the instructions below. Student B will follow the instructions on page 439.

STUDENT A

- The story below is missing some information. Your partner has the same story that contains your missing information. Ask your partner questions to find the missing information.

  EXAMPLE: **A:** What has been called the world's most famous painting?
  B: The *Mona Lisa* has been called the world's most famous painting.

- Your partner's story is missing different information. Answer your partner's questions so that he or she can fill in the missing information.

  EXAMPLE: **B:** When was the *Mona Lisa* stolen from the Louvre Museum in Paris?
  A: It was stolen from the Louvre Museum on August 21, 1911.

_____, which has been called the world's most famous painting, was stolen from the Louvre Museum in Paris on August 21, 1911. Amazingly, the theft was not even noticed until _____. Vincenzo Peruggia, a handyman, was eventually discovered to be the thief. Peruggia had been hired by the museum to _____. How did he manage to steal the painting? He first hid in a closet overnight. After the museum had been closed for the day, Peruggia took the painting off the wall. He then hid it under his coat and walked out of the building. No one stopped him because at this time, _____ was not given much attention by museum authorities. Also, the actions of the police investigating the crime were unimpressive, to say the least. Peruggia was named a suspect and was questioned twice before it became clear that he had perpetrated the crime. _____ was even treated as a suspect for a time. Two years later, after he tried to sell the *Mona Lisa*, Peruggia was caught in a successful police operation. He was finally arrested and was sentenced to seven months of jail time, and the painting _____.

EXERCISE 10 SOLVE THE CRIME

A CRITICAL THINKING You are going to try to solve a possible crime. First, read this article about the discovery of some buried coins found in California.

Saddle Ridge Gold

In February 2013, a married couple were walking their dog on their California farm in an area they called Saddle Ridge. They came across a mysterious, battered old can sticking up out of the ground. When they dug up the can, they discovered it was full of gold. They eventually dug up a total of eight cans that contained 1,400 gold coins, worth about $10 million in 2015 dollars. The couple have chosen not to reveal their identities or the exact location of their home. They say they have no idea where the coins came from or who buried them on their property.

Saddle ridge gold coins and rusted cans on display

Where did these coins come from? One possibility is that they are none other than those stolen from the San Francisco Mint in 1901. Those coins were valued at about $30,000 at the time of the theft and would be worth millions of dollars today. Walter N. Dimmick, a clerk at the San Francisco Mint who had previously been caught forging and stealing, was arrested for the crime, tried, and found guilty. However, the coins he was accused of stealing were never recovered. Had Dimmick buried the coins on the farm before he was captured? Nobody knows for sure. In any case, the prosecution team eventually admitted that Dimmick had been convicted on circumstantial evidence that did not prove his guilt. Additionally, the U.S. government has stated that the coins in the cans probably do not come from one single source: they have different face values, and some are in worse condition than others.

It has also been suggested that the coins were loot that was buried by famous Wild West gangsters like Jesse James or Black Bart. Another less glamorous theory is that the coins simply belonged to a person who did not trust banks. He or she decided to bury the coins to keep them safe instead of depositing them in a bank account. Indeed, several people have already demanded a share of the coins, claiming that their relatives were the ones who hid the treasure.

Many questions remain about the Saddle Ridge gold. Are the married couple telling the truth about their discovery? Why haven't their identities or location been revealed? Could these coins have been stolen from the mint? Was Dimmick really the thief? If not, are any of the other explanations that have been offered about the coins possible or plausible? If the coins were hidden by someone who hated banks, should they be given to the relatives of that person? What do you think?

B Work with a partner. Discuss the questions posed in the last paragraph of the article. Then share your opinions with the class.

Go to MyEnglishLab for more communication practice.

FROM GRAMMAR TO WRITING

A **BEFORE YOU WRITE** You are going to write about a crime. Do some Internet research to find a crime you are interested in. Take notes about the crime.

B **WRITE** Using your ideas in A, write a five-paragraph essay about your topic. Remember to use passive constructions. Try to avoid the common mistakes in the chart. Use the example below to help you begin your essay.

EXAMPLE: Stradivarius violins were made in Italy in the 1600s and 1700s. They are considered the best violins in the world because they produce an excellent sound, and they are very beautiful. They are found in such places as the Library of Congress and the Smithsonian Museum. They are also sometimes stolen.

In 1995, a Stradivarius that was valued at $3 million was stolen from the apartment of violinist Erica Morini in New York. Morini died not long after the robbery at the age of ninety-one. The violin has not been recovered. Was it stolen for the money it might bring? Or is it still being played by the thief who took it?

Here's what investigators know . . .

Common Mistakes in Using the Passive Voice

Don't use *being* in **simple passives**. Use *been*.	That crime hasn't **been** solved. **NOT** That crime hasn't ~~being~~ solved.
Don't use *been* in **progressive passives**. Use *being*.	That building is **being** demolished. **NOT** That building is ~~been~~ demolished.
Don't use *get* for **non-action passives**. Use *be*.	More teachers **are** needed in our schools. **NOT** More teachers ~~get~~ needed in our schools.
Don't use incorrect past participles in passive sentences. Make sure you use **correct past participles**.	The ship was **sunk** by the iceberg. **NOT** The ship was ~~sank~~ by the iceberg.

C **CHECK YOUR WORK** Look at your essay. Underline the passive constructions. Use the editing checklist to check your work.

Editing Checklist

Did you use . . . ?

- [ ] the past participle of the verb in all passive constructions
- [ ] *been* in simple passive sentences
- [ ] *being* in progressive passive sentences
- [ ] *by* phrases where appropriate
- [ ] the correct past participles in all passive constructions

D **REVISE YOUR WORK** Read your essay again. Can you improve your writing? Make changes if necessary.

Go to MyEnglishLab for more writing practice.

UNIT 6 REVIEW

Test yourself on the grammar of the unit.

A Complete the sentences. Circle the correct answers.

1. Right now, a new hotel is constructed / is being constructed downtown.

2. Tadao had his car serviced / had serviced his car because he couldn't do it himself.

3. The thieves were caught / caught when they tried to spend stolen money.

4. The driver of the car died / was died in the accident.

5. Evidence shows that the theory has been / being disproved.

6. The children were been / being driven to school when the accident happened.

7. The suspects won't have been / been being arrested by this weekend.

8. Without any help, I got the job done by noon / by an assistant.

B Complete the sentences with the verb *report*. Use passives and the forms in parentheses.

1. The news _____ daily. (simple present)

2. The news _____ right now. (present progressive)

3. The news _____ twice today. (present perfect)

4. The news _____ an hour ago. (simple past)

5. The news _____ when the robbery occurred. (past progressive)

6. The news _____ an hour before the robbery occurred. (past perfect)

7. The news _____ at 5:00 p.m. (simple future)

8. The news _____ by 3:30 p.m. (future perfect)

C Find and correct four mistakes.

The Turkish city of Trabzon has just being hit by a tsunami. The tsunami got caused by an earthquake centered in the Black Sea. At this time last year, international talks were been held on how to protect countries from tsunamis, but no significant decisions were agreed upon. U. N. officials said, "We must get these talks start again."

Now check your answers on page 428.

Go to MyEnglishLab to complete the review online.

Passives: Part 2
LEGENDS AND MYTHS

OUTCOMES
- Describe situations or states, and report ideas, beliefs, and opinions with the passive
- Identify the meaning of key concepts in an academic article
- Identify events in a news broadcast
- Participate in discussions on academic topics, expressing and supporting opinions with details
- Write an essay about a legend or myth

STEP 1 | **GRAMMAR IN CONTEXT**

BEFORE YOU READ

Discuss the questions.

1. The picture on page 106 shows a psychologist and his patient. In what parts of the world do people consult psychologists? What might people from other cultures think of this practice?

2. Why is the psychologist dressed in a tribal costume in this picture?

3. What is an aspect of your culture that might be hard for people from other cultures to understand? How would you explain it?

READ

 Read this article about an unusual tribe of people.

The Strangest of Peoples

For many years, anthropologists have studied strange and unusual peoples all over the world. One of the strangest is a group called the Nacirema, the predominant tribe of the North American continent. The territory of the Nacirema is located between the territories of the Canadian Cree and the Tarahumara of Mexico. In the southeast, their territory is bordered by the Caribbean. Relatively little is known of the origin of this people, though they are said to have come from somewhere to the east. In fact, the Nacirema may be related to certain European and African peoples.

Nacirema people spend a great deal of time on the appearance and health of their bodies. In Nacirema culture, the body is generally believed to be ugly and likely to decay. The only way to prevent this decay is through participation in certain magical ceremonies. Every Nacirema house has a special shrine room devoted to this purpose. Some Nacirema houses have more than one shrine room. In fact, it is felt in Nacirema culture that the more shrine rooms a family has, the richer it is.

What is in the shrine room? The focal point is a box built into the wall, inside of which is a large collection of magical potions, medicines, and creams. Below the box is a small fountain from which water is obtained. Every day, each member of the Nacirema family enters the shrine room, bows to the chest, and receives magic holy water from the fountain.

Several rituals in Nacirema culture are performed by one sex or the other, but not by both. Every morning, for example, a Nacirema man places a magic cream on his face and

then scrapes and sometimes even lacerates[1] his face with a sharp instrument. A similar ritual performed only by women involves the scraping of the legs and underarms.

In Nacirema culture, the mouth is regarded as a highly significant part of the body. The Nacirema are fascinated by the mouth and believe its condition has an important and supernatural effect on all social relationships. The daily body ritual involves an activity that would be considered repulsive in some cultures. It is reported that the Nacirema actually insert into their mouths a stick on one end of which are plasticized hairs covered with a magical paste! They then move these sticks back and forth in their mouths in highly ritualized gestures.

Among the most important individuals in the culture are the "holy-mouth-people." Naciremans visit these practitioners once or twice a year. They possess excellent sharp instruments for performing their magic ceremonies. They place these instruments in the mouths of the Naciremans. If there are holes in the teeth, they are enlarged with these tools. Then a supernatural substance is placed in each hole. It is said that the purpose of this practice is to prevent decay in the teeth and especially to help Nacirema people to find spouses.

Another significant person in Nacirema culture is the "listener," a witch doctor who is thought to have the power to get rid of the devils in the heads of people who have been bewitched.[2] Naciremans believe parents often bewitch their own children, especially while teaching the secret toilet rituals, and the listeners must "unbewitch" them. It is also believed that the secret to getting rid of these devils is simply to talk about them, usually while reclining on a sofa.

Clearly, the Nacirema are a magic-inspired tribe. Much more research is needed in order to understand this strange people.

---

1 *lacerates:* cuts
2 *bewitched:* "magically" placed under one's power

AFTER YOU READ

A VOCABULARY Choose the word or phrase that is closest in meaning to the word in **bold**.

1. The Nacirema are the **predominant** tribe of the North American continent.
   a. most intelligent   **b.** most energetic   **c.** most beautiful   **d.** most powerful

2. The only way to prevent this decay is through **participation in** magical ceremonies.
   a. starting   **b.** admiration of   **c.** sharing in   **d.** inventing

3. The **focal** point is a box built into the wall.
   a. beginning   **b.** unimportant   **c.** central   **d.** final

4. Every Nacirema house has a special shrine room **devoted to** this purpose.
   a. used for   **b.** coming from   **c.** kept from   **d.** caused by

5. Below the box is a small fountain from which water is **obtained**.
   a. seen   **b.** gotten   **c.** admired   **d.** purchased

6. Naciremans visit these **practitioners** once or twice a year.
   a. scientists   **b.** specialists   **c.** teachers   **d.** assistants

7. This is a practice that would be considered **repulsive** in some cultures.
   a. dangerous   **b.** unusual   **c.** attractive   **d.** disgusting

8. One **ritual** involves the scraping of the legs and underarms.
   a. thought   **b.** habitual act   **c.** illegal act   **d.** unusual event

B COMPREHENSION Complete the sentences based on the reading.

1. The Nacirema people are one of several _____ in North America.

2. The shrine room is in reality the _____.

3. The measure of a family's wealth in Nacirema culture is felt to be the number of _____ it has.

4. The activity of scraping the face, legs, or underarms is _____.

5. The stick that Naciremans insert in their mouths is a _____.

6. The holy-mouth-people are _____.

7. The listeners or witch doctors are in reality _____.

8. In reality, the devils in the heads of bewitched people represent mental _____.

C DISCUSSION Work with a partner. Compare your answers in B. Then discuss: Who are "the Nacirema" meant to represent in real life? Give reasons for your answer.

Go to MyEnglishLab for more grammar in context practice.

PASSIVES: PART 2

Describing Situations or States

Subject	*Be* + Past Participle	Prepositional Phrase
The people	**are related**	(**to** each other).
The country	**is composed**	**of** two regions.
The island	**is connected**	**to** the mainland.
The capital	**was located**	**in** the South.

Passive Sentences

*There is no active equivalent to this type of passive sentence. Therefore, there is also no agent that could be expressed with *by* + agent.

Reporting Opinions or Ideas

Active Sentences

Subject	Verb	*That* Clause
Some anthropologists	**say** **think** **believe** **allege**	(**that**) the people came from somewhere to the east.

Passive Sentences with *It* + *That* Clause

It	*Be* + Past Participle	(*By* + Agent)	*That* Clause
It	**is said** **is thought** **is believed** **is alleged**	(by some anthropologists)	(**that**) the people came from somewhere to the east.

Passive Sentences with *To* Phrase

Subject	*Be* + Past Participle	(*By* + Agent)	*To* Phrase
The people	**are said** **are thought** **are believed** **are alleged**	(by some anthropologists)	**to** have come from somewhere to the east.

GRAMMAR NOTES

1 Stative Passive

The passive is often used to describe **situations or states**. This use is called the **stative passive**.

To form the **stative passive**, use *be* + past participle.	These peoples **are related** to each other. St. Louis **is located** on the Missouri River.
In stative passive sentences, there is normally **no action taking place**. The past participle functions as an **adjective**. It is often followed by a prepositional phrase.	The United States **is composed** of 50 states. Cuba **is located** in the Caribbean.
Stative passive sentences are often used in everyday English. Examples of stative passive expressions are: *be bordered by* *be found in* *be composed of* *be located in* *be connected to* *be located on* *be connected with* *be made up of* *be connected by* *be related to* *be divided into* *be surrounded by* *be divided by*	A peninsula **is surrounded by** water on three sides. Curitiba **is found in** southern Brazil. Canada **is made up of** 10 provinces and three territories. South Africa **is bordered by** Namibia. Argentina and Uruguay **are divided by** the Uruguay River.
A few stative passive sentences have a corresponding **active sentence**. These include passives formed with **connect** and **surround**.	England and France **are connected** by the Chunnel. *(passive)* The Chunnel **connects** England and France. *(active)*
BE CAREFUL! Most stative passive sentences do not have a corresponding active sentence, and most do not contain a *by* phrase.	Our two families **are related**. **NOT** ~~Genealogists relate our two families.~~

2 Opinion/Belief Passives

We often use regular passives to report **ideas**, **beliefs**, and **opinions**.

To form this type of passive, use *it + be + past participle + that*. You can use these verbs to form the passives: *allege* *believe* *report* *think* *assume* *claim* *say*	It **is assumed that** this culture is very old. It **is believed that** Atlantis really existed.
Passive sentences of this type have corresponding **active** sentences.	Scholars **assume that** this culture is very old. Some people **believe that** Atlantis really existed.
These passive structures may take an optional **by phrase**.	It **is claimed (*by some scholars*) that** Shakespeare didn't write all his plays.
BE CAREFUL! Use this passive structure only with verbs that can be followed by a *that* clause. *That* is optional and is frequently omitted in informal English.	It **is said (*that*)** these people came from Asia. **NOT** ~~It is regarded (that) these people came Asia.~~

3 Opinion/Belief Passives + *To* Phrase

To form passives that report ideas, beliefs, and opinions, you can also use **subject +
be + past participle + *to* phrase**.

Passive + *to* phrase sentences can be formed from an equivalent **active** sentence with a *that* clause. A *by* phrase is optional.	**ACTIVE** Scholars **assume** *that* **the culture dates** from 5000 B.C.E. **PASSIVE** The culture **is assumed** (by scholars) **to date** from 5000 B.C.E. Bigfoot **is thought to live** in the Pacific Northwest.
The verb in the *to* phrase can be **present** or **past**.	He is said **to be** the author. The Japanese are thought **to have visited** the New World before Columbus.
USAGE NOTE Passives with *consider* can take an infinitive, but they are often followed by just a noun phrase or an adjective.	Native Americans **are considered (to be)** the real discoverers.
USAGE NOTE Passives with *regard* can be followed by a *to* phrase but are much more commonly followed by *as* + a noun phrase.	Columbus **is regarded** *as* the discoverer of America.

4 Passives in Academic Discourse and the News

Use passives with *that* clauses or *to* phrases in **academic discourse** and when reporting
the **news**. Passive sentences of this type create an objective impression by distancing the
author from the idea.

• + *that* clause	It **is believed that** the Abominable Snowman actually exists.
• + *to* phrase	The defendant **is alleged to have committed** the crime.
IN WRITING Authors can create the greatest distance between themselves and an idea by starting a passive sentence with *it* + *be* + **past participle** + *that* clause. This type of sentence is formal.	**It is thought that** the Vikings explored the New World long ago.
BE CAREFUL! *It* + *be* + past participle + *that* structures occur only with verbs that can be followed by a clause beginning with *that*.	**It is claimed that** Shakespeare didn't write all of his plays. **NOT** ~~It is regarded that~~ Shakespeare didn't write all of his plays.

REFERENCE NOTES

For more information on *that* **clauses**, see Unit 20 on page 337.

For more information on **infinitive (*to*) phrases**, see Unit 9 on page 143.

For a list of **passive verbs followed by a *that* clause**, see Appendix 12 on page 417.

For a list of **stative passive verbs + prepositions**, see Appendix 13 on page 417.

Go to MyEnglishLab to watch the grammar presentation.

EXERCISE 1   DISCOVER THE GRAMMAR

A   GRAMMAR NOTES 1–3   Read the sentences based on the reading. Look at each underlined passive structure. Check *Stative Passive* or *Opinion/Belief Passive*.

		Stative Passive	Opinion/Belief Passive
1.	The Nacirema territory is <u>located</u> between Mexico and Canada.	☑	☐
2.	Their territory is <u>bordered</u> by the Caribbean.	☐	☐
3.	They <u>are said</u> to be from somewhere to the east.	☐	☐
4.	The Nacirema may <u>be related</u> to European and African peoples.	☐	☐
5.	The body <u>is</u> generally <u>considered</u> ugly and likely to decay.	☐	☐
6.	It <u>is felt</u> that shrine rooms give a family high social status.	☐	☐
7.	The mouth <u>is regarded</u> as a significant part of the body.	☐	☐
8.	This activity <u>would be considered</u> repulsive in some cultures.	☐	☐
9.	The "listener" <u>is thought</u> to have great powers.	☐	☐
10.	Naciremans <u>are surrounded</u> by potions, medications, and creams.	☐	☐

B   GRAMMAR NOTES 1–3   Read the sentences based on the reading. For each sentence, answer the questions *yes* or *no*.

1. The Nacirema territory is located between Mexico and Canada.

    a. Could the sentence be rewritten with a *by* phrase?   _no_

    b. Could the sentence be rewritten in the active voice?   _no_

2. The Nacirema may be related to European and African peoples.

    a. Could the sentence be rewritten with a *by* phrase?   _____

    b. Could the sentence be rewritten in the active voice?   _____

3. The mouth is regarded as a significant part of the body.

    a. Could the sentence be rewritten with a *by* phrase?   _____

    b. Could the sentence be rewritten in the active voice?   _____

4. It is felt that shrine rooms give a family high social status.

    a. Could the sentence be rewritten with a *by* phrase?   _____

    b. Could the sentence be rewritten in the active voice?   _____

EXERCISE 2 STATIVE PASSIVES

GRAMMAR NOTE 1 Study the map. Complete the sentences with the stative passive forms of the verbs from the box. Some of the verbs may be used more than once, and some items have more than one possible answer.

border by	divide into	locate (in)	surround by
connect by	find (in)	make up of	

1. North and South America _____are connected by_____ the Isthmus of Panama.

2. The island nations of the region _____ the waters of the Caribbean.

3. The island of Hispaniola _____ two nations: Haiti and the Dominican Republic.

4. Cuba _____ about 90 miles south of Florida.

5. The nation of Trinidad and Tobago _____ two separate islands: Trinidad and Tobago.

6. On the north, Costa Rica _____ Nicaragua and on the south by Panama.

7. The nation of The Bahamas _____ many islands, some large and some small.

8. The nation of Panama _____ two parts by the Panama Canal.

9. Jamaica _____ west of Hispaniola.

10. The French-speaking islands of Guadeloupe and Martinique _____ the eastern Caribbean, north of South America.

EXERCISE 3 OPINION/BELIEF PASSIVES + *AS* OR *TO* PHRASE

GRAMMAR NOTES 3–4 Complete the sentences with a present or past passive form of the verbs in parentheses. Add *as* or *to be* as needed.

1. For centuries before Copernicus, the earth _____was thought to be_____ the center of
   (think)
   the universe.

2. Atlantis _____ a continent off the coast of Spain with a rich,
   (claim)
   technologically advanced civilization.

3. In some circles, the Basques _____ the descendants of people
   (consider)
   from Atlantis.

4. Mother Teresa and Albert Schweitzer _____ great humanitarians.
   (regard)

5. In the Middle Ages, fairies and other spirit creatures _____ real.
   (believe)

6. Since the nineteenth century, George Washington and Abraham Lincoln

   _____ the greatest American presidents by many.
   (consider)

7. Bigfoot _____ a large, mysterious forest creature who lives in the
   (say)
   Pacific Northwest.

8. In the fifteenth century and afterwards, King Richard III of England

   _____ a monstrous king. Today, he has a better reputation.
   (regard)

9. Today, William Shakespeare, perhaps the most famous playwright ever,

   _____ the author of the plays credited to him, but some have
   (assume)
   suggested he couldn't have written them all.

10. From time to time, certain people _____ criminals, but some are
    (allege)
    later proved innocent by DNA evidence.

EXERCISE 4 OPINION/BELIEF PASSIVES + *THAT* CLAUSE

GRAMMAR NOTE 4 Rewrite each sentence with *it* + *be* + past participle + *that* clause.
Change the verb in the *that* clause as necessary.

1. For centuries before Copernicus, the earth was thought to be the center of the universe.
   For centuries before Copernicus, it was thought that the earth was the center of the universe.

2. Flying saucers are claimed by many people to actually exist.

   _____

3. The yeti is said by some to inhabit the Himalayas.

   _____

4. At the time of Plato, Atlantis was thought to have been hit by a series of earthquakes.

_____

5. Atlantis was believed to have sunk into the ocean without a trace.

_____

6. At one time in history, the earth was assumed to be flat.

_____

7. The Greek poet Homer is believed by some to have been a composite of several people.

_____

EXERCISE 5 OPINION/BELIEF PASSIVE CONSTRUCTIONS

GRAMMAR NOTES 2–4 Answer each question about your country with the verb in parentheses. Use a passive construction in each sentence.

1. Who is one of the most famous mythical characters in your country's past? (regard)
The Yellow Dragon is regarded as one of the most famous mythical creatures in China.

2. What strange event do people say happened in the distant past in your country? (allege)

3. What well-known creature do people think lives in your country today? (say)

4. What do people think is the most beloved or popular legend in your culture? (feel)

5. Who do people think was the founder of your nation? (assume)

6. Who do people think is the greatest leader in your country's history? (consider)

7. Who do people believe is the best writer or artist in your country's history? (believe)

8. Who do people think was the most famous criminal in your country's history? (claim)

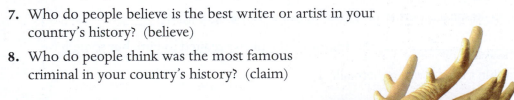

EXERCISE 6 EDITING

GRAMMAR NOTES 1–4 Read this student essay about a creature that may or may not be real. There are nine mistakes in passive constructions. The first one is already corrected. Find and correct eight more.

The Snowman

Every area of the world has its own legends, and Asia is no different. One of the most famous Asian legends is about the Abominable Snowman, also called the yeti.

believed
The yeti is ~~believe~~ to live in the mountains of the Himalayas. He thought to be a huge creature—perhaps as tall as eight feet. His body is supposed to be covered with long, brown hair. He says to have a pointed head and a hairless face that looks something like a man's. It is claimed that he lives near Mount Everest, the highest mountain in the world, which locates on the border of Nepal and Tibet.

Sightings of the yeti have been reported for centuries, but the yeti was introduced to the rest of the world only in 1921. In that year, members of an expedition to climb Mount Everest saw very large tracks in the snow. They looked like prints of human feet, but no conclusive evidence of the yeti's existence was found.

In 1969, Sir Edmund Hillary, who is regarded one of the greatest climbers ever, arranged an expedition in the region. He planned not to only see the yeti but also to capture him. Once again, tracks were discovered, but that was all. Hillary eventually decided the footprints might simply considered normal animal tracks. He thought the tracks might have been enlarged by the daytime melting of the snow.

Despite the lack of evidence, some scientists continued to believe that the yeti actually exists. Boris F. Porshnev, a Russian scientist, theorized that the yeti is a surviving descendant of Neanderthal Man. Neanderthal Man is believed to live from 200,000 to 25,000 years ago and is thought by some to be an ancestor of modern humans. If this is true, the yeti may be related us!

The mystery continues. Does the yeti really exist? It seems to me that there must be more to this mystery than just melted tracks. Centuries of reports by Himalayan trail guides must mean something. Besides, other yeti-type creatures have reported—most notably, Bigfoot in North America. Time will tell, but maybe we shouldn't be so quick to dismiss the Abominable Snowman as nothing more than an entertaining story.

Go to **MyEnglishLab** for more focused practice.

EXERCISE 7 LISTENING

▶ 07|02 **A** **Listen to the news bulletin. What has happened?**

_____

▶ 07|02 **B** **Listen again. Read each statement. Check (✓) *True* or *False*.**

		True	False
1.	It is claimed that one of the earthquakes registered a 9 on the Richter scale.	✓	☐
2.	The epicenter of the quakes was located in the Pacific Ocean.	☐	☐
3.	The exact number of drowned people is known.	☐	☐
4.	Coastal areas were hit by a tsunami.	☐	☐
5.	It is thought that severe flooding has occurred inland.	☐	☐
6.	The president was reported to be vacationing at his seaside retreat.	☐	☐
7.	So far, no looting has been reported.	☐	☐
8.	According to the president, it is to be hoped that citizens of the country will stay calm and law-abiding.	☐	☐
9.	Citizens are advised to go to low areas.	☐	☐

C **Work with a partner. It is assumed in the Listening that the lost continent of Atlantis was real. In your opinion, how should the Atlantis story be regarded? Should it be thought of as just an entertaining story, or should it be considered something more?**

EXERCISE 8 TEST YOUR TRIVIA IQ

GAME Form two teams. With your team, use the prompts on page 117 to write six passive-voice questions. Put verbs in the past where necessary. Then ask the other team each question. They guess the answer, choosing from the words in the box. Take turns. Check answers on page 435.

EXAMPLE: **Prompt:** continents / connect by / Isthmus of Panama

> **TEAM A:** Which continents are connected by the Isthmus of Panama?
> **TEAM B:** North and South America.

Albert Schweitzer and Mother Teresa	George Washington and Abraham Lincoln
Atlantis	Hispaniola
Bigfoot	the Bahamas
Costa Rica	the Basque people
Cuba	the yeti
Earth	William Shakespeare

Team A's Prompts:

1. island / compose of / the nations of Haiti, the Dominican Republic

_____?

2. Central American country / border by / Panama, Nicaragua

_____?

3. people / consider by some / be / the descendants of Atlanteans

_____?

4. legendary creature / think / live / the Himalayas

_____?

5. man / claim / be / the greatest playwright ever

_____?

6. individuals / regard / great humanitarians

_____?

Team B's Prompts:

1. Caribbean nation / compose of / many islands

_____?

2. Caribbean nation / locate / about 90 miles south of Florida

_____?

3. forest creature / say / live / the Pacific Northwest

_____?

4. lost continent / think / be located / the Atlantic Ocean

_____?

5. planet / think / be / the center of the universe / before Copernicus

_____?

6. two presidents / regard / the greatest American presidents

_____?

EXERCISE 9 MORE ABOUT THE NACIREMA

A CRITICAL THINKING You are going to discuss the Nacirema with a partner. First, read more about the tribe.

The focal point of the shrine is a box, or chest, which is built into the wall. Many charms and magical potions are located in this chest. It is believed that natives cannot live without these preparations. They are obtained from a variety of specialized practitioners. The most powerful of these are the medicine men. They are regarded as very important people in the tribe, and their assistance must be rewarded with substantial gifts. However, the medicine men do not provide the curative potions for their clients. They decide what the ingredients should be and then write them down in an ancient and secret language. This writing is understood only by the medicine men and by the herbalists, who, for another gift, provide the required charm.

The charm is not disposed of after it has served its purpose. It is placed in the charm box of the household shrine. As these magical materials are alleged to cure different types of sicknesses, and the real or imagined illnesses of the people are many, the charm box is usually full to overflowing. The magical packets are so numerous that people forget what their purposes were and fear to use them again. While the natives are very vague on this point, it is assumed that they believe that if they keep the old magical materials in the charm box, in front of which their body rituals are performed, they will in some way be protected from harm.

B Work with a partner. What do you think the following items are supposed to represent in the article in A? Discuss.

1. the charm box
2. the medicine men
3. the magical packets
4. herbalists
5. substantial gifts

C Dr. Horace Miner, an anthropologist, is the author of *Body Ritual Among the Nacirema*, the original article on which this reading is based. Discuss the following questions.

1. In your opinion, what characteristics are the American people thought to have? In general, are they regarded as scientific and rational, or as spiritual and naïve?
2. How does Dr. Miner's article portray the "Nacirema" (the American people)?
3. Why do you think Dr. Miner chose to describe the American people in this way? What do you think he wanted to say or show by doing this?

EXERCISE 10 UFO?

A PICTURE DISCUSSION Work in a group. Look at the photos. Then answer these questions, doing research on the Internet if necessary.

1. What are these two photos alleged to show? Where are the objects in the photos believed to have come from?

2. What is reported to have happened in Roswell, New Mexico, in 1947? What is claimed by the U.S. government to have happened?

3. It is believed by some people that the government doesn't want people to know what really happened in Roswell. Do you think the public has been told the truth about it?

4. UFOs and aliens are considered by some people to be real. What do you think? Is the universe composed of many different planets with their own life forms? Are we surrounded by aliens, and if so, have they visited us on Earth? Will they visit us in the future?

A UFO

Aliens

B Present your conclusions to the class.

Go to MyEnglishLab for more communication practice.

FROM GRAMMAR TO WRITING

A **BEFORE YOU WRITE** You are going to write about a legend or myth from your culture or another culture you are familiar with. Write a few sentences describing the legend or myth.

B **WRITE** Using your ideas in A, write a five-paragraph essay on the legend or myth you have chosen. Remember to use stative and opinion/belief passive constructions. Try to avoid the common mistakes in the chart. Use the example below to help you begin your essay.

EXAMPLE: My favorite American myth is the story of Paul Bunyan. Paul was a gigantic lumberjack who was thought to have great strength. It is said that he lived in the North Woods of Minnesota with his enormous blue ox named Babe. The story of Paul and Babe is certainly considered one of the most famous American myths. . . .

Common Mistakes in Using the Passive

Don't mix the passive and the active in the same sentence. Be sure to put **passive** items in a **series** in **parallel structure**.	The fugitive was **captured**, **tried**, and **convicted** of the crime. **NOT** The fugitive was captured, tried, and ~~they~~ convicted ~~him~~ of the crime.
Be sure to use a form of the verb *be* in each passive construction.	Bigfoot **is said** to live in the Northwest. **NOT** Bigfoot ~~says~~ to live in the Northwest.
Don't use *that* with the verb *regard*. Use *as*.	Einstein **is regarded as** a great scientist. **NOT** Einstein is regarded ~~that he is~~ a great scientist.

C **CHECK YOUR WORK** Look at your essay. Underline the passive constructions. Use the Editing Checklist to check your work.

Editing Checklist

Did you . . . ?

- [ ] use passives in a series in parallel structure
- [ ] use a form of the verb *be* in each passive construction
- [ ] use *as*, not *that*, with the verb *regard*

D **REVISE YOUR WORK** Read your essay again. Can you improve your writing? Make changes if necessary.

Go to **MyEnglishLab** for more writing practice.

UNIT 7 REVIEW

Test yourself on the grammar of the unit.

A Complete the sentences. Circle the correct answers.

1. Spain bordered by / is bordered by Portugal to the west and France to the north.

2. Europeans and Africans are regarded as / that the ancestors of the Nacirema.

3. It claims / is claimed that the Loch Ness Monster actually exists.

4. The body is believed to be / is considered that it is ugly in Nacirema culture.

5. Gebru and I are related to / by marriage.

6. The capital locates in / is located in the center of the nation.

7. Ben Jonson is thought / thinks by some to have written some of Shakespeare's plays.

8. The Basqucs allege / are alleged to have come from Atlantis.

B Complete each sentence with the correct forms of the words in parentheses.

1. Native Americans _____ from Asia originally.
   (think / have / come)

2. _____ by scholars that Basque is unrelated to other languages.
   (It / say)

3. The yeti _____ to be covered with long, brown hair.
   (claim / witnesses)

4. The culture _____ from the year 3000 B.C.E.
   (assume / experts / date)

5. Fifteenth- and sixteenth-century artist and scientist Leonardo da Vinci

   _____ left-handed.
   (believe / have / be)

C Find and correct seven mistakes.

Hawaii is regarded by one of the most beautiful places in the world. It is composed from a number of islands, some large and some small. An island is an area of land that surrounds on all sides by water, so Hawaii is not bordered of any other country. It is claiming by some that mythical creatures live in Hawaii. For example, the Menehune say to be very small people who live deep in the forests there. They are allege to have lived in Hawaii since before the Polynesians arrived from Tahiti many centuries ago.

Now check your answers on page 428.

Go to MyEnglishLab to complete the review online.

Gerunds and Infinitives

PART 4

OUTCOMES

- Use gerunds as subjects, objects, and complements
- Identify key concepts in an article
- Identify key details in a telephone conversation
- Talk about personal interests, likes, and dislikes
- Discuss the topic of friendship, expressing opinions, agreeing and disagreeing
- Write an essay describing a close friendship

OUTCOMES

- Use infinitives as subjects and objects in the simple, past, and passive forms
- Use verbs with infinitives and/or gerunds
- Recognize and respond to key details in an article and recorded news bulletin
- Conduct an interview and report answers to the group
- Discuss the topic of procrastination, expressing opinions, agreeing and disagreeing
- Write an essay describing a personal experience

OUTCOMES
- Use gerunds as subjects, objects, and complements
- Identify key concepts in an article
- Identify key details in a telephone conversation
- Talk about personal interests, likes, and dislikes
- Discuss the topic of friendship, expressing opinions, agreeing and disagreeing
- Write an essay describing a close friendship

STEP 1 GRAMMAR IN CONTEXT

BEFORE YOU READ

Discuss the questions.

1. What do you value in friendships?

2. Are all of your friends the same type of friend (for example, long-term friends, special-interest friends), or are some different types of friends?

READ

▶08|01 Read this article about types of friends.

Friends

I was having trouble finding a subject for this week's column until my wife, Amanda, said, "What about friendship? Talk about that. You have lots of friends." I thought about that a while and realized my perspective on friendship has changed considerably. When I was a boy, I had the naïve notion that friends were either true or false, but now I recognize the complexity of friendship. There are many types of friends. In fact, I can identify at least five types.

TYPE 1: Convenience Friends

These are the friends we make when our schedules and activities coincide. Years ago, I was starting a new job and didn't have a way of getting to work easily. I tried taking the bus, but the commute was ridiculously long. Then I learned that Andrés, a co-worker, lived near me. He had a car, and it was convenient for him to pick me up. We became friends by riding with each other and developed a good relationship. We didn't get together outside the work context, though.

TYPE 2: Special-Interest Friends

My brother, whose passion is kayaking, belongs to a kayaking club. He's made several good buddies at meetings and on river trips. They have exciting times when they go kayaking. Likewise, living through dangerous experiences has made them close. Once the trips are over, though, they don't socialize with each other. Their special interest is the only thing that holds them together.

TYPE 3: Online Friends

Online friendship is a new phenomenon made possible by technology. Communicating with people online has never been easier. Many people today have a rather wide circle of friends that they rarely or never meet in person but whom they regularly talk to or exchange messages with online. But there can be a downside: if someone says something upsetting on social media, for example, it's easy to abandon the relationship just by unfriending that person. However, if one is willing to commit to staying friends, the friendship can be rewarding and fulfilling. We can be online friends with interesting people all over the world that we might never be able to meet in person.

TYPE 4: Part-of-a-Couple Friends

My wife, Amanda, and Gretta, the wife of my buddy Bill, are good examples of this common type of friendship. When our partner has a friend in another couple, we have to go through the often difficult process of getting to know the "other person" in that couple. People may feel they have little or nothing in common with their counterpart and may even resent having to socialize with a "friend" they don't find compatible. Fortunately, Amanda and Gretta have become good friends on their own through their common interest in running.

TYPE 5: "Best" Friends

To me, a best friend is a person with whom we don't have a problem being honest or vulnerable. It's someone who will never desert you, who keeps no record of wrongs, who doesn't spare your feelings or avoid telling you what you need to hear. I have two best friends. One is Ken, whom I met in the military. Our having gone through difficult experiences has bonded us for life. The other is Amanda. We love having long conversations that can wander everywhere and nowhere. Sometimes we talk for hours. We both love being listened to. Other times, we like being together without saying much of anything. I would have a hard time living without my two "best" friends, but it's important to have the others, too.

AFTER YOU READ

A VOCABULARY Match the words in **bold** with their meanings.

_____ **1.** When I was a boy, I had a **naïve** notion about friendship.

_____ **2.** These are the friends we make when our schedules and activities **coincide**.

_____ **3.** We didn't get together outside the soccer **context**, though.

_____ **4.** **Likewise**, living through dangerous experiences has made them close.

_____ **5.** It's easy to **abandon** the relationship by unfriending the person.

_____ **6.** We most often **seek** friends in our own age group.

_____ **7.** They may resent having to socialize with a "friend" they don't find **compatible**.

_____ **8.** A friend is someone with whom we don't have a problem being **vulnerable**.

a. in the same way

b. give up

c. easy to harm

d. innocent

e. like-minded

f. happen at the same time

g. conditions in which something occurs

h. try to find

B COMPREHENSION Complete the sentences based on the reading.

1. If you have the same schedule as someone, that person can become a _____ friend.

2. The author's brother met a lot of friends through _____, his special interest.

3. The _____ of social networking websites has made online friendships possible.

4. One downside of an online _____ is that it's perhaps too easy to abandon an online friend.

5. It's not easy to be friends with someone if you have little or nothing _____ with that person.

6. Some people may not feel like _____ with friends of their spouses.

7. If someone is your best friend, you can be _____ with that person.

8. The author and his wife both place great importance on being _____ to.

C DISCUSSION Work with a partner. Compare your answers in B. Then talk about a friend who fits into one of the categories in the reading. Describe your experiences and explain why you feel your friend fits into that category.

Go to **MyEnglishLab** for more grammar in context practice.

GERUNDS

Gerund as Subject

Gerund (Subject)	Verb	Object
Kayaking	involves	some risks.
Swimming	builds	endurance.
Not inviting him	will cause	resentment.

Gerund as Object

Subject	Verb	Gerund (Object)
They	enjoy	**kayaking**.
I	went	**swimming**.
We	don't advise	**excluding** him.

Gerund as Subject Complement

Subject	Verb	Gerund (Subject Complement)
My sport	is	**skiing**.
His problem	is	**not exercising**.

Gerund as Object Complement

Subject	Verb	Object	Gerund (Object Complement)
He	spends	time	**reading**.
She	found	him	**not working**.

Gerund as Object of a Preposition

	Preposition	Gerund	
She insists	**on**	**going out**	every weekend.
He's accustomed	**to**	**giving**	parties.
They have a reason	**for**	**not inviting**	Michael.

Possessive + Gerund

	Possessive	Gerund	
Bob and Helen worry about	**Emily's** / **her** / **the children's** / **their**	**having**	so few friends.

Active and Passive Gerunds

	Active Gerunds	Passive Gerunds
Simple	**Inviting** them to her wedding was a nice gesture on her part.	**Being invited** to her wedding was a great surprise to them.
Past	**Having invited** them to her wedding made her feel good.	**Having been invited** to her wedding is a fond memory for them.

GRAMMAR NOTES

1 Form and Function of Gerunds

A **gerund** is a **noun made from a verb**. Gerunds and gerund phrases perform the same functions as nouns.

To form a gerund, add *-ing* to the **base form** of the verb.	**Cooking** is my hobby. I like **eating**, too.
Add *not* before a gerund to make a **negative** statement.	**Not calling** her was a big mistake.
Many words in English end in *-ing*. Don't confuse gerunds with verbs in the progressive form or with present participles used as adjectives or in adverbial phrases.	I've been **making** friends at work. *(progressive form)* Mary is enrolled in a **cooking** class. *(as adjective)* **Walking on the beach**, I wondered why she was angry at me. *(adverbial phrase)*
BE CAREFUL! Be sure to spell gerunds correctly.	**Smoking** is not good for your health. **NOT** ~~Smokeing~~ is not good for your health. **Swimming** is very good exercise. **NOT** ~~Swiming~~ is very good exercise.

2 Gerunds as Subjects and Subject Complements

Gerunds and gerund phrases often function as **subjects** and **subject complements**.

They act as **subjects** of a sentence.	**Gardening** is one of my hobbies.
They act as **subject complements**. Subject complements occur after the verb *be* and other linking verbs such as *seem*. They describe or add information about the subject of the sentence.	*Star Wars* is a movie worth **seeing**.

3 Gerunds as Objects and Object Complements

Gerunds and gerund phrases often function as **objects** and **object complements**.

They act as **objects** of a sentence.	I like **playing** soccer.
They act as **object complements**. Object complements describe or add information about the object of the sentence.	Melanie has trouble **making** new friends.
Common examples of verbs and verb phrases that have gerunds as objects are: avoid consider feel like mind can't help enjoy keep	I **enjoy meeting** new people. You should **avoid working** late. I **can't help feeling** sorry for her.
We often use *go* + **gerund** to talk about recreational activities: *go skiing, go swimming, go hiking*, etc. In this type of sentence, *go* has the basic meaning of "do the activity of."	We **go skiing** every weekend in the winter. We **went swimming** yesterday afternoon.

4 Gerunds as Objects of Prepositions

Gerunds and gerund phrases often function as **objects of prepositions**.

Many preposition combinations are followed by gerunds:	
• **verb + preposition**	They **insisted on giving** us a present.
• **adjective + preposition**	She's **good at making** friends.
Note that the word *to* can be a preposition or part of an infinitive.	He will adjust *to* **working** hard. *(preposition)* He tries *to* **work** hard. *(part of the infinitive)*
BE CAREFUL! Don't confuse *be used to* and *used to*. The *to* in *be used to* is a preposition. The *to* in *used to* is part of the infinitive.	**I'm used to getting** up early. *(accustomed to)* **I used to get up** early, but I don't anymore. *(habitual past)* **NOT** ~~I'm used to~~ get up early.

5 Possessive Gerunds

In writing and more formal speaking, use a **possessive** noun or pronoun **before a gerund** to show possession.	**Pete's dominating** every conversation bothers me. **His dominating** every conversation bothers me.
USAGE NOTE In conversation and informal writing, we often use a **name** or an **object pronoun before a gerund** instead of a possessive. We don't use subject pronouns before gerunds.	I don't like **Pete dominating** every conversation. I don't like **him dominating** every conversation.

6 Simple and Past Gerunds

Gerunds can occur in **simple** or **past** form.

We often use a **simple gerund** (without a past participle) to make a **generalization**.	**Making** friends is a natural thing to do. **Eating** a good diet is important.
We often use a **past gerund** (*having* + past participle) to show an **action** that **occurred before** the action of the main verb in the sentence.	**Having met** Jane in my first week of college **helped** me throughout my college career.
USAGE NOTE You can also use a **past gerund** to **emphasize** the **difference in time** between two actions. The simple gerund is also correct in many situations.	I realize now that my **having gone** to college is the reason I got this job. **or** I realize now that my **going** to college is the reason I got this job.

7 Passive Gerunds

Gerunds and gerund phrases can occur in **passive** form.

• **present passive**: *being* + past participle	She hates **being ignored**.
• **past passive**: *having been* + past participle	She's still angry about **having been ignored**.

REFERENCE NOTES

For a list of common **verbs followed by gerunds**, see Appendix 14 on page 417.

For a list of common **adjective + preposition combinations followed by gerunds**, see Appendix 18 on page 419.

Go to MyEnglishLab to watch the grammar presentation.

STEP 3   FOCUSED PRACTICE

EXERCISE 1 DISCOVER THE GRAMMAR

A GRAMMAR NOTE 1   Read each sentence based on the reading. Check (✓) *Yes* if the *-ing* word is a gerund. Check *No* if it isn't a gerund.

		Yes	No
1.	I've long since stopped thinking about friendship in these terms.	✓	☐
2.	These are the friends we make by engaging in some specific activity.	☐	☐
3.	He belongs to a kayaking club.	☐	☐
4.	We enjoy just catching up on each other's activities.	☐	☐
5.	I have been kayaking for years.	☐	☐
6.	Online friendships are worth pursuing.	☐	☐
7.	He was my teacher in a writing class.	☐	☐
8.	They have a common interest in running.	☐	☐
9.	We are having dinner with another couple next week.	☐	☐
10.	I would have a hard time being single again.	☐	☐

B GRAMMAR NOTES 2–4   Read each sentence based on the reading. Underline the gerund. Then write *S* if the gerund is being used as a subject, *O* if it is being used as an object, *OP* if it is the object of a preposition, or *C* if it is a subject or object complement.

__C__ **1.** I was having trouble <u>finding</u> a subject.

_____ **2.** I remembered learning a rhyme.

_____ **3.** I didn't have a way of getting to the practices.

_____ **4.** My brother's passion is kayaking.

_____ **5.** We can go months without contacting each other.

_____ **6.** Making new friends is sometimes not easy to do.

_____ **7.** My teacher supported my becoming a writer.

_____ **8.** I would have a hard time living without my two "best" friends.

EXERCISE 2 SIMPLE GERUNDS

GRAMMAR NOTES 1–4, 6 Maria Roybal is constantly tired and dissatisfied. She has gone to a doctor to see if there is anything physically wrong with her. Use words from the box to complete the conversation with gerunds. Some words will be used twice.

do	meet	not sing	rest	ski	work
make	not have	not work	sing	socialize	

DOCTOR: Well, Maria, what seems to be the problem?

MARIA: I'm tired all the time. Some nights when I come home from work, I'm so

exhausted I don't feel like _____*doing*_____ anything but collapsing on the sofa
                1.

and _____ in front of the TV. Is there anything physically wrong
       2.

with me?

DOCTOR: No, I've looked at your test results, and you're healthy. How long have you been

feeling like this?

MARIA: Oh, two or three months, I guess. Long enough so that I've started to worry about

_____ any energy.
    3.

DOCTOR: How much are you working?

MARIA: Well, I'm putting in a lot of overtime—all in all, at least 60 hours a week, I'd say.

DOCTOR: Why are you doing this? Are you trying to make yourself sick?

MARIA: Well, at this point, _____ overtime is out of the question. I've got a
                    4.

lot of bills to pay off. The other thing is that my company recently transferred me

to the office here, and I hardly know anyone, so my focus is on

_____ money right now. I like _____, but I don't
    5.   **6.**

know quite how to go about _____ new people.
                      7.

DOCTOR: You're not married, then?

MARIA: No, I'm not.

DOCTOR: Well, I think you need to stop _____ so much and start to enjoy
                            8.

yourself a little—to put things in balance. I'd say you need a hobby—and

some friends.

MARIA: A hobby? You mean some tiring thing like gardening?

DOCTOR: No. That's an OK hobby if you like it, but I think you need a more social one.

MARIA: Like what?

DOCTOR: Oh, maybe like karaoke. Do you like _____?
                            9.

MARIA: I love music, but I don't have much of a voice. Also, I think that

_____ at all is better than _____ badly.
    10.   **11.**

DOCTOR: Have you ever gone cross-country _____ ?
12.

MARIA: Well, yes. I used to do a lot of cross-country when I lived in Utah. I loved it.

DOCTOR: I have a friend who runs a cross-country ski club. I think there are a lot of people your age in it. I'll give you her cell-phone number.

MARIA: That would be great. Thanks a lot.

EXERCISE 3 POSSESSIVE GERUNDS

GRAMMAR NOTE 5 Complete each sentence with a possessive noun or pronoun and a gerund. Use the correct forms of the words in parentheses.

1. I have two best friends, Bob and Mary. Bob is my co-worker. I'm grateful for

   _____ *his giving* _____ me a ride to work every day.
   (he / give)

2. I'm new to the firm, so I also appreciate _____ me learn my job.
   (Bob / help)

3. _____ my work is hard to deal with, so Bob's encouragement is vital.
   (My boss / criticize)

4. Mary is my neighbor. _____ so close is wonderful.
   (She / live)

5. I especially appreciate _____ me on tough issues.
　　　　　　　　　　　　　　　(Mary / advise)

6. She knows how to deal with _____ discouraged.
　　　　　　　　　　　　　　　　　　(I / become)

7. I couldn't ask for two better friends than Bob and Mary. I'm thankful for

_____ there for me when I need them.
　　(they / be)

8. _____ together frequently helps us stay close.
　　　(We / get)

EXERCISE 4　SIMPLE AND PAST GERUNDS

GRAMMAR NOTE 6　Complete the sentences with simple gerunds or past gerunds with *having* + past participle. Use a past gerund if it is possible to do so.

　　Martha, who is 20 years older than I am, is one of my best friends. One of the best

things that ever happened to me was my _____*having met*_____ her long ago
　　　　　　　　　　　　　　　　　　　　　　1. (meet)

when I was an unhappy college sophomore. Martha and I have stayed friends. I look

forward to _____ her whenever our schedules permit. Our
　　　　　　2. (see)

relationship hasn't always been smooth, though. Martha and I were both in the same

calculus class. I was having a lot of difficulty and was angry at myself for

_____ in a class I didn't need for my degree. It was too late to
　　3. (enroll)

drop the class, though. Since I was frustrated, I often complained to the teacher during

class. Once, I told her she was unfair for _____ so much difficult
　　　　　　　　　　　　　　　　　　　　4. (assign)

homework the week before. Martha stopped me one day after class. She said she was tired

of my continual _____ with the teacher. "You need to grow up,"
　　　　　　　5. (argue)

she said. I was offended at first, but soon I realized that she was right. I had to get rid of

my negative attitude. I did need to grow up. In fact, the older I get, the clearer it is to me

that her _____ that changed the course of my life. Anyway, a
　　　　　6. (say)

few days later, I asked Martha if she would mind _____ with me
　　　　　　　　　　　　　　　　　　　　　　　　　7. (study)

and _____ me with the homework. She agreed. With a lot of
　　8. (help)

patient work, I succeeded in _____ the course. Eventually,
　　　　　　　　　　　　　　9. (pass)

Martha and I became great friends. I will always be thankful for Martha's

_____ me what I needed to hear when I needed to hear it. She
　　10. (tell)

has certainly made a difference in my life.

EXERCISE 5 ACTIVE AND PASSIVE GERUNDS

A **GRAMMAR NOTES 6–7** Write questions using the words in parentheses. Write a passive gerund and an active gerund in each sentence.

1. (like / awaken / by an alarm clock) (wake up / on your own)
   <u>*Do you like being awakened by an alarm clock or waking up on your own?*</u>

2. (prefer / ask / out on a date / by someone) (ask / someone / yourself)

   _____

3. (more interested in / entertain / yourself) (in / entertain / by others)

   _____

4. (prefer / cook dinner / yourself) (invite / to dinner / by friends)

   _____

5. (like / tell / what to do / by others) (give / people / orders)

   _____

6. (like / figure things out / yourself) (show / how to do things / by others)

   _____

7. (prefer / give / advice / by friends) (give / your friends / advice)

   _____

B Write true answers to your questions from A.

I like waking up on my own. I hate being awakened by an alarm clock.

EXERCISE 6 EDITING

GRAMMAR NOTES 1–7 Read this letter from a woman on vacation. It has ten mistakes in the use of gerunds. The first mistake is already corrected. Find and correct nine more.

ENCHANTED DESERT RANCH

Dear Adam,

I've been here for three days and am having a great time, but I can't help ~~wish~~ *wishing* you were here, too. Tell your boss I'm really angry at him. His not let you take any vacation time qualifies him for the Jerk-of-the-Year Award. (Just kidding. Don't say that!)

Believe it or not, the first night I missed hearing all the city noises, but I haven't really had any trouble to get used to the peace and quiet since then. Everything's so relaxed here—there's no rush around or check things on your cell phone. Get out of New York City was definitely what I needed, even if it's only for two weeks. The ranch has lots of activities—horseback ride, river raft on the Rio Grande, hiking in the wilderness—you name it. The ranch employees do everything for you. Being taken care of is nice for a change, and I love being chauffeured around Santa Fe in the ranch limousine. Tonight, a group of us are going out to a country-and-western dance place called Rodeo Nites in Santa Fe, so we having taken those two-step dance lessons last summer will come in handy. It's just too bad you couldn't come along so we could both have a good time. Tomorrow, we're all going to Taos Pueblo to watch some weaving being done and to see some Native American dancing. That's great because I'm really interested in learn more about Native American culture. And I'm looking forward to see <u>Carmen</u> at the Santa Fe Opera on Saturday.

I'll write again in a day or two. Miss you lots.

Love,
Louise

Go to MyEnglishLab for more focused practice.

EXERCISE 7 LISTENING

08|02 **A** Brian Hansen and Jane Travanti are having a telephone conversation. Listen. What is Brian's main reason for joining the orienteering club?

_____

08|02 **B** Listen again. Check (✓) *True* or *False*.

		True	False
1.	Brian has tried orienteering before.	☐	☑
2.	Brian thinks he should stop working.	☐	☐
3.	Being experienced in orienteering is necessary to join Jane's club.	☐	☐
4.	Jane's club tries to go orienteering at least twice a month.	☐	☐
5.	In the summer, they get around by biking.	☐	☐
6.	In the winter, they get around by cross-country skiing.	☐	☐
7.	Brian has gone cross-country skiing before.	☐	☐
8.	Being single is a requirement for joining the club.	☐	☐
9.	The club collects dues to pay for organizing their activities.	☐	☐
10.	On the 15th, they'll get to the forest by carpooling.	☐	☐

C Work with a partner. Brian thinks that joining the orienteering club will help him meet new people. Do you agree? What are other ways of meeting new people?

EXERCISE 8 ALL ABOUT YOU

A CONVERSATION You are going to talk about yourself with a partner. First, complete the sentences about your own life with gerunds or gerund phrases.

1. I spend a lot of time _____.

2. I especially enjoy _____.

3. I've always avoided _____ because _____.

4. I strongly dislike _____.

5. On weekends, I don't feel like _____.

6. I have stopped _____ recently.

7. I have trouble _____.

8. I'm still not used to _____.

9. I'm looking forward to _____.

10. If you visit my country, I recommend _____.

B Work with a partner. Talk about your lives. Share some or all of your answers to the questions in A.

EXAMPLE: **A:** I spend a lot of time playing computer games. I especially enjoy playing fantasy baseball games. What do you enjoy doing?

B: I enjoy hiking. I've always avoided playing computer games because I spend a lot of time working on the computer at my job! What do you dislike doing?

A: I dislike . . .

EXERCISE 9 YOU'VE GOT TO HAVE FRIENDS!

A QUESTIONNAIRE What do you value in friendships? Add your own item to the chart. Then complete the chart for yourself by rating each item.

People show they are friends by . . .	Rating
Giving each other presents	
Always being honest with one another	
Not hurting each other's feelings	
Giving help whenever it is asked for	
Lending money if it is asked for	

1 = Not Important in a Friendship
2 = Somewhat Important in a Friendship
3 = Very Important in a Friendship

B Work with a group. Discuss your answers to the questionnaire. Do you agree on what is important in a friendship? What kinds of things do people show they are friends by doing?

EXAMPLE: **A:** I think that people show they are friends by giving each other presents.

B: I don't think that giving presents is important in a friendship. I think that always being honest with each other is more important . . .

EXERCISE 10 MAKING FRIENDS AROUND THE WORLD

CROSS-CULTURAL COMPARISON Work in a group of students from different countries. Discuss the topic of making friends around the world. Using gerunds and gerund phrases, answer the questions.

1. How do people make friends in your country? What might be unique about the process of making friends there? Do you think making friends is easy or difficult?

   EXAMPLE: **A:** In my country, making friends is easy. It's easy to start talking to a stranger in the street. Soon, that stranger is your friend.

   B: In my country, making friends with men is easy if you are a man. But making friends with women is nearly impossible . . .

2. If you are now living in a country you were not born in, is making friends in your new country easy or difficult? Have you had trouble making friends in this country? Do you think getting to know people from a different country is challenging?

Go to MyEnglishLab for more communication practice.

A **BEFORE YOU WRITE** Think about a friendship that has been meaningful for you. Write a few sentences on each of the following points:

• We became friends by . . .
• We've made our friendship stronger by . . .
• We've stayed friends by . . .

B **WRITE** Using your ideas in A, write a five-paragraph essay about your friendship. Remember to use different kinds of gerunds. Try to avoid the common mistakes shown in the chart. Use the example below to help you begin your essay.

EXAMPLE: One of the most meaningful friendships I've ever had is the one with my friend Sarah Rodriguez. We became friends by going to the same school. Making friends wasn't that easy at first . . .
   Ever since Sarah and I became friends, we've enjoyed sharing all kinds of experiences. We can't go more than a month or so without contacting or even visiting each other . . .

Common Mistakes in Using Gerunds

Don't mix gerunds with infinitives in the same sentence. Keep **gerunds** and gerund phrases in **parallel structure**.	All my best friends love **going** to movies, **having** dinner together, and **taking** short trips. **NOT** All my best friends love going to movies, having dinner together, and ~~to go~~ on short trips.
Don't use subject pronouns before gerunds or gerund phrases. Use **possessive pronouns** in more formal English.	John's a good friend, but **his** constantly **interrupting** people is annoying. **NOT** John's a good friend, but ~~he~~ constantly interrupting people is annoying.
In **less formal English**, you can use **object pronouns** before gerunds or gerund phrases.	John's a good friend, but **him** constantly **interrupting** people is annoying.

C **CHECK YOUR WORK** Look at your essay. Underline the gerunds. Use the Editing Checklist.

Editing Checklist

Did you . . . ?
- [ ] use gerunds in parallel structure
- [ ] use possessive pronouns before gerunds as appropriate
- [ ] use object pronouns before gerunds in informal English

D **REVISE YOUR WORK** Read your essay again. Can you improve your writing? Make changes if necessary.

Go to MyEnglishLab for more writing practice.

UNIT 8 REVIEW

Test yourself on the grammar of the unit.

A Complete the sentences. Circle the correct answers.

1. Thank you very much for not smoke / not smoking.

2. Maria is extremely good at to make / making new friends.

3. I'm bothered by Emiko's / Emiko is talking so loudly.

4. She insisted on giving / to give me a present.

5. Carlos is used to have / having his family near him.

6. People with glaucoma have difficulty to see / seeing.

7. Most people dislike being awakened / being awaken by an alarm clock.

8. Pavlina was annoyed at not having been invited / not to be invited.

B Complete each sentence with a gerund phrase that is correct for formal English. Use the correct forms of the words in parentheses.

1. _____ them to the get-together was a mistake.
   (Mary / invite)

2. _____ to her party was a big surprise.
   (Be / invite)

3. Bob is feeling sad about _____ you when he was in town.
   (not / have / call)

4. Asha is concerned about her _____ any friends.
   (children / not / have)

5. I sometimes _____ my teacher when she speaks quickly.
   (have / trouble / understand)

6. Hassan is not _____ so much homework.
   (used to / be / assign)

C Find and correct six mistakes.

A: Going to that movie was a good idea; it's definitely worth to see.

B: I agree! It was great. So, how's it going at work these days? Are you excited about having hiring your friend Jack to work with you?

A: Well . . . no! I thought I'd enjoy to work with him, but I'm kind of upset with him right now. First of all, he has trouble finish his work on time. And sometimes he's rude. At a meeting yesterday, I was bothered by he coming in without asking permission. Also, he seems to hate told what to do; he prefers making his own decisions.

Now check your answers on page 429.

Go to MyEnglishLab to complete the review online.

STEP 1   GRAMMAR IN CONTEXT

BEFORE YOU READ

Discuss the questions.

1. What is procrastination?

2. What are the dangers of procrastination?

3. Do you ever procrastinate? If so, in what situations?

READ

▶ 09|01   Read this article about procrastination.

Seize the Day

Picture this scenario: It's late Sunday afternoon. Jane is making dinner. Ben needs the paperwork for this year's taxes. It has to be given to the accountant tomorrow.

BEN: Jane, have you got the paperwork ready for the taxes? I have to take it to the accountant first thing in the morning.

JANE: Ben, the Garcias are coming in about an hour. I'm trying to get dinner into the oven. I can't stop to find the paperwork now.

BEN: But honey, I've got to have it. You said you'd do it.

JANE: Why didn't you tell me you needed it tonight? I didn't know I had to get it together so soon.

BEN: I really did plan to remind you about it, but I forgot to. What are we going to do? Can't you stop for a little while?

JANE: If I stop cooking, I won't have enough time to finish before the Garcias get here. Tell you what: you go look for it, and if you can't find it, I'll help you later this evening.

Does this kind of situation ring a bell?[1] It illustrates the problem of procrastination. I interviewed psychiatrist Robert Stevens to find out more about this problem.

REPORTER: Dr. Stevens, I want to ask you if there's such a thing as a procrastination syndrome.

STEVENS: Well, I don't know if we can call it a syndrome, but procrastination is widespread and can be a very serious problem for some people.

REPORTER: Can we start with a definition of procrastination?

---

1 *ring a bell:* remind you of something

STEVENS: Of course. To procrastinate is literally to put things off until tomorrow. It's a postponing of events until a later time. But unlike the word "postpone," which has a neutral sense, the word "procrastinate" has a negative connotation. There are sometimes good reasons to postpone things, but never to procrastinate. Procrastinating has the sense of avoidance.

REPORTER: All right. Now what causes people to procrastinate? Laziness?

STEVENS: That's a popular idea, but I'd have to say that laziness isn't the major cause. No, I think that fear is really the most important force that motivates people to put things off.

REPORTER: Fear? Can you explain?

STEVENS: Well, procrastinators want to live up to other people's expectations. They're afraid to fail or make mistakes, or maybe they don't want to be rejected. Interestingly, procrastination has nothing to do with education. Some of the most learned people are among the worst procrastinators.

REPORTER: What would be an example of that?

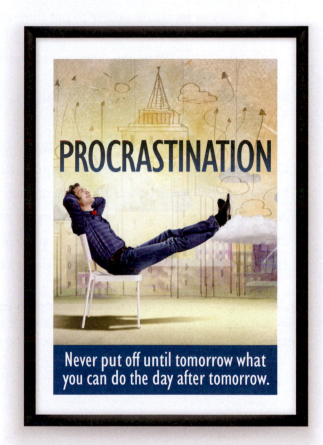

PROCRASTINATION

Never put off until tomorrow what you can do the day after tomorrow.

STEVENS: Well, let's see . . . Suppose a professor—a woman we'll call Blanche—has been planning a lecture. She's mentioned the lecture to colleagues but hasn't told them the time and date it will take place, which would be the straightforward thing to do. Either consciously or subconsciously, she expects to fail, so she delays telling people until the very last moment. Her colleagues expected her to have told them before now. When she didn't, they forgot about the event and made other plans. It's too short notice for most of them to come. Blanche's fear has caused things to turn out like this. She feels bad about it, but she doesn't know how to change.

REPORTER: Well, what if a procrastinator would like to change? What would you advise that person to do?

STEVENS: Getting a procrastinator to change can be a tough nut to crack,[2] but I recommend three principles for my clients. The first is never to put off until tomorrow what needs to be done today. Not to avoid painful or difficult things is the second. They're part of life. The third is contained in the Latin phrase *carpe diem*—"seize the day." I try to consider every experience an opportunity. I don't want people to take unnecessary or foolish risks, but I do advise them not to put off living. They may not get another chance.

REPORTER: Well, Dr. Stevens, thanks for a stimulating discussion.

---

2 *a tough nut to crack:* a difficult problem to solve

AFTER YOU READ

A VOCABULARY Match the words in **bold** with their meanings.

_____ 1. Picture this **scenario**.

_____ 2. The word *postpone* has a **neutral** sense.

_____ 3. Procrastination is **widespread**.

_____ 4. The word *procrastinate* has a negative **connotation**.

_____ 5. This situation **illustrates** the problem of procrastination.

_____ 6. That would be the **straightforward** thing to do.

_____ 7. Is there such a thing as a procrastination **syndrome**?

_____ 8. Fear can **motivate** people to put things off.

a. cause

b. direct and simple

c. meaning

d. common

e. possible situation

f. shows the meaning of

g. not showing feelings

h. pattern of behavior

B COMPREHENSION Read the statements. Check (✓) *True* or *False*.

	True	False
1. Jane is not going to stop dinner preparations.	☐	☐
2. The word *postpone* has a positive sense.	☐	☐
3. To procrastinate is literally to put things off until tomorrow.	☐	☐
4. Dr. Stevens believes it is sometimes appropriate to procrastinate.	☐	☐
5. Dr. Stevens believes that fear is the major cause of procrastination.	☐	☐
6. According to Dr. Stevens, procrastinators are afraid to fail.	☐	☐
7. Dr. Stevens believes it is permissible to avoid difficult or painful things.	☐	☐
8. Dr. Stevens thinks it is good to consider every experience an opportunity.	☐	☐

C DISCUSSION Work with a partner. Compare your answers in B. Justify your answers. Then discuss this question: Do the psychiatrist's explanations seem plausible? If you procrastinate, do you think fear is the reason you do it?

Go to MyEnglishLab for more grammar in context practice.

INFINITIVES

Infinitive as Subject

Infinitive (Subject)	Verb	Object
To procrastinate	causes	a lot of problems.
Not to go ahead	proved	a mistake.

Infinitive as Object

Subject	Verb	Infinitive (Object)
Not everyone	wants	**to procrastinate**.
He	decided	**not to go ahead**.

Infinitive as Subject Complement

Subject	Verb	Infinitive (Subject Complement)
His job	is	**to motivate** people.
Their real intention	is	**not to succeed**.

It + *Be* + Adjective + Infinitive

It	*Be*	Adjective	(*For*/*Of* + Noun/Pronoun)	Infinitive
It	is	foolish	(for Alice/her)	**to procrastinate**.
It	was	wrong	(of Hal/him)	**not to go ahead**.

Verbs Followed by Infinitives

	Verb	(Noun/Pronoun)	Infinitive
They	**decided**	Ø*	
	convinced	Steve/him	**to call**.
	expected	(Steve/him)	

*Ø = When *decide* is used with an infinitive, it cannot be followed by a noun or object pronoun.

Adjectives Followed by Infinitives

	Adjective	Infinitive	
Hal is	**reluctant**	**to complete**	his work on time.
He's	**careful**	**not to make**	mistakes.
They're	**happy**	**to hear**	the test has been postponed.

Nouns Followed by Infinitives

	Noun	Infinitive	
He can always think of	**reasons**	**to put off**	studying.
It seems like	**the thing**	**to do**.	
She always shows	**reluctance**	**to finish**	a job.

Too/Enough with Infinitives

	Too + Adjective/Adverb	Infinitive	
The project is	**too** complicated	**to finish**	on time.
Alice types	**too** slowly	**to meet**	the deadline.

	Adjective/Adverb + Enough	Infinitive	
Steve is	intelligent **enough**	**to understand**	the situation.
He didn't call	quickly **enough**	**to get**	the job.

	Enough + Noun	Infinitive	
They have	**enough** intelligence intelligence **enough**	**to pass**	the test.

Active and Passive Infinitives

	Active Infinitives	Passive Infinitives
Simple Past	She plans **to invite** them.	They expect **to be invited**.
	She was glad **to have invited** them.	They were happy **to have been invited**.

GRAMMAR NOTES

1 Form and Function of Infinitives

An **infinitive** is *to* + **the base form of a verb**. Infinitives and infinitive phrases often perform the same functions as **nouns**.

Infinitives and infinitive phrases can be:

- **subjects**

  To finish what you started is advisable.

- **objects**

  I'd like **to invite** you to dinner.

- **subject complements**

  A teacher's job is **to create** a desire to learn.

To make an infinitive **negative**, place *not* before *to*.

It's advisable **not to get** behind in your homework.
The teacher asked her students **not to be** late.

USAGE NOTE Using an infinitive as the subject of a sentence is relatively formal. *It* + *be* + **adjective** + **an infinitive** is more common. We often use *for* + a noun or pronoun to say who or what does the action.

It's advisable **to finish** what you started.
It's important **for a student to take** good notes in class.

USAGE NOTE To avoid repeating an infinitive just mentioned, replace the verb with *to*. This is called **ellipsis**.

Steve knew he had to go to work, but he didn't want **to**.

BE CAREFUL! Don't confuse *to* as part of an infinitive with *to* as a preposition. *To* in an infinitive is followed by the base form of the verb. *To* as a preposition is followed by a gerund, regular noun, or pronoun.

I plan **to *work*** hard.
NOT I plan to working hard.
I'm used **to *working*** hard.
NOT I'm used to work hard.

2 Verbs + Infinitives and Gerunds

Some verbs can be followed only by infinitives, others only by gerunds, and others by either infinitives or gerunds. These verbs fall into four patterns:

- **verbs followed only by infinitives**

appear	manage	want
decide	need	would like
expect	pretend	
hope	seem	

They **managed to find** new jobs.
She **pretended to be** busy.

- **verbs followed only by gerunds**

avoid	enjoy	keep
be worth	feel like	mind
can't help	have trouble	miss
consider	have a hard time	spend (time)

We **considered hiring** him.
I don't **feel like working** today.

- **verbs followed by infinitives or gerunds; no real meaning change**

begin	hate	prefer
can't stand	like	start
continue	love	

They **began to encourage** her.
or
They **began encouraging** her.

- **verbs followed by infinitives or gerunds; significant meaning change**

forget	regret	try
go on	remember	
quit	stop	

I **stopped to buy** a soda.
  (I stopped another activity in order to buy a soda.)
I **stopped buying** sodas.
  (I stopped the activity of buying sodas. I don't buy them anymore.)
Maria **didn't remember to call**.
  (She didn't call.)
Alicia **doesn't remember calling**.
  (She called but doesn't remember doing it.)

3 Verbs + Nouns + Infinitives

Certain **verbs** are followed only by **infinitives**.

She **offered to help** me.
Jama **decided to accept** the job.

Other verbs must be followed by a **noun or pronoun + an infinitive**:

advise	encourage	order	tell
allow	force	persuade	urge
convince	invite	require	warn

I **warned** *Stan* **to make** the payments.
NOT I ~~warned to make~~ the payments.
We told *Nancy* **to come** early.
NOT We ~~told to come~~ early.

Still other verbs may be followed by an **infinitive** or by a **noun or pronoun + an infinitive**:

ask	expect	need	want
choose	get	pay	would like

We **expected to finish** on time.
We **expected** *Asha* **to finish** on time.
I **would like to visit** you this week.
I **would like** *her* **to drive** me to your house.

4 Adjectives + Infinitives

Certain **adjectives** can be followed by **an infinitive**. These adjectives usually describe people, not things. They often express **feelings** about the action described in the infinitive.

George is *afraid* **to make** mistakes.
Mary is *not willing* **to help** us.

Common adjectives followed by infinitives are:

afraid	*fortunate*	*important*	*reluctant*
amazed	*glad*	*likely*	*sorry*
excited	*happy*	*proud*	*willing*

Helen was *fortunate* **to get** a job.
Martin is *reluctant* **to tell** us what happened.

5 Nouns + Infinitives

Nouns are often followed by **an infinitive**. When this occurs, the infinitive gives **information about the noun**.

Cozumel is a good *place* **to spend** a vacation.
Generosity is a good *trait* **to have**.

A noun + infinitive often expresses **advisability** or **necessity**.

Starting immediately is the *thing* **to do**.
Honesty is the best *policy* **to pursue**.

6 *Too* and *Enough* + Infinitives

We often use the words *too* and *enough* before infinitives.

Use *too* in the pattern *too* + **adjective/adverb** + **infinitive**. It implies a negative result.

We were *too* **tired to do** any work today.
  (So we didn't work.)
Sam started *too* **late to finish** on time.
  (So he didn't finish.)

Use *enough* + **infinitive** after an adjective or adverb.

Ken is **strong** *enough* **to lift** 80 kilos.
Mia is running **fast** *enough* **to win** the race.

We often use *enough* **before a noun** + infinitive.

There's not *enough* **money to pay** for the repairs.

You can also use *enough* **after a noun** in more formal English.

There is not **money** *enough* **to purchase** the automobile.

Add *for* + **a noun or pronoun** to show who performs the action of the infinitive.

There's not **enough money** *for Jane* **to pay** for the repairs.

Infinitives can occur in **simple**, **past**, and **passive** forms.

Use a **simple infinitive** (without a past participle) to indicate an action in the **same general time frame** as the action in the main verb.	I **expected** you **to call**. We **asked** you **not to do** that.
Use a **past infinitive** (*to* + *have* + past participle) to show an action or state that **occurred before** the action of the main verb.	You **seem to have forgotten** the report that was due today. Arnie **appears not to have understood** what you said.
Infinitives can occur in **passive** form. In the present, use *to* + *be* or *get* + past participle. In the past, use *to* + *have* + *been* + past participle. Use the **past passive** form to indicate an action or state that occurred before the action of the main verb.	The work is supposed **to be finished** by tomorrow. The work was **to have been done** before now.

REFERENCE NOTES

For a list of **verbs followed by infinitives**, see Appendix 15 on page 418.

For more information on **verbs followed by gerunds or infinitives**, see Unit 8 on page 127 and Appendices 16 and 17 on page 418.

For a list of **verbs followed by noun/pronoun + infinitives**, see Appendix 19 on page 419.

For a list of **adjectives followed by infinitives**, see Appendix 20 on page 419.

EXERCISE 1 DISCOVER THE GRAMMAR

A GRAMMAR NOTE 1 Read these sentences based on the reading. How is the underlined infinitive or infinitive phrase used in each sentence? Write *S (subject)*, *O (object)*, or *SC (subject complement)*.

___O___ **1.** I really did plan <u>to remind</u> you about it.

_____ **2.** I want <u>to ask</u> you if there's such a thing as procrastination.

_____ **3.** <u>To procrastinate</u> is literally to put things off until tomorrow.

_____ **4.** It's not a good idea <u>to delay</u> doing important tasks.

_____ **5.** Maybe they don't want <u>to be rejected</u>.

_____ **6.** She expects <u>to fail</u>.

_____ **7.** The first is never <u>to put off</u> until tomorrow what needs to be done today.

_____ **8.** <u>Not to avoid</u> painful or difficult things is the second.

_____ **9.** I try <u>to consider</u> every experience as an opportunity.

B GRAMMAR NOTES 2–3, 5, 7 Read the first sentence in each pair. Check (✓) *True* or *False* for the second sentence.

	True	False
1. "I can't stop to find the paperwork now." The speaker doesn't have time to find the paperwork.	✓	☐
2. "I really did plan to remind you about it, but I forgot to." The speaker doesn't remember reminding someone.	☐	☐
3. "Maybe they don't want to be rejected." Maybe they're worried about rejecting someone.	☐	☐
4. "Maybe they just don't want to be told *no*." Maybe they always want to be given *yes* answers.	☐	☐
5. "Her friends no doubt expected her to have called them." Her friends probably thought she was going to call them before now.	☐	☐
6. "The second piece of advice is not to avoid painful or difficult things." The advice is to stay away from painful or difficult things.	☐	☐

EXERCISE 2 VERBS AND ADJECTIVES + INFINITIVES

GRAMMAR NOTES 2–4 Complete the sentences with the verbs or adjectives in parentheses. Use infinitives, and add pronouns if necessary. See Appendices 19 and 20 on page 419 for help.

I'm basically a procrastinator. I've always _____*wanted to stop*_____
1. (want / stop)

procrastinating but didn't know how. It started when I was a teenager and I had trouble getting

my schoolwork done. My parents always _____ doing my
2. (warn / not / put off)

assignments. However, they also _____ my own decisions. I guess
3. (want / make)

they thought it was _____ the consequences of my actions, so
4. (important for / experience)

they never _____ hard . . . and I didn't. I guess I was
5. (force / study)

_____ from high school, and then from college. Later, when I
6. (fortunate / graduate)

started working, I still _____ my tasks by doing things at the last
7. (expect / finish)

minute. However, I soon learned that that strategy wouldn't work anymore. There were 20

employees in my department, and my boss _____ sales reports
8. (require / write)

every month. I was nervous about the reports, so I put them off, of course, and didn't even start

them until the day they were due. When I tried to turn in one report a week late, my boss got

angry. He said it was _____ the reports on time, and he
9. (important / submit)

_____ a report late again. He _____
10. (tell / not / turn in)   11. (advise / change)

my whole attitude toward finishing necessary tasks. He _____ my
12. (encourage / complete)

reports quickly, without worrying about whether they were perfect or not, and then check them

before submitting them to him. I took his advice and, many painful months later, I am starting

to conquer the procrastination demon.

EXERCISE 3 *TOO* AND *ENOUGH* + INFINITIVES

GRAMMAR NOTE 6 For each situation, write a sentence with *too* + adjective or adverb + infinitive or with *enough* + infinitive.

1. It's 5:15. Jill's flight leaves at 5:45, and it takes 45 minutes to get to the airport. (enough)

   Jill doesn't have enough time to get to the airport.

2. Jack's 10-page report is due in an hour. He types only 25 words a minute. (too)

   _____

3. Marcy wants to buy her friend's used car, which costs $5,000. She has $4,000 in the bank and is able to save $400 a month. Her friend must sell the car within three months. (enough)

   _____

4. Eve invited guests to dinner. She waited until 6:45 to start cooking the meal. The guests are expected by 7:00. (too)

   _____

5. Sally's doctor advised her to eat three meals a day to stay healthy. To lose weight, Sally ate only one small meal a day. She became quite sick. (enough)

   _____

6. Carlos has a very difficult problem to solve, but he is a very intelligent man and can solve it if he applies himself. (enough)

   _____

EXERCISE 4 PAST INFINITIVES

GRAMMAR NOTE 7 Complete the paragraph with past infinitives. Use the words in parentheses. One sentence will be in the passive.

My husband and I took a five-day trip out of town and left the kids in charge. On the morning we were returning, we called our son and daughter. We expected them

_____*to have cleaned*_____ the house because we were having dinner guests that evening.
　　　　1. (clean)

When I asked Jennifer about this, she at first seemed _____ me, and
　　　　　　　　　　　　　　　　　　　　　　　　　　　　2. (not / hear)

quickly changed the subject. I persisted in the question, and this time Jennifer pretended

_____ what I'd said. "You mean the house needs to be clean tonight?"
3. (not / understand)

she said. "Yes," I said. "Did you clean it?" "Well, sort of. Josh was supposed

_____ some cleaning supplies, but I can't find them anywhere. I did
4. (get)

what I could, Mom." "Well, this is important, Jen. We expect you two

_____ the cleaning by the time we get home," I said in my
5. (finish)

firmest voice.

When we got home, the house appeared _____ by a tornado. The
 **6.** (hit)

kids were nowhere to be found. Dirty dishes were everywhere. Jennifer and Josh appeared

_____ the animals, but they seemed _____
 **7.** (feed) **8.** (not / do)

anything else. Next time, we won't trust the kids to take care of the house!

EXERCISE 5 PASSIVE INFINITIVES

GRAMMAR NOTE 7 Read the sentences. Then complete the questions with passive
infinitives. Use the words in parentheses.

1. On your second day of a new job, you are an hour late to work. (fire / by the company)

   Would you expect *to be fired by the company* _____?

2. You have a flat tire on a busy freeway. (help / by a passing motorist)

   Would you expect _____?

3. You have put off paying your phone bill for three months. (your phone service / disconnect)

   Would you expect _____?

4. Your son or daughter has been stopped for speeding. (notify / by the police)

   Would you expect _____?

5. You are going 10 miles over the speed limit. (stop / by a police officer)

   Would you expect _____?

6. Your report was due three days ago. (question / by your boss)

   Would you expect _____?

EXERCISE 6 EDITING

GRAMMAR NOTES 1–7 Read the entry from Amanda's journal. There are ten mistakes in the use of infinitives. The first mistake is already corrected. Find and correct nine more.

I just had ^to write tonight. Until now, I've never had the courage do this, but now I do. I've decided to have confronted Sarah about her irresponsibility. This is something that has been bothering me for a long time now, but somehow I've always been reluctant force the issue. So here's the situation: Sarah invites people to do things, but she doesn't follow through. Last week, she asked my fiancé, Al, and me have dinner, and she also invited our friends Mark and Debbie. The four of us made plans go to her house on Friday evening. Something told me I should call Sarah asking what we should bring, and it's a good thing I did. Sarah said, "Dinner? I'm not having dinner tonight. I guess I mentioned it as a possibility, but I never settled it with you guys. You misunderstood me." Well, that's just silly. She told us planning on it for Friday evening at 7 p.m. When I told the others, they were furious. Al said, "I don't expect being treated like royalty. I do expect to be treated with consideration." So tomorrow, I'm going to call Sarah up and make my point. I'm not going to allow her make my life miserable.

Enough for now. Time for bed.

Go to MyEnglishLab for more focused practice.

EXERCISE 7   LISTENING

09|02   **A**   Listen to the news bulletin. What is reported to have happened in Grandview?

_____

09|02   **B**   Read the questions. Listen again. Answer each question in a complete sentence.

1. How many prisoners are reported to have escaped?

   Three prisoners are reported to have escaped.

2. How are they thought to have escaped?

   _____

3. By whom are they believed to have been helped?

   _____

4. When was the new security system supposed to have been installed?

   _____

5. Why wasn't the new security system installed?

   _____

6. What are the prisoners thought to have?

   _____

7. In what direction are they believed to be heading?

   _____

8. What are listeners warned not to do?

   _____

9. What are they asked to do if they have any information?

   _____

  C   Work with a partner. Discuss these questions.

1. Do you think prisoners should be allowed to serve a reduced sentence in return for good behavior?

2. Do you think it is too easy for criminals to escape from prison?

3. What can prisons do to make it more difficult to escape?

4. Why are listeners warned not to approach the escaped prisoners?

EXERCISE 8 ALL ABOUT A CLASSMATE

Ⓐ INTERVIEW You are going to interview a partner about experiences in his or her life. Ask your partner these questions and record his or her responses.

1. What is something you are proud to have done?
2. What is something that you have always been reluctant to do?
3. What is something that you are willing to do if necessary?
4. What is something that your parents always encouraged you to do?
5. What is something that you were warned not to do but did anyway?

Ⓑ Report your findings to the class.

EXAMPLE: Peichi is proud to have gotten good grades in all her classes this year.

EXERCISE 9 FAMOUS QUOTATIONS ABOUT PROCRASTINATION

Ⓐ CRITICAL THINKING You are going to discuss famous quotations related to procrastination. First, work with a partner. Talk about what each quotation means. Then put the quotation in your own words, using infinitives.

1. The early bird catches the worm. — *Unknown*

    It is better to get to a place earlier than everyone else, because then you will get a reward.

2. Procrastination is the thief of time. — *Edward Young, poet*

    _____

3. Someday is not a day of the week. — *Janet Dailey, procrastination expert*

    _____

4. Never put off till tomorrow what may be done the day after tomorrow just as well.
    — *Mark Twain, author*

    _____

5. What is deferred is not avoided. — *Thomas More, philosopher and statesman*

    _____

6. Don't ask for directions if you're not going to start the car. — *Rob Liano, author*

    _____

7. Perfection is man's ultimate illusion. It simply doesn't exist. — *David D. Burns, psychologist*

    _____

Ⓑ Work in a group. Evaluate the quotations. Do you think they are true or not? Give reasons for your answers. Then report interesting conclusions to the class.

EXAMPLE: "The early bird catches the worm."

> **A:** I find this quotation to be true. I agree that it is better to get somewhere before others do. The early bird does usually earn the reward.
>
> **B:** It's not always better to get somewhere first. Sometimes it's better to wait . . .

EXERCISE 10 HOW TO GET SOMETHING DONE

(A) **PICTURE DISCUSSION** Work in a group. Look at the two photos below. The people in both pictures have been told to complete an important task. Answer the questions.

1. What is the man in Photo 1 doing? What do you think he wants to do right now? Does he need to do anything different in order to complete the task he has been assigned?

2. What are the people in Photo 2 doing? What does their attitude toward the task appear to be? Do they need to do anything different in order to complete the task they have been assigned?

3. Which people seem to be more likely to complete their task? Why?

(B) Report back to the class.

EXAMPLE: The man in Photo 1 is playing with a paper airplane. We think he doesn't want to work on the task he is supposed to do. To complete the task, he needs to . . .

Photo 1

Photo 2

Go to MyEnglishLab for more communication practice.

FROM GRAMMAR TO WRITING

A BEFORE YOU WRITE Most of us have procrastinated at one time or another. Think of a situation in which you put off doing something that needed to be done. Write a few sentences on each of the following aspects of the situation.

- How you managed to get into the situation
- Why and how you put off the task that needed to be done
- What the consequences turned out to be

B WRITE Using your ideas in A, write a five-paragraph essay about the situation in which you procrastinated. Remember to use different kinds of infinitives. Try to avoid the common mistakes shown in the chart. Use the example below to help you begin your essay.

EXAMPLE: There have been lots of times when I didn't do things that needed to be done, but one that sticks in my mind is the time I had to get my car tuned up. I was scheduled to go on a cross-country trip, and I knew I needed to take my car in for a tune-up. One thing led to another, though, and I continued to procrastinate. To put things off never works, as you will see. Here's what happened. . . .

Common Mistakes in Using Infinitives

Don't use gerunds after **verbs** and **adjectives** that are followed by **infinitives**. If you are unsure, check Appendices 14–18 on pages 417–419.	Carlos **managed to earn** a scholarship. **NOT** Carlos managed ~~earning~~ a scholarship.
Don't confuse *to* as part of an infinitive with *to* as a preposition. When *to* is part of an **infinitive**, it is followed by the **base form** of the verb. When *to* is a **preposition**, it is often followed by a **gerund**.	She never **used to work** hard. **NOT** She never used to ~~working~~ hard. She wasn't **used to working** hard. **NOT** She wasn't used to ~~work~~ hard.

C CHECK YOUR WORK Look at your essay. Underline the infinitives. Use the Editing Checklist to check your work.

Editing Checklist

Did you . . . ?

- ☐ avoid using gerunds after adjectives and verbs followed by infinitives
- ☐ use *to* as part of the infinitive with the base form of the verb
- ☐ use *to* as a preposition with a gerund

D REVISE YOUR WORK Read your essay again. Can you improve your writing? Make changes if necessary.

Go to **MyEnglishLab** for more writing practice.

UNIT 9 REVIEW

Test yourself on the grammar of the unit.

A Complete the sentences. Circle the correct answers.

1. What did Carlos decide to do / doing about his job?

2. He quit accepting / to accept a position at Windale's.

3. Did Ben ever manage giving up / to give up tobacco?

4. Yes. He actually stopped to smoke / smoking two months ago.

5. Did you remember to have locked / to lock the front door?

6. Yes, it's locked. I remember to lock / locking it when I left.

7. Alicia is afraid to confront / confronting Jaime about the problem.

8. That's because he hates to be criticized / to be criticizing.

B Complete the sentences with the correct forms of the verbs in parentheses.

1. My accountant warned me _____ doing my taxes.
   (not / put off)

2. I was _____ which project I wanted to work on.
   (allow / choose)

3. The work was supposed to have been done, but that seems _____.
   (not / happen)

4. The town was a mess. It appeared _____ by a tornado.
   (be / hit)

5. Berta was too _____ her assignment.
   (tired / finish)

6. Sayid never came; he seems _____ about the meeting.
   (forget)

C Find and correct six mistakes.

   I decided buy an apartment last year. My friends warned not to procrastinate. They told me buying the apartment as soon as possible before prices went up. But there are occasionally good reasons postpone big decisions. I found an apartment I liked on the beach, but it wasn't enough cheap to buy. So I procrastinated . . . and the prices went down! I'm lucky to gotten my apartment for a very low price.

Now check your answers on page 429.

Go to MyEnglishLab to complete the review online.

Nouns

OUTCOMES

- Use regular and irregular count and non-count nouns, and nouns that are only plural
- Make certain non-count nouns countable
- Identify the interviewee's opinion in an interview transcript
- Comment on important details from a conversation
- Discuss health habits, supporting opinions with examples
- Write a five-paragraph essay about personal health habits

OUTCOMES

- Use indefinite, definite, and zero articles in a variety of different situations
- Identify key information in a scientific article
- Identify and comment on key details from a conversation on a topic of nature conservancy
- Discuss nature conservancy
- Write a five-paragraph essay about an endangered species

OUTCOMES

- Describe quantities and use quantifiers with count and non-count nouns
- Identify key information in an advice column
- Identify key details in a conversation about a student's academic difficulties
- Talk about your life now compared to your life in the past
- Discuss the meaning and implications of research data on a foreign country
- Write an essay about improving study habits

OUTCOMES

- Add more information about nouns with adjective and noun modifiers
- Identify an author's attitude in a magazine article
- Identify key details in a conversation
- Engage in a literary analysis of a short story
- Discuss experiences with overcoming obstacles
- Write an essay discussing expectations about life events

DREAMS

OUTCOMES

- Use regular and irregular count and non-count nouns, and nouns that are only plural
- Make certain non-count nouns countable
- Identify the interviewee's opinion in an interview transcript
- Comment on important details from a conversation
- Discuss health habits, supporting opinions with examples
- Write a five-paragraph essay about personal health habits

STEP 1 **GRAMMAR IN CONTEXT**

BEFORE YOU READ

Discuss the questions.

1. What are the most important health issues these days?

2. What should people do to stay healthy?

READ

 Read this transcript of part of a TV program about health.

Concerned About Health? Ask the Expert.

MIRANDA OLSON: Good afternoon. Welcome to *Ask the Expert*. I'm Miranda Olson. My guest today is Dr. Mel Brand, an authority on everyday health issues, and we're going to devote today's entire program to your questions about health. So let's get right to it with our first caller. . . . Tell us your name and where you're from.

SALLY MATTHEWS: Hi, Dr. Brand. I'm Sally Matthews from San Diego, California. We hear a lot of negative stuff about fast food, but my husband and kids love hamburgers and fries and sodas. How bad is fast food?

DR. MEL BRAND: Sally, it's OK in moderation—but I wouldn't make a habit of eating it. Most fast food is full of salt, sugar, cholesterol, and lots of calories. An occasional trip to a fast-food place won't hurt you, especially if you can offset the junk food with healthy salads or sandwiches. But I wouldn't eat it more than once or twice a week.

MIRANDA OLSON: OK. Next question?

BOB GONZALES: Dr. Brand, I'm Bob Gonzales from Tampa, Florida. I'm twenty-five years old, and my question is about sun. My lovely wife is a wonderful woman, but she's also a member of the sunblock police. She won't let me go out the door without putting sunblock on. I've always been able to get a good tan, so is this really necessary? It's a pain.

DR. BRAND: Bob, I've got to side with your wife. The sun makes us feel wonderful, and we love its warmth, but it has its dangers. I've treated patients with skin cancer. The most telling example was an older man who hiked for forty years and refused to wear a hat. He developed skin cancer and didn't survive it.

I'm not trying to scare you, but I do advocate sunblock if you're going out in the sun for more than a few minutes. And you should definitely wear a brimmed[1] hat that protects your face and your neck. And that's all of us, not just fair-skinned people.

MIRANDA OLSON: OK. Let's go to the next question now.

MARTINA SMITH: Dr. Brand. I'm Martina Smith from Toronto, Canada. My question is about weight. My husband has gotten enormous. He's 5 feet 11 inches tall and weighs about 250 pounds. He used to be in good shape when he was a tennis champion, but now he doesn't get any exercise. When I try to get him to go to the gym, he either says he's too tired or he doesn't have time. Any suggestions?

DR. BRAND: Martina, it's evident that your husband is way too heavy. Have you heard of body mass index? Anyone with a BMI[2] of more than 25 is considered overweight. Hence, your husband would have a BMI of about 35, which puts him in the obese[3] category. He's got to start exercising and taking off the pounds. Have him start slowly and build up to at least three times a week and not deviate from that plan. Get him to play a game of tennis with you. But don't delay.

MIRANDA OLSON: All right. Do we have another question?

FRANK LEE: Hi, Dr. Brand. I don't know if this is a health question or not, but is there a cure for baldness? I've been losing my hair since I was thirty-five, and . . .

---

1 *brimmed:* with an edge that gives protection or shade
2 *BMI:* body mass index; a numerical measurement of body fat
3 *obese:* extremely overweight

AFTER YOU READ

A VOCABULARY **Complete the sentences with the words from the box.**

advocate	category	hence	in moderation
authority	deviate	imperative	offset

1. Someone who is an accepted expert in a certain field is a(n) _____.

2. The word _____ means basically the same as *for this reason*.

3. To do something in order to make something bad have a smaller effect is to _____ it.

4. To _____ from a plan or course of action is to turn away from it.

5. When you do something _____, you don't do it too much.

6. When it is extremely important to do something, it is _____ to do it.

7. To _____ something is to support or recommend it.

8. A(n) _____ is a general class of things or ideas.

B COMPREHENSION **Complete the sentences based on the reading. Choose the correct answers.**

1. According to Dr. Brand, consuming fast food is _____ OK.
   a. usually   **b.** occasionally   **c.** never   **d.** always

2. Dr. Brand suggests that too much _____ in food is not beneficial.
   a. protein   **b.** calcium   **c.** fiber   **d.** sugar

3. Dr. Brand says _____ should wear sunblock if they spend time in the sun.
   a. fair-skinned people   **b.** dark-skinned people   **c.** people over forty   **d.** everyone

4. Exposure to the sun _____ cause skin cancer.
   a. will   **b.** shouldn't   **c.** can   **d.** won't

5. Anyone with a BMI exceeding _____ is considered overweight.
   a. 40   **b.** 35   **c.** 25   **d.** 20

6. Dr. Brand believes exercise is of _____ importance to someone who is overweight.
   a. no   **b.** great   **c.** some   **d.** minimal

C DISCUSSION **Work with a partner. Compare your answers in B. Then discuss: What health issue are you most concerned about personally?**

Go to MyEnglishLab for more grammar in context practice.

NOUNS

Proper Nouns
Mel Brand is a physician.

Common Nouns
The **doctor** is an **expert**.

Count and Non-Count Nouns

Count Nouns			
Article or Number	Noun	Verb	
A One	**snack**	is	refreshing.
The Two	**snacks**	are	

Non-Count Nouns		
Noun	Verb	
Rice	is	nourishing.
Nutrition		important.

Nouns with Count and Non-Count Meanings

Count Meaning
There's **a hair** in my soup!
A chicken escaped from the henhouse.
How many **times** did you eat out?
Please bring us **two coffees**.
Brie is **a soft cheese**.
I see **a light** in the window.
Her new novel is **a work** of art.

Non-Count Meaning
Sandra has black **hair**.
We had **chicken** for dinner.
It takes **time** to prepare a good meal.
I'd like some **coffee**.
Cheese is produced in France.
The sun provides **light**.
Ideally, **work** should be fulfilling.

Non-Count Nouns Made Countable

Non-Count Noun
You need **advice**.
Let's play **tennis**.
There's not enough **salt** in the soup.
I like **bread** with my meal.
It's unhealthy to eat **meat** every night.
Please put more **paper** in the printer.

Made Countable
Let me give you **a piece of advice**.
Let's play **a game of tennis**.
Add **one spoonful of salt**.
Please get **a loaf of bread** at the store.
The recipe takes **three pounds of meat**.
Two packages of paper are all we have.

GRAMMAR NOTES

1 Definition of Nouns

Nouns name persons, places, or things. There are two types of nouns: **proper** nouns and **common** nouns.

Proper nouns name particular persons, places, or things. They are usually unique and are **capitalized** in writing. For example: *Dr. Brand, Kinshasa, China, the United Nations*	**Dr. Brand** has an office in this building. She comes from **China**.
Common nouns refer to people, places, or things but are **not** the **names** of particular individuals. For example: *scientist, athlete, city, country, building*	My uncle is a **scientist**. This is the biggest **city** in this area.

2 Types of Common Nouns

There are two types of common nouns: **count** nouns and **non-count** nouns.

Count nouns refer to things that you **can count separately**. They can be singular or plural.	**One woman** lives in this apartment. There are **eight planets** in our solar system. Some **vegetables** are tasty.
You can use *a* or *an* before singular count nouns.	I'd like **a sandwich**. Do you want **an apple**?
Non-count nouns refer to things that you **cannot count separately**. In their basic sense, they have **no plural form**. We do not use *a* or *an* with them.	You should avoid **cholesterol**. **NOT** You should avoid ~~a cholesterol~~.
The definite article *the* and the quantifiers *some* and *any* often precede non-count nouns.	Let me give you **some advice**. Sally said she didn't need **any advice**. **NOT** Sally said she didn't need ~~an advice~~.
We often use a **singular verb** with a **non-count noun**. We use a **singular pronoun** to refer to the noun.	**Rice** feeds millions. **It** feeds millions.

3 Categories of Non-Count Nouns

Non-count nouns fall into a number of different categories.

• **abstractions:** *beauty, energy, honesty, love*	**Honesty** is the best policy.
• **diseases:** *AIDS, cancer, influenza, malaria*	She is undergoing treatment for **cancer**.
• **fields of study/languages:** *Arabic, engineering, English, physics, Spanish*	He learned **Arabic** in Saudi Arabia.
• **food and drink:** *bread, coffee, fish, meat, tea, water*	They don't eat **fish**.
• **natural phenomena:** *electricity, heat, lightning, rain, sun*	I got too much **sun** today.
• **particles:** *dust, pepper, salt, sand, sugar*	This food needs some **salt**.
• **others:** *equipment, furniture, money, news, traffic*	Do you have enough **money** in your account?

4 Count and Non-Count Meanings of Nouns

Many nouns have **both a non-count** and **a count meaning**.

When we add the indefinite article, *a/an*, to a **non-count noun** or make the noun **plural**, the noun **becomes a count noun**, and its **meaning changes**. It generally changes from a mass that cannot be counted to one or more examples that can be counted.	**Film is** a major art form.
	 I've seen a lot of interesting **films** lately.
	   (individual movies)
	 I used to be a professor of **history**.
	 I read **a history** of the Civil War.
	   (a single book)
	 Mandy gets a lot of **exercise** every day.
	 I always start my workout with **a warm-up exercise**.
	   (a specific exercise that has a beginning and an end)

When we place *a/an* before non-count nouns or make the nouns plural, they also take on these meanings: *type of*, *kind of*, or *variety of*.	In Italy, I tasted **a** new **pasta**. That shop sells many different **teas**. Many tasty **cheeses** are produced in France. I drank **a soda**.
BE CAREFUL! Not all non-count nouns can be made countable. See Appendix 7 on page 415.	We were stuck in **traffic** for hours. **NOT** We were stuck in ~~a traffic~~ for hours. We had **fun** yesterday. **NOT** We had ~~a fun~~ yesterday.

5 Making Non-Count Nouns Countable with Phrases

We can make certain non-count nouns countable by adding a **phrase** that gives them a **form**, a **limit**, or a **container**.

	NON-COUNT NOUN	MADE COUNTABLE
• a form	rain	**a drop of** rain
	rice / sand	**a grain of** rice / sand
• a limit	advice	**a piece of** advice
	news	**a news item**
• a container	coffee / tea	**a cup of** coffee / tea
	soda	**a can of** soda

USAGE NOTE We often use phrases that make nouns countable instead of *some* or *any*. We use them when we want to be **more precise** and emphatic. They are commonly found in writing.

May I give you **some advice**? *(less precise)*
May I give you **a piece of advice**? *(more precise)*

6 Irregular Nouns

Certain nouns are **irregular**.

- **non-count nouns** ending in -*s*:
  news, mathematics, economics, physics

  The **news is** not good tonight.
  Mathematics is a difficult subject for me.

- **count nouns** with **irregular plurals**:
  criterion, criteria
  stimulus, stimuli
  phenomenon, phenomena
  species, species

  Thunder is **an** atmospheric **phenomenon**.
  Thunder and lightning are atmospheric **phenomena**.

- nouns that are **normally plural** only:
  people
  police

  People are funny.
  NOT People is funny.
  The **police are** coming.
  NOT The police is coming.

USAGE NOTE In the singular, we normally use *person* and *police officer*. *People* can also be used in the singular when it means an ethnic group.

Tilahun is **an** interesting **person**.
My daughter became **a police officer**.
The Hutu are **a people** living in Rwanda and Burundi.

REFERENCE NOTES

For a list of **irregular noun plurals**, see Appendix 4 on page 414.
For a list of **non-count nouns**, see Appendix 5 on page 414.
For a list of **ways of making non-count nouns countable**, see Appendix 6 on page 415.
For a list of **nouns with non-count and count meanings**, see Appendix 8 on page 416.

Go to MyEnglishLab to watch the grammar presentation.

EXERCISE 1 DISCOVER THE GRAMMAR

GRAMMAR NOTES 1–6 Read the sentences based on the reading. Underline the count nouns. Circle the non-count nouns.

1. We're going to devote the entire program to your questions about health.

2. It's OK in moderation, but I wouldn't make a habit of it.

3. Most fast food is full of salt, sugar, cholesterol, and calories.

4. We love its warmth, but it has its dangers.

5. I've treated patients with cancer.

6. You should wear sunblock if you're going out in the sun for more than a few minutes.

7. He used to be in good shape when he played tennis every day, but now he doesn't get any exercise.

8. Your husband would have a BMI of about 35, which puts him in the obese category.

9. Is there a cure for baldness?

10. I've been losing hair for several years.

EXERCISE 2 COUNT AND NOUN-COUNT NOUNS

GRAMMAR NOTE 4 Look at the word in bold in each pair of sentences. What kind of noun is it? Check *Count* or *Non-count*.

			Count	Non-Count
1	a.	You need to get more **exercise**.	☐	☑
	b.	Have you finished the **exercise** yet?	☑	☐
2.	a.	There's a **hair** in my soup!	☐	☐
	b.	Bruce has short black **hair**.	☐	☐
3	a.	**Work** can be boring, but it can also be fulfilling.	☐	☐
	b.	Samantha's new novel is a **work** of art.	☐	☐
4.	a.	Please bring us four **sodas**.	☐	☐
	b.	Drinking too much **soda** is not good for you.	☐	☐
5.	a.	The **history** I'm reading about World War I is interesting.	☐	☐
	b.	**History** has always been my favorite subject.	☐	☐
6.	a.	**Film** is my favorite art form.	☐	☐
	b.	My uncle recommended this **film**.	☐	☐
7.	a.	The last **time** I saw Helena, she was sick.	☐	☐
	b.	I never have enough **time** to do the things I want.	☐	☐

EXERCISE 3 COUNT AND NON-COUNT NOUNS

GRAMMAR NOTES 4, 6 Complete the event postings on the website. Choose the correct count or non-count form.

SHOUT

FIND: [   ]

NEAR: [   ]

JEFFERSON JUNG: POETRY READING

WEDNESDAY, AUGUST 28, 2018, 7 P.M. • BURLINGTON CIVIC CENTER

Poet Jefferson Jung will give reading / (a reading) from his latest book of poems, which he describes as
$\overline{\hspace{3cm}}$
1.

work / a work in progress.
$\overline{\hspace{2cm}}$
2.

HELEN HAMMOND: HEALTH IN THE TWENTY-FIRST CENTURY

FRIDAY, AUGUST 30, 2018, 8 P.M. • BURLINGTON CITY HALL

Professor Helen Hammond will give talk / a talk on health / a health in the twenty-first century.
$\hspace{4.5cm}\overline{\hspace{1.5cm}}\hspace{1.3cm}\overline{\hspace{1.5cm}}$
3.   4.

Professor Hammond has written history / a history of public health care in the United States. At
$\hspace{4.5cm}\overline{\hspace{2cm}}$
5.

time / a time when some people think that Americans are unhealthier than ever, she will discuss
$\overline{\hspace{1.5cm}}$
6.

all the government's criterion / criteria for making budget cuts to Medicaid and other health
$\hspace{3cm}\overline{\hspace{2cm}}$
7.

care programs.

LABOR DAY PICNIC

MONDAY, SEPTEMBER 2, 2018, 5-9 P.M. • PATTON PARK

Work / A work on the renovation of Patton Park is now complete, and we're all set for the annual
$\overline{\hspace{2cm}}$
8.

Labor Day picnic! If you haven't bought your tickets yet, time / a time is running short! As usual, we'll
$\hspace{6cm}\overline{\hspace{1.8cm}}$
9.

have hamburgers / hamburger and hot dogs, as well as soda / a soda and milk / a milk for the kids.
$\overline{\hspace{2.5cm}}\hspace{3cm}\overline{\hspace{1.5cm}}\hspace{1cm}\overline{\hspace{1.5cm}}$
10.   11.   12.

BURLINGTON FILM FESTIVAL

TUESDAY AND WEDNESDAY, SEPTEMBER 3-4, 2018, 7-12 P.M. • BURLINGTON CIVIC AUDITORIUM

Local theater owner Anna Waters will open this year's festival with film / a film by the
$\hspace{6.5cm}\overline{\hspace{1.5cm}}$
13.

famous director Maximilian Garcia. The following evening, Ms. Waters will introduce Sophia

Chiwetel, local filmmaker / a local filmmaker, who will present her own new movie about
$\hspace{1.5cm}\overline{\hspace{2.5cm}}$
14.

an intercultural romance / intercultural romance between a Nigerian woman and an American man.
$\overline{\hspace{3cm}}$
15.

EXERCISE 4 NON-COUNT NOUNS MADE COUNTABLE

GRAMMAR NOTE 5 Complete the pairs of sentences. In the sentences on the left, use *some* or *any*. In the sentences on the right, use a phrase that makes the non-count noun countable. Look at Appendix 7 on page 415 for help.

Less Precise

1. **a.** When we moved to the new office, we lost ___*some*___ equipment.

2. **a.** Look! I just saw _____ lightning in the sky.

3. **a.** We didn't play _____ tennis after all.

4. **a.** Let me give you _____ advice: Don't eat that doughnut.

5. **a.** There hasn't been _____ rain here for over a month.

6. **a.** There wasn't _____ rice left on the plate.

7. **a.** I bought _____ meat at the supermarket.

8. **a.** We bought _____ furniture at the mall.

9. **a.** I always have _____ coffee when I wake up in the morning.

10. **a.** I got _____ sand in my shoes when I was at the beach.

More Precise

1. **b.** When we moved to the new office, we lost ___*two pieces of*___ equipment.

2. **b.** Look! I just saw _____ lightning in the sky.

3. **b.** We didn't play _____ tennis after all.

4. **b.** Let me give you _____ advice: Don't eat that doughnut.

5. **b.** There hasn't been _____ rain here for over a month.

6. **b.** There wasn't _____ rice left on the plate.

7. **b.** I bought _____ meat at the supermarket.

8. **b.** We bought _____ furniture at the mall.

9. **b.** I always have _____ coffee when I wake up in the morning.

10. **b.** Some people think you can see the world in _____ sand.

EXERCISE 5 COUNT AND NON-COUNT NOUNS WITH *A*, *AN*, *THE*

GRAMMAR NOTES 2–6 For each noun, write a sentence in which the noun is used in a non-count sense and another sentence in which it is used in a count sense. Make sure that the count sentences include *a*, *an*, or the plural form of the count noun.

1. **time**

   Non-count: *Time passes much too quickly.*

   Count: *We had a great time in Mexico last summer.*

2. **film**

   Non-count: _____

   Count: _____

3. **equipment**

   Non-count: _____

   Count: _____

4. **advice**

   Non-count: _____

   Count: _____

5. **work**

   Non-count: _____

   Count: _____

6. **talk**

   Non-count: _____

   Count: _____

7. **experience**

   Non-count: _____

   Count: _____

8. **fish**

   Non-count: _____

   Count: _____

9. **light**

   Non-count: _____

   Count: _____

10. **history**

    Non-count: _____

    Count: _____

EXERCISE 6 EDITING

GRAMMAR NOTES 1–6 Read the email. There are ten mistakes in the use of count and non-count nouns. The first mistake is already corrected. Find and correct nine more.

Hi Kendra!

Your mom and I are having ^a^ wonderful time in Brazil. We landed in Rio de Janeiro on Tuesday. On Wednesday, we walked and sunbathed on the Copacabana and Ipanema beaches. Unfortunately, I didn't put on any sunblock and got a bad sunburn. There's a good news, though; it's better today. Actually, there's one other problem: We don't have enough furnitures in our hotel room. There's no place to put anything. But everything else has been great. We went to samba show, too. It was a lot of fun.

The Brazilian people is very friendly and helpful. On Friday, we had a flight to São Paulo at 9 a.m., and we couldn't get a taxi. But we were saved by one of the hotel employees, who gave us a ride to the airport. We got there just in time. Now we're in São Paulo. It's an exciting place, but I can't get over the traffics. It took two hours to get from our hotel to the downtown area.

Yesterday we ate *feijoada*, a typical Brazilian food. It was delicious. Tonight we're going to have dinner at very famous restaurant where they serve every kind of meats you can think of. I'm going to have to go on a diet when we get home!

You wouldn't believe the amount of coffees the Brazilians drink. They have little cups of coffee several times a day. It's very strong and sweet.

I'm happy to report that your mom hasn't had a time to go shopping yet. You know I hate shopping!

Love, Dad

EXERCISE 7 LISTENING

▶10|02 **A** Listen to the conversation. How is Joe Hanson's health?

_____

_____

▶10|02 **B** Listen again. Answer each question with a complete sentence.

1. What is Joe Hanson concerned about?

   He is concerned about his weight.

2. Does Joe have high, medium, or low cholesterol?

   _____

3. Which meal does Joe skip daily?

   _____

4. Does he have enough time to eat that meal?

   _____

5. How much exercise does he get?

   _____

6. What kind of food does he eat for lunch?

   _____

7. What health issue is Joe at high risk for?

   _____

8. What kind of change is the doctor suggesting regarding Joe's eating habits?

   _____

9. What foods will Joe still be able to eat?

   _____

10. How many times a week will Joe need to exercise at the beginning?

   _____

C Work with a partner. Talk about the health habits of someone you know. Discuss these questions.

1. How much exercise does the person get?

2. Does he or she have any bad habits?

3. Does he or she eat regular meals?

4. What kind of diet does the person follow?

5. Does the person have any specific health problems?

EXERCISE 8 HEALTHY VS. UNHEALTHY

A **CRITICAL THINKING** You are going to compare the habits of Jack Gonzales and Marvin Hamner. First, read the descriptions.

Jack Gonzales gets up about 7 a.m. each morning and starts his day by taking his dog for a walk. When they return, Jack fixes a big breakfast. After breakfast, he reads the newspaper and then bikes to work. He's fortunate to have a workplace that believes in the benefits of exercise, so he's able to take a half hour off at 11:00 a.m. and visit the gym located in his building. At 12:30 p.m., he generally has lunch with his colleagues. He usually takes a sack lunch consisting of a sandwich, two pieces of fruit, and a glass of V-8 juice. When his workday ends at 5:00 p.m., he bikes back home and makes his dinner. He goes out two evenings a week: One evening he volunteers at an animal shelter, and the other he plays the clarinet in a band. When he gets home, he usually reads for an hour or so. Occasionally, he watches TV. He's normally in bed by 11:00 p.m.

Jack's co-worker Marvin Hamner usually doesn't get up until about 8:15. Since he's almost always pressed for time, he generally skips breakfast. His morning meal, in fact, is usually a doughnut and coffee, topped off with a cigarette. He doesn't have time to bike or walk to work, so of course he drives. Sometimes, he doesn't make it there on time. Most days he's tired and sleepy, so he depends on coffee to keep him awake. At midday, he goes out to a fast-food restaurant and eats a meal full of fatty foods with lots of cholesterol. Marvin doesn't use the company's gym. At 5:00 p.m., he leaves the office and heads for his car. At home, he often orders pizza, his favorite food, for dinner. After dinner, he watches TV until about midnight. He smokes quite a few cigarettes while he's engrossed in the TV. It's usually 1 a.m. by the time he gets to bed.

B Work in a group. Compare Jack and Marvin using the following criteria. Give each person a rating on a scale of 1 to 5, 5 being the healthiest. Discuss their differences, giving reasons for your answers.

Criteria	Jack	Marvin
Regularity of meals		
Quality of food at meals		
Exercise		
Good habits		
Bad habits		

C Report your ratings to the class.

EXAMPLE: In our group, we gave Jack a rating of 5 for regularity of meals, and we gave Marvin a rating of 3. Both Jack and Marvin eat meals at around the same time every day, but Marvin usually doesn't eat breakfast. . . .

EXERCISE 9
MY HEALTH

A QUESTIONNAIRE
Complete the questionnaire. Choose the answers that best apply to you.

1. In general, I'd say I'm in _____ health.
   a. excellent **b.** good **c.** fair **d.** poor

2. Exercise is _____ to me.
   a. very important **b.** important **c.** somewhat important **d.** not important

3. The best exercise for me is _____.
   a. running **b.** swimming **c.** walking **d.** weight lifting

4. My favorite kind of food is _____.
   a. meat **b.** pasta **c.** dessert **d.** salad

5. The drink I like the best is _____.
   a. water **b.** soda **c.** milk **d.** coffee

6. I never miss _____.
   a. a meal **b.** a party **c.** exercising **d.** watching TV

7. It's difficult for me to _____.
   a. lose weight **b.** gain weight **c.** avoid stress **d.** get enough sleep

8. I _____ smoke.
   a. never **b.** seldom **c.** sometimes **d.** often

9. I'm _____ ill.
   a. often **b.** sometimes **c.** seldom **d.** never

B Work in a group. Discuss your questionnaire answers. What health habits do you have in common with your classmates? What health trends do you see in your class?

EXAMPLE: **A:** I think I'm in good health. Exercise is important to me, and I swim twice a week. My favorite drink is water, and I love salad.

B: I'm in good health, too. I think exercise is very important, and I run every day. What about you, Kimiko?

C: I think I'm in fair health. I drink a lot of soda, and I don't get enough exercise . . .

EXERCISE 10 THE NOUN GAME

A **GAME** Divide into two teams. First, work with your own team. Look at the words in the word box. Match them with their definitions in the chart.

~~advice~~	a space	baldness	fast food	people	talk	work
~~a criterion~~	a talk	cancer	film	rice	the police	
a film	a tan	cholesterol	lightning	space	thunder	
a people	a work	criteria	news	sunblock	traffic	

a. _____ :
an art form that involves moving pictures on a screen

f. _____ :
a brownish color that the sun gives to the skin

k. _____ :
a cream used on the skin to protect it from burning by the sun

p. _____ :
a sudden electrical discharge in the atmosphere

u. _____ :
a movie

b. *advice* _____ :
an opinion about what could or should be done about a situation

g. _____ :
movement of people or vehicles along routes of transportation

l. _____ :
a substance found in the human body and in various foods

q. _____ :
people who are responsible for capturing criminals, etc.

v. _____ :
a booming sound that occurs with an electrical discharge in the air

c. _____ :
conversation

h. _____ :
a disease involving the abnormal growth of cells in the body

m. _____ :
standards, rules, or tests on which judgments can be made

r. _____ :
a grain that many people eat, grown in warm climates

w. _____ :
a particular ethnic group

d. _____ :
a condition that involves the loss of hair on the head

i. _____ :
a blank or empty area

n. _____ :
hamburgers, fries, and fried chicken, for example

s. _____ :
your job or activities that you do regularly to earn money

x. _____ :
the area beyond the atmosphere of the earth

e. _____ :
a painting, book, play, or piece of music, for example

j. *a criterion* _____ :
a standard, rule, or test on which judgments can be made

o. _____ :
information about events that have happened recently

t. _____ :
human beings

y. _____ :
a formal discussion

B Work with the other team. Take turns asking and answering *what* questions about each word or phrase in the word box. Then check your answers on page 435. Which team got the most answers correct?

EXAMPLE: **TEAM A:** What is *advice*?
TEAM B: *Advice* is an opinion about what could or should be done about a situation.

TEAM B: What is *a criterion*?
TEAM A: *A criterion* is a standard, rule, or test on which judgments can be made.

Go to MyEnglishLab for more communication practice.

FROM GRAMMAR TO WRITING

A BEFORE YOU WRITE Think about your own health. Write a few sentences about each of the topics below.

- Your diet
- Your approach to exercise
- Your approach to work

B WRITE Using your ideas in A, write a five-paragraph essay in which you evaluate your own health. Remember to use count and non-count nouns. Try to avoid the common mistakes shown in the chart. Use the example below to help you begin your essay.

EXAMPLE: How is my health? Overall, I think it is reasonably good, though there's certainly room for improvement.

My diet is good in general, though I should cut down on sugar. . . .

As for exercise, I visit the gym at least five days a week. I do lots of different kinds of exercise: weight training, swimming, and biking. . . .

The area in which my health needs improvement is work. I've been told by friends that I work too many hours every week. . . .

Common Mistakes in Using Count and Non-Count Nouns

Don't use *a* or *an* with non-count nouns or plural count nouns. Use *a* or *an* with **singular count** nouns.	I had **a sandwich**, **an apple**, and **a glass of juice**. **NOT** I had a sandwich, an apple, and ~~glass~~ of juice. Both **work** and **play** are important in life. **NOT** Both ~~a~~ work and ~~a~~ play are important in life.
Don't use plural verbs with **singular nouns** that end in *-s*. Use **singular verbs**.	**Mathematics is** difficult for me. **NOT** Mathematics ~~are~~ difficult for me.
Don't use the word *people* with a singular verb. Use a **plural verb**.	A lot of **people live** in this neighborhood. **NOT** A lot of people ~~lives~~ in this neighborhood.

C CHECK YOUR WORK Look at your essay. Underline the count and non-count nouns. Use the Editing Checklist to check your work.

Editing Checklist

Did you . . . ?

- [ ] use *a* or *an* with singular count nouns
- [ ] avoid using non-count nouns with *a* or *an*
- [ ] use singular verbs with singular nouns ending in *-s*
- [ ] use the word *people* with plural verbs

D REVISE YOUR WORK Read your essay again. Can you improve your writing? Make changes if necessary.

Go to MyEnglishLab for more writing practice.

UNIT 10 REVIEW

Test yourself on the grammar of the unit.

A Look at the underlined word in each sentence. Write *C* (*count noun*) or *NC* (*non-count noun*).

_____ 1. Jack Sanderson describes his latest novel as a <u>work</u> in progress.

_____ 2. Let me give you some <u>advice</u>: Walk for half an hour every day.

_____ 3. My favorite dinner is fried <u>chicken</u> and mashed potatoes.

_____ 4. We saw an interesting new <u>film</u> at our local movie theater last night.

_____ 5. I don't care much for potatoes, but I do like <u>rice</u>.

_____ 6. My favorite professor is giving a <u>talk</u> tonight.

_____ 7. In my view, <u>reading</u> is one of the most beneficial activities.

B Complete the sentences with the correct count or non-count form of the words in the box. Add phrases like *a piece of* if necessary.

advice	cheese	exercise	rice

1. **a.** There is no doubt that _____ provides many benefits to the body.

   b. We always start off our English class with a couple of grammar _____ .

2. **a.** I've given you several _____ , but you haven't followed any of them.

   b. The _____ you gave me sounded good but turned out to be unrealistic.

3. **a.** There wasn't a single _____ left in the bowl.

   b. _____ is a very important type of grain grown in Asia.

4. **a.** _____ is one of my absolute favorite foods.

   b. Gouda is _____ made from whole or skimmed milk.

C Find and correct five mistakes.

Many people needs to lose weight these days. I do too. My doctor gave me an advice to help me lose weight. He said I should improve my diet. But it takes a work to prepare a nutritious meal. Also, I dislike cauliflower, carrots, beans, and most other vegetable. And I like to drink a can of sodas with every meal. What can I do?

Now check your answers on page 429.

Go to MyEnglishLab to complete the review online.

UNIT 11

Definite and Indefinite Articles

DISAPPEARING SPECIES

STEP 1   GRAMMAR IN CONTEXT

BEFORE YOU READ

Discuss the questions.

1. Is the disappearance of animal and plant species a serious problem?

2. What do you think could be done to stop the disappearance of species?

READ

 11|01 Read this article about disappearing species.

Going, Going … Gone?

WHAT DO THE AUROCH, the passenger pigeon, and the western black rhinoceros have in common? The answer: They've all gone extinct. These vanished animals typify the problem of the disappearance of species. Several grim statistics indicate the seriousness of the issue. Today more than 18,000 species are thought to be in danger of extinction. This means that over 40 percent of the world's animals are considered at risk. It is also estimated that about one-half of the world's animal species have disappeared since 1970. Many feel that something must be done to stop this, and soon. But what?

Some animals have been extinct for a considerable time. Aurochs, large wild oxen that lived in Europe and Asia, had died out by the early 1600s. The passenger pigeon was once the most common bird in North America. Historically it populated the eastern U.S. and Canada, but by the end of the nineteenth century it had almost disappeared because of habitat destruction and excessive hunting. The last known passenger pigeon, a female named Martha, died at the Cincinnati Zoo on September 1, 1914. More recently, we have lost the western black rhinoceros, which lived in the southeastern part of the African continent. It declined greatly over the twentieth century and was last seen in 2008. It was officially declared extinct on November 6, 2013.

Which animals are presently in danger of extinction? There are three significant categories: critically endangered, endangered, and vulnerable. Those considered critically endangered include the mountain gorilla of central Africa and the California condor. Those termed endangered include the Asian elephant and the blue whale. Those considered vulnerable include the African lion and the polar bear of northern North America.

Critically endangered   Endangered   Vulnerable

The picture looks bleak[1] overall. Nevertheless, the situation is not hopeless. There have been a few successes in bringing animals back from the edge of extinction. The whooping cranes of Canada and the United States are one example. In 1941, there were only twenty-one cranes in captivity and two in the wild. By 2015, there were estimated to be 603 birds in the wild. Their story can be considered a limited recovery, though there is still a potential problem of species diversity. The humpback whale is another species that has made something of a comeback, particularly since the ban on commercial whaling was instituted.

Human activity is by far the most significant cause of animal extinction. The most crucial problem is loss of habitat caused by the increase of human population and its associated development. This includes expanded farming, excessive hunting, poaching,[2] and man-made pollution. To that we can add climate change and the effects of invasive species that overwhelm[3] the native animals of an area.

What can we do? Several strategies have been suggested: (1) reduce our use of meat and dairy products; (2) focus on renewable energy; (3) change our shopping habits; (4) support laws that restrict development; and (5) support efforts to protect the rain forests, wetlands, coral reefs, and grasslands. There is need for alarm. If we're concerned about the loss of species, we need to make our voices heard. Once an animal is gone, it is gone forever.

---

1 *bleak:* giving no encouragement
2 *poaching:* taking by illegal hunting
3 *overwhelm:* completely defeat

AFTER YOU READ

A VOCABULARY   Match the words in **bold** with their meanings.

_____ 1. Sadly, these animals have **vanished** from the earth.

_____ 2. Some animals have been extinct for a **considerable** time.

_____ 3. **Nevertheless**, the situation is not hopeless.

_____ 4. A ban on whaling was **instituted** decades ago.

_____ 5. There is still a problem of species **diversity**.

_____ 6. The most **crucial** aspect is loss of habitat.

_____ 7. Several **strategies** have been suggested.

_____ 8. We need to support laws that **restrict** development.

a. plans of action

b. extremely important

c. variety

d. disappeared

e. introduced

f. limit

g. in spite of that

h. long, extensive

COMPREHENSION Read the statements. Check (✓) *True* or *False*.

	True	False
1. More than 18,000 species are believed to be in danger of extinction.	☐	☐
2. About one-fourth of the world's species have disappeared since 1970.	☐	☐
3. Aurochs had gone extinct by the early 1600s.	☐	☐
4. The passenger pigeon once populated the western U.S. and Canada.	☐	☐
5. At present, the mountain gorilla is considered vulnerable.	☐	☐
6. The habitat of the polar bear is in the southern hemisphere.	☐	☐
7. Whooping cranes have made a partial recovery.	☐	☐
8. Climate change is considered the most significant cause of extinction.	☐	☐

C **DISCUSSION** Work with a partner. Which of the strategies mentioned in the last paragraph of the article do you think are most likely to succeed in preventing the disappearance of species? Give reasons for your answer.

> Go to MyEnglishLab for more grammar in context practice.

STEP 2 GRAMMAR PRESENTATION

INDEFINITE AND DEFINITE ARTICLES

A/An: Indefinite Article

	Non-Specific	Generic
Singular Count Nouns	The mountain gorilla is **an** endangered **species**.	**A species** is a particular type of animal or plant.

Zero Article (No Article)

	Non-Specific	Generic
Plural Count Nouns	Africa has thousands of animal **habitats**.	**Habitats** are environments inhabited by individual animal groups.
Non-Count Nouns	Water **pollution** has a negative impact on animal habitats.	**Pollution** is the introduction of harmful substances into the environment.
Proper Nouns	**Ms. Rodriguez** spent a year in **Africa**. She worked in **Cameroon** and **Nigeria**. She now lives in **New York City**.	

The: Definite Article

	Specific	Generic
Singular Count Nouns	Our zoo recently acquired **a polar bear**. **The polar bear** it acquired is gigantic. It's **the largest animal** in **the zoo**.	**The polar bear** is a vulnerable species.
Plural Count Nouns	**The rain forests** in South America are being cut down.	We need to protect **the rain forests** everywhere.
Non-Count Nouns	**Poaching** has become a serious problem in those countries.	**Poaching** is the taking of animals by illegal hunting.
Proper Nouns	Ms. Rodriguez crossed **the Sahara**, visited **the Pyramids**, and sailed down **the Nile**.	

GRAMMAR NOTES

1 Indefinite and Definite Nouns

Nouns can be **indefinite** or **definite**.

We use **indefinite** nouns when we **do not have a particular** person, place, or thing in mind.

A wolf is **a** wild **animal**.

Indefinite nouns can be **non-specific** or **generic**.

A noun is **non-specific** when it is **one out of many** members of the same group or class.

We saw **a** gigantic **lion** on today's excursion. We also saw **a giraffe**.

A noun is **generic** when it represents **all members** of a class or category of persons, places, or things. Generic nouns talk about **things in general**.

Giraffes are native to the African continent. **Lions** normally have tawny yellow coats.

We use **definite** nouns when we **know which particular** person, place, or thing is being talked about.

The food we had for lunch was terrible. **The island** used to be the habitat of many animals.

A noun or noun phrase is normally **definite** if you can ask a *which* **question** about it. Nouns of this type are often followed by a phrase with *of*.

A: **Which food** was terrible?
B: *The* **food** we had for lunch was terrible.
A: **Which country** is Nairobi the capital of?
B: Nairobi is **the capital *of* Kenya**.

A noun is often **indefinite** the first time we mention it. It is usually **definite** after the first mention.

I'm reading about *an* endangered **animal**. *The* **animal** lives in West Africa.

2 Indefinite Article *A/An*

Use the indefinite article, *a/an*, with **indefinite singular count nouns**.	Our city needs **a** good **zoo**. She wants to be **an anthropologist**.

3 Zero Article

Use **zero article** (= no article) with indefinite plural count nouns, indefinite non-count nouns, names of people, names of most countries, and habitual locations.

• **indefinite plural count nouns**	This area used to have wild **animals**.
• **indefinite non-count nouns**	**Platinum** and **gold** are valuable minerals.
• **names of people**	**Mr. Jama** is a zoologist.
• **names of most countries**	Ngorongoro Crater is found in **Tanzania**.
• **habitual locations**	People spend most of their time at **work**, at **school**, or at **home**.

4 Definite Article *The*

Use the **definite article** *the* in a variety of different situations.

Use *the* with **non-count nouns** and **singular and plural nouns** that are **definite** for you and your listener or reader.	**The food** we had for lunch was terrible. **The island** used to be the habitat of many animals. **The animals** who lived there have become extinct.
Use *the* with nouns that describe something **unique**. An **adjective** can often make a noun represent something unique:	**The world** is certainly an interesting place. **The sun** gives us light and heat.
• *first*, *last*, *only*, *right*, *wrong*	**The** *last* **passenger pigeon** died in 1914.
• **comparative** forms of adjectives	**The** *stronger* of the two animals is **the** *older* one.
• **superlative** forms of adjectives	It was **the** *worst* **disaster** in the country's history.
You can also use *the* to talk about the following categories:	
• **inventions**	**The wheel** was invented thousands of years ago.
• **musical instruments**	Helen plays **the piano**.
• **parts of the body**	**The brain** is the seat of intelligence.
The is also used with the following:	
• **public places**	**the** bank, **the** post office, **the** library, **the** gym
• the names of many **geographical features**	**the** Grand Canyon, **the** Congo (River), **the** Pacific (Ocean), **the** Persian Gulf, **the** Atlas Mountains
• the names of a few **countries**	**the** Netherlands, **the** United States, **the** Dominican Republic, **the** Bahamas, **the** United Kingdom
• the names of **ships**	**the** *Titanic*, **the** *Queen Mary*

There are **five principal ways** to use nouns **generically**.

• **indefinite article + count noun**	**A whale** is a large marine mammal that inhabits the world's oceans.
• **zero article + plural count noun**	**Dogs** are domestic mammals related to **wolves** and **foxes**.
• **definite article + singular count noun**	The **mountain gorilla** is considered critically threatened.
• **definite article + plural count noun**	**The whooping cranes** are making a comeback.
• **zero article + non-count noun**	**Water** is essential for survival of animals, humans, and plants.
You can also make a generic statement with the **definite article + adjective**. In this kind of statement, a noun such as *people* is implied. The adjective is plural in meaning and takes a plural verb.	**The rich are** fortunate. They need to help **the poor**, who **are** not so fortunate.

REFERENCE NOTE

For more complete lists of **nouns used with the definite article**, see Appendices 9–11 on pages 416 and 417.

Go to MyEnglishLab to watch the grammar presentation.

STEP 3 **FOCUSED PRACTICE**

EXERCISE 1 DISCOVER THE GRAMMAR

Ⓐ GRAMMAR NOTES 1–5 Read the sentences based on the reading. For each sentence, identify the underlined word or phrase as *non-specific* (*N*), *generic* (*G*), or *definite* (*D*).

D 1. These vanished species typify <u>the problem</u> of the disappearance of species.

_____ 2. <u>The passenger pigeon</u> was once the most common bird in North America.

_____ 3. About one-half of <u>the world's</u> animal species have disappeared since 1970.

_____ 4. The last passenger pigeon that died was <u>a female</u>.

_____ 5. Recently we lost <u>the western black rhinoceros</u>.

_____ 6. The humpback whale has made something of <u>a comeback</u>.

_____ 7. This comeback was positively influenced by <u>the ban</u> on commercial whaling.

_____ 8. Invasive species can overwhelm the native animals of <u>an area</u>.

_____ 9. We need to support efforts to protect <u>the rain forests</u> throughout the world.

_____ 10. Once <u>an animal</u> is gone, it is gone forever.

B GRAMMAR NOTES 1, 5 Read the sentences based on the reading. Then circle the answer that correctly explains the meaning of the sentence.

1. A giraffe is a long-necked mammal native to Africa.
   (a.) All giraffes are long-necked mammals.
   b. Some giraffes are long-necked mammals.

2. The auroch had died out by the beginning of the 1600s.
   a. Some of the aurochs had died out.
   b. All of the aurochs had died out.

3. The passenger pigeon populated the eastern United States and Canada.
   a. Passenger pigeons in general populated this area.
   b. One particular passenger pigeon populated this area.

4. The whooping crane is doing much better these days.
   a. Some whooping cranes are doing much better.
   b. Whooping cranes in general are doing much better.

5. On our African trip, we saw hippopotamuses.
   a. We saw some hippopotamuses.
   b. We saw all the hippopotamuses.

6. We need to protect the world's grasslands.
   a. We need to protect some of the grasslands.
   b. We need to protect all of the grasslands.

EXERCISE 2 INDEFINITE AND DEFINITE ARTICLES

GRAMMAR NOTES 1–2, 4–5 Complete the sentences with *a*, *an*, or *the*.

1. _____The_____ earth has only one moon. It has two sides. We never see _____ dark side
   a.   b.
   of _____ moon.
        c.

2. _____ planet Saturn has many moons. Titan is _____ moon of Saturn. It is
   a.   b.
   _____ largest of Saturn's moons.
   c.

3. On our first morning in Rwanda, we saw _____ gorilla far off in the distance.
                                            a.
   _____ gorilla we saw was _____ silverback.
   b.   c.

4. _____ last confirmed sighting of _____ individual dodo bird occurred on the
   a.   b.
   island of Mauritius in 1662.

5. We saw _____ humpback whale. It was _____ largest whale I have ever seen.
            a.   b.

6. Our friends are taking _____ trip around _____ world. _____ trip will
                           a.   b.   c.
   last four months.

7. We saw _____ elk being pursued by _____ wolf. _____ elk managed to
            a.   b.   c.
   escape from _____ wolf.
                d.

EXERCISE 3 ARTICLES: *A, AN, THE,* AND ZERO ARTICLE

GRAMMAR NOTES 1–5 Complete the paragraph. Circle the correct articles (Ø = *zero article*).

We are losing many species, and a major contributor to the loss of species is pollution.
One of a / (the) / Ø most serious causes of pollution is plastics. Did you know that a / the / Ø
____1.____ ____2.____
plastics represent about 10 percent of all pollution on a / the / Ø earth today?
____3.____

How can a / the / Ø product that is so essential to the lifestyle of a / the / Ø twenty-first
____4.____ ____5.____
century also be one of a / the / Ø worst polluters? Obviously, the answer is complex, but we
____6.____
can begin by noting that plastic is everywhere. It's in landfills; it's on city streets; it's in forests;
it's in lakes and oceans.

Consider the following facts about products made with plastic. One of the most polluting
plastic products is a / the / Ø disposable diaper. It requires about 450 years to biodegrade.
____7.____
Fishing line takes about 600 years. It was originally thought that plastics in a / the / Ø ocean
____8.____
would take a / an / the extremely long time to decay, but researchers have recently discovered
____9.____
that water currents make plastic degrade faster. However, the vast increase in the amount of
plastic reaching the ocean makes a / the / Ø process slower.
____10.____

When plastic products do decay
in the ocean, the chemicals in them
gradually enter the water and can sicken
animals like birds, whales, and sea
turtles, which eat them. A / The / Ø
____11.____
whale, for example, might eat pieces
of plastic and become ill or even die.
A / The / Ø seagull might get tangled
____12.____
in fishing line. Even more seriously,
a / the / Ø large netting, which of
____13.____
course contains plastic, captures larger
animals. Normally, they are unable to
escape and end up drowning or starving
to death. These examples show us that
a / the / Ø problem of plastic pollution
____14.____
is becoming increasingly acute.

EXERCISE 4 GENERIC NOUNS

GRAMMAR NOTE 5 Write two sentences about each noun, using the correct forms of the words given. In sentence *a*, use zero article + the plural. In sentence *b*, use the definite article. Add necessary articles and prepositions along with the word *that*.

1. Mountain gorilla

   a. *Mountain gorillas are great apes that inhabit forest areas in three central African countries.*
   (be / great ape / inhabit forest areas in three central African countries)

   b. *The mountain gorilla is a critically endangered species.*
   (be / critically endangered species)

2. African elephant

   a. _____
   (be / very large mammal / inhabit forests, woodlands, and desert areas in many parts of Africa)

   b. _____
   (be / endangered species)

3. California condor

   a. _____
   (be / very large land bird / became extinct in the wild in 1987)

   b. _____
   (be / critically endangered species)

4. wheel

   a. _____
   (be / circular device / turn around a central point)

   b. _____
   (be / invented 5,000 to 6,000 years ago)

5. telephone

   a. _____
   (be / communication device / convert sound signals into waves)

   b. _____
   (be / invented in 1878 by Alexander Graham Bell)

6. guitar

   a. _____
   (be / stringed instrument / typically have six strings)

   b. _____
   (be / invented in the 1400s in Spain)

7. clarinet

   a. _____
   (be / woodwind instrument / use reeds)

   b. _____
   (be / invented around 1700 in Europe)

8. library

   a. _____
   (be / place / lend people books to read)

   b. _____
   (be / important institution in every town or city)

9. eye

   a. _____
   (be / part of the body / allow us to see)

   b. _____
   (be / vulnerable to injury)

GRAMMAR NOTES 1–5 Read the student composition about poaching. There are nine mistakes in the use of articles. The first mistake is already corrected. Find and correct eight more.

Down with Poaching!

Last summer, our family took a wonderful trip to several countries in Africa. I learned a lot about all the amazing animals that inhabit African continent. The most upsetting thing I learned about, though, was the problem of poaching. Poachers are hunters who capture or kill animals illegally. Main reason they do this, of course, is to earn money. The majority of poachers are paid by organized crime groups that sell the poached animals' body parts worldwide for large amounts of cash. Consider elephants, for example. Elephant tusks, bones, and skin can be illegally sold for great profits. In August of the 2014, it was estimated that about 100,000 African elephants were being killed each year by poachers. Another animal that is target of poachers is the black rhinoceros. In recent decades, its population has decreased by 97.6 percent.

Why are these animal products so much in demand? The main reason is that there is a mistaken belief these animal body parts have powers they do not really have. For example, rhino horn can supposedly be used to treat the hangovers, fever, and cancer. But it has not been proven that the product will cure any of these. The ivory from elephants' tusks is made into jewelry, eating utensils, and religious objects. One pound of ivory will sell for $30,000 a pound. Compare that to the gold, which sells for about $22,000 a pound. Another main reason for poaching is that animals and animal parts are extremely popular as trophies. Some people love the idea of having a set of elephant tusks to display over their fireplace. That seems like very selfish idea to me.

Poaching is having a very negative effect on the survival of certain species, especially species that are endangered. I don't want to see any more species die. In my opinion, we must do everything within our power to stop the illegal activity of the poaching.

Go to MyEnglishLab for more focused practice.

EXERCISE 6   LISTENING

▶11|02   **A**   Listen to the conversation between a husband and a wife. What are they talking about doing with wolves?

_____

_____

_____

_____

A herd of elk

Wolves

▶11|02   **B**   Read the statements. Then listen again to the conversation. Complete the sentences. Circle the correct answers.

1. According to the husband, the newspaper is on the side of _____.
   a. an environmentalist   **b.** the environmentalists

2. The husband thinks _____ point of view is not being considered.
   a. the ranchers' and hunters'   **b.** the environmentalists'

3. The husband supports the point of view of _____.
   a. both ranchers and hunters   **b.** only hunters

4. The husband _____ a hunter.
   a. is   **b.** is not

5. The husband thinks _____ are dangerous creatures.
   a. wolves in general   **b.** some wolves

6. The husband says that wolves kill _____.
   a. a lot of people   **b.** a few people

7. The wife supports the point of view of _____.
   a. the ranchers and hunters   **b.** the environmentalists

8. Before 1995, _____ in Yellowstone were too numerous.
   a. elk   **b.** wolves

9. According to the wife, _____ elk have been killed off.
   a. a number of old and sick   **b.** all old and sick

10. The wife thinks _____ are intelligent and helpful.
    a. some wolves   **b.** wolves in general

C   Work with a partner. What is your viewpoint on the controversy discussed in the Listening? Is the wolf a dangerous animal? Is the husband's view of wolves a stereotype? Should wolves be placed in national parks?

EXERCISE 7 THE MOUNTAIN GORILLA

INFORMATION GAP Work with a partner. Student A will follow the instructions below. Student B will follow the instructions on page 440.

Student B will follow the instructions on page 440.

STUDENT A

- The article below is missing some information. Your partner has the same article that contains your missing information. Ask your partner questions to find the missing information.

  EXAMPLE: **A:** What is the mountain gorilla?
  B: The mountain gorilla is a great ape.

- Your partner's story is missing different information. Answer your partner's questions so that he or she can fill in the missing information.

  EXAMPLE: **B:** What kind of ape is the mountain gorilla?
  A: It is the largest of the great apes.

THE MOUNTAIN GORILLA is _____; in fact, it is the

largest of the great apes. Mountain gorillas inhabit national parks in three countries in central Africa:

Uganda, Rwanda, and _____.

Mountain gorillas have _____, a

characteristic that enables them to live in cold, mountainous areas. An adult male is

called a silverback and can grow as tall as 6 feet 3 inches, or 1.9 meters. Adult

males can weigh up to 430 pounds, or 195 kilograms. Mountain gorillas live

together in social groups dominated by _____.

A group is composed mainly of a dominant male and several females and young

gorillas. The mountain gorilla is an intelligent creature; silverbacks can often

remove the traps left by _____.

Since these animals are herbivores, they need a good deal of food daily in order to

support their great bulk.

The mountain gorilla is a critically endangered species. There are two principal

causes of its endangerment: _____.

Mountain gorillas are sometimes hunted for food, and they are pursued by poachers for

their fur and for sale to zoos. It is clear that human development and encroachment on

locales where mountain gorillas have traditionally lived has split their habitat into widely

separated areas. There were only 254 mountain gorillas in 1981, and there are now about 880.

This sounds positive, but since particular groups of mountain gorillas are not able to interact

with other gorilla groups, the result is _____

within the species. This is a serious problem indeed.

EXERCISE 8 TEST YOUR TRIVIA IQ

GAME Work in a group. Complete the chart below. First, read each answer in the chart. Choose a word from the word box that matches the answer. Then use the word to form a *what* or *who* question with the correct article and verb. Then check your answers on page 435. Which group got the most answers correct?

auroch	brain	humpback whale	poaching	post office	silverback	sun	water
bank	elk	plastic	poor	rich	species	telephone	wolves

Questions	Answers
1. What is an auroch?	It's a now-extinct wild ox that lived in Europe and Asia.
2.	It's a place in a town or city where one keeps one's money.
3.	They're the people who have very little money.
4.	It's capturing or killing animals by hunting illegally.
5.	It's something that is useful and that also pollutes the earth.
6.	They're animals that have been reintroduced in national parks.
7.	It's an ocean-dwelling mammal that is now less endangered than in the past.
8.	It's the part of the human body that you use to think.
9.	They're the people who have a great deal of money.
10.	It's the device invented in 1878 by Alexander Graham Bell.
11.	It's a particular type of animal or plant.
12.	It's a type of animal killed by wolves in Yellowstone National Park.
13.	It's an adult male gorilla that is in charge of his own group.
14.	It's the source of heat and light on the earth.
15.	It's something that is essential for the survival of humans, animals, and plants.
16.	It's the place in a city or town where one can mail letters and packages.

EXERCISE 9 HOW DO YOU FEEL ABOUT IT?

A **SURVEY** Complete the survey. Walk around the class and ask people their opinions. Keep track of how many people think each proposed action is *Not Important*, *Important*, or *Very Important*.

EXAMPLE: **A:** How do you feel about saving the mountain gorilla and other endangered species?

 B: I think saving the mountain gorilla is important . . .

Proposed Actions	Not Important	Important	Very Important
Saving the mountain gorilla and other endangered species			
Protecting the rain forests from farming and other development			
Stopping plastic pollution			
Developing industry to give people jobs and end poverty			
Stopping animal poaching and trade of animal body parts			
Expanding farmland to feed more people			

B Rank the proposed actions in the chart above in order of importance. Then work in a group. Discuss why you ranked the actions in the order you did. Then share your survey results and your rankings with the class.

EXAMPLE: In our group, we ranked "Stopping plastic pollution" as "very important." We feel that plastic pollution is a serious problem. There is too much plastic pollution in the oceans and on our beaches . . .

Go to MyEnglishLab for more communication practice.

Definite and Indefinite Articles **191**

FROM GRAMMAR TO WRITING

A **BEFORE YOU WRITE** Think of an animal species that is critically endangered, endangered, or vulnerable. Write a few sentences about each of the following points. Do some research on the Internet if necessary.

- the species that is endangered
- the habitat of the species
- the outlook for saving the species

B **WRITE** Using your ideas in A, write a five-paragraph essay about the endangered species that you have chosen. Remember to use generic nouns and definite and indefinite articles with nouns. Try to avoid the common mistakes shown in the chart. Use the example below to help you begin your essay.

EXAMPLE: The endangered species that I am most interested in is the mountain gorilla. Mountain gorillas live in Rwanda, Uganda, and the Democratic Republic of the Congo. There are only about 880 of them left in the wild.

The main threats that the gorillas face are loss of habitat and illegal hunting, especially poaching. . . .

Common Mistakes in Using Nouns with Articles

Use *a/an* with **indefinite count nouns**.	The mountain gorilla is **an endangered species**. **NOT** The mountain gorilla is ~~endangered species~~.
Use *the* before **definite nouns**.	**The food** we ate at that restaurant was terrible. **NOT** ~~Food~~ we ate at the restaurant was terrible.
Don't use *the* before **indefinite non-count nouns**. Use **zero article** in this situation.	**Poaching** is a big problem. **NOT** ~~The~~ poaching is a big problem.
Don't use *the* with count nouns unless they are **generic nouns**.	**Antelopes** are commonly hunted by lions. **NOT** ~~The~~ antelopes are commonly hunted by lions.

C **CHECK YOUR WORK** Look at your essay. Underline nouns used with *a*, *an*, or *the* and generic nouns with zero article. Use the Editing Checklist to check your work.

Editing Checklist

Did you . . . ?

- [ ] use *a* or *an* with indefinite count nouns
- [ ] use *the* before definite nouns
- [ ] use zero article before non-count nouns
- [ ] avoid using *the* before count nouns unless they are generic

D **REVISE YOUR WORK** Read your essay again. Can you improve your writing? Make changes if necessary.

Go to MyEnglishLab for more writing practice.

UNIT 11 REVIEW

Test yourself on the grammar of the unit.

A Identify each underlined word or phrase as *non-specific* (*N*), *definite* (*D*), or *generic* (*G*).

_____ **1.** The clarinet was invented around the year 1700.

_____ **2.** My parents bought me a trumpet when I started band in middle school.

_____ **3.** The moon is Earth's only satellite.

_____ **4.** Water is an extremely valuable commodity, especially in desert areas.

_____ **5.** In my view, we need to help the poor in whatever way we can.

_____ **6.** The man who is giving the lecture is my next-door neighbor.

_____ **7.** The ship was hit by an iceberg on its maiden voyage.

_____ **8.** The kids spilled juice all over the kitchen floor.

B Complete the sentences with *a*, *an*, or *the* where necessary. Write Ø if no article is needed.

Disaster at Sea: Many Lives Lost

April 16, 1912. In the latest news, _____ *Titanic*, _____ British steamer, sank in
                      1.   **2.**

_____ North Atlantic last night after hitting _____ iceberg, disproving its
   3.   **4.**

builders' claims that it couldn't be sunk. Ironically, _____ ship was on its maiden
                                       5.

voyage from Southampton, England, to _____ New York City. More than 1,500 people
                                   6.

perished, in large part because it was felt that _____ lifeboats took up too much deck
                                               7.

space, so there were only twenty of them.

C Find and correct five mistakes.

One of the most famous animals in the history of Earth is a dinosaur. The extinction of

the dinosaurs is still a matter of debate in scientific community. Why did they die out? Many

scientists now believe that giant meteorite flew through the space and hit our planet very

hard. This changed an earth's climate, making it too cold for dinosaurs to survive.

Now check your answers on page 429.

Go to MyEnglishLab to complete the review online.

OUTCOMES
• Describe quantities and use quantifiers with count and non-count nouns
• Identify key information in an advice column
• Identify key details in a conversation about a student's academic difficulties
• Talk about your life now compared to your life in the past
• Discuss the meaning and implications of research data on a foreign country
• Write an essay about improving study habits

STEP 1   **GRAMMAR IN CONTEXT**

BEFORE YOU READ

Discuss the questions.

1. Do you enjoy studying? What do you consider your greatest challenge in studying?
2. What study habits do you think successful students have?

READ

▶ 12|01   Read this article about study skills.

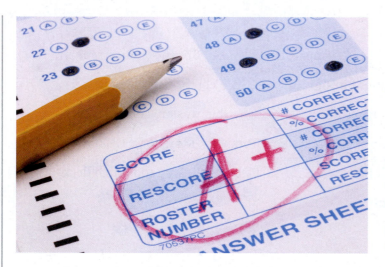

The Study Habits of Successful Students

College students face many challenges. They have to take care of a large number of responsibilities in a limited amount of time. There are plenty of distractions that can divert students' attention from their studies. Most students struggle at one point or another to maintain focus on their schoolwork. But if you're a student, don't despair. All of the study tips listed below have been proven to help students to be successful in their studies.

TIP 1: Figure out how much time you need to devote to each subject. The general recommendation is to study two hours outside of class for every hour spent in class. If you're taking fifteen credits, plan to allocate approximately thirty hours a week to school study. That may sound like a lot of hours, but that's just the general recommendation. Bear in mind that you shouldn't study constantly either. All the aspects of your life—work, recreation, socializing, study, exercise—need to be kept in balance. If you find yourself overloaded, take fewer classes the next time around.

TIP 2: Make yourself a study schedule. There are basically two types of schedule: time orientation and task orientation. In time orientation, you get out your weekly calendar and list the precise time and number of hours you will devote to each subject. So, for example, if you're taking a zoology class, you might write down something like this: *Tuesdays/Thursdays 2 to 4 p.m.: study zoology.* In task orientation, you delineate[1] the number of tasks you have to accomplish each week but don't specify times or exact numbers of hours. Instead, you might lay out the week's tasks like this:

History: read chapters 1 and 2.

English: write draft 1 of next week's essay. By the end of the week: write the final draft.

Chemistry: do lab experiments on Monday. Thursday: write up the results. . . .

I personally have found task orientation to be the superior method, but that's just me. Determine which method works better for you. Both types of orientation are basically "to do lists." The trouble with lists, though, is that people sometimes spend a lot of time writing down what they need to do and little time actually doing it. Just make a general outline of what you want to accomplish in a particular week so that you won't forget any important things.

TIP 3: Put things in order of priority, from most important to least important. Study the harder subjects first, when you have more energy and focus. If your grade needs improvement in a certain class, put in more work on that class. If you have a large project, such as a major term paper, break it down into smaller, more manageable segments. Get started and do a bit of work on it each day. That way you can avoid the misery of having an assignment due imminently[2] with not enough time to finish it. While you're doing this, avoid perfectionism. You can refine things later.

TIP 4: Find yourself some study partners. If you join a study group, you will complete assignments more quickly because you will be working with several other people who have the same goal. You can ask for help when you are having a little trouble understanding something. If you understand a topic well, explaining it to your study partners will help you to remember it better. However, make sure that you choose the right study partners. No study partner is preferable to the wrong study partners. You don't want to waste any time studying with people who are not prepared or who aren't serious about their work.

TIP 5: Find yourself the right study environment. A great many people work well in quiet locales[3] with few distractions. Many find they accomplish little real work when they are interrupted by cell phone calls and text messages. But not everyone is like this. Some people actually work well in situations where there's a great deal of noise, music, or other activity going on around them. If you're like this, that's fine. Any locale that allows you to put in quality study time will ultimately help you succeed in your classes.

TIP 6: Always remember why you are doing all this studying. If you don't already have a positive attitude toward learning, adopt one. Be eager to learn. Participate in class as much as possible. Above all, make the most of your present opportunity. It may not come around again.

---

1 *delineate:* outline
2 *imminently:* very soon
3 *locales:* places

AFTER YOU READ

A VOCABULARY   Match the words in **bold** with their meanings.

_____ **1.** If you feel stressed, don't **despair**.

_____ **2.** **Allocate** thirty hours a week to study.

_____ **3.** That amount of study is **approximate**.

_____ **4.** Each **aspect** of your life needs to be in balance.

_____ **5.** Two strategies are time and task **orientation**.

_____ **6.** List the **precise** time and number of hours.

_____ **7.** You can **refine** things later.

_____ **8.** Good study locales will **ultimately** help you succeed.

a. in the end

b. improve

c. decide to use

d. direction or type of thought

e. close but not quite exact

f. exact

g. lose hope

h. part

B COMPREHENSION   Complete the sentences based on the reading.

1. Students have to take care of many responsibilities in a limited _____ of time.

2. It's not how much or how little time you have; it's how you _____ your time that's important.

3. If you feel overloaded this term, take _____ classes next term.

4. For the author, _____ orientation is the superior method to make a schedule.

5. The author's recommendation is to study the _____ subjects first.

6. The author recommends avoiding _____ when studying day by day.

7. The author says some people work well when there's _____ going on around them.

8. The author says that a student should _____ in class as much as possible.

C DISCUSSION   Work with a partner. Compare your answers in B. Do you agree that the study habits described in the article are effective? How many of the study habits do you personally have?

Go to **MyEnglishLab** for more grammar in context practice.

QUANTIFIERS

Quantifiers	With Count Nouns	With Non-Count Nouns
One	**One class** is open.	Ø*
Each	**Each subject** is challenging.	Ø
Every	**Every day** is different.	Ø
Two	**Two classes** are open.	Ø
Both	**Both subjects** are challenging.	Ø
A couple of	I have **a couple of** hard **classes**.	Ø
Several	I study with **several** good **friends**.	Ø
Few	He has **few friends**.	Ø
A few	She has **a few good friends**.	Ø
Many	Are you taking **many classes**?	Ø
A great many	He has earned **a great many credits**.	Ø
A number of	She has earned **a number of credits**.	Ø
Little	Ø	They have **little money**.
A little	Ø	She has **a little money**.
Much	Ø	Does he do **much studying**?
A great deal of	Ø	She does **a great deal of studying**.
A bit of	Ø	I have **a bit of trouble** with math classes.
No	They have **no vehicles** of their own.	They have **no spare time**.
Any	They don't have **any vehicles** of their own.	They don't have **any spare time**.
Some	They have **some friends**.	They have **some money**.
Enough	You have **enough friends**.	You have **enough money**.
A lot of	He has **a lot of good teachers**.	He has **a lot of self-confidence**.
Lots of	I have **lots of appointments** today.	I have **lots of** spare **time** this week.
Plenty of	She has **plenty of good teachers**.	She has **plenty of patience**.
Most	**Most students** are motivated.	**Most work** is useful.
All	**All students** are important.	**All work** can be tiring.

*Ø: The quantifiers *little, a little, much, a great deal of,* and *a bit of* are not used with count nouns. The quantifiers *one, each, every, two, both, a couple of, several, a few, few, many, a great many,* and *a number of* are not used with non-count nouns.

GRAMMAR NOTES

1 Definition of Quantifiers

Quantifiers state the **number** or **amount** of something.

Quantifiers can be single **words** or **phrases**.	There are **forty** people in my calculus class. I'm spending **a great deal of** time studying.
Quantifiers are used with both **nouns** and **pronouns**.	I'm taking **six** *classes* this semester. **All of** *them* are challenging.
Quantifiers are often used **alone** if a noun or pronoun has just been mentioned, as in a question.	**A:** Have you made **many friends** here at school? **B:** Yes, I've made **a lot**.

2 Quantifiers + Nouns

Use quantifiers with all types of **nouns**.

• with **singular count** nouns: *one, each, every*	***Each** student* in the class has a computer. I was able to solve ***every** problem* on the exam.
• with **plural count** nouns: *two, both, a couple of, a dozen, several, a few, few, many, a great many, a number of*	***Many** students* earned scholarships. ***A number of** students* in the class come from other countries.
• with **non-count** nouns: *a little, little, much, a great deal of, amount of, a bit of*	I had ***a great deal of** difficulty* getting to class today. The ***amount of** traffic* on the roads was amazing.
• with both **plural** and **non-count** nouns: *no, any, some, enough, a lot of, lots of, plenty of, most, all*	He had ***no** friends* before he came here. He had ***no** money* either. ***All** students* have to pay tuition. ***All** work* is potentially worthwhile.

3 *Amount, Number*

Use *amount* with **non-count** nouns.	The ***amount** of stress* in people's lives seems to be growing.
Use *number* with **count** nouns.	The ***number** of mistakes* I made on the exam was incredible.

Use *a few*, *few*, *a little*, *little*, and *a bit* to describe **small amounts** or **numbers** of things.

Use *a few* and *few* with **count** nouns. Use *a little* and *little* with **non-count** nouns.	Sayid has *a few* good **friends**. He has *few* **problems** at school. Asha has *a little* **trouble** with math classes. She has *little* **difficulty** with English, though.
There are **meaning differences** between *a few* and *few* and between *a little* and *little*.	

Use *a few* and *a little* to give a statement a **positive** sense. They mean "a small number or amount, but probably **enough**."	I have *a few* **investments**.
	  (a small number, but probably enough)
	We have *a little* **food** at home.
	  (a small amount, but probably enough)

Use *few* and *little* to give a statement a **negative** sense. They mean "a small number or amount, but probably **not enough**."	Hank has *few* **friends**.
	  (a small number, but probably not enough)
	He also has *little* **self-confidence**.
	  (a small amount, but probably not enough)

Note that if we add *only* to *a few* or *a little*, the **positive** sense **disappears**.	I have *only* **a few** friends. *(I would like more.)* I have *only* **a little** money. *(I would like more.)*
In comparisons, use *fewer* with **count** nouns and *less* with **non-count** nouns.	I have *fewer* **problems** than I used to. I earn *less* **money**, though.
You can use *as many* + **count** noun as a quantifier.	Helen doesn't have *as many* **health issues** now.
In positive comparisons, use *more* with both count and non-count nouns.	I have *more* **friends** now than I used to. I also have *more* **self-confidence**.
A little and *a bit* are similar in meaning. *A bit* must be used with *of* if a noun follows.	Ellen had *a little* **trouble** with the exam. I had *a bit of* **difficulty** myself.
You can also combine *a little* and *bit* in a single sentence.	Our team had *a little bit of* **luck** and won the game.

5 Much, Many, A Great Many, A Lot, Lots, A Great Deal

Use *much*, *many*, *a great many*, *a lot*, *lots*, and *a great deal* to describe **large amounts** or **numbers** of things.

Use *much* and *a great deal* with **non-count** nouns.	I don't have *much* free **time**. Presidents are under *a great deal of* **stress**.
Use *many* and *a great many* with **count** nouns.	There are *many* job **opportunities** for college graduates. The government employs *a great many* **workers**.
USAGE NOTE We don't often use *much* in affirmative sentences, especially in conversation. We usually replace it with *a lot of* or *lots of*. Use *a lot of* and *lots of* both with count and non-count nouns.	We spend *a lot of* **money** on rent. There's *lots of* **construction** going on. There are *a lot of* **books** for this class. The professor gives *lots of* **quizzes**.
However, *much* is common in **questions**, **negative** statements, and in combination with the adverb *too* in affirmative sentences.	Did they spend *much* **money**? She doesn't watch *much* **TV**. I ate *too much* for dinner.
IN WRITING The quantifiers *a great deal* and *a great many* are somewhat formal. We use them more in writing than in conversation.	I have had to do *a great deal of* **work** for my physics class. There are *a great many* **students** in lecture classes.

6 Some, Any

Use *some* and *any* with both **count** and **non-count** nouns.

In **affirmative** statements, use *some* in its basic sense.	Bill bought *some* new **textbooks**. He borrowed *some* **money** from me.
In **negative** statements, use *any* in its basic sense.	Alice didn't take *any* **trips** last year. She didn't have *any* spare **time**.
Use both *some* and *any* in **questions**.	Did you buy *some* **clothes**? Did you see *any* good **movies**?
In general, use *some* in **offers** and *any* in **negative** questions.	Would you like *some* **soda**? *(an offer)* Didn't you send *any* **postcards**? *(a negative question)*
In affirmative sentences, *any* sometimes carries the expectation that the statement described is **not expected** or not very likely.	If you still have **any questions**, we can talk about them after the review is finished. *(The speaker thinks it's not very likely that the students will still have questions.)*
In affirmative sentences, *any* can also have a meaning similar to *every*, with the emphasis on one item in particular.	I would recommend **any professor** in the history department. *(Every professor in the department is good.)*
BE CAREFUL! Don't use two negatives in the same simple sentence.	Jack **didn't** understand **anything** in the lecture. **NOT** Jack didn't understand ~~nothing~~ in the lecture.

7 Quantifiers in Phrases with *of*

Many **quantifiers** appear in **phrases** with the preposition *of* before plural nouns or non-count nouns.

Use a **quantifier** + *of* + *the* or another determiner when you are **specifying** particular persons, places, things, or groups.	**Many *of the* students** in my class got good grades. *(a specific group of students)* I've already spent **a lot *of the* money** I earned. *(a specific amount of money)*
We often use **quantifiers without *of*** when we have **no particular** person, place, thing, or group in mind.	***Many* businesses** take credit cards. *(businesses in general)* ***Most* people** don't understand the Theory of Relativity. *(people in general)*
USAGE NOTE Quantifiers such as *most of* and *many of* can be followed by a singular or a plural verb, depending on the noun that follows *of*.	**Most of the information** we heard *was* useful. **Most of the students** *were* paying attention.
BE CAREFUL! Don't use quantifiers with *of* before a **singular** noun.	**A few of the students** did well on the exam. **NOT** A few of the ~~student~~ did well on the exam.

PRONUNCIATION NOTE

 Reducing *of* in Quantifiers

Quantifiers containing the preposition *of* are often reduced in rapid speech and in conversation. The word *of* is often reduced to "a." This reduction often happens when the word following *of* begins with a consonant. When the word following *of* begins with a vowel, full forms are generally used.

a couple of	→	"a couple a"	We met **"a couple a"** new people at the party.
a lot of	→	"a lotta"	I had **"a lotta"** work to do tonight.
lots of	→	"lotsa"	There are **"lotsa"** great movies playing.
plenty of	→	"plentya"	There's **"plentya"** time to get there.
a number of	→	"a numbera"	I had **"a numbera"** problems with the homework.
amount of	→	"amounta"	The **"amounta"** traffic today was incredible.
a bit of	→	"a bitta"	He had **"a bitta"** trouble hearing the lecture.
most of	→	"mosta"	I was able to solve **"mosta"** the problems.

IN WRITING The forms *couple a, lotta, lotsa, plentya, a numbera, amounta, bitta,* and *mosta* are **not used in writing**.	We have **a lot of** work left to do. There's **plenty of** food for everyone. We had **lots of** fun at the amusement park. The **amount of** money she earns is amazing.

REFERENCE NOTE

For more information on **count and non-count nouns**, see Unit 10 on page 163.

Go to MyEnglishLab to watch the grammar presentation.

EXERCISE 1   DISCOVER THE GRAMMAR

GRAMMAR NOTES 1–7   Read the sentences based on the reading. Could the underlined quantifiers be replaced with the words in parentheses without changing the basic meaning or creating an incorrect sentence? For each sentence, write *Y* (*Yes*) or *N* (*No*).

_N_   **1.** Students have a limited <u>amount</u> of time. (number)

____   **2.** We get twenty-four hours <u>each</u> day. (every)

____   **3.** I think I can offer you <u>some</u> reasonable suggestions. (any)

____   **4.** Figure out how <u>much</u> time you need to devote to each subject. (many)

____   **5.** That may sound like <u>a lot of</u> hours. (a great many)

____   **6.** You list the <u>number</u> of hours you have to devote to each task. (amount)

____   **7.** Take <u>fewer</u> classes the next time around. (less)

____   **8.** People sometimes spend <u>a lot of</u> time writing down what they have to do. (a great deal of)

____   **9.** Get started and do <u>a bit of</u> work on your assignment each day. (a little)

____   **10.** Many people accomplish <u>little</u> real work when they're interrupted by distractions. (a little)

____   **11.** <u>Some</u> people work well in noisy situations. (Any)

____   **12.** <u>Any</u> locale where you can study easily will help you succeed in your classes. (Every)

EXERCISE 2   QUANTIFIERS

GRAMMAR NOTES 2–6   Complete the paragraph. Circle the correct answers.

I just got back from my year of study in Germany. I had less /(fewer) difficulties
$\underline{}$
1.
with the language than I expected. I didn't take <u>some / any</u> classes that were given
2.
in English. All year long, I spent <u>less / fewer</u> money than I expected I would. During the
3.
week, I had to spend <u>a great deal of / much</u> time studying. I didn't have <u>many / much</u> spare hours,
4.   **5.**
so I couldn't do anything but hit the books. I did have <u>some / any</u> time to visit tourist attractions
6.
on the weekends, though. I lived in an apartment with <u>any / several</u> other students who were also
7.
at the university. We would study together almost <u>all / every</u> evening. We had <u>a little / little</u> trouble
8.   **9.**
getting along with each other because everyone was friendly. In fact, the <u>amount / number</u> of
10.
friendships I made during the year was amazing. It was really a wonderful year.

EXERCISE 3 MORE QUANTIFIERS

GRAMMAR NOTES 2–7 Diego and Alicia Marquez are trying to save money for their college tuition. They are examining their budget. Complete their conversation with quantifiers from the box, using each expression once.

$50	a few	any	both of	few	more	one of
a couple	~~a lot of~~	as many	every	less	much	some

ALICIA: Diego, we're still spending _____*a lot of*_____ money on things we don't really need.
    1.
After I pay the bills this month, we're going to have even _____ cash left over
                                                                2.
than we did last month. We've got to save for next semester's tuition, remember? We're not
saving enough money. If we don't start saving _____, one of us is going to
                                              3.
have to take the semester off.

DIEGO: OK, but what have we bought that we don't need?

ALICIA: That exercise machine, for one thing. We've only used it _____ times. We
                                                                4.
could get a year's membership at the gym for what it cost and still have something left over.

DIEGO: You mean _____ us could get a membership, don't you?
                  5.

ALICIA: No, _____ us could. That's what I'm saying. The machine cost $600, and
            6.
memberships are $250 each. How about selling the thing and going to the gym?

DIEGO: Hmm. Maybe you're right. What else?

ALICIA: Well, we're spending about _____ extra a month on those premium cable
                                    7.
channels. We wouldn't have _____ channels to choose from if we went back
                            8.
to the basic coverage, but we don't watch very _____ TV anyway. We're
                                                9.
always studying.

DIEGO: Yeah, you're right. . . . And you know, I'd say we could get rid of the land line. We've used it
very _____ times in recent months, and it's expensive. We wouldn't have
     10.
_____ telemarketing calls, either, because telemarketers don't call cell
    11.
phone numbers.

ALICIA: OK. Let's cancel it, then. And here's one more suggestion. We should start taking a sack
lunch to the college _____ of times a week instead of eating out at noon. If
                      12.
we did these four things, we'd have _____ money left _____
                                     13.   14.
month, and we could use it to pay next semester's bills.

DIEGO: Oh no! Not my lunches with the guys! Lunchtime is when I get to see them.

ALICIA: Invite them over to study and then have dinner afterwards.

EXERCISE 4 QUANTIFIERS AND NUMBERS

GRAMMAR NOTES 2, 4–5, 7 Imagine that you are researching statistics for a class assignment. Study the chart. Then complete each sentence with the appropriate quantifier from the box.

Categories	The World in 1960	The World in 2009–2015
Population	3,020,100,000	7,315,000,000 (2015)
Birth rate per thousand people	31.2	19.15 (2012)
Death rate per thousand people	17.7	8.37 (2009)
Female life expectancy at birth	51.9 years	68.07 years (2009)
Male life expectancy at birth	48.6 years	64.29 years (2009)
World literacy (the number of people 15 and older who can read and write)	42%	83% (2010)
Female literacy	42%	80% (2012)
Male literacy	58%	89% (2012)

Notes: The figures above are based on the most recent statistics available and are approximations.
Literacy = the number of people 15 and older who can read and write
Illiteracy = the inability to read and write

a great deal	all	a lot of	fewer	less	~~many~~	more	the number of

1. There were more than twice as _____ *many* _____ people in the world in 2015 as there were in 1960.

2. There were _____ births per thousand people in 2012 than in 1960, which shows that global efforts to avoid overpopulation have been successful.

3. There were _____ deaths per thousand people in 1960 than in 2014. This statistic proves that we have made great progress in improving world health.

4. Since 1960, there has been _____ progress in increasing the life expectancy of both men and women.

5. Today, as in 1960, there is _____ male illiteracy than female illiteracy. In other words, more men can read than women.

6. _____ literate females in the world is still lower than that of men, an indication that there is still a lot of work to be done in educating women around the world.

7. Literacy in the world has increased _____ since 1960, which is very encouraging to those involved in global education reform.

8. Literacy rates have been rising, but they need to rise even more. When _____ the people in the world know how to read and write, we will have achieved our goal.

EXERCISE 5 REDUCING *OF* IN QUANTIFIERS

▶ 12|03 **PRONUNCIATION NOTE** Listen to each sentence. How is the quantifier pronounced? Check (✓) *Full Form* or *Reduced Form*.

		Full Form	Reduced Form
1.	I've made lots of friends in my classes.	☐	✓
2.	I've got plenty of assignments to finish this weekend.	☐	☐
3.	The amount of traffic on the freeway was discouraging.	☐	☐
4.	I did a number of exercises in my grammar book.	☐	☐
5.	There are a lot of amazing professors at our school.	☐	☐
6.	I was able to answer most of the questions on the exam.	☐	☐
7.	Mary bought a couple of apples for us to eat.	☐	☐
8.	Bill had a bit of trouble finishing his term paper.	☐	☐
9.	Most of the students passed the exam.	☐	☐
10.	Many of the examples are difficult to understand.	☐	☐

EXERCISE 6 EDITING

GRAMMAR NOTES 1–7 Read the excerpt from a college student's speech in an "If I Were President" debate. There are ten mistakes in the use of quantifiers. The first one is already corrected. Find and correct nine more.

My fellow citizens: We are at a time in our history when we need to make some real sacrifices.
                                                                          many
Recent presidents have made a great ~~deal of~~ promises they didn't keep. Tonight you deserve

to hear the truth. On the economy, we've made little progress, but we still have a great many

work to do. That's why I'm proposing several measures. First, I want to raise taxes on the very

wealthy because a few of them really pay their share. Second, many members of the middle class

are carrying an unfair tax burden, so I'm asking for a tax cut for them. Third, there are much

loopholes in the current laws that allow any people to avoid paying any taxes at all. I want to close

these loopholes.

We have more problems to deal with. One major one is this: We have relatively few money

available for education reform, and we've also made a little progress in decreasing pollution and

meeting clean air standards. Therefore, as my final measure, I am asking Congress to approve a

50-cent-a-gallon increased tax on gasoline. This will create great deal of additional revenue. My

goal is to make a college education affordable for every people who desire it.

Go to MyEnglishLab for more focused practice.

EXERCISE 7   LISTENING

 A Listen to the conversation between a college student and his professor. What is Luis's problem?

_____

_____

B Listen again. Then complete the sentences about the Listening. Circle the correct answers.

1. Luis has missed a lot of / (a few) assignments.

2. Luis has failed a number of tests / one test.

3. Luis can understand few / most of the short stories he has read.

4. Luis feels he understands some / a little of the poetry he has read.

5. The professor thinks Luis is taking too many / few classes this term.

6. The professor recommends that Luis take few / fewer classes next term.

7. Luis works many / a few hours every week.

8. There are no / a couple of students who are willing to help Luis.

9. The professor thinks Luis can pass the class if he does a bit / a lot of work.

10. Luis will also have to turn in most / all of his regular assignments.

C Work with a partner. Discuss the questions.

1. Should professors or tutors be available to help students who are having difficulty in classes? If so, what would be a reasonable number of hours of availability per week?

2. What should be the maximum number of classes a student may take each semester?

3. How many hours a week should students be permitted to work while taking classes?

EXERCISE 8   WHAT ABOUT YOU?

A CONVERSATION You are going to have a conversation comparing your life now to your life before you started studying English. Write eight sentences using each of the quantifiers from the box.

a few	a great deal of	a little	a lot of	fewer	less	many	more

B Work with a partner. Talk about the changes in your life. Compare them with your partner's changes. Then report interesting examples to the class.

EXAMPLE: A: I have more work to do now than I did before I started studying English.
          B: I have less work now. Before I started studying, I had a lot of work to do . . .

EXERCISE 9 CHINA HAS MANY PEOPLE

A PRESENTATION Imagine you are a student in a geography class. You are going to give a presentation about a country. Look at the chart about China. Then pick a country from the box, or choose another country. Complete the chart about that country. Do research on the Internet if necessary.

Argentina	Egypt	Nicaragua
Australia	India	Nigeria
Brazil	Kenya	Somalia
Canada	Libya	United States

Country	China	
Number of people	1.3 billion	
Size/Land area	3.705 million sq miles (9.597 million sq kilometers)	
Number of cities with over one million people	160 cities	
Literacy	96.4 %	
Number of rivers	Almost 50,000	
Number of mountains	Thousands	
Amount of oil produced	4.189 million barrels daily	

B Work with a partner. Present your information on the country you researched. Listen to his or her presentation.

C Compare the country you researched with your partner's country. Ask and answer the following questions. Then report your answers to the class.

1. Which country has more people?

   EXAMPLE: **A:** Your country is China, and my country is Argentina. Which country has more people?
   B: China has more people than Argentina.

2. Which country has a greater land area?

3. Which country has a larger number of cities over one million people?

4. Which country has a higher amount of literacy?

5. Which country has fewer rivers?

6. Which country has fewer mountains?

7. Which country produces less oil?

EXERCISE 10 STUDY SKILLS

INFORMATION GAP Work with a partner. Student A will follow the instructions below.
Student B will follow the instructions on page 441.

STUDENT A

- The article below is missing some information. Your partner has the same article that contains your missing information. Ask your partner questions to find the missing information.

  EXAMPLE: **A:** Who feels most alert early in the morning?
  B: Many people feel most alert early in the morning.

- Your partner's article is missing different information. Answer your partner's questions so that he or she can fill in the missing information.

  EXAMPLE: **B:** Who is at their best late at night?
  A: A few people are at their best late at night.

Want to be the best student you can be? Here are several suggestions.

■ Do your studying when you are the most awake and alert. _____

feel most alert early in the morning. A few people, however, are at their best late at night.

Identify your own particular characteristics.

■ Take _____ in class. Some students prefer just to listen to a

lecture, believing that note-taking distracts them from what the professor is saying. Relatively

_____, however, learn effectively by following this strategy.

You interact with the course material when you take notes about it, and that kind of active

learning is highly beneficial.

■ Review your notes regularly. Do this every day if possible. You don't have to spend

_____ doing this. Going over your notes for a few minutes

daily can really help you to learn and retain information.

■ Examine your lifestyle and make improvements in it if necessary. According to a well-known

English proverb, "_____ makes Jack a dull boy." You need to

work hard, but your life will be dull indeed if you never have any fun. Build in time for

entertainment and socializing. And while you're at it, make sure you eat healthy food and get

_____. You'll have fewer problems and less stress if you do.

■ Finish whatever you start. Once you start something, keep working at it until you've made a

visible amount of progress. Then stay with the project until it's done. If you don't do this, you'll

simply waste _____. Don't worry if this takes a long time.

Rome wasn't built in a day, but it did get built.

Go to **My**English**Lab** for more communication practice.

FROM GRAMMAR TO WRITING

A **BEFORE YOU WRITE** You are going to write about your study habits and how you would like to improve them. Write a few sentences about the ways in which you study and what you would like to change.

B **WRITE** Using your ideas in A, write a five-paragraph essay about improving your study habits. Remember to use quantifiers with nouns and pronouns. Try to avoid the common mistakes in the chart. Use the example below to help you begin your essay.

EXAMPLE: I need to improve my study habits. The first thing I need to do is to get more sleep. I do most of my studying in the late evening, and I don't get to bed until about 1:00 a.m. I get up at 6:30 a.m., so I'm tired all day. When I try to study, I have very little energy, so I don't remember many of the things I work on.

Another thing I need to work on is to take more notes in class. All of my teachers have said I can use my laptop to take notes in class, so I'm going to start using it. I have enough speed as a typist to take down everything my professors say. . . .

Common Mistakes in Using Quantifiers

Don't use *amount* with **count nouns**. Use *number*.	I was amazed by **the number of** people there. **NOT** I was amazed by the ~~amount~~ of people there.
Don't use *less* with **count nouns**. Use *fewer*.	I made **fewer mistakes** on this week's exam. **NOT** I made ~~less~~ mistakes on this week's exam.
Avoid using *much* in **affirmative sentences** except in very formal English. Use *a lot of*, *lots of*, or *a great deal of*.	I have **a lot of energy** in the morning. **NOT** I have ~~much~~ energy in the morning.
Don't use *a few* and *a little* in sentences with a **negative sense**. Use *few* and *little*.	He's lived here for years, but he has **few friends** and **little social interaction**. **NOT** He's lived here for years, but he has ~~a few~~ friends and ~~a little~~ social interaction.

C **CHECK YOUR WORK** Look at your essay. Underline quantifiers and the nouns they occur with. Use the Editing Checklist to check your work.

Editing Checklist

Did you . . . ?

- ☐ use *amount* with non-count nouns and *number* with count nouns
- ☐ use *less* with non-count nouns and *fewer* with count nouns
- ☐ avoid using *much* in affirmative sentences
- ☐ use *few* and *little* in sentences with a negative sense

D **REVISE YOUR WORK** Read your essay again. Can you improve your writing? Make changes if necessary.

Go to MyEnglishLab for more writing practice.

UNIT 12 REVIEW

Test yourself on the grammar of the unit.

(A) Complete the sentences. Circle the correct answers.

1. Most / Most of people can study more easily in quiet places.

2. I can't believe the number / amount of homework we have to do in this class.

3. I have a big test tomorrow, but I don't have some / any time to study today.

4. My friend Ali earned a lot of / much money at his part-time job.

5. Can you please get me few / a couple of candy bars at the store?

6. The number / amount of students at this college has increased.

7. About how much / many people are in your biology class?

8. Bob's problem is that he has little / a little motivation to pass his classes.

9. We have plenty / plenty of glasses and plates, so don't bring any.

10. We have any / no money left after our night on the town.

(B) Look at each underlined word or phrase. Write a quantifier that has a similar meaning to it.

1. I have made a lot of friends in my English class. _____

2. I don't have a lot of homework to finish this afternoon. _____

3. He has a great deal of money in the bank. _____

4. Andrea has some problems in her Chinese class. _____

5. There are many problems with your plan. _____

6. Each person in the class earned a good score on the test. _____

(C) Find and correct four mistakes.

On the whole, I have lot of fun at my new job. I earn less money than I used to, but I have a lot fewer stress. Most of my co-workers are responsible and work hard, but a few of them do a little if any work. The majority of my colleagues have a lot of experience, so I can ask them for advice and help. The only real negative about my new position is the number of traffic on the roads in the morning and afternoon.

Now check your answers on page 429.

Go to MyEnglishLab to complete the review online.

OUTCOMES
- Add more information about nouns with adjective and noun modifiers
- Identify an author's attitude in a magazine article
- Identify key details in a conversation
- Engage in a literary analysis of a short story
- Discuss experiences with overcoming obstacles
- Write an essay discussing expectations about life events

STEP 1	GRAMMAR IN CONTEXT

BEFORE YOU READ

Discuss the questions.

1. What is the difference between hoping for something to happen and expecting it to happen?

2. In your experience, does what you expect to happen usually happen? Give an example.

3. How can expectations be a negative force? How can they be a positive force?

READ

 13|01 Read this article about expectations.

I Hope for It, but I Don't Expect It

It's the 22nd Winter Olympics in Sochi, Russia. Slovenian skier Tina Maze has emerged as a strong favorite to medal in the super-combined women's downhill in alpine skiing. In her record-breaking season of 2012–2013, Maze had won eleven World Cup medals, and she had previously earned two silver medals in the 2010 Vancouver Winter Olympics. Many expect her to win this downhill race, but she doesn't. After finishing in the number four position, she says, "Somebody had to finish fourth." Two days later, however, the situation is different. Few if any are expecting Maze to take a gold medal in the women's downhill race, but take one she does. Amazingly, Tina ends up tied with Swiss skier Dominique Gisin. The two skiers finish with exactly the same time, the first time this has happened in a Winter Olympics. Maze later says she'd thought she'd blown her chance[1] for a gold medal because in the second part of the race she'd made some small mistakes. But the 30-year-old Maze wins Slovenia's first gold medal ever—even though after her supposed "mistakes" she hadn't expected to win at all.

Tina Maze kisses the snow after her win

---
1 *blown her chance:* lost her opportunity

It's the weekend, and you and your friend feel like going to a movie. You search the local movie listings, but nothing sounds particularly interesting. Then you remember that a film website has recommended the Academy Award-nominated film *Her*. The website raves about its fascinating plot, its excellent color photography, and its awesome commentary on our culture's technological addiction. The movie is about a man who writes love letters for others and ends up falling in love with the operating system on his computer. You find this an amusing idea and are curious to see how the movie storyline will be developed. So you go to the movie, expecting to like it . . . but as you watch it you find it full of increasingly preposterous[2] and unconvincing events. Contrary to your expectations, you end up disliking the movie. Your friend, who didn't read any reviews prior to seeing the movie, winds up having much more positive feelings about it than you do.

In the movie *Her*, Theodore Twombly falls in love with his computer's operating system

These two situations illustrate what we might call "the mystery of expectations." On the one hand, events often have surprising outcomes that turn out much more positively than we had expected. On the other hand, events often do not turn out as we feel they will or should. Sometimes children do not meet their parents' career expectations of them; athletes do not win the contests people expect them to win; great literature doesn't live up to its reputation. I asked a psychology instructor at a local university whether she thought expectations can actually make things turn out negatively, or whether we're merely talking about an unpleasant, frustrating irony[3] of the human condition. She observed that the mind has immense power to control outcomes. In sporting competitions, for instance, she noted that athletes sometimes concentrate too hard and make mistakes they wouldn't normally make. They miss the basket, don't hit the ball, or lose the race. In effect, they're letting their expectations control them.

I then asked the professor if she had ever experienced this phenomenon in her everyday life. She said she had, many times: "Let me give you a personal example from skiing that shows the mind's tremendous power. There are days when I feel like a tense, cautious intermediate skier, and I stand at the top of a steep, icy slope, plotting my every move down the course. I fear that I'll fall, thereby ensuring that

---

2 *preposterous:* ridiculous, absurd
3 *irony:* a condition that is the opposite of what is expected

I do fall. Other days I feel different. My expectations are miles away. I forget about myself, ski well, and don't fall. To be successful, people should concentrate on the process instead of the goal. When they persist in placing an excessive focus on goals, they often fail. Have you heard the phrase 'trying too hard'? That's what people often do."

I asked the professor about her overall recommendation for dealing with the phenomenon of expectations. Her concluding statement was this: "It's better to hope for things than to expect them." Good suggestion, I thought.

AFTER YOU READ

A VOCABULARY Match the words in **bold** with their meanings.

_____ 1. Tina Maze has **emerged** as a favorite to win a medal.

_____ 2. The website **raves about** the movie's fascinating plot.

_____ 3. **Contrary** to your expectations, you dislike the picture.

_____ 4. The mind has the power to control any **outcome**.

_____ 5. It's caused by **intense** concentration.

_____ 6. I become afraid, **thereby** guaranteeing that I'll fall.

_____ 7. My fear will **ensure** my eventual fall.

_____ 8. We sometimes **persist** in focusing too much on goals.

a. make certain to happen

b. opposite

c. because of that

d. continue

e. praises highly

f. appeared

g. effect or result

h. very strong

B COMPREHENSION Read the statements. Check (✓) *True* or *False*.

	True	False
1. Tina Maze was expected to medal in the super-combined race.	☐	☐
2. Maze had never had a record-breaking season before 2014.	☐	☐
3. Maze had earned silver medals in an earlier Winter Olympics.	☐	☐
4. Few people expect Maze to take a gold medal in the downhill.	☐	☐
5. The movie *Her* is about a writer who falls in love with a woman.	☐	☐
6. *Her* makes a commentary on our present-day addiction to technology.	☐	☐
7. The human mind often controls outcomes of situations.	☐	☐
8. People usually fail because they are not trying hard enough.	☐	☐

C DISCUSSION Work with a partner. Compare and justify your answers in B. Then discuss this question: Do you find the author's arguments about expectations convincing? Give an example from your personal experience that supports or opposes the arguments.

Go to MyEnglishLab for more grammar in context practice.

MODIFICATION OF NOUNS

	Adjective Modifier	Noun Modifier	Head Noun
I remember the		Winter	Olympics.
	wonderful		athletes.
	amazing	downhill	races.
	unexpected	Slovenian	victory.

Order of Modifiers

	Opinion	Size	Age	Shape	Color	Origin	Material	Purpose	
I saw a	great		new			French		action	movie.
I met its	fascinating		young			Chinese			director.
She had		large		round			jade		earrings.
She wore a		long			red		silk	party	dress.

Several Modifiers

Different Modifier Categories	Same Modifier Category
A **great new epic** movie	A **serious**, **profound**, and **heartwarming** movie A **serious**, **profound**, **heartwarming** movie A **heartwarming**, **profound**, **serious** movie

Compound Modifiers

The movie has lots of	**computer-generated** **strange-looking**	scenes. creatures.
The main character is a	**thirteen-year-old** **long-haired**, **short-legged**	girl. boy.

GRAMMAR NOTES

1 Types of Modifiers

Nouns can be **modified** both by **adjectives** and by **other nouns**.

Adjective and noun modifiers usually come before the noun they modify. The noun they modify is called the **head noun**.

ADJECTIVE MODIFIERS	NOUN MODIFIER	HEAD NOUN

Neymar is a **famous Brazilian   soccer   player**.

Noun modifiers usually come **directly before** the **noun** they modify.

Milk chocolate is chocolate made with milk.
Chocolate milk is milk with chocolate in it.

When there are **both adjective** and **noun modifiers** in a sentence, the **noun modifier comes closer** to the head noun.

ADJECTIVE MODIFIER	NOUN MODIFIER	HEAD NOUN

She is a **good   tennis   player**.

2 Adjective Modifiers

Two common types of adjective modifiers are **present participles** and **past participles**.

Present participial modifiers, which end in -*ing*, often describe someone or something that **causes a feeling**.	It was a **boring** movie.
	  (*The movie caused the viewers to be bored.*)
	We heard some **shocking** news today.
	  (*The news caused people to be shocked.*)

Past participial modifiers, which end in -*ed* or -*n*, often describe someone who **experiences a feeling**.	The **bored** viewers left the movie.
	  (*The viewers experienced the feeling of boredom.*)
	There were a lot of **shocked** people who heard the news.
	  (*The people experienced the feeling of shock.*)

3 Order of Modifiers

When there is **more than one modifier** of a noun, the modifiers occur in a **fixed order**.

The following is the usual order of modifiers, from first to last position:

POSITION	CATEGORY OF MODIFIER	
1	opinion	**ugly**, **beautiful**, **dull**, **interesting**
2	size	**big**, **tall**, **long**, **short**
3	age or temperature	**old**, **young**, **hot**, **cold**
4	shape	**square**, **round**, **oval**, **triangular**
5	color	**red**, **blue**, **pink**, **purple**
6	origin, nationality, social class	**computer-generated**, **Congolese**, **middle-class**
7	material	**wood**, **cotton**, **denim**, **silk**, **glass**
8	purpose	**action**, **party**, **sports**, **residential**

The order can be changed to reflect the emphasis a speaker or writer wants to give to a particular adjective.	He was a **young, interesting** man.
	  (*emphasis on* **young**)
	He was an **interesting young** man.
	  (*emphasis on* **interesting**)

4 Modifiers in the Same Category

When a noun has **two or more modifiers** in the **same category**, separate the adjectives with a **comma**. If the modifiers are in **different** categories, **do not separate** the modifiers with a comma.	He is a **serious, hardworking** student.
	  (*same category*)
	I bought a **beautiful denim** shirt.
	  (*different categories*)

One way to determine whether adjectives are in the same category is to add the word *and* between the modifiers. If the resulting statement is **logical**, the modifiers are in the same category.	He is a **serious and hardworking** student.
	  (*logical—same category*)
	NOT I bought a ~~beautiful and denim~~ shirt.
	  (*not logical—different categories*)

The **order** of adjectives in the **same category** can **vary**.	He is a **serious, hardworking** student. He is a **hardworking, serious** student.

5 Compound Modifiers

Compound modifiers are constructed from **more than one word**.

There are four common kinds of compound modifiers: • **number + noun** • **noun + present participle** • **noun + past participle** • **adjective + past participle**	I work in a **twelve-story** building. It's a **prize-winning** film. It's a **crime-related** problem. The actor plays a **long-haired, one-armed** pirate in the movie.
Compound modifiers that **precede** a noun are usually **hyphenated**. If they occur **after** a noun, they are usually **not hyphenated**.	It's a **computer-generated** program. The program is **computer generated**.
BE CAREFUL! Plural nouns used as modifiers become **singular** when they come **before** the noun.	Her daughter is ten years old. She has a **ten-year-old** daughter. **NOT** She has a ~~ten-years-old~~ daughter.

6 Number of Modifiers

In general, the **number** of adjective and noun modifiers in a sentence should be **limited**.

Avoid using more than **three adjective modifiers** in a sentence.	That **tall, beautiful, energetic** woman is my sister.
Avoid using more than **one or two noun modifiers** in a sentence.	We went to a **baseball** game last night.
BE CAREFUL! Sentences containing more than two noun modifiers can be confusing. Break up a string of noun modifiers with prepositional phrases or rearrange the modifiers in some other way.	**Student** Jerry Gonzales won the award for painting portraits. **OR** Jerry Gonzales won the award for **portrait** painting. **NOT** Jerry Gonzales won the ~~student portrait painter~~ award.

 13|02 ## PRONUNCIATION NOTE

Pausing With Modifiers of Nouns

When the **modifiers** of a noun are in the **same category**, we normally **pause** between them in speaking. In writing, we place a **comma** between them. When modifiers of nouns are in **different categories**, we **do not normally pause** between them in speaking, and we do not separate the modifiers with commas in writing.

• modifiers in the **same category**	It was an **icy, dark, stormy** evening. He is an **arrogant, opinionated, proud** man.
• modifiers in **different categories**	I'm going to wear my **round blue sapphire** earrings. He is an **elderly middle-class** man.

Go to MyEnglishLab to watch the grammar presentation.

EXERCISE 1 DISCOVER THE GRAMMAR

GRAMMAR NOTES 1–6 Read the sentences based on the reading. Circle all head nouns that have noun or adjective modifiers before them. Underline adjective modifiers once and noun modifiers twice.

1. It's the 22nd <u>Winter</u> <u><u>Olympics</u></u>.

2. Maze is a favorite to medal in the women's downhill.

3. Few if any are expecting Maze to take a gold medal.

4. Maze ends up tied with a Swiss skier.

5. Your friend has recommended the Academy Award-nominated *Her*.

6. The website raves about its awesome commentary on our technological addiction.

7. The movie is full of preposterous, unconvincing events.

8. Children sometimes do not meet their parents' career expectations for them.

9. I stand at the top of a steep, icy slope.

10. We sometimes have an excessive focus on goals.

EXERCISE 2 MULTIPLE MODIFIERS

GRAMMAR NOTES 3–5 Bill and Nancy are dressing for a party being thrown by Nancy's new boss. Nancy isn't sure what is expected and is worried about making a bad impression. Complete their conversation. Unscramble the modifiers in parentheses. Place commas where they are needed.

BILL: This is a _____*formal office*_____ party, isn't it? What if I wear my
                 1. (office / formal)

_____ tie?
    2. (silk / new)

NANCY: That's fine, but don't wear that _____ shirt with it.
                      3. (purple / denim / ugly)

People will think you don't have any _____ clothes.
                          4. (formal / suitable)

BILL: So what? Why should I pretend I like to dress up when I don't?

NANCY: Because there are going to be a lot of _____
                             5. (interesting / important)

people there, and I want to make a _____
                      6. (memorable / good)

impression. It's my job, remember? I don't want people to think my husband is a

_____ dresser. Humor me just this once, OK?
    7. (unstylish / sloppy)

Hmm. . . . I wonder if I should wear my _____
                      8. (round / sapphire)

earrings or the _____ ones.
         9. (green / oval / emerald)

(Later, at the party.)

NANCY: Hi, Paul. This is Bill, my husband.

PAUL: Welcome. Bill, I'm glad to meet you. Help yourselves to snacks. There are some

_____ sandwiches.
10. (tomato-and-cheese / excellent)

NANCY: Thanks!

PAUL: Nancy, I guess you expected this to be a _____ party.
11. (formal / fancy)

Sorry I didn't make it clear that it's casual. I hope you won't feel out of place.

BILL: Thanks. We'll be fine. By the way, Paul, that _____ shirt
12. (beautiful / denim / purple)

you're wearing is great. Where did you get it?

EXERCISE 3 COMPOUND MODIFIERS

GRAMMAR NOTE 5 Complete the sentences with compound modifiers. Use the words in parentheses. Add the indefinite articles *a* or *an* where necessary.

Pam and Allen Murray took their daughter Heather to a reading specialist because Heather

could not read aloud in class. Heather told Dr. Parker, the specialist, that she got frustrated in

her reading class because the teacher was having the students read aloud every day. Even though

it was only ___*a fifty-minute*___ period, to Heather, it seemed like a year. When the
1. (fifty minutes)

teacher called on Heather to read aloud, Heather would panic every time, even if it was only

_____ assignment. Dr. Parker asked Heather if she had any
2. (one paragraph)

problems with silent reading. Heather said she didn't, adding that she loved to

read to herself and could finish _____ book in a day or two.
3. (300 pages)

Dr. Parker asked how long this problem had been going on. Allen said it had

begun when Heather was in the first grade. Since Heather was now twelve, the

situation had become _____ ordeal. Dr. Parker wondered
4. (six years)

how the problem had started. Pam replied that she felt it was definitely

_____ problem, since Heather had lisped when she started
5. (related to stress)

school. Heather added that she had felt bad when the other children would

laugh at her when she pronounced her "s" sounds as "th" sounds. Dr. Parker

agreed that teasing might have caused Heather's problem but

suggested another possibility—that Heather's inability to read

aloud could be _____ problem. She asked if
6. (related to eyesight)

it would be all right to test Heather's vision. When the Murrays

agreed, Dr. Parker asked Heather to read two eye charts, which she was able to read perfectly. She then asked Heather to read a sentence that she held at a distance. "The gunfighter walked down the street wearing _____ hat." Heather read the sentence with no
7. (ten gallons)
difficulty at all.

After this test, Dr. Parker told Heather's parents that Heather had _____
8. (induced by performance)
anxiety. Since Heather had often failed before, she expected to fail again . . . unless she was distracted and encouraged to think about something else before she read. During the test, Dr. Parker had distracted Heather by referring to her vision.

Dr. Parker said that she had _____ program that would teach Heather
9. (two months)
to read aloud proficiently. Heather was more than willing to try it, so the Murrays made arrangements to start the program soon.

EXERCISE 4 MODIFIERS IN SENTENCES

GRAMMAR NOTES 2–5 Write a sentence for each phrase, changing the phrase so that the modifier appears before the head noun. Use correct punctuation.

1. a flight that takes ten hours

   Last month, I was on a ten-hour flight from Bogotá to Buenos Aires.

2. a project for work that was stressful

   _____

3. a jacket that is old and comfortable

   _____

4. an experience that surprises and amuses me

   _____

5. a child who is eleven years old

   _____

6. a movie that wins an award

   _____

7. an outcome that was disappointing and unexpected

   _____

8. expectations that are unrealistic and naïve

   _____

9. a skirt that is made of cotton, is short, is blue, and is expensive

   _____

EXERCISE 5 PAUSING WITH MODIFIERS OF NOUNS

▶13|03 **A** PRONUNCIATION NOTE Listen to the sentences. Then write each sentence, placing commas and hyphens where necessary.

B Work in pairs. Compare your sentences in A. Discuss why you think your punctuation and spelling are correct. Then check the answers on page 436.

EXERCISE 6 EDITING

GRAMMAR NOTES 1–6 Read the entry from medical student Jennifer Yu's computer journal. There are nine mistakes in the use of modifiers. The first mistake is already corrected. Find and correct eight more.

FRIDAY: It's midnight, the end of a long day. My first week of ~~school medical~~ *medical school* is over, and I'm exhausted but happy! Everything has exceeded my expectations. I knew I'd be working hard, but my classes are a lot more interesting than I thought they'd be. I'm not completely sure yet, but I think I want to go into psychiatry child because I love working with children—especially nine- and- ten-years-old kids.

Yesterday our psychiatry class visited a large new hospital where many middle-class troubled children go for treatment. I expected to see a lot of boys and girls behaving badly, but most of them were pretty quiet and relaxed. They just looked like they needed some warm, personal attention.

Today in our surgery class we had a bright, hardworking teacher, a Brazilian young doctor who was substituting for our usual professor. I didn't expect a whole lot from a substitute, but this guy gave us an international helpful viewpoint on things.

The only thing I don't like about medical school is the cafeteria disgusting food. I'm going to have to start getting some Chinese hot tasty food from my favorite local place.

I just downloaded a computer new program, and I hope it works correctly. But it's time for me to get some sleep now, so I'll try it out tomorrow.

Go to MyEnglishLab for more focused practice.

EXERCISE 7   LISTENING

13|04 **A** Listen. What is Josh's problem, and, according to the coach, what is causing it?

_____

_____

13|04 **B** Read the statements. Then listen to the conversation again. Check (✓) *True* or *False*.

		True	False
1.	Josh is having a difficult time right now.	✓	☐
2.	Josh thinks he's no longer a good baseball player.	☐	☐
3.	Josh is now playing on a high school baseball team.	☐	☐
4.	Josh's strong point used to be throwing the ball.	☐	☐
5.	Josh's batting average is OK in practices.	☐	☐
6.	The coach says few other players have had the same problem as Josh has.	☐	☐
7.	The coach says Josh should stop being afraid.	☐	☐
8.	The coach says it's a good idea for Josh to compare himself to others.	☐	☐
9.	Josh has been considering leaving the team.	☐	☐
10.	Josh should have a higher batting average if he worries less.	☐	☐

C DISCUSSION   Work with a partner. Do you think the strategy that the coach suggests is an effective way of dealing with an expectation-based problem? Why or why not? Discuss.

EXERCISE 8 A FAMOUS STORY

A **CRITICAL THINKING** You are going to analyze a famous Arabic story. First, read the story.

Death Speaks

Long ago, a kind, wealthy nobleman lived in Baghdad. One day, he sent his chief servant to the crowded marketplace to buy food. Before long, the frightened servant returned. "Master," he said, "when I was in the marketplace just now, I had a terrifying experience. I was about to pay for things when a strange woman bumped me, and I turned to see that it was Death. She was wearing a single-piece black garment, and she waved her bony white hands and put a spell on me. Master, may I please borrow your strongest horse? It is not my time to die, so I will ride to Samarra to avoid my fate. Please let me have the horse; I must ride quickly." The nobleman gave the servant his best horse, and the servant rode away as fast as he could.

The curious, worried nobleman went to the marketplace and soon encountered me in the crowd. "Why did you wave your arms at my servant and cast a wicked spell on him?" he asked me.

"I did not cast a wicked spell on him, or any other kind of spell," I answered. "When I saw him, I waved my hands because I couldn't believe my eyes. You see, I was very surprised to see him in Baghdad since I am to meet him tonight in Samarra."

B Work with a partner. Answer the questions.

1. Who is the narrator of the story?
2. How would you describe the narrator's physical appearance?
3. How did the servant feel when he returned from the marketplace? Why did he feel this way?
4. Why did the servant want to ride to Samarra?
5. What does the story suggest about escaping from fate?

C Work in a group. What do you think the story shows about expectations? Discuss.

EXAMPLE: **A:** I think the poor, frightened servant expects to die because he thinks Death cast a spell on him.

  B: I agree, but I also think the servant expects to escape that fate....

EXERCISE 9 OVERCOMING A PROBLEM

A DISCUSSION Work in a group. Has anyone in your group dealt with one of the problems listed below? If not, does someone know a person who has? What was the problem? How did the person overcome it?

- dealing with public-speaking anxiety
- not being able to get hired for a worthwhile job
- failing tests even though you have studied hard
- losing athletic competitions because you were nervous
- dealing with a problem of unfair treatment

B Work with another group. Discuss your findings. What similarities or differences do you see in the ways people dealt with their problems?

EXAMPLE: **A:** I have dealt with public-speaking anxiety. I couldn't participate in classroom discussions because I didn't think I had interesting things to say. I expected people to get bored when I talked. I overcame my anxiety problem by forcing myself to say one small thing every day in class.

B: I know someone else who had public-speaking anxiety. He felt anxious about public speaking because his English pronunciation wasn't very good. . . .

EXERCISE 10
NO ONE EXPECTED
IT TO SINK . . .

A PICTURE DISCUSSION
Work with a partner. Look at the picture of the sinking of the *Titanic* in April 1912. Describe what you see, using as many modifiers as possible. Write down your sentences. Then share your sentences with another pair.

The ship was sinking into the dark, icy ocean waters.

B Work in a group. Discuss what the picture and the situation suggest about expectations.

EXAMPLE: The *Titanic* was supposed to be an unsinkable ship. Its builders didn't expect it to sink. . . .

Go to MyEnglishLab for more communication practice.

FROM GRAMMAR TO WRITING

A **BEFORE YOU WRITE** You are going to write an essay about the kinds of expectations people have about major life experiences. Choose one of the following topics and write a few sentences about it.

- marriage
- family
- career
- education

B **WRITE** Using your ideas in A, write a five-paragraph essay about your view of people's expectations about a major life experience. Remember to use adjective and noun modifiers with head nouns. Try to avoid the common mistakes shown in the chart. Use the example below to help you begin your essay.

EXAMPLE: Many people have very traditional marriage expectations. First, they expect to find the perfect husband or wife that they'll always be in love with. . . .

Second, many expect their marriage to be a never-ending honeymoon. They think nothing will ever go wrong. . . .

Third, many newly married people expect that they'll soon live in a nice house and have intelligent, beautiful children. . . .

Common Mistakes in Using Adjective and Noun Modifiers

Don't separate **modifiers in different categories** with commas. Separate **modifiers in the same category** with **commas**.	I bought my wife a **beautiful silk blouse**. **NOT** I bought my wife a beautiful, silk blouse. *Hugo* is a **heartwarming, substantive film**. **NOT** *Hugo* is a ~~heartwarming substantive~~ film.
Don't use plural compound modifiers when they come **before** a **head noun**. Use **single** compound modifiers.	It's **a three-hour trip**. **NOT** It's a ~~three-hours~~ trip.
Don't use multiple noun modifiers of a head noun in a single sentence. Use **one or two noun modifiers**.	Bill won the high school award for basketball players. **NOT** Bill won the ~~high school basketball player~~ award.

C **CHECK YOUR WORK** Look at your essay. Underline adjective modifiers once and noun modifiers twice. Circle head nouns. Use the Editing Checklist to check your work.

Editing Checklist

Did you . . . ?

- [ ] avoid separating modifiers in different categories with commas
- [ ] separate modifiers in the same category with commas
- [ ] use singular compound modifiers before a head noun
- [ ] use no more than two noun modifiers of a head noun

D **REVISE YOUR WORK** Read your essay again. Can you improve your writing? Make changes if necessary.

Go to MyEnglishLab for more writing practice.

UNIT 13 REVIEW

Test yourself on the grammar of the unit.

Ⓐ Complete the sentences by putting the modifiers in the correct order.

1. It was a _____ day.
   (humid / summer / sweltering)

2. She was nervous about the _____ interview.
   (job / challenging / five-hour)

3. I'm going to wear my _____ shirt.
   (cotton / striped / new)

4. We were introduced to the _____ actor.
   (Asian / young / handsome)

5. I didn't think the team would do so well in the _____ game.
   (soccer / World Cup / last)

6. She lived in a _____ cabin.
   (little / dirty / old)

Ⓑ Rewrite each phrase so that the modifiers come before the noun.

1. a son who is eleven years old   _____

2. a pleasure that was unexpected   _____

3. a new experience that was surprising _____

4. six periods of fifty-five minutes each _____

5. a proposal initiated by voters   _____

6. a building with forty-five stories   _____

7. a statue from China made of ivory   _____

8. a cat that is gray and heavy   _____

Ⓒ Find and correct six mistakes.

Over the weekend, I attended a film wonderful festival. As I expected, the films were excellent in general, with one major exception. This one exception was a horror terrible movie with a lot of special silly effects and strange looking creatures. The best film overall, surprisingly, was a digitally remastered version of *Gone with the Wind*. I'd seen it previously and wasn't all that excited about seeing it again. I was pleasantly surprised. Even though it's a nearly four-hours-long movie, it never gets boring. Everyone should see this awesome exciting movie at least once.

Now check your answers on page 430.

Go to MyEnglishLab to complete the review online.

Adjective Clauses

226

PART 6

OUTCOMES

- Modify subjects and objects of sentences with adjective clauses
- Identify key details in a psychology article
- Identify and comment on key details from a conversation about university life
- Discuss personality traits of various people
- Conduct research about a famous person and present findings to the class
- Write an essay about the personality type that fits you

OUTCOMES

- Form and use adjective clauses with prepositions, quantifiers, and nouns
- Form and use adjective phrases
- Identify key details in an sociology article
- Identify key details of a conversation in an academic setting
- Discuss culture and culture shock
- Write an essay describing a cultural experience

Adjective Clauses: Introduction

PERSONALITY

OUTCOMES

- Modify subjects and objects of sentences with adjective clauses
- Identify key details in a psychology article
- Identify and comment on key details from a conversation about university life
- Discuss personality traits of various people
- Conduct research about a famous person and present findings to the class
- Write an essay about the personality type that fits you

STEP 1   **GRAMMAR IN CONTEXT**

BEFORE YOU READ

Discuss the questions.

1. Complete the sentence with an adjective that describes your personality well: "I am a person who is _____."

2. Is it helpful to classify people into personality types or to place yourself in a personality category? Why or why not?

READ

▶ 14|01   Read this article about personality.

What Type Are You?

IMAGINE YOU'RE AT A PARTY where you know several people well. The hosts have a new party game that involves comparing each person to a flower. Which flower would you choose for each person and which flower for yourself? Are you the kind of person who resembles a daisy, open to the world most of the time? Or are you more like a morning glory, which opens up only at special moments?

Why do we enjoy party games like these that reveal our personality traits and help us to classify people's personalities? Classifying personalities can enable us to understand both ourselves and others better. Moreover, it can assist us in working together effectively and minimizing conflict. For these reasons, over the last century, many personality types have been recognized, and tests have been devised that help us to identify these types. Personality identification has become a science.

Carl Jung, a Swiss psychiatrist who is regarded as one of the fathers of modern psychiatry, published a famous work on personality in 1921. Isabel Briggs Myers, an American author who studied and admired Jung's theories, felt that Jung's ideas were important and should be made understandable to the general public. Briggs Myers was very disturbed by the global conflict of World War II and had a strong desire to help people to understand each other better. Along with her mother, Katharine Briggs, Briggs Myers created the Myers-Briggs Type Indicator, or MBTI. The MBTI, which

Daisy

Morning glory

is constantly being revised and improved, has become the world's most popular test of personality identification. The MBTI is now used for a variety of purposes, such as marital counseling, training of executives, and career decisions.

In the 1950s, cardiologists Meyer Friedman and Ray Roseman proposed two new personality categories, Type A and Type B, based on the idea that some people (Type As) were more likely to suffer from heart disease than others (Type Bs). This idea has now been discounted, but the basic outlines of these personality types have become popular, and Type C and D categories have followed them into common use.

What type of personality do you have? What about your co-workers, friends, and family? Try to place yourself and people you know into the following categories. Bear in mind, though, that most people don't fit perfectly into a single category.

TYPE A
Self-driven, competitive

Type As are "drivers," competitive individuals who have a no-nonsense approach to life. They're the kind of people who tell you exactly what they think without mincing words.[1] They embrace risk and change and often turn out to be entrepreneurs.[2] Nancy, who started her own greeting card business three years ago, is the perfect example. However, Nancy is impatient with detail and routine, which is why she has hired Paul and Mandy to manage her business.

TYPE B
Charismatic, easy-going

Type Bs are socializers. They're extroverts, the kind of people who love the spotlight. They love to entertain people. They often gravitate toward jobs in sales or marketing or as performers on radio and TV. Nancy's husband, Jack, whom most people consider a charismatic[3] person, is a good example. He's the host of a two-hour talk radio show.

TYPE C
Introverted, stress-prone

Type Cs are lovers of detail and data. They tend to be individuals who become accountants, programmers, or engineers. Paul, an accountant, is an example. He's the type of person who loves the details that Nancy hates. Type Cs are sensitive, which can cause them to have trouble communicating with others.

---

1 *without mincing words:* speaking of something negative with plain, direct language
2 *entrepreneurs:* people who own and run a business
3 *charismatic:* having personal qualities that attract and hold people

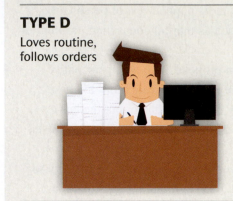

TYPE D

Loves routine, follows orders

Type D people are those who like routine and tend not to enjoy adventure. Not surprisingly, they usually resist change. They feel secure when they're told what to do. They're often compassionate. Mandy, who loves her office job, is Type D. She wouldn't be happy as the boss. Nor would Paul. But they both appreciate working for Nancy.

What did you learn by classifying personalities in this way? Did it give you any insight into yourself and others?

AFTER YOU READ

A VOCABULARY Complete the sentences with the words in the box.

conflict	data	discount	enable	gravitate	insight	moreover	secure

1. Myers was disturbed by the global _____ in the 1940s.

2. That idea has been proven wrong, and people now _____ it.

3. Type Ds feel _____ when they're told what to do.

4. Type Bs often _____ towards sales jobs.

5. Type Cs enjoy working with _____.

6. Did your research give you any _____ into the problem?

7. Understanding personality types can _____ us to understand others better.

8. Linda is very confident. _____, she is aggressive and extroverted.

B COMPREHENSION Read the statements. Check (✓) *True* or *False*.

	True	False
1. Carl Jung was important in the development of modern psychiatry.	☐	☐
2. Isabel Briggs Myers wanted to help people understand each other better.	☐	☐
3. The Myers-Briggs inventory has not been changed since it was devised.	☐	☐
4. Most people belong to only one personality category.	☐	☐
5. A Type A person likes change.	☐	☐
6. A Type B person generally doesn't like to be the center of attention.	☐	☐
7. A Type C person sometimes has trouble communicating with others.	☐	☐
8. A Type D person does not like to be told what to do.	☐	☐

C DISCUSSION Work with a partner. Compare your answers in B. Give reasons for your answers. Then describe a person you know who fits closely into one of the personality categories.

Go to MyEnglishLab for more grammar in context practice.

ADJECTIVE CLAUSES

Adjective Clauses: Placement

Main Clause		Adjective Clause	
	Noun / Pronoun	Relative Pronoun	
They met a	woman	**who**	**teaches psychology**.
This is the	personality test	**that**	**I took**.

Main Clause	Adjective Clause		Main Clause Continued
Noun / Pronoun	Relative Pronoun		
The woman	**who**	**teaches psychology**	is also a writer.
The personality test	**that**	**I took**	was very revealing.

Relative Pronouns as Subjects: *Who, Which, That*

People		
I have friends	**who**	love to talk.
I have a friend	**that**	loves to talk.

Things		
This is a book	**which**	is useful.
These are books	**that**	are useful.

Relative Pronouns as Objects: *Who(m), Which, That, Ø**

People		
This is the doctor	**who(m)** **that** **Ø**	we consulted.

Things		
This is the test	**which** **that** **Ø**	he gave us.

* Ø = no pronoun

Whose + Noun to Indicate Possession

People
She is the woman **whose son** is so famous.
She is the woman **whose son** I am tutoring.

Things
It's the book **whose reviews** were so good.
It's the book **whose reviews** I have just read.

Where and *When* in Adjective Clauses

Where		
Place		
I remember the café	**where**	we met.

When		
Time		
I remember the day	**(when)** **(that)** **Ø**	we parted.

Adjective Clauses: Identifying or Nonidentifying

Adjective Clauses That Identify
No Commas
The woman **who created the test** studied psychology. The test (**that**) **she created** describes personality types.

Adjective Clauses That Do Not Identify
Commas
Sara Gomez, **who created the test**, studied psychology. The Gomez test, **which she created**, describes personality types.

GRAMMAR NOTES

1 Definition of Adjective Clauses

A **clause** is a group of words that contains at least one **subject** and a **verb** showing past, present, or future time.

Clauses are either independent or dependent.

Independent clauses can stand alone as **complete sentences**.	The house is in the suburbs. *(independent)*
Dependent clauses **cannot stand alone**. They need to be linked with another clause to be fully understood.	that we bought *(dependent)* The house **that we bought** is in the suburbs. *(dependent clause linked to independent clause)*
An **adjective clause** is a **dependent** clause that **modifies a noun or a pronoun** in a main (independent) clause.	The elderly lady **who lives down the street** is a very interesting personality. *(The dependent clause modifies "elderly lady.")*
A sentence with an adjective clause can be seen as a combination of two sentences. An adjective clause can occur **after** or **inside** a main clause.	John is a man. + He works hard. John is a man **who works hard**. Mary is interesting. + I like her a lot. Mary, **whom I like a lot**, is interesting.
An adjective clause commonly begins with a relative pronoun: *who*, *whom*, *which*, *whose*, or *that*. It can also begin with *when* or *where*. For a list of pronouns that can introduce adjective clauses, see Appendix 22 on page 420.	Frank, *who is quite shy*, spends a lot of time alone. Let's do something *that* **is fun**. I can remember a time *when* **I was carefree**.
The word that begins an adjective clause usually comes **directly after the noun** or **pronoun** that the clause modifies.	**Toronto**, *which* is the largest city in Canada, is a beautiful place.

2 Subjects in Adjective Clauses

The **subjects** in adjective clauses can refer to **people or things**.

To refer to **people**, use *who* and *that* as the subjects of verbs in adjective clauses. *That* is less formal than *who*.	The Ings are the **people** *who* bought the house. Sam is the **man** *that* lives next door to me.
To refer to **things**, use *which* and *that* as the subjects of verbs in adjective clauses.	Math is the **subject** *which* is the hardest for me. This is the **car** *that* is the nicest.
The **verb** in an adjective clause **agrees** with the **noun** or pronoun that the clause modifies.	There are many *people* who **have taken** this personality test. Myers-Briggs is the ***test*** that **is** the best known.
BE CAREFUL! Do not use a **double subject** in an adjective clause.	Type C individuals are **people who** love detail and data. **NOT** Type C individuals are people who ~~they~~ love detail and data.
BE CAREFUL! Do not use *which* to refer to **people**. Use *who* or *that*.	Ann is a **person** *who* spends a lot of time alone. **NOT** Ann is a person ~~which~~ spends a lot of time alone.

3 Objects in Adjective Clauses

The **objects** in adjective clauses can refer to **people** or **things**.

To refer to **people**, use *whom*, *who*, or *that* as the **objects** of verbs in adjective clauses. *Whom* is quite formal and is more common in writing than in speech. *Who* and *that* are used in both formal and informal situations. When it refers to people, *that* is less formal than *who* and is commonly used in conversation and informal writing.	Mr. Pitkin, ***whom I mentioned yesterday***, is my boss. Mr. Pitkin was the person *who* I mentioned. Mr. Pitkin was the person *that* I mentioned.
To refer to **things**, use *which* and *that* as the **objects** of verbs in adjective clauses. *Which* is a bit more formal than *that*.	The test *which* **I took** was difficult. The test *that* **James took** was easy.
USAGE NOTE In conversation and informal writing, you can **omit** the **relative pronoun** if it is an **object**. This is the most common spoken form for sentences containing adjective clauses. (See Note 7 for more information on omitting relative pronouns.)	Mrs. Gomez is the woman **I met**. The car **we bought** was cheap.
BE CAREFUL! Make sure that the **verb agrees** with the **subject**, not the object of the clause.	The Wangs are the people that ***Sally* knows**. **NOT** The Wangs are the people that Sally ~~know~~.

4 *Whose* in Adjective Clauses

Use *whose* to introduce an adjective clause that indicates **possession**.

Use *whose* to replace *his/her/its/their* + a **noun**. An adjective clause with *whose* can modify people or things:	
• **people**	Ken is the man. + We met his wife. = Ken is the man ***whose* wife we met**.
• **things**	It's a theory. + Its origins go back many years. = It's a theory ***whose* origins go back many years**.
BE CAREFUL! The relative pronoun *whose* **cannot be omitted**.	Harvey, ***whose* house we're renting**, is a lawyer. **NOT** Harvey, ~~house we're renting~~, is a lawyer.

5 *Where* in Adjective Clauses

Use *where* to introduce an adjective clause that modifies a noun of **place**.

Use *where* to replace the adverb *there*.	This is the restaurant. + We ate there. This is the restaurant ***where* we ate**.
You can replace *where* with **which or that** + **a preposition**, such as *in*, *at*, or *for*. In this type of adjective clause, *which/that* can be omitted.	
• *which*	This is the building ***where* she works**. This is the building (***which***) she works **in**.
• *that*	This is the hotel ***where* we stayed**. This is the hotel (***that***) we stayed **at**.
BE CAREFUL! Use an adjective clause with *where* only if you can restate the location with the word *there*. Do not use an adjective clause with *where* if the location cannot be stated in this way.	Chihuahua is the town ***where* I was born**. = Chihuahua is the town. I was born ***there***. Stockholm is a city ***that* has beautiful scenery**. **NOT** Stockholm is a city ~~where has beautiful scenery~~.

6 *When* and *That* in Adjective Clauses

Use *when* and *that* to introduce an adjective clause that modifies a noun of **time**.	I can't think of a **time *when*** I wasn't happy. She told us about a **time *that*** she was carefree.
USAGE NOTE In conversation and informal writing, you can **omit *when*** and ***that*** in this type of adjective clause.	I can't think of a **time I wasn't happy**. She told us about a **time she was carefree**.

7 Identifying and Nonidentifying Adjective Clauses

Two types of adjective clauses are **identifying** and **nonidentifying**.

An **identifying adjective clause** (also called **essential**) is **necessary to identify** the **noun** that it refers to.	People **who embrace risk and change** are classified as Type A people. *(shows which kind of people are called Type A people)*
Identifying adjective clauses **are not enclosed in commas**.	People **who love the spotlight** are classified as Type B people. *(shows which kind of people are called Type B people)*
A **nonidentifying adjective clause** (also called **nonessential**) **gives additional information** that is not necessary to identify the noun or pronoun to which it refers. Nonidentifying adjective clauses **are enclosed in commas**.	Maryam, **who is undoubtedly a Type A person,** is the student body president. *(does not distinguish Maryam from any other person but gives extra information about her)*
BE CAREFUL! You can **omit** relative pronouns only in **identifying** adjective clauses. You **cannot omit** the relative pronoun in **nonidentifying** adjective clauses.	The man **you met on Friday** is Tarik. Tarik, *who* **just took the personality inventory**, is originally from Lebanon. **NOT** Tarik, ~~just took the personality inventory~~, is originally from Lebanon.
BE CAREFUL! You can use **that** as a relative pronoun only in an **identifying** clause. Don't use *that* as a relative pronoun in a **nonidentifying** clause. Use *which* in this type of clause.	The Myers-Briggs test, *which* **I took a long time ago**, has proved to be accurate. **NOT** The Myers-Briggs test, ~~that~~ I took a long time ago, has proved to be accurate.

8 Special Use of *Which* in Adjective Clauses

In conversation and informal writing, you can use the relative pronoun *which* to refer to an **entire previous idea**.	Jamal is a socializer. + That quality impresses me = **Jama is a socializer**, *which* impresses me. Paris is beautiful and exciting. + Those qualities are why I like going there = **Paris is beautiful and exciting**, *which* is why I like going there.
IN WRITING In more formal speaking and in writing, use a **noun** at the **beginning** of a *which* or *that* clause.	Jamal is a socializer, **a quality** *which* impresses me. Paris is beautiful and exciting, **qualities** *that* make me like going there.

PRONUNCIATION NOTE

Pausing in Identifying and Nonidentifying Clauses

Sentences with identifying adjective clauses and nonidentifying adjective clauses are not pronounced in the same way.

Identifying clauses have **no pauses** before and after them.	The woman **who is wearing a red skirt and a green blouse** is my friend's mother. The tie **which has a stain on it** needs to be dry-cleaned.
Nonidentifying clauses have **pauses** before and after them. The pauses correspond to **commas** in written sentences.	The woman, **who is wearing a red skirt and a green blouse**, is my friend's mother. The tie, **which has a stain on it**, needs to be dry-cleaned.

Go to MyEnglishLab to watch the grammar presentation.

STEP 3   FOCUSED PRACTICE

EXERCISE 1   DISCOVER THE GRAMMAR

A GRAMMAR NOTES 1–8 Read these sentences based on the reading. Could the underlined words be replaced by the words in parentheses without creating a different meaning or making an incorrect sentence? Write *Y* (Yes) or *N* (No).

___Y___ **1.** Are you the kind of person <u>who</u> resembles a daisy? (that)

_____ **2.** Or are you more like a morning glory, <u>which</u> opens up only at special moments? (that)

_____ **3.** Try to place yourself and people <u>whom</u> you know in these categories. (Ø)

_____ **4.** Type As are competitive individuals <u>who</u> take a no-nonsense approach to life. (that)

_____ **5.** They're the kind of people <u>who</u> tell you exactly what they think. (Ø)

_____ **6.** Nancy is impatient with detail and routine, <u>which</u> is why she has hired Paul and Mandy to manage her business. (that)

_____ **7.** Type Bs are the kind of people <u>who</u> love the spotlight. (whom)

_____ **8.** Mandy, <u>who</u> loves her office job, wouldn't be happy as the boss. (that)

B GRAMMAR NOTE 7 Read the sentences based on the reading. Underline the adjective clause in each sentence. Then identify the clause as *identifying* (*I*) or *nonidentifying* (*NI*).

___I___ **1.** Imagine you're at a party <u>where you know several people well</u>.

_____ **2.** Try to place yourself and people you know into one or more categories.

_____ **3.** Nancy, who started her own business several years ago, is the perfect example.

  Unit 14

_____ **4.** Type Cs tend to be the kind of people who become accountants, programmers, or engineers.

_____ **5.** He's the type of person who loves details.

_____ **6.** Nancy is impatient with detail and routine, which is why she has hired Paul and Mandy to manage her business.

_____ **7.** Nancy's husband, Jack, whom most people consider a charismatic person, is a good example.

_____ **8.** Type Cs are sensitive, which can translate into trouble communicating with others.

_____ **9.** Type D people are those who like routine and tend not to enjoy adventure.

EXERCISE 2 RELATIVE PRONOUNS

GRAMMAR NOTES 2–4, 8 Complete the paragraph. Circle the correct answers.

I come from a family (which) / whom has eight members. I have three sisters and two
　　　　　　　　　　　　　　1.
brothers, who / which made a lot of noise in the house when we were growing up. Our
　　　　　　2.
house, which / that is four stories high, has eight bedrooms. The members of my family,
　　　　3.
who / whom are all interesting, fit nicely into the Type A to D categories of personality
4.
types. My mother and father, who / whom both like to be with people a great deal, are
　　　　　　　　　　　　　5.
extroverts. My favorite brother, with who / whom I still spend a lot of time, is an introvert.
　　　　　　　　　　　　　　　　6.
My other brother, who / which is a Type A, is a great guy, but always has to be right. My
　　　　　　　　7.
favorite sister, who / whose fiancé is the same age as I am, is a Type A. Of my other two
　　　　　　8.
sisters, the one Ø / which I am closer to is a Type C. I'm less close to the sister who / Ø is
　　　　　　9.　　　　　　　　　　　　　　　　　　　　　　　**10.**
much older than I am. She's a Type D.

EXERCISE 3 IDENTIFYING AND NONIDENTIFYING CLAUSES

GRAMMAR NOTES 2–7 Combine each pair of sentences into one sentence with an adjective clause, using the word in parentheses. Use the first sentence in each pair as the main clause. Add commas where necessary. The sentences are connected as a story.

1. The company makes computers. I work for the company. (that)

The company that I work for makes computers.

2. The company has existed for fifteen years. It is named Excelsior Computer. (which)

_____

3. The building is located downtown. We do most of our work in the building. (where)

_____

4. The office has been remodeled. I work in the office. (that)

_____

5. Darren Corgatelli is the perfect Type A boss. His wife is my aunt. (whose)

_____

6. Darren is an excellent manager. I've known him since I was a child. (whom)

_____

7. Darren's wife, Sarah, keeps the company running smoothly. She is a perfect Type C. (who)

_____

8. I joined the company in 1995. I graduated from college then. (when)

_____

9. I really admire the personalities of my colleagues. Their advice has been invaluable. (whose)

_____

10. I have to do some telemarketing. I don't like telemarketing. (which)

_____

EXERCISE 4 FORMAL AND INFORMAL ADJECTIVE CLAUSES

GRAMMAR NOTES 2–3, 7–8 Read two reports by an attorney. Using the words in parentheses, complete the spoken report with informal adjective clauses. Omit relative pronouns if possible and use contractions. Then complete the written report with formal adjective clauses. Do not omit relative pronouns and do not use contractions. Put all verbs in the correct forms.

Spoken Report

Our client is a guy _____*who's been in trouble*_____ for minor offenses in the past,
                          1. (have / be / in trouble)

but I don't think he's a murderer, _____ I feel comfortable
                                      2. (be / why)

defending him. He did time in the penitentiary from 2008 to 2010, and according to all the reports

he was a really social Type B person _____. Since he got
                                        3. (the other prisoners / respect)

out of jail in 2010, he's had a good employment record with Textrix, an electronics company

_____. The psychological reports on him show that when
4. (he / have / be working for)

he was in prison he was a person _____ well-balanced
                                    5. (the psychiatrists / consider)

and even-tempered, _____ I don't think he's guilty.
                      6. (be / why)

Written Report

EAGER, BARNES, AND KIRBY
ATTORNEYS-AT-LAW
555 NORTH LIBERTY • BOSTON MA 02110

Our client is a man _____ *who has been in trouble* _____ for minor
                                                      7. (who / be / in trouble)

offenses in the past, but I do not believe that he is a murderer,

_____ comfortable defending him. He
                8. (an opinion / make / me)

served time in the penitentiary from 2008 to 2010, and according to all the reports he

was a highly social Type B person _____ .
                                     9. (the other prisoners / respect)

Since he was released from prison in 2010, he has had a good employment record with

Textrix, an electronics company _____ . His
                            10. (have / employ / him)

psychological profile suggests that when he was in prison he was a person

_____ well balanced and even-tempered,
              11. (the psychiatrists / consider)

_____ believe that he is not guilty.
              12. (evidence / make / me)

EXERCISE 5 PAUSING IN IDENTIFYING AND NONIDENTIFYING CLAUSES

14|03 **A** PRONUNCIATION NOTE Listen for the pauses in the sentences. Place commas around the adjective clauses if necessary. Then identify each clause as *identifying* (*I*) or *nonidentifying* (*NI*).

_NI_ **1.** The man, who lives down the street from me, is a friend of my father.

_____ **2.** The man who lives down the street from me is a friend of my father.

_____ **3.** The teacher who handed out the awards is really a well-known scientist.

_____ **4.** The teacher who handed out the awards is really a well-known scientist.

_____ **5.** The student who lives close to the campus has low gasoline bills.

_____ **6.** The student who lives close to the campus has low gasoline bills.

_____ **7.** The garden which Mary planted is the most beautiful one of all.

_____ **8.** The garden which Mary planted is the most beautiful one of all.

B Work with a partner. Read the sentences in A aloud in a different order. Your partner guesses which type of adjective clause is in each sentence—identifying or nonidentifying.

EXERCISE 6 EDITING

GRAMMAR NOTES 1–8 Read the message from a college student to her parents. There are eleven mistakes in the use of adjective clauses. The first mistake is already corrected. Find and correct ten more.

TO: grants36@yoohoo.com
FR: AliceG@yoohoo.com
RE: My first week at college

Dear Mom and Dad,

Well, the first week of college has been kind of tough, but it's turned out OK. My advisor, who ~~he~~ is also from Winnipeg, told me about growing up there, so we had something who we could talk about.

Since I'm still thinking about what my major is going to be, my advisor had me take one of those tests show you what you're most interested in. It was called the Strong Interest Test. I found out that I'm most interested in things involve being on the stage and performing in some way, that doesn't surprise me a bit. I always liked being in school plays. Remember? So I signed up for two drama courses seem like they're going to be really interesting.

My advisor also had me do one of those personality inventories that they tell you what kind of person you are. This is something that is all new to me, but I found out some things whose are really interesting. According to the test I took, I'm a person whom is classified as a Type B person. I had no idea what that meant, but I've learned that a Type B person is someone which likes people a lot and likes to socialize. That fits me pretty well, I think.

Classes start on Wednesday, and I'm getting to know the other people in the dormitory which I live. It's pretty exciting being here. That's it for now. I'll call in a week or so.

Love,
Alice

Go to **My**English**Lab** for more focused practice.

EXERCISE 7 LISTENING

▶14|04 **A** Listen to a telephone conversation that Al had with his parents. What is Al doing these days?

_____

▶14|04 **B** Read the pairs of sentences. Then listen again to the conversation. Circle the answer that correctly describes what you heard.

1. **a.** Al likes his dormitory.
   b. Al doesn't like his dormitory.

2. **a.** The dormitory has one supervisor.
   b. The dormitory has more than one supervisor.

3. **a.** Both of Al's roommates are from Minnesota.
   b. One of Al's roommates is from Minnesota.

4. **a.** There is one group of girls living in the dormitory.
   b. There is more than one group of girls living in the dormitory.

5. **a.** The girls live on the same side of the building as Al.
   b. The girls live on the other side of the building from Al.

6. **a.** Al has one English class.
   b. Al has more than one English class.

7. **a.** Al has one history class.
   b. Al has more than one history class.

8. **a.** Al's writing class is going to be easy.
   b. Al's math class is going to be easy.

9. **a.** Al has one advisor.
   b. Al has more than one advisor.

C Work with a partner. Discuss these questions.

1. What is the best place that you've lived since you became a student? The worst?

2. What are benefits that you have gained in living with others?

3. What is the easiest course you have taken? The hardest?

4. Have you had advisors who have been helpful? How did they help you?

EXERCISE 8 A NIGHT AT THE MOVIES

A PICTURE DISCUSSION Work in a group. Carefully examine the picture. Describe the people in the picture. What are they doing? What kinds of personalities do you think they have? Write sentences with adjective clauses.

EXAMPLE: The man who is talking on his cell phone is annoying some of the people near him. He seems to be a person that is loud and inconsiderate.

B Share your results with the rest of the class. Which group has created the most sentences?

EXERCISE 9 WHAT TYPE ARE YOU?

Ⓐ SURVEY Walk around the classroom and find four people who believe they fit into one of these personality types: Type A, Type B, Type C, or Type D. Find out why they think they have one of these personality types. Write the name of the student in the chart and the reasons that they gave you.

Personality Type	Name	Reasons
Type A Self-driven, competitive		
Type B Charismatic, easy-going		
Type C Introverted, stress-prone		
Type D Loves routine, follows orders		

Ⓑ Read your sentences about each person aloud. Add other facts you may know about the person. Don't say the person's name. The class attempts to guess the name of the student you are describing.

EXAMPLE: **A:** This is a person who considers himself or herself a Type A person. This person, who is very competitive, has been studying English for five years.

      B: Is it Carlos?

      A: Yes!

EXERCISE 10
HE WAS A GREAT SCIENTIST WHO . . .

A **PRESENTATION** You are going to give a presentation about the personality of a famous person in the world, either in the present or the past. Choose a person from the box, or choose another person who interests you. Do research on the Internet to find information about the personality of the individual you have chosen. Then complete the chart.

Albert Einstein	Lionel Messi
Lady Gaga	Marilyn Monroe
Nelson Mandela	Mother Teresa
Angela Merkel	Kanye West

Name	
Occupation	
Nationality	
Life Dates	
Accomplishments	
Personal Characteristics	

B Write a presentation about the person you researched in A. Use adjective clauses in your sentences.

Albert Einstein, who was a theoretical physicist and one of the greatest scientists of all time, was born in Ulm, Germany in 1879. He died in Princeton, New Jersey in the United States in 1955. Einstein, whose theory of relativity is considered a major contribution to scientific knowledge, left Germany when Adolf Hitler came to power. He was a peace-loving individual who . . .

C Make your presentation to the class.

Go to MyEnglishLab for more communication practice.

A **BEFORE YOU WRITE** Consider the personality categories that have been mentioned in this unit and choose the one that fits you best. Write a few sentences about why you believe you fit into this particular category.

B **WRITE** Using your ideas in A, write a five-paragraph essay about the personality type that best fits you. Remember to use identifying and nonidentifying adjective clauses. Try to avoid the common mistakes shown in the chart. Use the example below to help you begin your essay.

EXAMPLE: No single personality type applies perfectly to a person, but for me one comes closer than all the others. The personality category that fits me most closely is Type B. First, Type Bs are social people who are basically extroverts. I've always enjoyed my friends, which is why I think this category fits me quite well. . . .

Common Mistakes in Using Adjective Clauses

Use *who*, not *which*, to refer to **people**.	The neighbor **who** is the nicest is Mrs. Lopez. **NOT** The neighbor ~~which~~ is the nicest is Mrs. Lopez.
Don't use a **double subject** in an adjective clause.	I'm impressed by people **who** are kind and helpful. **NOT** I'm impressed by people who ~~they~~ are kind and helpful.
Don't enclose identifying adjective clauses with **commas**.	People who put others before themselves are admirable. **NOT** People_x who put others before themselves_x are admirable.
Don't use *that* to introduce a **nonidentifying** adjective clause. Use *who*, *whom*, or *which*.	Hussein, **who** is my best friend, was born in Tanzania. **NOT** Hussein, ~~that~~ is my best friend, was born in Tanzania.

C **CHECK YOUR WORK** Look at your essay. Underline adjective clauses. Use the Editing Checklist to check your work.

Editing Checklist

Did you . . . ?

☐ use *who* or *whom* to refer to people and *which* to refer to things

☐ avoid using a double subject in adjective clauses

☐ enclose nonidentifying clauses with commas

☐ avoid using *that* to introduce a nonidentifying adjective clause

D **REVISE YOUR WORK** Read your essay again. Can you improve your writing? Make changes if necessary.

Go to **MyEnglishLab** for more writing practice.

UNIT 14 REVIEW

Test yourself on the grammar of the unit.

A Complete the sentences. Circle the correct answers.

1. The lady who / which is my teacher is the third from the right.

2. Hong Kong is the city that / where I was born.

3. Elena, that / whom I met at the conference, has a Type A personality.

4. The man whose / which car we borrowed is my father's boss.

5. Boris Popov is very detail-oriented, that / which is why we should hire him.

6. I can't remember a time where / when he wasn't helpful.

7. Lions are the animals that Lea like / likes the best.

8. Chuy is a person who / who he prefers to be alone.

B If necessary, place commas in the correct places in the sentences.

1. The man who lives next door is very talkative.

2. The book Sara bought was written by Junot Díaz.

3. Mrs. Ching whose dog is always barking is very wealthy.

4. The people I work with all have Type D personalities.

5. Yaoundé is the city in which I was born.

6. Ms. Voicu who is a student is from Romania.

7. Tumba whose children are very energetic is always exhausted.

C Find and correct five mistakes.

Last week in my psychology class, we took a personality test who is designed to determine what kind of person you are. The test, that I found interesting, took a couple of hours to complete. Today I got my results, whose were pretty much what I expected. I have many friends whom mean a lot to me, so it's not surprising that I'm classified as an extrovert. I would recommend that everyone wants to find out more about himself or herself should take a test like this.

Now check your answers on page 430.

Go to MyEnglishLab to complete the review online.

Adjective Clauses and Phrases
CULTURE SHOCK

OUTCOMES
- Form and use adjective clauses with prepositions, quantifiers, and nouns
- Form and use adjective phrases
- Identify key details in a sociology article
- Identify key details of a conversation in an academic setting
- Discuss culture and culture shock
- Write an essay describing a cultural experience

| STEP 1 | GRAMMAR IN CONTEXT |

BEFORE YOU READ

Discuss the questions.

1. What problems do you think that someone who moves to a new country might face?
2. Have you ever lived in a different culture from the one you grew up in? If so, what was your experience like?

READ

 15|01 Read this article about culture shock.

What Is Culture Shock?

Jamal is a young man who has been in New York City for five months and is studying at an American university. When he first got to the United States, everything seemed exciting and wonderful. He met a lot of new students that he immediately became friends with. He got acquainted with a number of Americans, most of whom were kind and helpful to him. He fell in love with many aspects of New York, including its towering downtown skyscrapers and its amazing subway system. That was five months ago. Now things have changed considerably. The Americans he has met don't seem as kind or helpful as they did at the beginning. His friends, some of whom he continues to see regularly, are still here, but many of them don't have time to get together anymore. The subway, which he was initially so impressed with, now just seems dirty, noisy, and much too crowded. The skyscrapers which had previously seemed so magnificent now make him feel dwarfed. New York simply just isn't as wonderful as it was at the beginning.

What has happened? Jamal is suffering from culture shock, a type of disorientation often resulting from a change to a new locale, a new social setting, or a new country. We can identify four stages of culture shock: honeymoon, negotiation, adjustment, and mastery.

HONEYMOON: Jamal has had the honeymoon stage, but just as newly married couples discover after their honeymoon, the initial period of joyful excitement experienced by people in a new culture doesn't last. The delight they felt with the new and perhaps exotic food, the new language, and their new surroundings is replaced by the feelings of frustration that will characterize the next stage.

NEGOTIATION: Three months or more after one has made an entry into a new culture, the honeymoon stage is generally replaced by the negotiation stage. This stage is normally characterized by negative feelings, examples of which include anxiety, loneliness, and homesickness. Jamal is lacking the support of his parents, his extended family, and his friends. Even worse, he has been having trouble communicating with others. Whereas Americans were previously impressed with his mastery of English, suddenly people don't seem to understand him very well. He can't find the kinds of food he wants to eat. He longs for the friends, family, and the customs he has been accustomed to in his native land. Jamal's stage of negotiation is probably the most difficult of the four stages for anyone experiencing culture shock to get through.

ADJUSTMENT: Somewhere between six and twelve months, there usually begins a period of adjustment characterized by a gradual acceptance of the new culture. Jamal, tiring of his months of negativity, has come around to the idea that New York City might be worth living in after all. His several months of discontent have gradually given way to a kind of maturity involving acceptance of the culture and adopting a more normal lifestyle.

MASTERY: Sometime in his second year of living in New York, Jamal reaches the stage of mastery, in which he feels comfortable with the culture and is again content to be here. In this period, often called the bicultural stage, Jamal has attained the ability to participate completely in the New York culture and regard it favorably. This does not mean that he has been converted into an American. It does mean that he is flexible enough to keep many aspects of his native culture while adopting those parts of his new culture that appeal to him. Jamal wasn't able to avoid culture shock, but he was able to master it.

AFTER YOU READ

A VOCABULARY Match the words in **bold** with their meanings.

_____ **1.** The skyscrapers cause him to feel **dwarfed**.

_____ **2.** Jamal is experiencing **disorientation**.

_____ **3.** He is **flexible** enough to keep his native culture.

_____ **4.** Negotiation is followed by a time of **adjustment**.

_____ **5.** Jamal has now gained a kind of **maturity**.

_____ **6.** He has **attained** the ability to participate completely.

_____ **7.** Jamal has not been **converted** into an American.

_____ **8.** **Whereas** people used to be impressed with his English, now they don't understand him well.

a. changed

b. although

c. full development

d. adaptation to a new situation

e. made to appear small

f. able to change easily

g. confusion

h. succeeded in getting

COMPREHENSION Complete the sentences based on the reading.

1. Jamal quickly became friends with other _____.

2. He fell in love with the New York City _____ system.

3. The New York City skyscrapers seemed _____ at first.

4. The first stage of culture shock is the _____ stage.

5. In culture shock, initial feelings of delight are replaced by feelings of _____.

6. The _____ stage is probably the most difficult stage to get through.

7. The period of adjustment involves a gradual _____ of the new culture.

8. The bicultural stage is also called the _____ stage.

DISCUSSION Work with a partner. Compare your answers in B. Give reasons for your answers. Then discuss this question: Do you agree that people who experience culture shock go through the four stages described in the article?

Go to MyEnglishLab for more grammar in context practice.

STEP 2 GRAMMAR PRESENTATION

ADJECTIVE CLAUSES AND PHRASES

Adjective Causes with Prepositions

Main Clause	Adjective Clause with Preposition			
People/Things	Preposition	Relative Pronoun		Preposition
He's the man	to	whom	she was talking.	
		who(m) that Ø*	she was talking	to.
It's the company	for	which	he works.	
		which that Ø	he works	for.
That's the professor		whose	classes I told you	about.
That's the teacher			class I spoke	of.

*Ø = no pronoun

Adjective Clauses with Quantifiers

Main Clause	Adjective Clause with Quantifier			
People/Things	Quantifier	*Of*	Relative Pronoun	
I have many friends,	all most many a number	of	whom	are colleagues.
I played in a lot of games,	some a few several		which	were victories.
I've met new colleagues,	a couple both two		whose	relatives live nearby.

Adjective Clauses with Nouns

Main Clause	Adjective Clause with Noun		
Things	Noun	*Of which*	
Professor Brown writes mysteries,	an example	of which	is *The Ghosts in the Tower*.
I love her books,	a chapter		I just read.

Reducing Adjective Clauses to Adjective Phrases

	Adjective Clause
She's the student	**who's from Nigeria.**
I saw the film	**which is about culture shock.**
That's the man	**who was in charge of personnel.**
That's the gym	**that's near my house.**

	Adjective Phrase
She's the student	**from Nigeria.**
I saw the film	**about culture shock.**
That's the man	**in charge of personnel.**
That's the gym	**near my house.**

Changing Adjective Clauses to Adjective Phrases

	Adjective Clause
Bob's the colleague	**who lives** downtown.
I read a book	**which describes** World War II.
We saw a movie	**that takes** place in Pakistan.

	Adjective Phrase
Bob's the colleague	**living** downtown.
I read a book	**describing** World War II.
We saw a movie	**taking** place in Pakistan.

GRAMMAR NOTES

1 Adjective Clauses with Prepositions

An **adjective clause** is a dependent clause that modifies a noun or pronoun in a main (independent) clause. (See Unit 14.) The relative pronouns *who(m)*, *that*, *which*, and *whose* can be used after a noun as **objects of prepositions** in adjective clauses.

The **preposition** can appear at the beginning or end of the adjective clause.	
Sentences with the preposition at the **beginning** of the clause are **formal**.	Bill is the man *to whom* I spoke. That's the book *to which* he referred.
Sentences with the preposition at the **end** of the clause are **informal**.	Dr. Gomez is the professor **who(m)** I spoke *to*. New York City is the place **which** he referred *to*.
A preposition can come at the **beginning** of a clause with *who(m)* or *which*. It cannot come at the beginning of a clause with *that*.	It's the firm *for* **which** he works. **NOT** It's the firm ~~for that~~ he works.

Identifying (essential) and **nonidentifying** (nonessential) clauses can also occur with prepositions.	The company **for which I work** is Excelsior.
	    (identifying)
	Excelsior, **which I work for**, is an excellent firm.
	    (nonidentifying)

We can **omit** the relative pronouns *who(m)*, *that*, and *which* **after** a preposition. When we do this, the preposition moves to the **end** of the clause.	She is the friend *to* **whom I was referring**. She's the friend **I was referring** *to*. That is the film *about* **which he was lecturing**. That's the film **he was lecturing** *about*.
BE CAREFUL! The relative pronoun *whose* cannot be omitted.	She's the friend **whose car I ran into**. **NOT** She's the friend ~~car I ran into~~.

2 Adjective Clauses with Quantifiers

Some adjective clauses have the pattern **quantifier + *of* + relative pronoun**.

IN WRITING **Quantifiers** occur only in clauses with *whom*, *which*, and *whose*. These clauses may refer to **people** or **things**. They are formal and are found mostly in writing and in careful speech.	He has made many friends at the university, *all* of **whom** he likes. His university has many beautiful buildings, *most* of **which** are old. My degree requires four science courses, *none* of **which** I've taken yet.
If a clause with a quantifier occurs **within** the main clause, it is enclosed in **commas**. If it occurs **after** the main clause, a comma **precedes** it.	Her novels, **most of which I've read,** are popular. I like her novels, **most of which I've read**. My Swahili professor has written two books, **neither of which is available yet in this country**.

3 Adjective Clauses with Noun + *of which*

Some adjective clauses have the pattern **noun + *of which***. Adjective clauses with this pattern refer to **things**.	New York City has many impressive tourist attractions, **an example of which** is the Empire State Building.
If a clause with a noun + *of which* occurs **within** the main clause, it is **enclosed in commas**. If it occurs **after** the main clause, a **comma precedes** it.	International celebrations, **occurrences of which are common at my university,** are a welcome change to the usual routine. Our faculty has won numerous awards, **examples of which include the Nobel and Pulitzer Prizes.**
BE CAREFUL! Adjective clauses with the pattern noun + *of which* refer **only** to **things**. They do not refer to people.	There are many students living in my dormitory, **a few of whom** are from other countries. **NOT** There are many students living in my dormitory, a few of which are from other countries.

4 Reducing Adjective Clauses to Adjective Phrases

Unlike a clause, a **phrase** is a group of words that **does not have both a subject and a verb showing time**. Adjective **clauses** with a *be* verb can be **reduced** to adjective phrases.

To reduce an adjective clause with a *be* verb, **delete** the **relative pronoun** and the *be* verb.	Any student **who is studying abroad** must learn the language of the country. *(adjective clause)* Any student **studying abroad** must learn the language of the country. *(adjective phrase)*
If an adjective clause needs **commas**, the corresponding adjective phrase also needs commas.	The Guggenheim Museum, **which was founded in 1939,** is very popular. The Guggenheim Museum, **founded in 1939,** is very popular.
BE CAREFUL! **Don't reduce** adjective clauses with a *be* verb when *whose* is the subject pronoun.	We met Professor Mandel, **whose classes are very popular**. **NOT** We met Professor Mandel, classes are very popular.

5 Changing Adjective Clauses without a *Be* Verb

If there is **no *be* verb** in an adjective clause, it is often possible to **change** the adjective clause to an adjective phrase. To do this, **delete** the **relative pronoun** and **change** the **verb** to its *-ing* form. You can do this only when *who*, *which*, or *that* is the **subject pronoun** of the clause.	Frank Okawilo, **who currently studies at Harvard University**, is going to graduate this year. Frank Okawilo, **currently *studying* at Harvard University**, is going to graduate this year. The tenants **who currently live in that apartment building** will have to move soon. The tenants **currently *living* in that apartment building** will have to move soon.

Go to **My**English**Lab** to watch the grammar presentation.

EXERCISE 1   DISCOVER THE GRAMMAR

Ⓐ GRAMMAR NOTES 1–5 Look at the sentences based on the reading. Underline the adjective clauses containing prepositions. Circle the noun referred to in each adjective clause and draw an arrow between the noun and the clause.

1. He met a lot of (students) that he immediately became friends with.

2. He also met many Americans, most of whom were kind and helpful to him.

3. This stage is normally characterized by negative feelings, examples of which include anxiety, loneliness, and homesickness.

4. Jamal reaches the stage of mastery, in which he again feels comfortable with the culture.

5. The subway, which he was initially so impressed with, now seems dirty and noisy.

6. He longs for the things he has been accustomed to in his native land.

Ⓑ GRAMMAR NOTES 4–5 Look at the underlined adjective phrases based on the reading. Change each phrase to a clause by adding a relative pronoun and the correct form of a verb.

1. He fell in love with many aspects of New York, including its skyscrapers and its subway system.

            which included   its skyscrapers and its subway system

2. Culture shock is a kind of disorientation resulting from a change to a new locale.

     _____ from a change to a new locale

3. The initial period of excitement experienced by people in a new culture doesn't last.

     _____ by people in a new culture

4. The negotiation stage is probably the most difficult of the four stages for anyone experiencing culture shock to get through.

     _____ culture shock

5. He is experiencing a number of negative feelings, including depression and frustration.

     _____ depression and frustration

6. There is a period of adjustment characterized by acceptance of the new culture.

     _____ by acceptance of the new culture

7. Jamal, tiring of his negativity, has come around to the idea that New York might be worth living in.

     _____ of his negativity

8. He has developed a kind of maturity involving acceptance of the culture.

     _____ acceptance of the culture

EXERCISE 2 PREPOSITIONS AT THE END OF CLAUSES

GRAMMAR NOTE 1 Change the following formal sentences to more informal sentences by moving the preposition to the end of the clause and deleting the relative pronoun.

1. Asha is happy in the new country to which she moved.

   Asha is happy in the new country she moved to.

2. She got a job at a company about which she had heard good things.

   _____

3. She appreciates the kindness of the supervisor to whom she reports.

   _____

4. She is fond of the other employees with whom she works.

   _____

5. She is amazed at the variety of countries from which they come.

   _____

6. However, the long commute is the one thing of which she is tired.

   _____

7. Nonetheless, Asha is happy with the company at which she works.

   _____

EXERCISE 3 ADJECTIVE CLAUSES WITH QUANTIFIERS

GRAMMAR NOTE 2 Complete the statements with the correct form of the words in parentheses. Use adjective clauses with the pattern quantifier + preposition + relative pronoun.

1. People from other countries, _____*some of whom have never lived abroad before*_____, often
   (some / have never / live / abroad before)

   experience culture shock in the United States.

2. These people, _____, eventually get
   (most / become homesick for their native country)

   through their difficulties.

3. Most problems of culture shock, _____,
   (all / seem serious at the time)

   fade away after the negotiation stage.

4. People from other countries often have to take jobs in the United States,

   _____.
   (many / do not pay well)

5. Newcomers to the United States, _____,
   (most / their families / are not with them)

   often suffer loneliness as well as homesickness.

6. Newcomers to the United States, _____,
   (few / lose / their native languages and accents)

   generally become comfortable with the culture in the mastery stage.

EXERCISE 4 ADJECTIVE PHRASES

GRAMMAR NOTES 4–5 Combine each pair of sentences into one sentence with an adjective phrase and a main clause. Use the underlined sentence to write the adjective phrase. Use the correct forms of verbs and punctuate correctly.

1. Bi-Yun was born in a small town in South Korea. He has overcome his struggle with culture shock in the United States.

   Bi-Yun, born in a small town in South Korea, has overcome his struggle with culture shock in the United States.

2. Los Angeles is often a difficult place to adjust to. It has become Bi-Yun's new home.

3. Bi-Yun has had several jobs in the United States. These include driving a taxi and washing dishes.

4. At the university, he has participated in extracurricular activities. They involve music and sports.

5. Bi-Yun is currently dating a fellow student. She is in his history class.

6. Bi-Yun shares an apartment with four other students. He is a very social person.

7. Bi-Yun is currently on the university track team. He was a star athlete in South Korea.

EXERCISE 5 CLAUSES TO SENTENCES

GRAMMAR NOTES 2–5 Each of the following sentences was formed from an original pair of sentences. Write the original pairs. Include the words in parentheses in each answer.

1. People who live in foreign countries face many problems in their new culture, examples of which are language difficulties and homesickness. (these problems)

   People who live in foreign countries face many problems in their new culture. Examples of these problems are language difficulties and homesickness.

2. Sundar has made friends from many different countries, including South Africa and Japan. (these countries)

   _____

   _____

3. After he arrived in Seattle, Sundar faced a number of challenges, including finding an affordable place to live and making friends with his neighbors. (these challenges)

   _____

   _____

4. Sundar's favorite tourist attractions are the Seattle Art Museum and the Space Needle, both of which he has been to several times. (these attractions)

   _____

   _____

5. He got to know his landlord and his next-door neighbor, both of whom he greatly respects, very well. (these people)

   _____

   _____

EXERCISE 6 ADJECTIVE CLAUSES AND PHRASES

GRAMMAR NOTES 2–5 Read the example sentences. Then think about experiences relating to culture shock that you have had or know about. Write sentences about these experiences using the phrases in the box.

born and raised in	including	(quantifier) + *of which*
examples of which	involving	(quantifier) + *of whom*

My cousin Lin, born and raised in China, did not experience serious culture shock after he moved to the United States.

I met a lot of interesting people, most of whom were very helpful, when I lived in Canada.

EXERCISE 7 EDITING

GRAMMAR NOTES 1–5 Read the email from Elena Gutierrez to her sister Rosa in Colombia. There are eight mistakes in the use of adjective clauses and phrases. The first mistake is already corrected. Find and correct seven more. Delete verbs, change pronouns, or add words where necessary. Do not change punctuation.

TO: Rosa111@yoohoo.com
FROM: ElenaGut@gomail.com
RE: Life in L.A.

Hi Rosa,

I'm writing this in English because I think we both need the practice. How are you doing? Please

say "hi" to everyone back there, ~~included~~ *including* all our friends in the neighborhood.

I'm still having a hard time here in Los Angeles, but things are a little better than they were.

I'm not quite as lonely as before because I've met some people in my neighborhood, many of

which are friendly, but so far I don't know anyone really well. I do have some friends who from

my classes at the university, most whom are very interesting. I'm looking forward to getting to

know them better as time goes on. The hardest thing is the food, most of it I just don't like very

much. It's difficult to find quality food that's not too expensive.

I did do one really fun thing recently. One of my friends from school and I went to Universal

Studios. We took a tram tour around the park and saw several actors working, some of that

I recognized. I felt like jumping off the tram and shouting, "Would everyone is famous please

give me your autograph?" Universal is where

the last Indiana Jones movie was filmed—you

know, those movies starred Harrison Ford?

I've got to get back to studying. I can hardly

wait to see you and the family in the

summer. Email me.

Love,
Elena

Go to **MyEnglishLab** for more focused practice.

EXERCISE 8 LISTENING

▶ 15|02 **A** Listen to the conversation between a student and a guidance counselor. What is Miryam's major problem?

_____

_____

_____

▶ 15|02 **B** Read each statement. Then listen to the conversation again. Check (✓) *True* or *False*.

	True	False
1. Miryam is doing well in all of her classes.	✓	☐
2. Her personal life is something with which Miryam is not satisfied.	☐	☐
3. Miryam has met several girls, few of whom seem nice.	☐	☐
4. Miryam has something in common with most of the people she's met.	☐	☐
5. Miryam is upset about people laughing at her.	☐	☐
6. Miryam's problem is something experienced by few foreign students.	☐	☐
7. The counselor thinks that Miryam should spend more time with people who are from Tanzania.	☐	☐
8. The counselor gives Miryam tips, one of which is to learn more about American culture.	☐	☐
9. Another thing Miryam should do is to laugh at her American friends.	☐	☐
10. The counselor thinks that the feelings which Miryam has been experiencing will go away eventually.	☐	☐

C Work with a partner. Discuss the questions.

1. Have you ever been in a situation like Miryam's in which things that used to be interesting now seem boring? If so, describe it.

2. Have you ever been in a situation in which you met people with whom you had nothing in common? Describe the situation.

EXERCISE 9 REVERSE CULTURE SHOCK

Ⓐ **DISCUSSION** You are going to discuss the topic of reverse culture shock. First, read this article.

Reverse Culture Shock

Did you know that there is such a thing as reverse culture shock? There is indeed. This kind of culture shock has basically the same stages as people experience when they are first living in a foreign country. Here's how these stages go:

1. **The Honeymoon:** When you return to your native land, you may have built up in your mind a vision of your home country that is not completely accurate. No doubt you've missed your family and friends, all of whom are excited and glad to see you back. You've missed the food, the city or town, the neighborhoods of your native country—all of which are delightful at first. At this point, everything seems interesting and fulfilling.

2. **Reverse Shock:** After a while back home, you start to feel annoyed and sad and begin to be critical of your home country. You may feel "reverse homesickness," missing the country you've returned from. You've idealized your home country in your mind, but it's not measuring up to your expectations. You start comparing it negatively to the country left behind.

3. **Recovery:** This is similar to the adjustment stage experienced when you left your native land. It takes a while, but eventually you come to terms with the characteristics of your original culture.

4. **Reintegration:** This is similar to the mastery stage when you went abroad the first time.

If this type of situation applies to you, a few suggestions may be in order: One is to expect reverse culture shock. This will make it easier to get through. Don't expect it to be easy to return to your original culture. Thomas Wolfe, the author of *Look Homeward, Angel*, is famous for this saying: "You can't go home again." You can of course go home, but you shouldn't expect things to be the same as they were when you left. Your country has changed. More significantly, you have changed.

Ⓑ **Work in a group. Discuss the questions. Then share your conclusions with the class.**

1. How do people returning to their native country usually feel when they first arrive?

2. In the reverse shock stage, how do returning people compare their native country to the country they recently left?

3. How is the recovery stage similar to the adjustment stage experienced when people have left their native land?

4. Do you think Thomas Wolfe's statement that "you can't go home again" is true? Why or why not?

EXERCISE 10 ANOTHER CULTURE

A CROSS-CULTURAL COMPARISON You are going to discuss a foreign culture. Think about the United States and its culture, or another foreign culture that you have spent time in or are familiar with. Complete the chart below.

Positive Things About the Culture	Negative Things About the Culture

B Work in a group with other students who have completed charts about the foreign culture you chose. Compare your charts. Do you agree on what is positive and what is negative? Then answer the questions.

1. How much time has each person in your group spent in the foreign culture?

2. Do you see a connection between the amount of time each person has spent in the culture and his or her opinions about the culture? Do people who have been in the culture for a short time have more positive feelings about the culture, or more negative ones?

C Share your conclusions with the class.

EXAMPLE: **A:** One positive thing about American culture experienced by most of the members of our group is that American people are usually friendly.
B: In our group, people who have been in the United States for a long time think that Americans are friendly, but people who have been here a short time think they are unfriendly.
A: The people who think they are unfriendly may be experiencing culture shock. . . .

EXERCISE 11 WHAT'S BEEN YOUR EXPERIENCE?

A **DISCUSSION** You are going to discuss your personal experiences with culture shock. First, study the diagram. Compare your experiences with the ones shown here. Write sentences based on your own experiences that correspond to each stage of the process of adjustment. Try to include adjective clauses and phrases in your sentences.

1. I left South Africa, the country which is my home.

2. I arrived in Canada, the new country that I moved to.

3. After my honeymoon period, I began to feel somewhat unhappy. I'd met a lot of Canadians, many of whom were friendly and kind, but few of whom became long-term friends . . .

The Stages of Culture Shock and Reverse Culture Shock

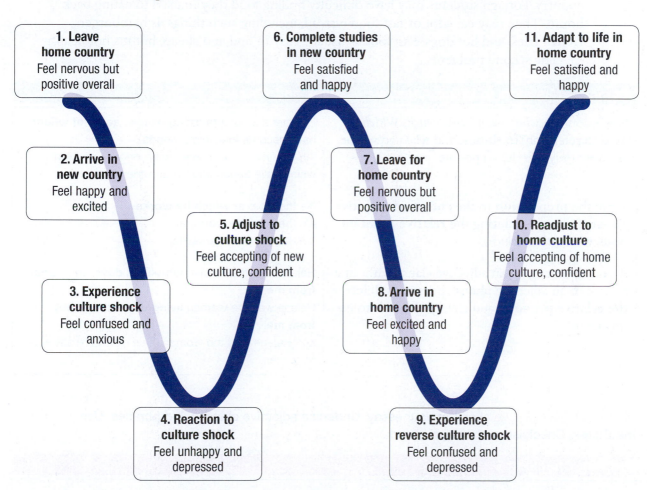

1. Leave home country
Feel nervous but positive overall

2. Arrive in new country
Feel happy and excited

3. Experience culture shock
Feel confused and anxious

4. Reaction to culture shock
Feel unhappy and depressed

5. Adjust to culture shock
Feel accepting of new culture, confident

6. Complete studies in new country
Feel satisfied and happy

7. Leave for home country
Feel nervous but positive overall

8. Arrive in home country
Feel excited and happy

9. Experience reverse culture shock
Feel confused and depressed

10. Readjust to home culture
Feel accepting of home culture, confident

11. Adapt to life in home country
Feel satisfied and happy

B Work in a group. Compare your experiences with the processes of culture shock and reverse culture shock.

EXAMPLE: **A:** I think I've experienced all the stages of culture shock and reverse culture shock described in this chart.
B: I haven't. I guess I had a few problems related to culture shock when I first moved to the United States, but . . .

Go to MyEnglishLab for more communication practice.

Adjective Clauses and Phrases   **261**

FROM GRAMMAR TO WRITING

A BEFORE YOU WRITE You are going to write an essay about the problems that foreign students might experience when moving to a different country and then returning home again. Write a few sentences about the problems students might expect to face.

B WRITE Using your ideas in A, write a five-paragraph essay about problems foreign students might expect to find when they move to another country. Remember to use adjective clauses and phrases. Try to avoid the common mistakes shown in the chart. Use the example below to help you begin your essay.

EXAMPLE: There are a few problems foreign students should be prepared for when they move to another country and then return to their home country.
      The first problem they should expect to encounter involves the food in the new country. Foreign students may have difficulty finding food they're used to eating back home. They may eat a lot of fast food instead, including such things as hamburgers, french fries, and hot dogs. Fast food is usually easy to find and cheap, but it's not healthy.
      The second problem . . .

Common Mistakes in Using Adjective Clauses and Phrases

Don't confuse *who/whom* with *which*. **Which** is used to refer only to **things**, and *who* and *whom* are used only to refer to **people**.	I've met a lot of interesting people, **some of whom** have become long-term friends. **NOT** I've met a lot of interesting people, some of ~~which~~ have become long-term friends.
Move the **preposition** to the **end** of an **adjective clause** if you are **deleting** the **relative pronoun** (*who, whom, that, which*).	It's the store **at which he works**. It's the store **he works at**. **NOT** It's the store ~~he works~~.
If you are changing an adjective clause without a *be* verb to an adjective phrase, be sure to **delete the relative pronoun** and change the verb to its *-ing* form.	Helene was the woman **who lived down the street from me**. Helene was the woman **living down the street from me**. **NOT** Helene was the woman ~~lived~~ down the street from me.

C CHECK YOUR WORK Look at your essay. Underline adjective clauses and phrases. Use the Editing Checklist to check your work.

Editing Checklist

Did you . . . ?

☐ use *which* to refer only to things and *who/whom* to refer only to people

☐ move prepositions to the end of their clauses if you have deleted the relative pronoun

☐ delete the relative pronoun and change the verb to its *-ing* form to form adjective phrases

D REVISE YOUR WORK Read your essay again. Can you improve your writing? Make changes if necessary.

Go to MyEnglishLab for more writing practice.

UNIT 15 REVIEW

Test yourself on the grammar of the unit.

A Complete the sentences. Circle the correct answers.

1. Dr. Brand and Dr. Wang, neither of <u>whom / which</u> I've met yet, are well-known professors.

2. Professor Meemook, <u>which / whose</u> classes I enjoy, is originally from Thailand.

3. My two roommates, both of <u>who / whom</u> are from Nigeria, are experiencing culture shock.

4. Hamburgers and hot dogs, neither of <u>them / which</u> I like, are not popular in my country.

5. Rashid and Hussein, <u>who / whom</u> are both newcomers to this country, work in a grocery store.

6. Anyone <u>interested / interesting</u> in culture shock should attend the lecture.

7. Pelé, <u>born / was born</u> in Brazil, used to be a great soccer player.

8. You can do several things to get over culture shock, <u>includes / including</u> befriending local people and learning more about their culture.

B Complete the sentences with words from the box. You will use some words more than once.

that	which	who	whom	whose

1. I've met five new colleagues, all of _____ I like.

2. I'm taking three new courses, none of _____ are very interesting.

3. I made two friends, both of _____ are teachers, this week.

4. I've lived in several countries, examples of _____ are Chile and Mexico.

5. Two famous authors, both of _____ books I've read, are here today.

6. I read a novel about a young man _____ is caught in a dead-end job.

7. The country _____ Emiko moved to is very different from Japan.

C Find and correct five mistakes.

   Newcomers to a country begin to suffer from culture shock often develop communication problems. They may be acquainted with many people, most of which they were previously able to talk with easily. Now they find it difficult to talk to these people. Moreover, aspects of the new culture, most of whom used to seem interesting and exciting, now begin to seem boring and unappealing. These newcomers may begin to experience negative emotions, included anger, hostility, and depression. Fortunately, this is only a temporary attitude is soon replaced by gradual acceptance.

Now check your answers on page 431.

Go to MyEnglishLab to complete the review online.

Adverbs

OUTCOMES

- Use adverbs to modify sentences and to bring focus to words or phrases in sentences
- Identify key details in conversations on controversial topics
- Discuss controversial topics, expressing opinions, agreeing and disagreeing
- Participate in a debate about a controversial topic
- Write an essay on a controversial topic

OUTCOMES

- Use adverb clauses to indicate when, where, why, or under what condition something happens
- Identify key arguments in a newspaper editorial
- Identify key details in an interview
- Discuss the topic of sports, expressing opinions, agreeing and disagreeing
- Write an essay about benefits and drawbacks of sports

OUTCOMES

- Form and use adverb and adverbial phrases
- Identify a sequence of events in a news story
- Comment on key details from a news broadcast
- Discuss the topic of compassion, expressing and supporting opinions with examples
- Write an essay about a compassionate act

OUTCOMES

- Use a range of connectors and transition words to connect ideas
- Identify key details in a scientific article
- Identify key points in a training workshop
- Discuss the topic of memory, expressing opinions, agreeing and disagreeing
- Write an essay about a memorable experience

Adverbs: Sentence, Focus, and Negative

CONTROVERSIAL ISSUES

OUTCOMES
- Use adverbs to modify sentences and to bring focus to words or phrases in sentences
- Identify key details in conversations on controversial topics
- Discuss controversial topics, expressing opinions, agreeing and disagreeing
- Participate in a debate about a controversial topic
- Write an essay on a controversial topic

STEP 1   GRAMMAR IN CONTEXT

BEFORE YOU READ

Discuss the questions.

1. What is military service?

2. Have you ever done military service? If not, would you like to? Why or why not?

READ

 16|01   Read this transcript of a radio call-in show.

Time to Sound Off

MIKE: Good evening, and welcome to *Sound Off*, the international talk show where you express your uncensored opinions on today's controversial issues. I'm Mike McGaffey. Tonight's topics: Should military service be required or voluntary? Should women join the military, and if they do, should they fight in combat? Let's see if we can shed some light[1] on these issues. Here's our first caller, Jerry Burns, from Kingston, Jamaica. Where do you stand, Jerry?

JERRY: Hi, Mike. Basically, I think military service should be voluntary. And I'm definitely against women being in combat.

MIKE: OK. Why should it be voluntary? Why shouldn't it be required of everyone?

JERRY: Because, overall, young people are not all the same. Some people have a military orientation. For them, military service is fine. Others aren't oriented that way. Compulsory military service interferes with their freedom, essentially.

MIKE: But many argue that we all owe our country something. It protects us and gives us benefits. Shouldn't we give something in return?

JERRY: We should if we're motivated to. But it shouldn't be an obligation. And I'd go further: Military forces have done a lot of evil. Maybe we shouldn't even have them.

MIKE: Hmm. I don't know, Jerry—I'm a pretty accepting guy, but even I find that suggestion extreme. But let's go to your second point. Why shouldn't women be in combat?

JERRY: We need to maintain the difference between the sexes. Men and women have inherent differences. If we put women in combat, we're saying that,

---

1 *shed some light:* provide new information that makes something easier to understand

fundamentally, they're the same as men. But women *just* aren't as physically strong and tough as men. Therefore, they aren't suited for combat.

MIKE: Are you saying that *only* men are strong enough? That's *clearly* an old stereotype.

JERRY: I'm not saying that. I *just* don't think fighting is feminine.

MIKE: Wow. All right, Jerry, very interesting. I expect we'll hear some pretty spirited responses to what you've said. Our next caller is Sarah Lopez from Toronto, Canada. Sarah, does Jerry have a valid point, or is this just fuzzy[2] thinking?

SARAH: Thanks, Mike. *Actually*, I couldn't disagree more with Jerry. It's not fuzzy thinking. He was clear in making his point, but I *just* don't agree with him.

MIKE: OK. So military service shouldn't be voluntary?

SARAH: No. If we're going to have it, it should be required.

MIKE: Why?

SARAH: It's the only way to ensure fair treatment for all. People in the military make major sacrifices—sometimes they risk their lives. That kind of risk should be spread out evenly. *Actually*, I'd go further: I'd support required national service. It wouldn't have to be *only* military.

MIKE: Expand a bit on that.

SARAH: There are lots of worthwhile things citizens can do for their country—like working in day care centers, hospitals, or the Peace Corps. National service has been started in a few countries, and *hopefully* it will be adopted in many more.

MIKE: All right. Now, Jerry opposes women being in combat. What's your position? Should it be allowed?

SARAH: *Not only* should it be allowed, *but* it should *also* be promoted. I should know: I've been in the military for eighteen months. *So* have several of my friends.

MIKE: You have?

SARAH: Yes. I disagree with the way Jerry characterizes women. *No way* is combat unfeminine!

MIKE: Have you ever been in combat?

SARAH: No, but if I'm ever called to combat, I'll be willing to go. Jerry also said we need to maintain the difference between the sexes. I don't agree with that, and *neither do* any of my friends.

MIKE: OK, Sarah. . . . Oops! *There goes* the buzzer. Time to hear from another caller. *Here*'s Lu Adijojo from Singapore. Lu, what's your view? . . .

---

2 *fuzzy:* unclear, confused

AFTER YOU READ

A VOCABULARY   Choose the answer that is closest in meaning to the word in **bold**.

1. On this show, people express their uncensored opinions on today's **controversial** issues.
   a. interesting
   b. causing disagreement
   c. well-known
   d. extremely important

2. Should military service be required or **voluntary**?
   a. done for money
   b. done for advancement
   c. done for enjoyment
   d. done willingly

3. The first caller doesn't think military service should be **compulsory**.
   a. optional
   b. required
   c. difficult
   d. unpleasant

4. He believes forced military service would **interfere with** people's freedom.
   a. limit
   b. increase
   c. have no impact on
   d. cancel

5. Men and women have **inherent** differences.
   a. natural
   b. accidental
   c. extreme
   d. slight

6. If we put women in combat, we're saying that, **fundamentally**, they're the same as men.
   a. partially
   b. definitely not
   c. possibly
   d. basically

7. That's an old **stereotype**, clearly.
   a. idea
   b. recording
   c. rule
   d. characteristic

8. Not only should it be allowed, but it should also be **promoted**.
   a. considered
   b. financed
   c. encouraged
   d. opposed

B COMPREHENSION   Complete the sentences based on the reading.

1. Jerry, the first caller, thinks _____ service should be voluntary.

2. Jerry thinks that only people who have a military _____ should have to join the military.

3. Jerry is _____ women being in combat.

4. Jerry doesn't think fighting is _____.

5. Sarah, the second caller, thinks military service should be _____.

6. In her opinion, it's the only way to ensure _____ treatment for everyone.

7. Sarah does not believe combat is _____.

8. If Sarah were called to combat, she would go _____.

C DISCUSSION   Work with a partner. Discuss your viewpoints on the questions.

1. Should military service be required or voluntary?

2. Should women fight in combat?

Go to MyEnglishLab for more grammar in context practice.

ADVERBS: SENTENCE, FOCUS, AND NEGATIVE

Sentence Adverbs: Placement

Beginning	**Clearly**, these are bitter controversies.
Middle	These are **clearly** bitter controversies.
End	These are bitter controversies, **clearly**.

Focus Adverbs: Placement and Meaning

Placement				Meaning
They	**just** don't	support what	he says.	They think he's wrong.
	don't **just**			They agree with him 100 percent.
Even	he	can do	that.	Almost anyone can do that task.
She	can do	**even**	that.	It's amazing how many things she can do.
Only	men	can	attend.	Women can't.
Men	can	**only**		They can't do anything else.

Negative Adverbs: Placement and Inversion

We	**rarely**	agree	on such things.
Rarely	do we		
I have	**seldom**	heard	that idea.
Seldom	have I		
They	**never**	disagreed	with him.
Never	did they	disagree	

Other Adverbs: Placement and Inversion

Here	comes	**the bus**.
Here	**it**	comes.
There	goes	**the train**.
There	**it**	goes.
Maria	has done	military service.
So	have	**I**.

GRAMMAR NOTES

1 Sentence Adverbs

Adverbs modify verbs, adjectives, and other adverbs.

Simple adverbs modify **single words** or phrases.	Sarah spoke **hopefully** about her future. *(simple adverb modifies the way in which she spoke)*
Sentence adverbs, also called **viewpoint adverbs**, modify entire **sentences**.	**Hopefully**, national service will be adopted in many more countries. *(sentence adverb modifies the entire sentence—It is to be hoped that this will happen.)*
Common sentence adverbs include the following: *absolutely essentially overall* *actually fortunately perhaps* *basically generally possibly* *clearly hopefully surely* *definitely obviously*	**Fortunately**, the Army paid for Bill's college education. *(It is fortunate that the Army paid for Bill's college education.)*
Some adverbs can function **either** as sentence adverbs or as simple adverbs.	**Clearly**, he is a good speaker. *(It's clear that he is a good speaker.)* He speaks **clearly**. *(simple adverb modifies speaks)*
You can use sentence adverbs in various places in a sentence: • If the adverb comes **first or last** in a sentence, we usually separate it from the rest of the sentence with a **comma**.	**Basically,** I'm in favor of that. I'm in favor of that**, basically**.
• If the adverb comes elsewhere in the sentence, it usually comes **after** the verb *be* and **before other verbs**.	I *am* basically in favor of that. I **basically** *agree* with the plan.

2 Focus Adverbs

Focus adverbs **focus attention** on a word or phrase.

Focus adverbs usually go **before the word or phrase focused on**.	**Even I** believe that. *(focuses on I)* I believe **even that**. *(focuses on that)*
Common focus adverbs are *even, just, only,* and *almost*.	We **almost** *spent* $50 but then didn't buy anything. *(focuses on spent)* We spent **almost** *$50*. *(focuses on $50—We spent between $47 and $49.)*
Changing the position of a focus adverb often **changes the meaning** of the sentence.	**Just** *teenagers* can attend the meetings. *(Teenagers are the only ones allowed to attend.)* Teenagers can **just** *attend* the meetings. *(Teenagers can't do anything else in the meetings.)*

3 Negative Adverbs

Negative adverbs are single words or expressions that are **inherently negative** in meaning.

We often place negative adverbs at the **beginning of a sentence** to emphasize the negative meaning. When a negative adverb begins a sentence, it **forces inversion** of the **subject** and the **verb** or auxiliary.

SUBJECT	VERB		ADVERB	
Women	**are**	drafted	**only**	in Israel.

ADVERB	VERB	SUBJECT	
Only in Israel	**are**	**women**	drafted.

SUBJECT	VERB	ADVERB	
He	**is**	**seldom**	on time.

ADVERB	VERB	SUBJECT	
Seldom	**is**	**he**	on time.

Common negative adverbs include the following:

barely	*never*
hardly	*not only*
in no way (informal *no way*)	*only*
little	*rarely*
neither	*seldom*

If the **verb** in the sentence (except for *be*) is in the **simple present** or **simple past**, use *do, does,* or *did* after an initial negative adverb.

Mothers rarely make a career of the military.
Rarely *do* mothers make a career of the military.

The negative adverb *not only* often combines with *but . . . also*. There is inversion after *not only* but **no inversion** between *but* and *also*.

Not only* should we** allow that, ***but we should also encourage it.

If the verb is in the **perfect** form, place the **auxiliary before** the **subject**.

I had never heard such a strange idea.
Never had I heard such a strange idea.

Sentences beginning with *neither* are common in both formal and informal English.

My grandfather didn't join the military. **Neither** did my father.

IN WRITING Sentences beginning with other negative adverbs often sound formal. Use them more in writing.

Seldom have women served in combat.

4 Other Adverbs

Here and *there* are other adverbs that **force inversion** when they come at the **beginning of** a sentence.

Here is your money.
There goes the bus.

So is another adverb that often **forces inversion** of subject and verb or auxiliary when it occurs at the beginning of a sentence. *So* is used to **connect two positive statements**, while *neither* is used to connect two negative statements.

Sarah is in favor of required military service. **So am I.**
My father supports capital punishment. **So does my brother.**

BE CAREFUL! In a sentence beginning with *here* or *there*, invert the subject and verb or auxiliary if the subject is a noun. **Don't invert** them if the subject is a **pronoun**.

Here comes *the bus*.
Here *it* comes.
NOT Here ~~the bus comes~~.
NOT Here ~~comes it~~.

PRONUNCIATION NOTE

Stressing Words After Focus Adverbs

In sentences with **focus adverbs**, the word following the focus adverb normally has the strongest stress in the sentence.

Even **I** like the cold weather.
I even **LIKE** the cold weather.
Only **TEENAGERS** can attend.
Teenagers can only **ATTEND**.

REFERENCE NOTE

For a list of **sentence adverbs**, see Appendix 21 on page 420.

Go to MyEnglishLab to watch the grammar presentation.

STEP 3 **FOCUSED PRACTICE**

EXERCISE 1 DISCOVER THE GRAMMAR

GRAMMAR NOTES 1–3 Underline the adverb in each sentence. Then identify the adverb as a *sentence adverb* (S), *focus adverb* (F), or *negative adverb* (N).

<u>F</u> **1.** Sarah doesn't <u>just</u> support the idea of women in combat.

_____ **2.** Basically, I think service should be voluntary.

_____ **3.** Young people aren't all the same, obviously.

_____ **4.** I'm an accepting guy, but even I find that suggestion extreme.

_____ **5.** Men and women are clearly different.

_____ **6.** Little do many people realize how dangerous military service can be.

_____ **7.** I just don't agree with the basic idea.

_____ **8.** In some countries, women are only allowed to perform medical duties in the military.

_____ **9.** Not only should it be allowed, but it should also be promoted.

_____ **10.** In Switzerland, only men are allowed to serve in combat.

EXERCISE 2 SENTENCE ADVERBS

GRAMMAR NOTE 1 Combine each pair of statements into one statement containing a sentence adverb. Use the adverb form of the word in parentheses. Vary your sentences so that the sentence adverb appears in different positions in the sentences: beginning, middle, and end.

1. National service is beneficial. (obvious)

   National service is obviously beneficial.

2. Military service can be dangerous. (unfortunate)

   _____

3. I'm against the death penalty because I consider it cruel. (essential)

   _____

4. There's a lot more violence in movies than in the past. (certain)

   _____

5. Nuclear weapons can be eliminated. (hopeful)

   _____

6. A vaccine against AIDS can be developed. (possible)

   _____

7. The prime minister's position is wrong. (clear)

   _____

EXERCISE 3 FOCUS ADVERBS

GRAMMAR NOTE 2 Complete the sentences. Circle the correct answers.

1. Bill believes that women should not fight. He feels _____ in noncombat roles.
   a. they should only serve   **b.** only they should serve

2. Carrie thinks women can do most jobs men can do, but she feels _____ in combat.
   a. men should serve only   **b.** only men should serve

3. Samantha is against gambling, but _____ the benefits of lotteries.
   a. even she can recognize   **b.** she can even recognize

4. I'm in favor of higher taxes. _____ taxing food and medicine.
   a. Even I'm in favor of   **b.** I'm even in favor of

5. My husband has some good reasons for supporting nuclear power. However, I _____.
   a. don't just agree   **b.** just don't agree

6. My father _____ the military draft; he's a military recruiter.
   a. doesn't just support   **b.** just doesn't support

7. My friend and I _____ $100 for the tickets, but the concert was worth the money.
   a. almost paid   **b.** paid almost

EXERCISE 4 NEGATIVE ADVERBS

GRAMMAR NOTE 3 Rewrite the sentences using the negative adverb in parentheses.

1. I didn't support the government's decision to invade that country last year. My friends didn't support the government's decision. (neither)

    I didn't support the government's decision to invade that country last year. Neither did my friends.

2. There are many women in the military worldwide. Women fight alongside men in combat. (rarely)

3. Some uninformed people oppose the military. Military service is useless. (in no way)

4. Violence won't ever be completely eliminated. Poverty won't be completely eliminated. (neither)

5. Climate change has become a popular topic. We heard about it in the past. (seldom)

6. I bought an SUV. It had occurred to me that SUVs could harm the environment, but I learned they can. (never)

7. We should support access to health care for everyone. We should take action to make it happen. (not only / but . . . also)

8. The political candidate gave a wonderful speech. I knew that he was being insincere. (little)

EXERCISE 5 NEGATIVE AND FOCUS ADVERBS

GRAMMAR NOTES 2–3 Study the chart. Then complete each sentence with the adverb
even, *just*, *only in*, or *not only/but . . . also* and the correct form of the verb in parentheses.

Country	Has a military	Has required military service	Allows women to serve in the military	Drafts women to serve in the military	Allows women to serve in combat
Brazil	X		X		X
Canada	X		X		X
China	X	X	X	X	
Costa Rica					
Israel	X	X	X	X	
Switzerland	X	X			
The United States	X		X		X
Venezuela	X		X		X

Facts about military service in eight countries:

1. (there / be)

   _____Only in_____ Costa Rica _____is there_____ no military.

2. (have)

   Though officially neutral, _____ Switzerland _____ a military.

3. (there / be)

   _____ three countries _____ required military service.

4. (they / allow)

   _____ do Brazil, Canada, the United States, and Venezuela allow women to

   serve in the military, _____ them to serve

   in combat.

5. (men / be required)

   _____ to serve in combat in Brazil, Canada, the United

   States, and Venezuela.

6. (women / be required)

   _____ Israel and China _____ to do

   military service.

Adverbs: Sentence, Focus, and Negative   **275**

EXERCISE 6 HERE, THERE, AND SO

GRAMMAR NOTE 4 Complete the conversation with the correct forms of the words in parentheses.

ILHAN: How long have we been waiting for our stupid bus? _____*Here comes another 44*_____ .
1. (come / here / another 44)

That's two 44s in the last half hour. I'm really getting tired of waiting.

PAVLINA: _____, but complaining about it won't make it get
2. (I / so)

here any faster.

ILHAN: Yeah, you're probably right. But these buses! They're always late, and they're way too

expensive. I think bus service should be free in the downtown area.

PAVLINA: _____, but the chance of that happening is pretty slim.
3. (I / so)

ILHAN: Hey, look—_____ now. Finally!
4. (come / here / it)

(One minute passes.)

PAVLINA: Oh, no! It's not stopping. . . . _____ . It says "NOT
5. (go / there / it)

IN SERVICE."

ILHAN: Hey, _____ . Let's take that instead.
6. (come / here / a taxi)

EXERCISE 7 STRESSING WORDS AFTER FOCUS ADVERBS

▶ 16|03 **Ⓐ PRONUNCIATION NOTE** Listen to the sentences. Underline the word that each adverb focuses on.

1. Bill can even <u>understand</u> this math.

2. Even Bill can understand this math.

3. I don't just agree with Nancy.

4. I just don't agree with Nancy.

5. We don't even like this food.

6. Even we don't like this food.

7. Only women can visit this club.

8. Women can only visit this club.

▶ 16|03 **Ⓑ** Listen again and repeat the sentences.

EXERCISE 8 EDITING

GRAMMAR NOTES 1–4 Read the email. There are nine mistakes in the use of adverbs. The first mistake is already corrected. Find and correct eight more.

TO: dave111@yoohoo.com
FR: ken0@yoohoo.com
RE: waiting for the train

Hi, Dad,

I'm waiting for the 5:25 train, so ~~just I~~ *I just* thought I'd drop you an email. I've been at the global warming conference. Actually, I almost didn't get to the conference because almost we didn't get our taxes done on time. Vicky and I stayed up late last night, though, and I mailed the forms this morning.

I hate income taxes! Only once in the last ten years we have gotten a refund, and this time the form was so complicated that Vicky got even upset, and you know how calm she is. Maybe we should move to Antarctica or something. No taxes there.

Besides that, we've been having problems with Donna. It's probably nothing more serious than teenage rebellion, but whenever we try to lay down the law, she gets defensive. Rarely if ever she takes criticism well. When we try to correct her, she usually says, "Why can't you just leave me alone?" Fortunately, Sam has been behaving like an angel, and Toby so has. But they're not teenagers!

Meanwhile, Donna's school has started a new open-campus policy. Students can leave the campus whenever they don't have a class. Even they don't have to tell the school office where they're going or when they'll be back. No way Vicky and I approve of that policy! School time, in our view, is for studying and learning, not for socializing. Little do those school officials realize how much trouble unsupervised teenagers can get into.

Well, Dad, here the train comes. I'll sign off now. Email or text me soon.

Love,
Ken

Go to MyEnglishLab for more focused practice.

EXERCISE 9
LISTENING

▶ 16|04   **A**   Listen to the radio call-in show. Overall, what does the caller think about human nature?

_____

_____

_____

▶ 16|04   **B**   Read each statement. Then listen to the talk show again. Check (✓) *True* or *False*.

	True	False
1. Capital punishment is used in every state in the United States.	☐	☑
2. The host of the radio show says that there clearly seems to be a worldwide movement to abolish capital punishment.	☐	☐
3. The caller is in favor of capital punishment, overall.	☐	☐
4. Capital punishment is apparently used in China.	☐	☐
5. Generally, the caller feels that people have gotten more civilized.	☐	☐
6. The caller believes that robbery is clearly a capital crime.	☐	☐
7. According to the caller, rehabilitation is clearly impossible for all criminals.	☐	☐
8. The caller hopes that the death penalty will not be abolished worldwide.	☐	☐

C   Work with a partner. Discuss the questions. Give reasons for your answers.

1. Do you basically agree or disagree with the viewpoint of the caller in the Listening?

2. Do you believe that, overall, people have become more or less civilized than they were in ancient times?

3. Do you believe that, generally, criminals are capable of rehabilitation?

EXERCISE 10   HOW DO YOU FEEL ABOUT...?

A   SURVEY   Work in a group. Ask your classmates for their opinions on the controversial issues in the chart on page 279. Then add up your group's responses, noting the number of students supporting and opposing each viewpoint.

EXAMPLE: **A:** How do you feel about making all schools coeducational?
     B: I'm absolutely in favor of it. Boys and girls should go to school together.
     C: I'm against it, overall. Coeducational schools are fine, generally, but some students do better in single-sex schools.

Topic	Absolutely in Favor	In Favor, Overall	Against, Overall	Absolutely Against
Making all schools coeducational				
Adopting children from foreign countries				
Requiring military service				
Cloning				
Government providing health care				

B Analyze the responses and draw conclusions from the data you collected. Report your conclusions to the class.

EXAMPLE: The people in our group are against making all schools coeducational, overall. Three people were completely in favor of this, but seven were against it, overall. Many of my classmates clearly believe that single-sex schools have some benefits.

EXERCISE 11 LET'S HAVE A DEBATE

A DEBATE You are going to have a debate. Work in a group. Choose a controversial topic that might be discussed on a TV or radio call-in show. Select a topic from the box or choose one of your own. Brainstorm points supporting both sides of the issue. Make a list of pros and cons.

Electric cars	Making voting compulsory	Using standardized tests in school
Gun control	Providing free education	

PROS:
- Gun control is clearly necessary.
- Apparently, people don't really know how to use guns safely, and they often shoot people accidentally.
- Not only are guns dangerous, but they are also . . .

CONS:
- Basically, everyone needs to have access to guns for protection.
- Clearly, strong enough guns laws already exist, but many times they're not even enforced. . . .

B Divide into two smaller groups. One group is for the topic (pro), and the other is against it (con). Further develop arguments for your list of points from A. Do research on the Internet if necessary.

EXAMPLE: Gun control is clearly necessary because, in the United States, more than 100,000 people are hurt or killed by guns every year. If we didn't have gun control, everyone would have guns, and many more people would obviously get injured. . . .

C Work in your original group from A again. Conduct the debate, using your arguments from B.

Go to MyEnglishLab for more communication practice.

FROM GRAMMAR TO WRITING

A **BEFORE YOU WRITE** You are going to write an essay on a controversial topic. Choose one of the topics in Exercise 11 or another topic. Write a few sentences on both sides of the issue. Then choose one viewpoint to focus on in your essay.

B **WRITE** Using your ideas from A, write a five-paragraph essay about the controversy you have chosen. Remember to use sentence, focus, and negative adverbs. Try to avoid the common mistakes shown in the chart. Use the example below to help you begin your essay.

EXAMPLE: Should we have national service in our country? Our government provides a lot of benefits to us, and we should certainly give something in return. Therefore, I think national service should be established in our nation. Not only should national service be available, but it should also be required of every citizen.

Here are the reasons why I believe this. . . .

Common Mistakes in Using Adverbs

Don't omit necessary **commas** next to **sentence adverbs**.	Gun control is a controversial **issue, clearly**. **NOT** Gun control is a controversial ~~issue clearly~~.
Invert the **subject** and the **verb** after **negative** adverbs at the **beginning** of a sentence.	*Rarely* **have I** heard such a bad idea. **NOT** Rarely ~~I have~~ heard such a bad idea.
Don't misplace the focus adverbs *almost*, *even*, *just*, and *only*. Place a **focus adverb** immediately **before** the word it focuses on.	She doesn't *even* **listen** to me. **NOT** She ~~even doesn't~~ listen to me. I don't *just* **like** that idea; I love it. **NOT** I ~~just don't~~ like that idea; I love it. **Only** students are eligible; adults are not. **NOT** ~~Students are only~~ eligible; adults are not.
Invert the **subject** and **verb** if the words *here*, *there*, or *so* begin a sentence and a noun follows.	Here **is *the book*** I borrowed from you. **NOT** Here ~~the book is~~ I borrowed from you.

C **CHECK YOUR WORK** Look at your essay. Underline sentence, focus, and negative adverbs. Use the Editing Checklist to check your work.

Editing Checklist

Did you . . . ?
- ☐ punctuate sentence adverbs correctly
- ☐ invert the subject and the verb after negative adverbs
- ☐ use correct word order with focus adverbs
- ☐ use correct word order after the words *here*, *there*, and *so*

D **REVISE YOUR WORK** Read your essay again. Can you improve your writing? Make changes if necessary.

Go to MyEnglishLab for more writing practice.

UNIT 16 REVIEW

Test yourself on the grammar of the unit.

A Complete the sentences. Circle the correct answers.

1. Mom tries to get me to eat oatmeal, but I don't just / just don't like it.

2. Never had we / we had seen such a fine performance.

3. Bill is pro-military; he even thinks / even he thinks the draft should be renewed.

4. In our club, members can only / only members can attend meetings.

5. I just don't / don't just love him; I want to marry him.

6. Pau is a terrible cook, but even he can / he can even boil eggs.

7. Rarely does Eva / Eva does arrive late at the office.

8. Here the train comes / comes the train.

B Complete the sentences with the correct forms of the words in parentheses.

1. Only in Australia _____ .
   (kangaroos / found)

2. _____ .
   (something / clear / have to / change)

3. _____ ,
   (not only / education / should / be / available to everyone)
   but it should also be free.

4. _____ .
   (seldom / our team / lose)

5. _____ ; non-citizens cannot.
   (citizens / only / can / vote)

6. _____ that I owe you.
   (here / the money / be)

7. _____ .
   (there / the plane / go)

C Find and correct five errors.

   Ben is my partner on our debate team, and he's one of my best friends, but sometimes he irritates me. Not only he is often late for debates, but I never know if he's going to be prepared. Rarely he will accept criticism, and at times even he won't listen. I never just know what kind of mood he's going to be in. He's an excellent debater fortunately. So, if his heart is in the debate, we usually win it.

Check your answers on page 431.

Go to MyEnglishLab to complete the review online.

STEP 1	GRAMMAR IN CONTEXT

BEFORE YOU READ

Discuss the questions.

1. What are some benefits of sports?

2. What are some negative aspects of sports?

READ

 Read this editorial about sports.

EDITORIAL

Are Sports Still Sporting?

AS I WRITE THIS EDITORIAL, preparations for the 2016 Summer Olympics are in full swing in Rio de Janeiro, Brazil. This international competition seems likely to be a big success, with 206 countries expected to participate in the first games ever to be played in South America. The 2012 Summer Games in London, England, and the 2014 Winter Olympics in Sochi, Russia, were artistic triumphs. The popularity of sports worldwide continues to rise. But while sports may look good on the surface, problems lurk underneath. For one thing, there's a vast overemphasis on fame and the worshipping of famous athletes. Then there's the increasingly large role money is playing in sports today, since there are ever-increasing possibilities for product endorsement by athletes. Finally, sports violence has certainly not diminished. In April of 2013, for example, a coach in an amateur soccer game in Salt Lake City was punched in the face by a player because he had penalized that player. The coach later died from the injury. What is wrong? I've concluded that the whole sports scene is in need of repair and have identified three major excesses:

FIRST EXCESS: Misplaced focus on fame. When the Olympics began about 2,700 years ago in Greece, the contests were derived from war. The javelin throw, for example, paralleled the throwing of a spear in a battle. Running paralleled the physical exertion you might have to make if an enemy was chasing you. When the modern Olympic games started in 1896, the philosophy had

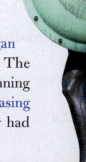

shifted to the promotion of peace. However, emphasis was still placed on demonstrating physical stamina[1] and excellence in challenging contests. How things have changed! Although athletes still try to achieve their personal best, the focus has shifted to the breaking of records and the achievement of fame. Can we really say that someone who finishes the 400-meter freestyle swim one-tenth of a second ahead of his or her nearest rival is a champion, while that rival is an also-ran[2]?

SECOND EXCESS: Money. Consider the cost of attending a major athletic competition. In the United States, the average cost of a ticket to a National Football League game in 2015 was about $84. If you add up the cost of taking a family of four to a game, the total was over $440. A ticket to an NBA basketball game is about $52. Baseball is cheaper, though it's not really a bargain at an average ticket cost of about $30. I wondered why tickets are so expensive until I remembered the key factor: players' salaries. NBA basketball star LeBron James earns about $23 million a year. Baseball player Alex Rodriguez made about $22 million in 2015. Is anyone worth that much money? Meanwhile, the president of the United States earns $400,000 a year, and U.S. public schoolteachers make a median yearly salary of about $53,000. We can infer a lot about what we value by looking at what we pay people. When we compensate professional athletes so highly, are we rewarding the people who are truly valuable to society?

LeBron James

THIRD EXCESS: Prevalence of violence. We see it wherever we look, and it's certainly not decreasing. Fights occur frequently in professional sports, with ice hockey one of the worst offenders. In one of the best-known cases, for instance, NHL player Steve Moore had to be hospitalized because another player hit him in the head with his hockey stick. Unfortunately, there seems to be increasing acceptance of violence as "just part of the game." But once we assume violence is inevitable, it will be almost impossible to stop. This sort of thing doesn't just happen in North America. We've all heard about the well-publicized violence surrounding soccer games in Europe. In another example that occurred in December of 2012, a Dutch amateur linesman was beaten to death after a youth match concluded.

Sports have enormous potential to benefit society, but somehow, in becoming big business entertainment, they have gone awry. What to do? Well, we can pay more attention to local athletics and events such as the Special Olympics. We can refuse to pay ridiculously high ticket prices. We can demand an end to violence. Above all, we need to get back to this idea: It's not whether you win or lose; it's how you play the game.

---

1 *stamina:* strength of body or mind to fight tiredness, illness, etc.
2 *also-ran:* a loser in a competition

AFTER YOU READ

A VOCABULARY   Complete the definitions with words from the box.

awry	derive	factor	infer	lurk	parallel	prevalence	shift

1. When you take something from an original source, you _____ it from that source.

2. When something changes in practice or position, it is said to _____.

3. To wait somewhere secretly is to _____.

4. Something that matches another situation is said to _____ it.

5. The common, general, or wide existence of something is termed _____.

6. An element, part, or ingredient of something is termed a(n) _____.

7. To _____ something is to deduce or draw a conclusion.

8. Something that has not happened the way it was planned is said to have gone _____.

B COMPREHENSION   Complete the sentences. Circle the correct answers.

1. When the Olympics began in ancient Greece, athletic contests were related to _____.
   a. politics   **b.** money   **c.** war

2. The modern Olympic Games were designed to promote _____.
   a. political harmony   **b.** peace   **c.** economics

3. According to the author, the emphasis in today's Olympic Games has shifted to _____.
   a. the pursuit of excellence   **b.** the achievement of fame   **c.** training for war

4. Tickets for _____ games are currently the least expensive of the three major U.S. sports.
   a. baseball   **b.** basketball   **c.** football

5. The author says that the high cost of tickets today is most directly related to the need to _____.
   a. pay taxes to the government   **b.** provide help for team owners   **c.** pay players' salaries

6. In the United States today, the average annual salary of _____ is about $50,000.
   a. the president   **b.** a public schoolteacher   **c.** a professional athlete

7. According to the author, sports violence is _____.
   a. decreasing   **b.** staying about the same   **c.** increasing

8. To improve the sports scene, the author recommends _____.
   a. supporting local athletics   **b.** making sports events more expensive   **c.** ignoring violence

C DISCUSSION   Work with a partner. Discuss: Do you agree or disagree with the author of the editorial about the excesses of sports? Give reasons for your answer.

Go to MyEnglishLab for more grammar in context practice.

ADVERB CLAUSES

Placement and Punctuation

Main Clause	Adverb Clause
We watched TV a lot	**when the Olympics were on.**
Tickets cost more	**because athletes earn so much.**

Adverb Clause	Main Clause
When the Olympics were on,	we watched TV a lot.
Because athletes earn so much,	tickets cost more.

Types

Adverb Clauses of Time	
Before I played basketball,	I was a soccer player.
The coach met with her players	**after the game was over.**
While the team was on the field,	the fans cheered continuously.

Adverb Clauses of Place	
I've seen children playing soccer	**everywhere I've been.**
Anywhere you go,	sports stars are national heroes.
I work out at a gym	**wherever I travel.**

Adverb Clauses of Reason	
Since she plays well,	I want her on our team.
He was unable to play in the final game	**as he had hurt his ankle.**
Now that TV covers the Games,	billions of people can see the Olympics.

Adverb Clauses of Condition	
Unless the tickets cost too much,	we'll go to the game next Saturday.
You'll be comfortable inside the dome	**even if it's cold and raining outside.**
Only if she wins the gold medal	will she get a professional contract.

Adverb Clauses of Contrast	
They won the game,	**though they didn't really deserve the victory.**
Although their team is talented,	they didn't win.
Swimmers are rarely injured,	**whereas hockey players are often hurt.**

GRAMMAR NOTES

1 Definition of Adverb Clauses

Remember that a **clause** is a group of words that contains at least one **subject** and a **verb** showing past, present, or future time. Clauses can be **independent** or **dependent**. (See Unit 14.)

Adverb clauses are **dependent** clauses that indicate **how**, **when**, **where**, **why**, or **under what conditions** things happen.

I went home **when the game was over.** *(when)*
She dropped out of the race **because she was injured.** *(why)*

Adverb clauses can also introduce a **contrast**.

They won the game, **although the score was very close.** *(contrast)*

Adverb clauses begin with **subordinating conjunctions** (also called subordinating adverbs), which can be either single words or phrases.

It began to rain *while* we were playing.
I have to practice *now that* I'm on the team.

Sentences containing both an independent clause and a dependent clause are called **complex sentences**. In a complex sentence, the **main idea** is normally in the **independent clause**.

DEPENDENT   INDEPENDENT
CLAUSE   CLAUSE (MAIN IDEA)
If we can get tickets, we'll go to the game.

Adverb clauses sometimes occur **inside independent** clauses.

The weather **when the game started** was terrible.

In a complex sentence, the clauses can come in either order. If the **dependent** clause comes **first**, we place a **comma** after it.

Whenever I exercise, I feel good.
I feel good **whenever I exercise.**

BE CAREFUL! In complex sentences, do not use *will* or *be going to* in the dependent clause to show future time.

We'll leave when they **get** here.
NOT We'll leave when they ~~will~~ get here.

2 Adverb Clauses of Time

Adverb clauses of time indicate **when** something happens.

To introduce an adverb clause of time, use *after*, *as*, *as soon as*, *before*, *by the time*, *once*, *since*, *until/till*, *when*, *whenever*, *while*, etc.

The race will start *as soon as* everyone is in place.
We always drink water *before* we start a game.
As we were walking, we heard shouts from the stadium.

The subordinating conjunction *once* means *starting from the moment something happens*.

She'll earn a good salary *once* she starts playing regularly.

The subordinating conjunctions *until* and *till* have the same meaning. *Till* is more informal and used more in conversation.

I will wait here *until* they arrive.
They won't be here *till* after the plane lands.

3 Adverb Clauses of Place

Adverb clauses of place indicate **where** something happens.

To introduce an adverb clause of place, use *anywhere*, *everywhere*, *where*, *wherever*, etc.	Professional sports are played *where* **there are big stadiums**. Star athletes are popular *wherever* **they go**.

4 Adverb Clauses of Reason

Adverb clauses of reason indicate **why** something happens.

To introduce an adverb clause of reason, use *as*, *because*, *now that* (= because now), *since*, etc.	She won *because* **she'd practiced tirelessly**. *Since* **he didn't register in time**, he can't play.
You can use *since* both in adverb clauses of reason and of time.	*Since* **Anna doesn't like sports**, she refused to go to the game. *(reason:* since = because*)* Barry has played sports *since* **he entered high school**. *(time:* since = starting from that point*)*
You can use *as* both in adverb clauses of reason and of time.	*As* **he was badly hurt**, he had to drop out of the game. *(reason:* as = because*)* He set a world record *as* **we were watching the Summer Olympics**. *(time:* as = while*)*

5 Adverb Clauses of Condition

Adverb clauses of condition indicate **under what conditions** something happens.

To introduce an adverb clause of condition, use *even if*, *if*, *only if*, *in case*, *unless*, etc.	You'll improve *if* **you practice daily**.
Even if means that the condition does not matter; the result will be the same.	*Even if* **he practices constantly**, he won't make the team.
Only if means that only one condition will produce the result.	Bi-Yun will make the team *only if* **another athlete drops out**.
Unless means that something will happen or be true if another thing does not happen or is not true.	*Unless* **you train a great deal**, you won't be a champion.
In case means that something should be done to prepare for a possible future happening.	We'd better take along some extra money *in case* **the tickets are more expensive than we thought**.
If the sentence begins with *only if*, invert the subject and verb of the main clause, and don't use a comma.	**Only if** another athlete drops out *will* **Bi-Yun** make the team.
BE CAREFUL! Don't confuse *even if* (or *even though*) with *even*.	**Even** my mother knows the rules of baseball. **Even if** they win, they won't be the champions. **NOT** ~~Even~~ they win, they won't be the champions.

Adverb clauses of contrast make a contrast with the idea expressed in the independent clause.

To introduce an adverb clause of contrast, use *although*, *even though*, *though*, *whereas*, *while*, etc.	He lost the race, *although* he was favored. *Even though* she is tall, she doesn't score much.
We often use *although*, *even though*, and *though* when we want to show an **unexpected result**.	*Although* he is young, he was selected for the team. *Though* he didn't start playing basketball until his senior year, he quickly became a star.
We often place a **comma before and after** a dependent clause of contrast.	We attended the Olympics, *even though it cost a lot*. *Even though it cost a lot,* we attended the Olympics.
To make a direct contrast, use *while* or *whereas*. *Whereas* is a bit more formal than *while*.	*While snowboarding is pricey*, skating is cheap. *Whereas my sister loves athletics*, my brother couldn't care less about them.
Use *while* to introduce both a clause of contrast and a clause of time.	*While they lost the game*, they played their best. *(contrast)* We ate *while we were watching the game*. *(time)*

REFERENCE NOTES

For a list of **subordinating conjunctions**, see Appendix 22 on page 420.
For more information on **future time clauses**, see Unit 3 on page 38.

Go to MyEnglishLab to watch the grammar presentation.

STEP 3   FOCUSED PRACTICE

EXERCISE 1 DISCOVER THE GRAMMAR

GRAMMAR NOTES 1–6 Read the sentences based on the reading. Underline the adverb clause in each sentence. Then identify the adverb clause as a clause of *contrast*, *place*, *time*, *reason*, or *condition*.

<u>*time*</u>   **1.** As I write this editorial, preparations are in full swing for the 2016 Olympics.

_____   **2.** While sports may look good on the surface, problems lurk underneath.

_____   **3.** Because he penalized a player, a British referee received death threats.

_____   **4.** When the Olympic Games started about 2,700 years ago in Greece, the contests held were basically those derived from war.

_____   **5.** Running paralleled the physical exertion you might have to make if an enemy was chasing you.

_____ **6.** Although athletes still try to achieve their personal best, the emphasis has shifted away from the individual pursuit of excellence.

_____ **7.** I wondered why tickets are so expensive until I remembered the key factor: players' salaries.

_____ **8.** Baseball is cheaper, though it's not really a bargain at an average ticket cost of $30.

_____ **9.** We see violence wherever we look.

_____ **10.** Once we assume violence is inevitable, it will be almost impossible to stop.

EXERCISE 2 SUBORDINATING CONJUNCTIONS IN ADVERB CLAUSES

GRAMMAR NOTES 2, 4–6 Read the sentences about various sports. Circle the correct subordinating conjunction in each sentence.

1. (Before) / Because you can ski, you need a lift ticket.

2. If / Although the overall score is forty love, one player's score is zero.

3. You can't play this game if / unless you have ice skates.

4. You go to the free-throw line before / after you've been fouled.

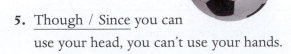

5. Though / Since you can use your head, you can't use your hands.

6. While / When you've finished the course, you've run 26.2 miles.

7. Your team can't bat until / in case the other team makes three outs.

8. Although / If your team scores a touchdown, it earns six points.

EXERCISE 3 MAIN CLAUSES AND ADVERB CLAUSES

GRAMMAR NOTES 2, 4–6 Combine each pair of sentences into one sentence containing an adverb clause and a main clause. Keep the clauses in the same order. Choose subordinating conjunctions from the box, using a different one in each sentence. Add necessary punctuation.

after	although	because	before	if	since	when	~~while~~

1. There are similarities between the ancient Olympics and modern Olympics. There are also differences.

   While there are similarities between the ancient Olympics and modern Olympics, there are also differences.

2. Greek city-states were often at war with one another. Olympic contestants stopped fighting during the games.

   _____

   _____

3. They had been held for over 1,000 years. The ancient Olympic Games were outlawed by the Roman Emperor Theodosius I.

   _____

   _____

4. Romans thought the Greeks wore too few clothes. Theodosius outlawed the games in 393.

   _____

   _____

5. French educator Pierre de Coubertin revived the Olympics. He thought they would promote international peace.

   _____

   _____

6. Tug-of-war was dropped from the Olympics in 1920. American and British athletes disagreed about how it should be played.

   _____

   _____

7. New Olympic sports often appear as demonstration events. They are adopted as medal sports.

   _____

   _____

8. Any sport can potentially become a medal event. It can be scored and fulfills certain criteria.

   _____

   _____

EXERCISE 4   CONDITION, CONTRAST, REASON, TIME

GRAMMAR NOTES 2, 4–6 Look at the pictures. Use the type of adverb clause given to complete the sentences describing each picture. Use a different subordinating conjunction in each clause.

1. CONDITION

The Sharks will win the game *if the player*
makes the basket.
_____

2. CONDITION

The other team can't win _____
_____
_____

3. CONTRAST

_____
_____
_____, their fans still love them.

4. CONTRAST

The players are doing their best _____
_____
_____

5. REASON

_____
_____
_____, the competition was postponed.

6. TIME

The competition won't be held _____
_____
_____ improves.

GRAMMAR NOTES 1–6 Read the student essay. There are ten mistakes in the use of adverb clauses. The first mistake is already corrected. Find and correct nine more.

Why Sports?

People are criticizing school athletics these days. Supposedly, there's too much emphasis on sports, ~~if~~ *while* there's not enough emphasis on education. People say that sports are too dangerous and encourage violence. I disagree. In my opinion, school sports are a positive force.

Sports are positive although they get students involved in something. We constantly hear that violence is increasing. But I think a lot of people get involved in crime when they don't have enough to do. After you'll play any kind of sport for two or three hours, it's hard to commit a violent act even you want to.

Second, sports teach people a lot of worthwhile things. If students play on a team, they learn to get along and work with others. Wherever their team wins, they learn how to be good winners. When their team loses they find out that they have to struggle to improve. They discover that winning a few and losing a few are part of the normal ups and downs of life. Also, students improve their physical condition unless they participate in sports.

Finally, sports are positive though they allow students who don't have enough money for college to earn sports scholarships and improve their chances for a successful life. Unless a young soccer player from a small village in Africa can get a scholarship, he will have a chance to get an education and probably make his life better. If a young woman with little money earns a scholarship to join a college swim team, she'll have the chance to earn a college degree and go on to a worthwhile job. Because school sports programs have some problems that need to be fixed, their benefits outweigh their disadvantages. I should know because I got a sports scholarship myself. School sports must stay.

Go to MyEnglishLab for more focused practice.

EXERCISE 6   LISTENING

▶ 17|02   **A**   Listen to the interview with Lillian Swanson, a sports star. Why does Lillian think she became successful?

_____

_____

▶ 17|02   **B**   Read the questions. Then listen again and answer each question with a complete sentence.

1. When did Lillian learn to swim?
   She learned to swim when she was four.

2. Why did Lillian and her family spend a lot of time at the beach?
   _____

3. What did Lillian decide when she was twelve?
   _____

4. Under what conditions did Lillian's parents agree to pay for lessons?
   _____

5. Although people know that sports make people physically stronger, what positive benefits of sports are they less aware of?
   _____

6. According to Lillian, what happens to kids whenever they play sports?
   _____

7. When did Lillian get discouraged?
   _____

8. Why can't Lillian imagine herself doing anything else?
   _____

C   Work with a partner. Discuss the questions.

1. Because Lillian loves swimming, she can't imagine doing anything else. Do you enjoy doing sports? If you do, why? Describe experiences you've had with sports.

2. In your opinion, should parents pressure their children to participate in sports?

3. Once Lillian had made the decision to try to get to the Olympics, her parents promised to support her if she stuck to her plan. Do you think that parents should require their children to stick to plans they've promised to carry out?

EXERCISE 7 FAMOUS SPORTS QUOTATIONS

CRITICAL THINKING   Work in a group. Read the quotations about sports. Choose five quotations and discuss them. What do they mean? Do you agree with them? Why or why not? Then report your conclusions to the class.

1. Champions keep playing until they get it right. —*Billie Jean King, tennis player*

    EXAMPLE: **A:** I think it's true that champions keep playing until they get it right. If you give up before you learn to do something well, you can never become a champion.

    B: That's true. But I think people shouldn't try to get something right unless they are good at it already. Not everyone can be a champion. . . .

2. The Six Ws: Work will win when wishing won't. —*Todd Blackledge, football player*

3. A good hockey player plays where the puck is. A great hockey player plays where the puck is going to be. —*Wayne Gretzky, hockey player*

4. You are never really playing an opponent. You are playing yourself, your own highest standards, and when you reach your limits, that is real joy. —*Arthur Ashe, tennis player*

5. Most people give up just when they're about to achieve success. They quit on the one yard line. They give up at the last minute of the game, one foot from a winning touchdown. —*Ross Perot, businessman and U.S. presidential candidate*

6. Good, better, best. Never let it rest—until your good is better and your better is best. —*Tim Duncan, basketball player*

7. When you lose a couple of times, it makes you realize how difficult it is to win. —*Steffi Graf, tennis player*

8. If it is a cliché to say athletics build character as well as muscle, then I subscribe to the cliché. —*Gerald Ford, U.S. president*

EXERCISE 8 SPORTS AND VIOLENCE

A DISCUSSION   Work in a group. Read the quotation from novelist George Orwell. Do you agree or disagree with his statements? Discuss the questions.

1. When athletes play sports seriously, are they concerned with fair play?

2. Although hatred, jealousy, and boastfulness can be found in the sports scene, do most athletes show these emotions when they compete?

3. Do a significant number of spectators take pleasure in witnessing violence whenever they watch sporting competitions?

4. Do you agree or disagree with Orwell's statement that sport is like war without the shooting? Why?

> **SERIOUS SPORT** has nothing to do with fair play. It is bound up with hatred, jealousy, boastfulness, disregard of all rules and sadistic pleasure in witnessing violence: in other words it is war minus the shooting.
>
> —*George Orwell*

B Share your group's conclusions with the class.

EXAMPLE: Our group felt that even though some athletes aren't concerned with fair play, the majority are concerned with it. They have to be because . . .

EXERCISE 9 THE SPORTS SCENE

A PICTURE DISCUSSION You are going to discuss different aspects of sports. First, study the photos. Then write *A* (*agree*) or *D* (*disagree*) for the statements below.

_____ **1.** Since too many athletes and fans are getting hurt, we need to solve the problem of sports violence as soon as possible.

_____ **2.** We should encourage young people to play sports. When young people play sports, they grow physically, mentally, and psychologically.

_____ **3.** Sports are worthwhile because they entertain people and provide enjoyment.

_____ **4.** Sports are beneficial for everyone. Even though some people have different abilities, they can still participate in them.

B Work in a group. Compare your answers to the questions in A. Give reasons for your answers.

EXAMPLE: **A:** I agree with Statement 1. I think that we should try to stop sports violence because too many athletes and fans are getting hurt.

B: I agree. We think that the police should always be at athletic events in case violence occurs. They should arrest people immediately if they start to act violently.

C: Well, although sports violence does happen sometimes, I don't think it's such a serious problem. I think that sports are positive overall because . . .

C Report your conclusions to the class. Then discuss: What do sports mean to you personally?

EXAMPLE: **A:** Sports mean very little to me personally. If I had the choice of going to a sporting event or staying home and reading a book, I'd stay home and read.

B: I have a different viewpoint. Sports mean a lot to me because . . .

Go to MyEnglishLab for more communication practice.

FROM GRAMMAR TO WRITING

A **BEFORE YOU WRITE** You are going to write an essay about the benefits and drawbacks of sports. Choose one of these topics and write a few sentences about it.

- Sports are valuable to society because they provide entertainment.
- Sports have become too violent.
- Sports stars earn ridiculously large salaries.
- Sports provide opportunities to people who have few other opportunities.
- Sports provide psychological and physical benefits for those who participate in them.

B **WRITE** Using your ideas from A, write a five-paragraph essay about the topic you have chosen. Remember to use adverb clauses. Try to avoid the common mistakes shown in the chart. Use the example below to help you begin your essay.

EXAMPLE: Though many people say that sports are too important in our culture, my view is that the advantages of sports outweigh their disadvantages. I strongly believe this because sports provide opportunities to people who don't have many other opportunities. Consider a boy from a poor family, for example. His parents can't afford to send him to college, even though he's a good student. He's very good at basketball. . . .

Common Mistakes in Using Adverb Clauses

Don't use *will* or *be going to* in **adverb clauses** expressing future **time**. Use the **simple present**.	As soon as Jomo **calls**, I'll get the tickets. **NOT** As soon as Jomo ~~will call~~, I'll get the tickets.
Don't use normal word order if an adverb clause begins with *only if*. **Invert** the subject and verb or auxiliary.	**Only if** she works hard *will she* succeed. **NOT** Only if she works hard ~~she will~~ succeed.
Don't confuse *even if* with *even*.	**Even if** Omar comes soon, we'll be late. **NOT** ~~Even~~ Omar comes soon, we'll be late.
Be sure to place a **comma** after an introductory adverb clause.	**If Jane makes the team,** I'll be happy. **NOT** If Jane makes the ~~team I'll~~ be happy.

C **CHECK YOUR WORK** Look at your essay. Underline the adverb clauses. Use the Editing Checklist to check your work.

Editing Checklist

Did you . . . ?

- [ ] use the simple present in adverb clauses expressing future time
- [ ] invert the subject and the verb in adverb clauses beginning with *only if*
- [ ] avoid confusing *even if* and *even*
- [ ] place a comma after an introductory adverb clause

D **REVISE YOUR WORK** Read your essay again. Can you improve your writing? Make changes if necessary.

Go to MyEnglishLab for more writing practice.

UNIT 17 REVIEW

Test yourself on the grammar of the unit.

A Complete the sentences. Circle the correct answers.

1. You won't be a champion if / unless you practice regularly.
2. Since / Even though the team is in the playoffs, I doubt they'll win the title.
3. We're taking along our racquets in case / although there's time to play.
4. Whenever / As Hai was running toward the goal line, he sprained his ankle.
5. Once / Because Bahdoon gets used to his new position, he'll start playing well.
6. Nelson and Elena don't go dancing once / now that they have children.
7. Famous athletes are in demand wherever / whereas they go.
8. We'll be leaving when / since she arrives.

B Complete the sentences with the words from the box.

although	as soon as	because	only if	unless	whenever	while

1. I visit my cousin _____ I'm in town.
2. _____ she arrives, we'll be leaving.
3. _____ I study for the next two weeks, I probably won't pass the exam.
4. _____ she's seldom at home, I don't often stop to see her.
5. _____ he exercises will he lose weight.
6. _____ they played with great skill, they lost the game.
7. _____ flying costs a lot, bus travel is inexpensive.

C Find and correct five mistakes.

A: As soon as Mom will get here, we can leave for the game.

B: You mean Mom is coming with us to the game? She won't understand what's going on even we give her a long explanation.

A: Unless we explain it slowly and carefully, she'll get the basic idea.

B: I'm not so sure. Only if we can take an hour or so to explain it she'll get the overall picture.

A: Even though she might not understand everything she'll enjoy being with us.

Check your answers on page 431.

Go to MyEnglishLab to complete the review online.

Adverb and Adverbial Phrases

COMPASSION

OUTCOMES
• Form and use adverb and adverbial phrases
• Identify a sequence of events in a news story
• Comment on key details from a news broadcast
• Discuss the topic of compassion, expressing and supporting opinions with examples
• Write an essay about a compassionate act

STEP 1   GRAMMAR IN CONTEXT

BEFORE YOU READ

Discuss the questions.

1. What is your definition of compassion?

2. How important a value is compassion in society?

READ

▶ 18|01   Read this article about compassion.

Compassion

Nicholas Green

It was the evening of September 29, 1994. Having spent a wonderful day exploring the ruins at Paestum in southern Italy, Reg and Maggie Green were driving south in the region of Italy known as the boot, their children Nicholas and Eleanor sleeping peacefully in the back seat. Suddenly an old, decrepit car pulled up alongside them. An Italian with a bandanna over his face yelled at them while motioning for them to stop. Not knowing what to do, Reg quickly considered the options. If they stopped, they risked a potentially deadly confrontation with criminals; if they sped away, they might escape. Guessing that their newer-model car could probably elude the old car the criminals were driving, Reg stepped on the gas. Shots rang out, shattering both windows on the driver's side of the car. The Greens' car took off, easily outdistancing the bandits' car. On checking the children, Reg and Maggie found them still sleeping peacefully in the back seat.

A bit farther down the road, Reg saw a police car parked on the shoulder and pulled over to alert the authorities. Upon opening the door, he saw blood oozing from the back of Nicholas's head. After being rushed to a hospital, Nicholas remained in a coma for two days, his status not changing. Then doctors declared him brain-dead. This was not the end of the story, however. As Nicholas lay on his deathbed, Reg and Maggie decided that something good should come out of the situation. Realizing that it would be far better to return good for evil than to seek revenge, they offered Nicholas's organs for transplant. "Someone should have the future he lost," Reg said. Profoundly moved by the gesture, Italians poured out their emotions. Maurizio Costanzo, the host of a talk show, summed up the common feeling by saying, "You have given us a lesson in civility . . . shown us how to react in the face of pain and sorrow."

The great irony of this tragedy was that it was a mistake. According to investigators' later determinations, Nicholas was killed by two petty[1] criminals who thought the Greens were jewelers carrying precious gems. The criminals were placed on trial after being turned over to the police.

People all over Europe and North America reacted in sorrow. Headlines in the Italian media spoke of *La Nostra Vergogna* ("Our Shame"). Wherever the Greens went, they met Italians who asked for their forgiveness. The Greens were given a medal, Italy's highest honor, by the prime minister.

Some good has indeed come out of Nicholas's death. Seven Italians received Nicholas's heart, liver, kidneys, islet cells, and corneas.[2] Perhaps more importantly, a blow was struck[3] for organ donation. Having heard Reg and Maggie speak on TV, 40,000 French people pledged to donate their organs when they died. On returning to the United States, the Greens began to receive requests to tell their son's story and speak about organ donation. "It gradually dawned on us," said Reg, "that we'd been given a life's work."

Nicholas Green is gone, but others live on because of his parents' compassionate act. How many of us would do the same thing, given the opportunity?

---

1 *petty:* small, unimportant
2 *corneas:* protective coverings on the outer surface of eyes
3 *a blow was struck:* progress was made

AFTER YOU READ

A **VOCABULARY** Match the words in **bold** with their meanings.

_____ 1. Suddenly an old, **decrepit** car pulled up.	**a.** flowing slowly
_____ 2. They risked a deadly **confrontation** with criminals.	**b.** became apparent to
_____ 3. Reg's vehicle could probably **elude** the criminals' car.	**c.** news sources
_____ 4. He saw blood **oozing** from Nicholas's head.	**d.** in bad condition
_____ 5. Nicholas lay in a coma, his **status** not changing.	**e.** politeness, courtesy
_____ 6. You have given us a lesson in **civility**.	**f.** condition, position
_____ 7. Headlines in the **media** spoke of "Our Shame."	**g.** angry or tense encounter
_____ 8. It **dawned on** us that we'd been given a life's work.	**h.** escape from

B COMPREHENSION Complete the sentences based on the reading.

1. The Greens were traveling in the region of Italy known as the _____.

2. The Greens' car was newer than the _____ car.

3. The shots _____ the windows on the driver's side of the car.

4. After the shooting, Nicholas lay in a _____ for two days.

5. The Greens thought it was better to return good for evil than to seek _____.

6. Italians were profoundly _____ by the Greens' donation of Nicholas's organs.

7. The ironic aspect of the Greens' tragedy was that it was a _____.

8. The criminals were placed on _____ after being turned over to the police.

C DISCUSSION Work with a partner. Compare and justify your answers in B. Then discuss this question: Do you feel it was the right thing for the Greens to offer Nicholas's organs for transplant? Give reasons for your answer.

Go to MyEnglishLab for more grammar in context practice.

STEP 2   GRAMMAR PRESENTATION

ADVERB AND ADVERBIAL PHRASES

Reducing Adverb Clauses of Time to Adverb Phrases

Adverb Clause		Adverb Phrase	
While they were in Italy,	they had trouble.	While in Italy,	they had trouble.
While I was in Italy,		Ø*	
When I am traveling,	I call her a lot.	When traveling,	I call her a lot.
When Sue is traveling,		Ø	

*Ø = no change possible

Changing Adverb Clauses of Time to Adverb Phrases

Adverb Clause		Adverb Phrase	
Before we left,	we visited Rome.	Before leaving,	we visited Rome.
Before Ann left,		Ø	
After they (had) investigated,	the police identified the killers.	After investigating,	the police identified the killers.
		After having investigated,	
When they heard Reg speak,	many Italians were moved.	On hearing Reg speak,	many Italians were moved.
		Upon hearing Reg speak,	

Changing Adverb Clauses of Time to Adverbial Phrases

Adverb Clause		Adverbial Phrase	
While they waited at the hospital,	they were deeply troubled.	Waiting at the hospital,	they were deeply troubled.
When they heard the news,	they decided what to do.	Having heard the news,	they decided what to do.

Changing Adverb Clauses of Reason to Adverbial Phrases

Adverb Clause		Adverbial Phrase	
As he saw the guns,	he chose to flee.	Seeing the guns,	he chose to flee.
Because they were unable to catch him,	the pursuers fired several shots.	Being unable to catch him,	the pursuers fired several shots.
Because I've been to Bari,	I hope to return.	Having been to Bari,	I hope to return.
Because I'd been to Bari,	I hoped to return.		I hoped to return.
Since they were accused by the police,	they had to appear in court.	Accused by the police,	they had to appear in court.

GRAMMAR NOTES

1 Definition of Adverb Phrases

A **phrase** is a group of words that does not have both a subject and verb showing time.
An **adverb phrase** is a group of words that often **modifies a main clause** in a sentence.

Adverb phrases commonly include:
- **present participles**
- **past participles**

Before *traveling* abroad, I had seldom seen poverty.

People will often help others **when *given* the chance.**

Negative adverb phrases contain the words *not* or *never* before the participle.

After *not* eating all day, we were very hungry.

2 Reducing Adverb Clauses with *Be*

Adverb clauses can be **reduced** to adverb phrases when the clause has a form of *be*.

To **reduce** an adverb clause to an **adverb phrase**, **omit** the **subject pronoun** and the form of *be*. If the original sentence has commas, keep the commas in the reduced sentence.	**ADVERB CLAUSE** **While they were driving,** they were attacked by bandits. **ADVERB PHRASE** **While driving,** they were attacked by bandits.
An adverb phrase can come **first** or **second** in the sentence. When it comes first, we usually place a **comma** after it.	**While driving,** they were attacked by bandits. They were attacked by bandits **while driving**.
BE CAREFUL! You can reduce an adverb clause to an adverb phrase *only if* the **subjects in both clauses** of the sentence refer to the **same person or thing**.	**Reg and Maggie** drove while **the children** were sleeping. **NOT** Reg and Maggie drove ~~while sleeping~~.

3 Changing Adverb Clauses of Time

Adverb clauses of time beginning with *after, before, since,* and *while* can be **changed to adverb phrases** when the clause has **no form of** *be*.

To change an adverb clause to an **adverb phrase**, **omit** the **subject pronoun** and change the verb to its *-ing* form. Keep the subordinating conjunction and original punctuation.	**ADVERB CLAUSE** **After they visited** Paestum, the Greens drove south. **ADVERB PHRASE** **After** *visiting* Paestum, the Greens drove south.
BE CAREFUL! You can change an adverb clause of time to an adverb phrase *only if* the subjects in the two clauses of the sentence refer to the same person or thing.	After **the bandits** saw the Greens' car, **the Greens** sped away. **NOT** ~~After seeing the Greens' car~~, the Greens sped away.

4 Changing Adverb Clauses with Past-Time Verbs

To change an adverb clause with a **simple past** or **past perfect verb** to an adverb phrase, change the verb to *having* + **past participle**. Keep the original punctuation.	**After they (had) opened** the door, they saw the blood. *Having* **opened** the door, they saw the blood.
In a sentence with a simple past or past perfect verb, you can also change the clause to a phrase by changing the verb to its *-ing* form and keeping the subordinating conjunction and the original punctuation.	After **opening** the door, they saw the blood.

5 Replacing *When* with *On* or *Upon* in Adverb Phrases

We don't use *when* in adverb phrases if the meaning is "at the time something occurred." If *when* has this meaning in an adverb clause, replace it with **on** or **upon** + *-ing* when you reduce the clause to an adverb phrase.

ADVERB CLAUSE
When they realized what had happened, they pulled to the side of the road.

ADVERB PHRASE
Upon *realizing* what had happened, they pulled to the side of the road.

On *realizing* what had happened, they pulled to the side of the road.

6 Definition of Adverbial Phrases

An adverb phrase **without a subordinating conjunction** is called an **adverbial phrase**.

We sometimes **omit** the **subordinating conjunction** in a phrase. When we do this, the adverb phrase changes to an **adverbial phrase**.

ADVERB PHRASE
While sitting on the porch, I thought about my future.

ADVERBIAL PHRASE
Sitting on the porch, I thought about my future.

7 Changing Adverb Clauses of Reason

Adverb **clauses of reason** can be changed to adverbial **phrases**.

To change an adverb clause of reason to an adverbial phrase, **omit** the subordinating conjunctions *because*, *since*, or *as* at the beginning of a clause. These conjunctions **must be omitted**.

ADVERB CLAUSE
Because the children were sleeping in the car, they were not aware of what was happening.

ADVERBIAL PHRASE
Sleeping in the car, the children were not aware of what was happening.

NOT ~~Because~~ sleeping in the car, the children were not aware of what was happening.

You can change *because/since/as* + a form of *be* to *being* in an adverbial phrase.

Since they were angry, they decided to do something about the problem.
Being angry, they decided to do something about the problem.

You can change a **present perfect** or **past perfect verb** in an adverb clause to *having* + past participle in an adverbial phrase. We generally use *having* + past participle to suggest that the action in the adverbial phrase occurred at an earlier time than the action in the independent clause.

Because they had been moved by the situation, people became organ donors.
Having **been moved** by the situation, people became organ donors.

8 Changing Passive Clauses

You can change a clause containing a **passive** verb to an adverbial phrase with a **past participle only**.

If you can omit the subordinating **conjunction** in an adverbial phrase **without changing the meaning** of the sentence, **delete the subject** and any auxiliaries in a passive sentence.	**Since I was given two options**, I chose the harder of the two. **Given two options**, I chose the harder of the two.
BE CAREFUL! Sometimes the subordinating conjunction **cannot be omitted without changing the meaning** of the sentence. In these cases, to form an **adverb phrase**, delete the subject and change the form of *be* to *being*.	**Before I was told** the nature of the problem, I had no idea what to do. **Before *being* told** the nature of the problem, I had no idea what to do. **NOT** ~~Told the nature of the problem~~, I had no idea what to do.

REFERENCE NOTE

For information on **shortening adjective clauses to adjective phrases**, see Unit 15 on page 249.

Go to MyEnglishLab to watch the grammar presentation.

STEP 3 FOCUSED PRACTICE

EXERCISE 1 DISCOVER THE GRAMMAR

A GRAMMAR NOTES 1–5 Look at the sentences based on the reading. Underline the adverb phrase in each sentence. Circle the subordinating conjunction.

1. An Italian screamed at them (while) signaling them to stop.

2. On checking the children, Reg and Maggie found them in the back seat.

3. Before speeding away, Reg quickly weighed his options.

4. Upon realizing the danger they were in, Reg floored the gas pedal.

5. The criminals were placed on trial after being turned over to the police.

6. On returning to the United States, Nicholas's parents received requests to tell their son's story.

B GRAMMAR NOTES 1–8 Read each pair of sentences based on the reading. Is the second sentence a correct rewriting of the first? Check *Yes* or *No*.

	Yes	No
1. Having spent the day exploring ruins, Reg and Maggie were driving south. Spending the day exploring ruins, Reg and Maggie were driving south.	☐	☑
2. Not knowing what to do, Reg carefully weighed the options. Because he didn't know what to do, Reg carefully weighed the options.	☐	☐

	Yes	No

3. Shots rang out, shattering both windows on the driver's side of the car. ☐ ☐
Having shattered both windows on the driver's side of the car, shots rang out.

4. The Greens' car took off, easily outdistancing the bandits' car. ☐ ☐
Having outdistanced the bandits' car, the Greens' car took off.

5. Upon opening the door, Reg saw blood oozing from Nicholas's head. ☐ ☐
When he opened the door, Reg saw blood oozing from Nicholas's head.

6. After being rushed to a hospital, Nicholas lay in a coma for two days. ☐ ☐
After he was rushed to a hospital, Nicholas lay in a coma for two days.

7. Nicholas lay in a coma for two days, his status not changing. ☐ ☐
Nicholas lay in a coma for two days because his status didn't change.

8. How many of us would do the same thing, given the opportunity? ☐ ☐
How many of us would do the same thing if we were given the opportunity?

EXERCISE 2 ADVERB CLAUSES TO PHRASES

GRAMMAR NOTES 1–5 Read the sentences. Circle the subjects in both clauses. If the subjects refer to the same person or thing, shorten the sentence by reducing or changing the adverb clause to a phrase. If the subjects are different, write *cannot be shortened*.

1. When ⓘ saw some hungry children working, ⓣⓗⓔⓨ asked me to buy them a meal.

cannot be shortened

2. While we were traveling in Europe, we had several opportunities to help people.

_____

3. Because the travelers had a flat tire, we stopped to help them fix it.

_____

4. When my friend saw an injured person on the roadside, he pulled over to help.

_____

5. While my roommate was recuperating in the hospital, I called her parents to inform them of the accident.

_____

6. Because we realized that our friends were running late, we gave them a ride to the airport.

_____

7. After the boy fell into the river, his friend dived into the water to rescue him.

_____

8. As she was trying to fix her computer, Anna realized that she needed her brother's help.

_____

EXERCISE 3 ADVERB CLAUSES; ADVERB AND ADVERBIAL PHRASES

A GRAMMAR NOTES 2–8 Read the article about animal emotion and compassion. There are ten adverb clauses in the article. The first has already been underlined. Find and underline nine more.

Animal Compassion and Emotion

MANY PEOPLE THINK that animals are fundamentally different from us. <u>Since they are not human</u>, animals supposedly cannot express emotions. Is this true? Are animals incapable of compassion and other emotions? Consider these accounts by Marc Bekoff, a professor emeritus of ecology at the University of Colorado and an expert on animal behavior. Bekoff recounts two situations in which elephants demonstrated compassion and other emotions.

In the first account, Bekoff describes a situation that took place at a reserve in Kenya. While Bekoff and a fellow researcher were observing elephants, they saw that a younger elephant named Babyl walked very slowly. She had trouble walking because she had been crippled some years previously. But Babyl was never allowed to fall too far behind while she was searching for food with her herd. The other elephants waited for Babyl because they sensed she needed protection from predators. Interestingly, Babyl's fellow elephants didn't seem to benefit in any material way from her presence. They seemed to change their regular behavior for her sake since they cared for her and wanted her to remain a part of the herd.

The second situation took place at an elephant sanctuary in Tennessee with two elephants, Shirley and Jenny. Compassionate individuals had brought both elephants to the sanctuary to live because they wanted the animals to recover from abuse they had suffered in the entertainment industry. When Shirley, an older female, arrived at the sanctuary, she was put in a stall next to Jenny, a younger female. To the keepers' astonishment, the two elephants reached out and touched each other through the bars separating them, and they roared in the typical elephant greeting. After their keepers checked the sanctuary records, they discovered that the elephants had been together in a circus twenty-two years previously. At that time, Jenny had been a calf and Shirley a twenty-something. It was obvious that the two elephants remembered each other, and they were happy to see each other. After they were reunited, the two elephants quickly became inseparable.

B | Complete the sentences by changing each adverb clause that you underlined in A to an adverb or adverbial phrase.

1. _Not being human_ _____, animals supposedly cannot express emotions.

2. _____,
   Bekoff and a fellow researcher saw that a younger elephant named Babyl walked very slowly.

3. She had trouble walking, _____.

4. But Babyl was never allowed to fall too far behind _____
   _____

5. The other elephants waited for Babyl, _____
   _____

6. They seemed to change their regular behavior for her sake, _____
   _____.

7. Compassionate individuals had brought both elephants to the sanctuary to live, _____
   _____.

8. _____
   _____, Shirley was put in a stall next to Jenny, an older female.

9. _____
   _____, they discovered that the elephants had been together in a circus 22 years previously.

10. _____, the two elephants quickly became inseparable.

EXERCISE 4 ADVERB AND ADVERBIAL PHRASES AND MAIN CLAUSES

GRAMMAR NOTES 1, 3–8 Look at the pictures, which are connected in a story. Write a sentence with a main clause and an adverb or adverbial phrase to describe the situation in each picture. Use the grammatical prompts and include any other necessary words.

1. (present participle)
   Coming out of the train station, the tourists
   saw a boy selling guidebooks.

2. (present participle)
   _____
   _____

3. (*not* + present participle)

_____

_____

4. (past participle)

_____

_____

5. (present participle)

_____

_____

6. (*having* + past participle)

_____

_____

7. (*after* + present participle)

_____

_____

8. (*having* + past participle)

_____

_____

GRAMMAR NOTES 1–8 Read the blog. There are ten mistakes in the use of adverb and adverbial phrases. The first mistake is already corrected. Find and correct nine more.

A Helping Hand

If you're at all like me, you hear a lot of requests to help others. ~~Barraging~~ *Barraged* by constant appeals for money to support homeless shelters, the Special Olympics, or the like, people tend to tune out. I certainly used to do that. I don't think I was selfish. But subjecting to so many requests, I felt overwhelmed, and my brain was numbed. After listening to yet another TV request asking viewers to sponsor a child overseas, I would say to myself, "I'll bet the money is pocketed by some local politician." Finally, convincing myself that I didn't have enough money to help others in any case, I was able to ignore all the requests. Or at least that was the way I thought before sent by my magazine to South America to do a human interest story on poor children. My opinions changed upon see the reality of the life of a poor child.

While landing in Santa Simona, I took a taxi to my hotel in the center of town, where I met Elena, a girl of ten or eleven. Sat on a dirty blanket on the sidewalk in front of the hotel, she caught my eye. Elena was trying to earn a living by selling mangoes. Smiled at me, she asked, "*Mangos, señor?*—Mangoes, sir?" I bought some mangoes and some other fruit, and we talked together. Elena's life had been difficult. Her parents were both dead, and she lived with an elderly aunt. Having polio at the age of five, she now walked with a limp. She and her aunt often went hungry.

Investigated the question the next day, I talked to several different authorities, and I learned that they were indeed trying to help. Having become convinced that money from sponsors does in fact get to those who need it, I knew my attitude had to change. Learning that I could sponsor Elena for less than a dollar a day, I began to feel ashamed. After all, I spend more than that on my dogs. But what remains most vivid in my mind is my vision of Elena. She didn't beg or feel sorry for herself. Sold her mangoes, she earned a living, and her spirit shone through in the process. So I say to all of you reading this: The next time you hear an ad about sponsoring a child, pay attention.

Go to MyEnglishLab for more focused practice.

EXERCISE 6 LISTENING

▶18|02 **A** Listen to the news broadcast. Check (✓) the two subjects that are *not* mentioned.

☐ political struggles in the nation of Franconia ☐ a new nation comes into existence

☐ an oil spill in the Mediterranean ☐ World Cup news

☐ a new vaccine for AIDS ☐ a rescue in a swimming pool

▶18|02 **B** Read the questions. Listen again to the news broadcast. Then answer each question in a complete sentence.

1. How did rebel leader Amalde respond when he was asked if he would go to the peace conference?

   He declined to commit himself to attending the conference.

2. What does the success of the upcoming conference depend on?

3. How has Mr. Tintor shown that he doesn't really want peace, according to Mr. Amalde?

4. What did an aide to President Tintor say in an interview about the upcoming peace conference?

5. What did researchers from the Global Health Foundation acknowledge?

6. What will the new nation be called?

7. When did the new government request billions of dollars in foreign aid?

8. What had Michaels nearly given up hope about?

9. How had Hutchinson become aware that Michaels was in trouble?

C Work with a partner. Discuss the questions.

1. Listening to the news broadcast in A, do you think the reporter shows compassion for the people he is reporting about? Give reasons for your answer.

2. Do you think journalists should show compassion while reporting the news?

3. When you consider the quality of news reporting today, what is your overall evaluation of it? What changes do you think would make it better?

EXERCISE 7 COMPASSIONATE ACTS

A DISCUSSION You are going to have a discussion about compassionate acts. First, think of a few examples of compassionate acts that you know about or have heard of. Why do these acts illustrate compassion?

B Work in a group. Tell your group members about your examples of compassionate acts. Then report interesting examples to the class.

EXAMPLE: Here's an example that happened to me. Driving through a rough neighborhood late one night with my friend, we saw a car accident. She insisted on stopping to help. I wanted to let the police handle it. We stopped, though, and it's a good thing we did. . . .

EXERCISE 8 GREYFRIARS BOBBY

A CRITICAL THINKING You are going to discuss whether animals can show compassion. First, read this short article about Greyfriars Bobby.

Greyfriars Bobby

A GREAT DEAL OF INFORMATION can be found today about Greyfriars Bobby, his name having been made famous in books and films. Bobby was a Skye terrier who lived in Edinburgh, Scotland. According to the most popular version of the story, Bobby belonged to John Gray, a night watchman for the Edinburgh police force. After having passed away, Gray was buried in Greyfriars Kirkwood, a cemetery in Edinburgh. Bobby is said to have spent fourteen years guarding Gray's grave, greatly mourning the loss of his master. Having become famous for his loyalty, Bobby was buried in the same cemetery upon dying in 1872. Residents of Edinburgh, feeling great admiration for Bobby's love and loyalty, erected a statue of the dog.

This traditional story of Bobby gradually came to be the most generally accepted version. But some people, not believing that the traditional story is accurate, point to different accounts. One such account claims that the real John Gray was a farmer, not a night watchman. Skeptics also claim that there are many documented stories of stray dogs living in European cemeteries. Fed by visitors to the cemeteries, the dogs came to be considered over time the guardians of the graves of their supposed masters.

B Work in a group. Discuss the questions.

1. After reading the article above, which version of the Greyfriars Bobby story do you feel is more accurate? Why?

2. Taking into account your own experiences with animals, do you think they have feelings? Are they capable of showing grief or any other kind of emotion?

3. If possible, give a personal example of an animal showing grief or another emotion.

C Share the main points of your discussion with the class.

EXAMPLE: **A:** Our group thinks it is obvious that Greyfriars Bobby waited at his master's grave, hoping that he would come back.

B: We disagree. Being animals, dogs can't understand death and loss. . . .

EXERCISE 9 HAVING VISITED ITALY . . .

A GAME Work in a group. Look at the beginnings of the sentences. For each item, make up at least three sentences that start with these words. Use your imagination.

EXAMPLE: Having visited Italy before . . .

A: Having visited Italy before, I didn't want to go to Rome again.
B: Having visited Italy before, I decided to go to France instead.
C: Having visited Italy before, I knew the best places to get ice cream!

1. Having visited Italy before . . .

2. While traveling in China . . .

3. Witnessing the accident . . .

4. Having seen the way animals behave . . .

5. Wanting to help people . . .

6. Upon completing my college degree . . .

7. Never having been to Africa . . .

8. After reading the article about refugees . . .

9. Presented with the opportunity to be in a movie . . .

10. Not having any money . . .

B Work with the class. Read some of your sentences aloud. Vote on the most interesting, amusing, or imaginative sentences.

Go to MyEnglishLab for more communication practice.

A BEFORE YOU WRITE You are going to write an essay about a compassionate act you witnessed. Write a few sentences about it.

B WRITE Using your ideas in A, write a five-paragraph essay about the compassionate act you have chosen. Remember to use adverb and adverbial phrases. Try to avoid the common mistakes shown in the chart. Use the example below to help you begin your essay.

EXAMPLE: The best example of compassion I have witnessed occurred about a year ago. Having been invited to an office party, I stayed at work late, and I finally managed to leave about 10:00 p.m. Driving home on the freeway, I suddenly felt the car slow down and heard a loud noise. Realizing that I probably had a flat tire, I quickly pulled over to the side of the road. I looked for the jack to change the flat but couldn't find it. Just then a group of teenagers slowed down and stopped. I thought to myself, "Uh-oh, I'm in trouble now." That's not what happened, though....

Common Mistakes in Using Adverb and Adverbial Phrases

Don't reduce an adverb clause to an adverb or adverbial phrase unless the **subjects** in the two original clauses are the **same**.	**Running into the room**, Janet announced her engagement. **NOT** Running into the room, ~~the engagement was announced by Janet~~.
Don't begin an adverb phrase with *when* if the meaning is "at the time something occurred." Use *on* or *upon* instead.	**On realizing** that a serious accident had happened, we stopped to help. **NOT** ~~When~~ realizing that a serious accident had happened, we stopped to help.
Don't use a present participle in an adverbial phrase when the time frame of the two original clauses is different. Use *having* + **past participle**.	**Having gone** to Spain on our last trip, we went to Portugal on this trip. **NOT** ~~Going~~ to Spain on our last trip, we went to Portugal on this trip.

C CHECK YOUR WORK Look at your essay. Underline adverb and adverbial phrases. Use the Editing Checklist to check your work.

Editing Checklist

Did you . . . ?

☐ make sure the subjects in the original clauses are the same before reducing one of them to an adverb or adverbial phrase

☐ use *on* or *upon* + present participle in adverb phrases if the meaning is "at the time something occurred"

☐ use *having* + present participle in adverbial phrases when the time frame of the two original clauses is different

D REVISE YOUR WORK Read your essay again. Can you improve your writing? Make changes if necessary.

Go to MyEnglishLab for more writing practice.

UNIT 18 REVIEW

Test yourself on the grammar of the unit.

Ⓐ Complete the sentences. Circle the correct answers.

1. Not knowing / Because not knowing how we could help, we called the volunteer line.

2. Having caught cheating / Caught cheating, she failed the course.

3. Getting the tickets / Having gotten the tickets, we decided to give them to kids who'd never seen a play.

4. Taksim turned off the lights before leaving / before left home.

5. On realizing / When realizing they had no money, we decided to pay their bill.

6. During relaxing / Relaxing at home, I remembered all the people who had helped me.

7. Having visited / Visiting Asia, I knew how beautiful it was.

8. We didn't know where to go before given / being given directions.

Ⓑ Complete the sentences with the correct forms of the words in parentheses.

1. _____ a noise downstairs, Melinda called 911.
   (hear)

2. Juan listens to music _____ his homework.
   (while / do)

3. _____ too fast, Bill got a bad case of indigestion.
   (eat)

4. _____ the project, the crew celebrated.
   (upon / finish)

5. _____ to Japan previously, we skipped it on our last trip.
   (be)

6. Sam recovered _____ to the hospital.
   (after / take)

7. _____ the choice, I decided to walk to work.
   (give)

Ⓒ Find and correct five mistakes in the paragraph.

When arriving at the Cairo airport, I was certain I had plenty of time to make the connection for my next flight. Not eating on the plane and feel very hungry, I stopped at a restaurant to get some food. Lost track of time, I enjoyed my meal. Then I glanced at my boarding pass and saw I had fifteen minutes to make it to my flight gate. I had a lot of heavy bags, so I grabbed them and started running toward the gate, known I'd never make it on time. Just then, out of the blue, a man I'd never met took a couple of my suitcases and got me to the gate with five minutes to spare. I wish I could have returned the favor.

Now check your answers on page 431.

Go to MyEnglishLab to complete the review online.

STEP 1 GRAMMAR IN CONTEXT

BEFORE YOU READ

Discuss the questions.

1. What is your earliest memory?

2. Do you ever have trouble remembering things? Are there any strategies that help you to remember?

READ

 Read this article about memory.

Try to Remember

You're with a friend, and suddenly up walks somebody you've known for a long time. You want to introduce this person to your friend. However, just as you say, "Nancy, I'd like you to meet . . . ," your mind goes blank, and you don't remember the person's name. It's embarrassing and worrisome enough to make you want to do something about it. If this has happened to you, though, don't be too concerned. It's a common problem. As people get older, they tend to become more forgetful. They can't remember everyday details like computer passwords, email addresses, and their friends' names.

I used to worry about memory loss myself. Therefore, I decided to do some research into the problem, and I learned a number of interesting things about memory and how it works. I also discovered that even though memory loss is probably unavoidable, there are things you can do to slow it down.

How does memory work? First of all, there are two types of memory: long-term and short-term. Long-term memory refers to our memories of things that we experienced some time ago and that form the core of our knowledge of ourselves. In contrast, short-term memory can be called "working" memory—the type we use in processing such things as passwords and the names of new people we meet.

As we grow older, our long-term memory holds up remarkably well. Thus, we are able to remember the highlight of the vacation we took to the Everglades at the age of ten and the alligators we saw there. Meanwhile, our short-term memory tends to deteriorate. We

Short-term memory   **Long-term memory**

have difficulty remembering things like where we put our house keys because our short-term memory fails us.

Why does short-term memory decline? Short-term memory operations occur in the frontal lobes[1] of the brain. As people age, these lobes tend to lose mass, as much as 5 to 10 percent per decade. Short-term memory operations require space in order to function correctly. Therefore, as the lobes become smaller, short-term memory gets worse.

It is difficult or impossible to completely avoid memory decline. However, it can be slowed. Maintaining a steady supply of glucose[2] can mitigate the problem of shrinking lobes. Consequently, elderly people would do well to eat several small meals each day rather than two or three big ones. There is evidence, moreover, that staying mentally active can help sustain our memory and keep it from deterioration.

Many companies feed on our fears of memory loss, and they attempt to induce us to buy products that will supposedly enhance our ability to remember. Do these products work? Well, sometimes. But it's important to keep in mind that all memory aids depend on the creation of a peg, or mental picture, on which to hang something we want to recollect. Suppose, for example, you have difficulty remembering names. Let's say you're at a party and are introduced to a woman named Sarah Baer. First, look for distinguishing features. You see that Sarah has long, thick hair, rather like a bear's fur. Second, think of words that will help you associate these features with this person. *Baer = Bear*. Furthermore, the first syllable of "Sarah" rhymes with "bear." *Sar* and *Baer*. It might work. The point is to create a mental picture you can relate to the person, place, or thing you want to recall. The more vivid the association is, the greater is the chance that you'll remember it.

Most importantly, memory improvement takes work. The real problem in remembering something we learned is often the fact that we weren't paying enough attention when we learned it. Think about the last time you were introduced to someone whose name you immediately forgot. Were you really paying attention to the person's name, or were you focusing on the impression you might be making? Memory courses can work, of course, but they depend on techniques we can create and perform for ourselves. The real trick lies in our willingness to tap[3] and use what's within us.

---

1 *lobes:* rounded parts of organs
2 *glucose:* a natural form of sugar
3 *tap:* take from an available source

AFTER YOU READ

A VOCABULARY Match the words in **bold** with their meanings.

_____ **1.** Companies often **induce** us to buy their products.

_____ **2.** Long-term memory forms the **core** of our self-knowledge.

_____ **3.** We are able to remember the **highlight** of our vacation.

_____ **4.** A steady supply of glucose can **mitigate** the problem.

_____ **5.** Meanwhile, our short-term memory tends to **deteriorate**.

_____ **6.** Memory aids can **enhance** our ability to remember.

_____ **7.** We need a peg to help us to **recollect** something important.

_____ **8.** The more **vivid** the image is, the better you'll remember.

a. remember

b. best aspect

c. cause, make

d. sharp, clear, colorful

e. improve

f. make less harmful

g. become worse

h. central part

B COMPREHENSION Read the statements. Check (✓) *True* or *False*. Correct the false statements.

	True	False
1. Forgetting things such as another person's name is quite uncommon.	☐	☐
2. Long-term memory refers to things we experienced some time ago.	☐	☐
3. Short-term memory can be termed "working" memory.	☐	☐
4. Our short-term memory holds up better than our long-term memory.	☐	☐
5. Memory problems are generally short-term memory problems.	☐	☐
6. Elderly people should eat several small meals daily.	☐	☐
7. There is no evidence that staying mentally active can slow memory deterioration.	☐	☐
8. A key reason we forget things is that we often weren't paying enough attention when we learned something.	☐	☐

C DISCUSSION Work with a partner. Compare and justify your answers in B. Do you agree with the statement in the reading that our long-term memory holds up better than our short-term memory? Discuss.

Go to MyEnglishLab for more grammar in context practice.

CONNECTORS

Connectors: Placement and Punctuation

Coordinating Conjunction	I was worried, **so** I did some research.
Subordinating Conjunction	**Because** I was worried, I did some research.
	I did some research **because** I was worried.
Transition	I was worried. **Therefore**, I did some research.
	I was worried. I, **therefore**, did some research.
	I was worried. I did some research, **therefore**.

Connectors: Functions

	Coordinating Conjunctions	Subordinating Conjunctions	Transitions
Addition	and, nor, or		besides, furthermore, indeed, in addition, moreover
Condition	or	if, even if, only if, unless	otherwise
Contrast	but, or, yet	although, though, even though, whereas, while	however, in contrast, meanwhile, nevertheless, nonetheless, on the contrary, on the other hand
Cause/Reason	for	as, because, since	
Effect/Result	so		consequently, otherwise, therefore, thus
Time		after, before, when, while	afterwards, meanwhile, next

Transitions: Connecting Sentences

Addition	She couldn't remember names.	**Furthermore**, she forgot addresses.
	Human brains lose mass.	**Indeed**, they may lose 10 percent a year.
Condition	Older people should eat several small meals a day.	**Otherwise**, their memory might deteriorate.
Contrast	I often have trouble with names.	**However**, I always remember faces.
	We all forget things.	**Nevertheless**, we shouldn't worry.
Effect/Result	I wasn't concentrating when we met.	**Consequently**, I couldn't recall her name.
	He wanted to improve his memory.	**Therefore**, he took a memory course.
Time	He studied for his course.	**Meanwhile**, his wife read a book.
	She completed the book.	**Next**, she bought a memory video.

Transitions: Connecting Blocks of Text

Listing Ideas in Order of Time/Importance	**First of all**, we need to distinguish between two types of memory.
Giving Examples	**For example**, you need to stay mentally active.
Summarizing	**To summarize**: Memory improvement requires work.
Adding a Conclusion	**In conclusion**, we can prevent the deterioration of memory.

GRAMMAR NOTES

1 Types of Connectors

Connectors (often called **discourse connectors**) are words and phrases that **connect ideas** both within sentences and between sentences and larger blocks of text.

Three types of connectors are:

- **coordinating conjunctions**

- **subordinating conjunctions**

- **transitions**

I try hard, **but** I can never remember new people's names.

I can't remember her name, **although** I can remember her face.

I spent a lot of money on a memory improvement course. **However**, it was a waste of money.

BE CAREFUL! Don't confuse subordinating conjunctions with transitions. They are often similar in their basic meaning but have different sentence patterns. **Subordinating clauses** begin **dependent clauses**. **Transitions** occur in **independent clauses** and often begin them.

Although I've been working on improving my memory, I haven't had much success.
   (subordinating conjunction introducing a dependent clause)

I've been working on improving my memory. **However**, I haven't had much success.
   (transition between two sentences)

NOT I've been working on improving my memory. ~~Although,~~ I haven't had much success.

2 Coordinating and Subordinating Conjunctions

There are two types of conjunctions: **coordinating conjunctions** and **subordinating conjunctions**.

Coordinating conjunctions join two **independent** clauses. Coordinating conjunctions come between independent clauses and are normally preceded by a comma.

The seven coordinating conjunctions are:

and	*for*	*or*	*yet*
but	*nor*	*so*	

I often forget things, **so** I write everything down.
I heard what you said, **but** what did you mean?

Subordinating conjunctions connect **ideas** within sentences. They come at the **beginning** of subordinate (**dependent**) clauses. If a subordinate clause comes first in a sentence, it is followed by a comma. If a subordinate clause comes second, it is not normally preceded by a comma.

Because I often forget things, I write everything down.
I write everything down **because** I often forget things.

BE CAREFUL! The coordinating conjunction *nor* is negative. Reverse the subject and verb after it.

Helena doesn't remember names consistently, ***nor* does she** remember passwords.
NOT Helena doesn't remember names consistently, nor ~~she does~~ remember passwords.

3 Definition of Transitions

Transitions are single words or expressions that **connect ideas** between **sentences** or larger sections of text.

Transitions that connect sentences can come at the **beginning** of a sentence, **within** it, or at the **end**. At the beginning of a sentence, a transition is preceded by a period or semicolon and followed by a comma. In the middle of a sentence, it is preceded and followed by a comma. At the end of a sentence, it is preceded by a comma.

Common transitions include:

besides	*in addition*	*otherwise*
consequently	*meanwhile*	*therefore*
however	*nevertheless*	

He said he would support the idea. **However,** I wouldn't count on him.

He said he would support the idea. I wouldn't**, however,** count on him.

He said he would support the idea. I wouldn't count on him**, however**.

BE CAREFUL! If a transition comes at the beginning of an **independent** clause, it must be preceded by a **period** or a **semicolon** and not by a comma.

I can remember people's names **easily; however**, I can't usually remember their phone numbers.
NOT I can remember people's names ~~easily, however~~, I can't usually remember their phone numbers.

There are five principal types of **transitions** that **connect sentences** and independent clauses.

These transitions show **addition**:			I remember her telephone number. **In addition**, I remember what street she lives on.
additionally	likewise	moreover	I live too far away to visit you; **besides**, I can never remember your address.
also	in addition	plus	
besides	in fact		
furthermore	indeed		

The transition *otherwise* shows **condition**. This transition indicates that a result **opposite** to what is **expected** will happen if a certain action isn't taken.

I need to write down your email address. **Otherwise**, I'll never remember it.

These transitions show **contrast**:		Her speech was good; **nevertheless**, I can't support her proposals.
however	nevertheless	Jim thinks I'm against his ideas. **On the contrary**, I'm one of his biggest supporters.
in contrast	nonetheless	
in spite of/despite that	still	
instead	though	

USAGE NOTE *Though* is a **contrast transition** when it occurs at the **end** of an **independent** clause and its meaning is equivalent to that of *however*. In other positions, it is a **subordinating conjunction**.

I carefully wrote down her name on a piece of paper. I lost the piece of paper, **though**. *(transition)*

Though I've told him my name many times, he never remembers it. *(subordinating conjunction)*

These transitions show **effect/result**:		I was not paying close attention when she was introduced. **Consequently**, her name escapes me.
accordingly	on account of this	This new memory technique is helpful; **therefore**, I can recommend it to you.
as a result	otherwise	
because of that	therefore	
consequently	thus	

USAGE NOTE *Otherwise* shows both **condition** and **effect/result**.

I need to say people's names when I'm introduced to them; **otherwise**, I forget them. *(condition)*

Maryam must take her medications; **otherwise**, she'll get sick. *(result)*

These transitions show **relationships** of actions, events, and ideas **in time**:			Bob spent three years in the military. **Meanwhile**, his brother was earning a college degree.
after that	in the meantime	next	I went to a memory workshop. **Afterwards**, I could remember almost everything I heard.
afterwards	meanwhile	then	

Some transitions connect **blocks of text**. They usually come at the beginning of a sentence and are commonly followed by a **comma**.

These transitions **list** ideas in **order of time** or **importance**: *finally*　　*most importantly*　　*second* *first (of all)*　　*next*　　　　　*third* (etc.)	**First of all**, let's consider the question of short-term memory. **Most importantly**, let's consider the issue of memory-improvement courses.
These transitions **give examples**: *for example*　　*to name/mention a few* *for instance*	I can remember lots of things about people. **For example**, I always remember what they're wearing. I remember many books I've read: *Middlemarch, War and Peace*, and *Things Fall Apart*, **to name a few**.
These transitions **summarize**: *all in all*　　*in summary*　　*to summarize* *in sum*　　　*overall*	**In sum**, these are the key points about memory loss. **All in all**, the key point is that memory can be improved.
These transitions **add a conclusion**: *in conclusion*　　*to conclude*	**To conclude**, let me just say that we can improve our memory if we work at it.

REFERENCE NOTES

For more information on **subordinating conjunctions**, see Unit 17 on page 285 and Appendix 22 on page 420.

For more complete lists of **transitions**, see Appendices 23–24 on page 421.

Go to MyEnglishLab to watch the grammar presentation.

STEP 3　FOCUSED PRACTICE

EXERCISE 1　DISCOVER THE GRAMMAR

A GRAMMAR NOTES 1–5　Read the sentences based on the reading. Identify each of the underlined words as a *coordinating conjunction (C)*, *subordinating conjunction (S)*, or *transition (T)*.

_C_ **1.** I decided to do some research into the problem, <u>and</u> I learned a number of interesting things.

_____ **2.** As we grow older, our long-term memory holds up remarkably well. <u>Thus</u>, we are able to remember the highlight of the vacation we took at the age of ten.

_____ **3.** <u>Meanwhile</u>, our short-term memory tends to deteriorate.

_____ **4.** We have difficulty remembering things like names and phone numbers <u>because</u> our short-term memory fails us.

_____ **5.** Suppose, <u>for example</u>, you have difficulty remembering names.

_____ **6.** Were you really paying attention, <u>or</u> were you focusing on the impression you might be making?

B GRAMMAR NOTES 3–5 Read the sentences based on the reading. Underline the transition in each sentence. Then identify it as a transition of *addition* (A), *contrast* (C), *effect / result* (R), *time* (T), or *order of importance or presentation* (O).

_C_ 1. <u>However</u>, just as you start to introduce your friend, your mind goes blank, and you don't remember the person's name.

_____ 2. The frontal lobes lose mass; therefore, short-term memory gets worse.

_____ 3. First of all, there are two types of memory, long-term and short-term.

_____ 4. Consequently, elderly people would do well to eat several small meals each day.

_____ 5. Meanwhile, things have been happening to our short-term memory.

_____ 6. It is difficult or impossible to completely avoid memory decline. However, it can be slowed.

_____ 7. Furthermore, the first syllable of "Sarah" rhymes with "bear."

_____ 8. Most importantly, memory improvement takes work.

EXERCISE 2 PUNCTUATING SENTENCES WITH CONNECTORS

GRAMMAR NOTES 2–3 Punctuate the sentences with connectors. Add commas or semicolons as necessary.

1. Frank has an excellent memory; however, he doesn't use it to good advantage.

2. Frank has an excellent memory but he doesn't use it to good advantage.

3. Marta was having trouble remembering things so she signed up for a memory course.

4. Marta was having trouble remembering things consequently she signed up for a memory course.

5. You need to start taking better notes otherwise you won't do well on the exam.

6. You need to start taking better notes or you won't do well on the exam.

7. I have difficulty remembering people's names yet I can always remember what they were wearing.

8. I have difficulty remembering people's names on the other hand I can always remember what they were wearing.

9. Amanda forgot to pay her bill so the power company turned off her electricity.

10. Amanda forgot to pay her bill therefore the power company turned off her electricity.

EXERCISE 3 CONNECTORS

GRAMMAR NOTES 2–5 Read this segment of a radio broadcast. Complete the sentences with the connectors from the box. Use each connector once.

first	in addition	meanwhile	otherwise	therefore
however	in fact	~~next~~	second	

_____*Next*_____, we focus on the aftermath of the recent earthquake. Investigators
1.

have determined that it will cost approximately eight billion dollars to rebuild damaged

highways. According to the governor, two actions have to be taken: _____, the
2.

federal government will have to approve disaster funds to pay for reconstruction;

_____, insurance investigators will need to determine how much their
3.

companies will have to pay in the rebuilding effort. With luck, the governor says, some key

highways could be rebuilt within six months. He cautioned, _____, that the
4.

six-month figure is only an estimate. The process cannot move forward without funds from

insurance companies, and certain insurance companies have been slow to approve such funds

in the past. The rebuilding effort could, _____, drag on for at least a year.
5.

_____, bad weather could prevent the speedy completion of the project.
6.

Listeners may remember that after the last earthquake, repair projects took much longer than

government officials had predicted. _____, it is taking some people as long as
7.

four hours to commute to work, and others haven't been able to get to work at all.

Interviewed by our news team, one commuter who works in an office downtown said, "It

took me three hours to drive to work last Friday. I knew I'd have to find some other way of

getting there; _____, I'd never make it. Well, yesterday the train got me there
8.

in fifty minutes, and the trip was really pleasant. I even had the chance to read the morning

paper. _____, I'm going to switch permanently to the train. Hopefully, my
9.

memories of traffic jams will be just that: memories."

EXERCISE 4 CONJUNCTIONS AND TRANSITIONS

GRAMMAR NOTES 2–4 Look at the pictures of Hank's stressful morning. Using the words in parentheses, write two sentences describing what happened in each picture. Use commas to join clauses connected by coordinating conjunctions. Use semicolons to join clauses connected by transitions.

1. (and / in addition)

Hank didn't take a shower, and he didn't have any breakfast.
Hank didn't take a shower; in addition, he didn't have any breakfast.

2. (but / however)

3. (so / consequently)

4. (and / moreover)

5. (in the meantime / meanwhile)

6. (or / otherwise)

EXERCISE 5 EDITING

GRAMMAR NOTES 1–5 Read the student composition. There are nine mistakes involving connectors. The first mistake is already corrected. Find and correct eight more. You may add or eliminate words, but do not change word order or punctuation.

My Car Is Moving to the Suburbs

Yesterday, I drove my car to the college. I usually have trouble finding a parking place, ~~however~~ *but* this time it was almost impossible. There were simply no parking places anywhere near the campus, so I had to park in the downtown mall. When I finished class, I walked back to the mall. Therefore, I couldn't remember where I'd parked my car! Believe it or not, it took me forty-five minutes to find it. I've had enough of this, yet I've decided that I'm going to send my car to a new home in the suburbs.

I used to think that a car was the most wonderful thing in the world. I loved the freedom of being able to drive to my job or to the college whenever I wanted. To cut down on costs, I joined a carpool with four other people. The carpool was OK, nevertheless I didn't like having to wait around when my carpool members weren't ready to leave. Consequently, I started driving alone, and that worked really well for a while.

Although, I've recently changed my mind about owning a car. Now it's clear to me that there are just too many disadvantages to having a car in town. For example, sitting stalled in your car in a traffic jam is stressful, besides it's a phenomenal waste of time. Whereas, there's always the chance my car will be vandalized when I park it on the city streets. I have to park on the streets because it would cost me $200 a month to park my car in a parking garage.

Nonetheless, I've decided to leave my car at my cousin Brent's house in the suburbs. Otherwise, I'll end up going broke paying for parking and a course in memory improvement. My car will have a good home, and I'll use it just for longer trips. When I'm in the city, though, I'll take the bus or the tram, otherwise I'll walk. They say you can meet some interesting people on the bus. Maybe I'll find the love of my life. My only problem will be remembering which bus to take.

Go to **MyEnglishLab** for more focused practice.

EXERCISE 6 LISTENING

▶19|02 **A** Listen to the excerpt from a memory training workshop. Check (✓) the two things that are true.

☐ The workshop visitor says he's from Hawaii.
☐ The visitor has a Hawaiian name.
☐ The visitor is wearing a tuxedo.
☐ The visitor is wearing brown shoes.

▶19|02 **B** Listen again. Complete the sentences. Circle the correct answers.

1. The workshop leader says clients like to be called by their names; therefore, _____.
   a. it's polite to do that   **b.** it's good business to do that

2. To get names into your short-term memory, first, the leader says that you should _____.
   a. call clients by their names   **b.** notice particular things about clients

3. A visitor interrupts the workshop, claiming that money has been stolen. However, _____.
   a. the thief is never identified   **b.** the story about the theft wasn't real.

4. One participant knows the visit wasn't real because the visitor wasn't in uniform. In addition, _____.
   a. the leader didn't seem surprised   **b.** visitors aren't allowed to interrupt meetings

5. The leader says the participants were able to remember the visitor's first name because _____.
   a. they repeated the name out loud   **b.** it's an unusual name

6. One participant was able to remember the visitor's last name because _____.
   a. the leader repeated his name   **b.** it's an easy name to remember

7. The visitor said good-bye in an unusual way. Consequently, the participants _____ .

    a. remembered it   **b.** didn't understand it

8. Summing up the main points of the experience, the leader says that, most importantly, the participants _____ .

    a. always need to write things down   **b.** need to focus their attention consistently

9. The leader says the participants remembered the unusual things, but they need to work on remembering _____ .

    a. the ordinary things   **b.** the complicated things

C   Work with a partner. Discuss the questions.

1. What are things that are relatively easy for you to remember? Why?

2. What are things that are difficult for you to remember? Why?

EXERCISE 7   FAMOUS QUOTATIONS ABOUT MEMORY

CRITICAL THINKING   Work in a group. Read the quotations about memory. Choose five quotations and discuss them. What do they mean? Do you agree with them? Why or why not? Then report your conclusions to the class.

1. Remembrance of things past is not necessarily the remembrance of things as they were. —*Marcel Proust, author*

    EXAMPLE: **A:** I think it is true that we can remember a lot of things from the past, even though we sometimes don't remember them right. I think we often remember things the way we think they should have been.

               B: I agree this is sometimes the case. However, I think that if we're really honest with ourselves, our memories can be very accurate.

2. There are some things one remembers even though they may never have happened. —*Harold Pinter, author*

3. Those who cannot remember the past are condemned to repeat it. —*George Santayana, philosopher*

4. Sometimes you can't let go of the past without facing it again. —*Gail Tsukiyama, author*

5. One of the keys to happiness is a bad memory. —*Rita Mae Brown, author*

6. People have an annoying habit of remembering things they shouldn't. —*Christopher Paolini, author*

7. If you tell the truth, you don't have to remember anything. —*Mark Twain, author*

8. Remember tonight . . . for it is the beginning of always. —*Dante Alighieri, author*

9. Always carry a notebook. And I mean always. The short-term memory only retains information for three minutes; unless it is committed to paper you can lose an idea forever. —*Will Self, author and political commentator*

EXERCISE 8 HOW MUCH CAN YOU REMEMBER?

A PICTURE DISCUSSION Study the painting for two minutes. Then close your book. Write down as many details as you can remember. Then open your book again and check your memory. Note the details you were able to remember and those you were not able to remember.

First, I remembered that there were dogs in the painting....

However, I didn't remember how many dogs there were....

Kitchen Still Life with a Maid and Young Boy
Frans Snyders (Flemish painter, 1579–1657)

B Work in a small group. Compare the details you were able to remember best with those that the other members of the group remembered. Then discuss the questions below with the class.

1. Why do you think you were able to remember certain things in the painting better than others?

2. What is your reaction to the painting? Do you like it, dislike it, or are you neutral about it? Why?

Go to MyEnglishLab for more communication practice.

FROM GRAMMAR TO WRITING

A **BEFORE YOU WRITE** You are going to write an essay about an experience that you remember well. Write a few sentences about each of the following points.

- What the memory is
- Why the memory is important to you
- Why you believe you remember it well

B **WRITE** Using your ideas in A, write a five-paragraph essay about the memory you have chosen. Remember to use connectors. Try to avoid the common mistakes shown in the chart. Use the example below to help you begin your essay.

EXAMPLE: One of my strongest, and most painful, memories is of my piano recital when I was thirteen years old. I had been taking piano lessons for three years. My piano teacher scheduled me for a recital. I was supposed to play two easy songs and one difficult one. My teacher had told me that I was making excellent progress; therefore, I was excited about the recital, and I practiced a lot for it. However, things didn't go at all as planned . . .

Common Mistakes in Using Connectors

Don't confuse subordinating conjunctions with transitions. **Subordinating conjunctions** begin **dependent** clauses. **Transitions** begin **sentences** and independent clauses.	I tried hard to remember everyone's name. **However,** I forgot a few of them. **NOT** I tried hard to remember everyone's name. Although, I forgot a few of them.
Don't connect **independent clauses** with just a comma. Use a **period** or **semicolon** between independent clauses.	Mo forgot her **phone; therefore,** she couldn't call. **OR** Mo forgot her **phone. Therefore,** she couldn't call. **NOT** Mo forgot her phone, therefore she couldn't call.
Don't confuse *though* as a transition with *though* as a subordinating conjunction. *Though* as a transition normally comes at the **end** of an independent clause.	I can remember faces. I have trouble remembering names, **though**. *(transition)* **Though** I can remember faces, I have trouble remembering names. *(subordinating conjunction)*

C **CHECK YOUR WORK** Look at your essay. Underline the connectors. Use the Editing Checklist to check your work.

Editing Checklist

Did you . . . ?

☐ use subordinating conjunctions in dependent clauses and transitions in independent clauses

☐ use periods or semicolons between independent clauses

☐ correctly use *though* as either a subordinating conjunction or a transition

D **REVISE YOUR WORK** Read your essay again. Can you improve your writing? Make changes if necessary.

Go to MyEnglishLab for more writing practice.

UNIT 19 **REVIEW**

Test yourself on the grammar of the unit.

A Complete the sentences. Circle the correct answers.

1. I never forget a face; and / however, I have trouble remembering names.

2. I never forget a face, besides / though I have trouble remembering names.

3. Because / Besides Hari forgot to pay his utility bill, the city turned off his water.

4. Hari forgot to pay his utility bill; and / therefore, the city turned off his water.

5. The house is too expensive for us; otherwise / besides, I don't really like it.

6. The house is too expensive for us, and / though I don't really like it.

7. You'd better get up right now, or / because you'll miss the bus.

8. You'd better get up right now; however / otherwise, you'll miss the bus.

B Add commas and semicolons to the sentences to give them correct punctuation.

1. I was exhausted so I went to bed at 8:00 p.m.

2. I've visited many exotic places for instance I've been to Bali, Marrakesh, and Tasmania.

3. We need to remember to get tickets otherwise we won't get seats.

4. Nora forgot her passport as a result she missed her flight.

5. Even though Bao has a degree he has a low-paying job.

6. As soon as I got off the train I took a taxi to the hotel.

7. You're too young to have a car besides cars are very expensive.

C Find and correct five mistakes in the conversation.

A: I heard you're taking a memory-improvement course, how's it coming along?

B: The course itself is fine. Although, it's pretty expensive. It's worth it, but.

A: I've been thinking about taking one, too, however, I wonder if I would really learn anything. Would you recommend your course?

B: Yes, I would, for why don't you sign up?

Now check your answers on page 431.

Noun Clauses

PART 8

OUTCOMES

- Form and use noun clauses as subjects, objects, and complements
- Identify key details in a psychology article
- Identify advice given in a counseling session
- Discuss the topic of birth order, responding to questions and presenting conclusions
- Write an essay on the topic of birth order

OUTCOMES

- Report what someone said, using direct and indirect speech, making necessary changes
- Identify key concepts in a transcribed interview
- Identify details in an interview
- Discuss the topic of communication, expressing opinions and reporting on what others said
- Write an essay about a past conflict

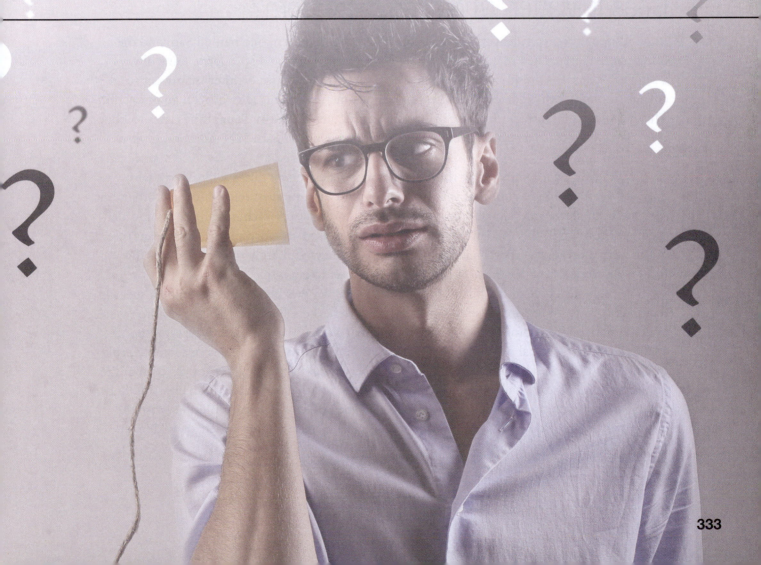

Noun Clauses: Subjects, Objects, and Complements

BIRTH ORDER

OUTCOMES
- Form and use noun clauses as subjects, objects, and complements
- Identify key details in a psychology article
- Identify advice given in a counseling session
- Discuss the topic of birth order, responding to questions and presenting conclusions
- Write an essay on the topic of birth order

STEP 1   **GRAMMAR IN CONTEXT**

BEFORE YOU READ

Discuss the questions.

1. In your view, can people change their character, or is it basically determined at birth?

2. Do you think the order in which children are born might affect their character? Why or why not?

READ

 Read this article about birth order.

Does It Matter When You Were Born?

Let's see if you can answer this question: There are two men, one named Sam and the other named Jerry. They're quite similar. Sam is a perfectionist, and so is Jerry. Jerry, always a high achiever, was president of his high school class. So was Sam. Neither man went to college, though both did become successful businessmen. Jerry has always been an innovator. This has made him a leader in most of his enterprises, just like Sam. Sam always tries to obey rules. Jerry does too. Jerry has never liked liberal ideas. Nor has Sam. The question is why they are so similar.

"Wait!" you say. "I know what the explanation is. They're identical twins. That's why they're so similar." Sorry, but that isn't it. They're not twins, or even related to each other, but they are both firstborns. Sam and Jerry are examples of what researchers call the birth-order theory. According to this theory, the order in which children are born plays a significant role in the formation of their personalities and in the way they ultimately turn out.[1] Does this sound like some crazy new idea? It isn't. It's been around for a while.

The main idea behind the birth-order theory is simple: Firstborn children enjoy a special relationship with their parents simply because they were there before any other children were. When other children come along, firstborns understand that these new arrivals represent a challenge to their special relationship. For this reason, firstborns tend to be conservative, rule-oriented, and opposed to change. They want to keep things as they are. Other children in the family have a different challenge. They must somehow adapt to the family dynamic and find a niche in their parents' affections. They sense that they have to become different from the oldest child, so they do. They learn to do whatever helps them establish their own identity.

---

1 *turn out:* develop in the end

One of the main supporters of the birth-order theory is Frank Sulloway, a researcher who did a twenty-six-year study of about 7,000 famous people in history and then performed a computer analysis. What he learned from the analysis led him to develop his theory that first-, middle-, and lastborns have very different characteristics. It is evident that firstborns are usually self-confident, assertive, and conscientious. They can also be jealous, moralistic, and inflexible. Winston Churchill, John Wayne, Oprah Winfrey, Saddam Hussein, and Joseph Stalin were all firstborns. Based on this idea, we might expect powerful political figures, such as U.S. presidents, to be firstborns. They often are, says Sulloway.

Sulloway observes that lastborns are usually more social, agreeable, and open to new and even revolutionary ideas. This is because, sensing the power of the already-established relationship between the oldest sibling[2] and the parents, they have to turn outward to establish their place in the world. Famous lastborns include Joan of Arc, Thomas Jefferson, and Leon Trotsky.

What about families in which there are more than two children? If there are three children in a family, the middle child is usually more flexible than the other two and often has a talent for compromise. Famous middle children include Nelson Mandela, Martin Luther King, Jr., and Jennifer Lopez.

A family in which there is only one child is the least predictable configuration, Sulloway says. An only child[3] isn't as inflexible as a firstborn. The fact that they are the sole child in the family, however, causes only children to identify with their parents as firstborns do.

Perhaps you're thinking this is all just too much of a generalization. That there are exceptions to the birth-order theory is clear. A child's temperament has a great deal to do

---

2 *sibling:* brother or sister
3 *only child:* the single child in a family

with how he or she turns out. Shy children, for example, may not become leaders even if they are firstborns. Sulloway notes that there have been famous firstborns who became revolutionaries as well as laterborns who became conservatives. Still, the theory of birth order is compelling even if its accuracy is controversial.

If we assume that there is some validity to the birth-order theory, how can parents achieve the best possible relationships with their children? What they should do, Sulloway says, is give each child unique time and attention. Whether or not they can significantly change the influences of birth order is an open question, but they will maximize the quality of those relationships.

AFTER YOU READ

Ⓐ VOCABULARY Complete the sentences with words from the box.

compelling	conscientious	innovator	sole
configuration	enterprises	niche	temperament

1. A person's _____ are his or her plans, businesses, and accomplishments.

2. A person who introduces something new is called a(n) _____.

3. A(n) _____ situation is one that attracts strong interest or attention.

4. A child who finds a(n) _____ in his or her parents' affections finds a suitable place.

5. A(n) _____ person is one who gives great attention or dedication to something.

6. The arrangement of children in a family is termed its _____.

7. The _____ child in a family is the only child in that family.

8. A child's _____ is his or her nature.

Ⓑ COMPREHENSION Read the statements. Check (✓) *True* or *False*.

	True	False
1. Both Sam and Jerry are firstborns.	☐	☐
2. The birth-order theory appeared very recently.	☐	☐
3. Firstborns tend to be conservative.	☐	☐
4. Powerful political figures are often lastborns.	☐	☐
5. Middle children are usually rebellious.	☐	☐
6. A family with only one child is the least predictable of the types.	☐	☐
7. According to Sulloway, there are no exceptions to the birth-order theory.	☐	☐
8. According to Sulloway, parents should give each child attention.	☐	☐

Ⓒ DISCUSSION Work with a partner. What forces do you think influence a person's character and personality? Discuss.

Go to MyEnglishLab for more grammar in context practice.

NOUN CLAUSES: SUBJECTS, OBJECTS, AND COMPLEMENTS

Noun Clauses Introduced by *That*

Subject
That he fits the category is obvious.
That they give the children so many gifts is unfortunate.

Object
You can see **(that) she loves her children.**
She knows **(that) they love her too.**

Complement	
Subject Complement	The problem was **(that) their son was a rebel.**
Adjective Complement	It is important **(that) people learn responsibility.**

Noun Clauses with Question Words

Subject
What I should tell her is obvious.
Why he did that wasn't evident.

Object
I wonder **what I should tell her.**
Can you explain **why he did that?**

Complement	
Subject Complement	The question is **why there are so many exceptions.**
Adjective Complement	It's interesting **who the exceptions are.**

Noun Clauses with *Whether* or *If*

Subject
Whether she'll outgrow her rebelliousness is hard to predict.
Whether the theory is valid is an interesting question.

Object
It's hard to predict **if she'll outgrow her rebelliousness.**
I care about **whether (or not) the theory accurate.**

Complement	
Subject Complement	The issue is **whether the categories are too broad.**
Adjective Complement	He's uncertain **whether he really believes it.**

Noun Clauses with *-ever* Words

Subject
Whatever you want to do is OK.
Whoever arrives first will get the job.
Whomever you recommend will be hired.
Whichever child is born first has advantages.
Wherever Mom wants to go will be OK with Dad.
Whenever you want to leave will be fine.
However you decide to proceed will be all right.

Object
It's OK to do **whatever you want to do.**
We'll hire **whoever arrives first.**
We'll hire **whomever you recommend.**
The advantages go to **whichever child is born first.**
Dad will be OK with **wherever Mom wants to go.**
I'll be fine with **whenever you want to leave.**
I'll be all right with **however you decide to proceed.**

GRAMMAR NOTES

1 Definition of Noun Clauses

Noun clauses are **dependent** clauses that perform the **same functions** as single **nouns**.

They can act as **subjects**.	**That firstborns identify with their parents** is apparent. **What laterborns must do** is become different from their siblings.
They can act as **objects**.	Laterborns sense **that they need to find a niche in their parents' affections.** We don't know **what her children's names are.**
They can act as **subject complements**. Remember that a complement is a word or phrase that describes or adds to the meaning of a subject, object, or adjective already mentioned in a sentence.	The *problem* is **that I don't understand the theory.** *(describes what the problem is)*
They can act as **adjective complements**. Adjective complements describe what is meant by the adjective used.	It's *obvious* **that she is a rebellious person.** *(describes what is obvious)*

2 *That* + Noun Clauses

Use the word ***that*** to **introduce** certain noun clauses.

When ***that*** begins a noun clause, it is a grammatical word that simply introduces the clause. It has **no concrete meaning**.	I believe **that** the birth-order theory is accurate in general.
You can omit *that* when it introduces an **object noun clause** or a **complement noun clause**. It is frequently omitted in speaking.	Firstborns realize **(that) siblings represent a challenge**. *(object noun clause)* It is evident **(that) firstborns are often conservative.** *(complement noun clause)*
When *that* introduces a **subject noun clause, do not omit** it.	**That there are exceptions to the theory** is clear. **NOT** ~~There are exceptions to the theory is clear.~~
It often functions as the subject of a sentence, with the noun clause coming later. Like the word *that*, *it* is sometimes a grammatical word that has no concrete meaning.	***It***'s funny **(that) you should say that**.
Subject noun clauses beginning with *that* are formal and are found mostly in writing.	**That birth order determines personality** is a controversial claim.
Don't confuse *that* and *what*. The word *that* simply introduces certain noun clauses. The word ***what*** refers to something definite. It serves as the object of a noun clause and **cannot be omitted**.	I know **(that) Maria is a middle child**. OBJECT SUBJECT VERB I don't know **what her future plans are**. **NOT** I don't know ~~her future plans are~~.

3 *The Fact That* + Noun Clauses

You can use the phrase ***the fact that*** in place of *that* in subject noun clauses. Sentences with *the fact that* are **less formal** than sentences with *that* introducing a subject noun clause.	**The fact that** Elena is rebellious might mean that she is a lastborn. *(less formal)* **That** Elena is rebellious might mean that she is a lastborn. *(formal)*
You **must** use *the fact that* in place of *that* in noun clauses that are **objects of prepositions**.	I'm impressed **by the fact that** Bob showed up. **NOT** I'm impressed by ~~that~~ Bob showed up.

4 Embedded Questions

A **question** that is **changed to a noun clause** is called an **embedded question**.

You can change both *wh-* questions and *yes/no* questions to noun clauses. Use **statement word order**, not question word order, in embedded questions.	Do you know **who their daughter is**? No, I don't know **who she is**. I don't know **if she's from around here**.
An embedded question can occur within a statement or within another question. An embedded question within a **statement** is followed by a **period**. An embedded question within another **question** is followed by a **question mark**.	I'm not sure **how many children they have.** Do you know **if Roberto is an only child?**
An embedded question is more polite than a direct question.	What time is it? *(direct)* Do you know **what time it is**? *(more polite)* What does "niche" mean? *(direct)* Do you know **what "niche" means**? *(more polite)*
Don't use question word order in an embedded question. Use **statement word order**.	Do you know **if they have children**? **NOT** Do you know ~~do~~ they have children? Can you tell me **what time it is**? **NOT** Can you tell me what time ~~is it~~?

5 *Wh-* Question Words + Noun Clauses

The *wh-* question words *what*, *who*, *whom*, *when*, *where*, *which*, *why*, and *how* introduce noun clauses (embedded questions) that are **formed from direct questions**.	Do you know **who their daughter is**? I'm not sure **when their son was born**.
The subject of an embedded *wh-* question takes a **singular verb**.	I'm not certain **who *is* going** with us.
Don't use *do*, *does*, or *did* in embedded questions.	I have no idea **what she meant**. **NOT** I have no idea what ~~did she mean~~.

6 If and Whether (or Not) + Noun Clauses

Use the words *if* and *whether (or not)* to introduce noun clauses (embedded questions) that are **formed from *yes/no* questions**.	Do you know **if they have any children**? Who knows **whether (or not) they have any children**? I have no idea **whether they have children**.
If and *whether (or not)* are similar in meaning and can be used interchangeably in many constructions.	We're not sure **if** Bob is married. We're not sure **whether** Bob is married **or not**.
Whether . . . or not can replace ***whether*** in all noun clauses.	We don't know **whether** Maria has any siblings. We don't know **whether** Maria has any siblings **or not**.
If . . . or not can replace ***whether*** in most clauses.	We don't know **if** Maria has any siblings **or not**.
BE CAREFUL! Don't use *if* to introduce a **subject noun clause**.	**Whether (or not) she understands** the issue is questionable. **NOT** ~~If she understands the issue is questionable.~~
BE CAREFUL! Don't omit *if* or *whether (or not)* in **embedded *yes/no* questions**.	I don't know **if** they are good parents. **NOT** I don't know ~~they are good parents~~.

7 -Ever Words + Noun Clauses

The *wh-* question words *what, who, whom, which, where, when,* and *how* often combine with the word ***ever*** to produce words that introduce noun clauses.	
• *whatever*	**Whatever she does** is acceptable to her parents.
• *whoever*	**Whoever interviews the best** will get the job.
• *whomever*	You can invite **whomever you want** to the picnic.
• *whichever (one)*	We can eat at **whichever restaurant you choose**.
• *wherever*	**Wherever you want to stay** will be fine with me.
• *whenever*	**Whenever you want to leave** will be agreeable.
• *however*	**However you want to handle this** will be OK.
USAGE NOTE *Wherever* and *whenever* can also introduce **adverb clauses**. (See Unit 17.) *However* is also a contrast transition word. (See Unit 19.)	We run into them **wherever we go**. She makes me laugh **whenever we're together**. I find the birth-order theory interesting. **However,** I don't totally understand how it works.

REFERENCE NOTES

For information on **noun clauses used to report speech**, see Unit 21 on page 355.

For information on **noun clauses in conditional sentences**, see Unit 22 on page 377.

For information on **noun clauses using the subjunctive**, see Unit 23 on page 395.

EXERCISE 1   DISCOVER THE GRAMMAR

A   GRAMMAR NOTES 1–5   Read the sentences based on the reading. Underline each noun clause. Then identify the way it is used: as *S* (a subject), *O* (an object), *SC* (a subject complement), or *AC* (an adjective complement).

_SC_   **1.** The question is <u>why they are so similar</u>.

_____   **2.** Sam and Jerry are examples of what researchers call the birth-order theory.

_____   **3.** I know what the explanation is.

_____   **4.** They sense that they have to become different from the oldest child.

_____   **5.** What he learned from the analysis led him to develop his theory.

_____   **6.** It is evident that firstborns are usually self-confident.

_____   **7.** That there are exceptions to the birth-order theory is clear.

_____   **8.** The fact that they are the sole children in their families makes them identify with their parents.

B   GRAMMAR NOTES 4–6   Read the sentences based on the reading. Underline the embedded question in each sentence. Then, for each embedded question, write the direct question it was derived from.

1. Let's see <u>if you can answer this question</u>.

    Can you answer this question? _____

2. The question is whether the theory is accurate.

_____

3. I know what that word means.

_____

4. What they should do is give each child unique attention.

_____

5. Whether or not they can change the influences of birth order is an open question.

_____

EXERCISE 2 THAT, THE FACT THAT, WHAT + NOUN CLAUSES

GRAMMAR NOTES 2–5 Complete the email with the correct forms of the words in parentheses and *that*, *the fact that*, or *what*. Use contractions where possible.

Hi, Sis,

You asked about the kids, so I thought I'd drop you an email and tell you

_____*what they've been doing*_____. I'll start with Bruce. I think you know
     1. (they / been doing)

_____ a senior in high school now. He's doing great in school
     2. (he / be)

and is planning for college. He's been accepted by the university, and we just found out

_____ a scholarship for his freshman year.
     3. (he / have / earn)

_____ well is a certainty; he's carrying a 4.00 grade point
     4. (he / be / going to do)

average. Mandy is a sophomore and is also doing well. She's in a college prep program, but so far she

doesn't know _____ when she gets to college. I guess
     5. (she / want / study)

_____ most middle children; she has a lot of friends. She
     6. (she / be / typical of)

always thinks _____ to get along with everyone. And then
     7. (it / be / important)

there's Jason. Al and I can't believe _____ so differently from
     8. (he / have / turn out)

the other two. He's in the eighth grade, and he isn't doing well in school. It's always been clear

_____ a rebellious streak, but now we're worried about
     9. (he / have)

_____. We love him dearly, but we aren't totally sure
     10. (it / be / getting worse)

_____ to keep him under control. We hope
     11. (we / can / do)

_____ as time goes on.
     12. (he / mature)

That's all for the moment. Email or text me, please. We hope

_____ well and happy.
     13. (you and Jaime / be)

Love,
Melanie

EXERCISE 3 EMBEDDED QUESTIONS

GRAMMAR NOTES 4–6 Read the following excerpt from a job interview. Then change each of the underlined questions to noun clauses that describe what the interviewer asked. Begin each clause with *if, whether or not,* or a *wh-* question word. Put the verbs in the embedded questions in the simple past or the past perfect. Do not use contractions.

LOPEZ: Good afternoon, Mr. Pei. I'm Blanca Lopez. Thanks for being here for this interview.

PEI: My pleasure. I'm happy to be here.

LOPEZ: So, Mr. Pei, <u>are you married?</u>
                      1.

PEI: Yes, I am.

LOPEZ: <u>Do you have any children?</u>
       2.

PEI: Yes, I do. My wife, Amy, and I have three children.

LOPEZ: You've indicated that you're working as a counselor. <u>How long have you been doing that?</u>
                                          3.

PEI: I've been working in counselling for ten years.

LOPEZ: Mr. Pei, you've written a great deal about birth order and family dynamics.

       <u>What made you start writing?</u>
              4.

PEI: I guess I just had a burning desire to communicate my ideas. The whole birth-order

       theory is pretty compelling.

LOPEZ: <u>How old are your children?</u>
       5.

PEI: Our oldest child is a girl who's sixteen years old. Our middle child is a boy who's

       fourteen. Our youngest child is a girl. She's twelve.

LOPEZ: <u>Does your family fit the theories you've written about?</u>
                  6.

PEI: Yes, basically, they do. For example, our older girl is a typical firstborn. She's always been

       conscientious about doing what needs to be done.

LOPEZ: <u>What can you tell me about the others?</u>
             7.

PEI: Well, our boy, the middle child, is very outgoing. Our younger girl is somewhat

       rebellious, or maybe we can call her free-thinking.

LOPEZ: Very interesting. <u>How do you deal with her rebelliousness?</u>
                     8.

W PEI: Well, it's complicated, but we limit her privileges, basically.

LOPEZ: All right. Now, Mr. Pei, <u>what do you consider your greatest strength as a counselor?</u>
                                 9.

PEI: I think my greatest strength is my ability to listen actively.

LOPEZ: All right, Mr. Pei. Thank you. . . .

1. Ms. Lopez asked *if he was married*   .

2. She asked _____ .

3. She asked _____ .

4. She asked _____ .

5. She asked _____ .

6. She asked _____ .

7. She asked _____ .

8. She asked _____ .

9. She asked _____ .

EXERCISE 4 -*EVER* WORDS AND NOUN CLAUSES

GRAMMAR NOTE 7 Complete the answers to the questions. Use the correct forms of the words in parentheses and the words from the box.

however	whatever	~~whenever~~	wherever	whichever	whoever	whomever

1. **Q:** Bob, what time shall we leave for the family picnic?

   A: _____ *Whenever you'd like to leave* _____ will be fine with me.
   (you'd like / leave)

2. **Q:** Dad, where should we go on our vacation?

   A: _____ will be great.
   (you kids and your mother / want to go)

3. **Q:** Mom, should I invite my school friends to the dinner?

   A: You can invite _____ .
   (you / want)

4. **Q:** Who's going to be our math teacher this year?

   A: It'll be _____ .
   (not / already have / a full teaching load)

5. **Q:** Which of these three books should I get Dad for his birthday?

   A: _____ is the least expensive.
   (you / should get / one)

6. **Q:** Alice, how do you think we should deal with this issue?

   A: _____ is OK with me.
   (you / want / deal with it)

7. **Q:** What would you like to do this weekend?

   A: I'll go along with _____ .
   (you'd / like to do)

EXERCISE 5 EDITING

GRAMMAR NOTES 1–7 Read this letter to Mr. and Mrs. Chen from their son James's teacher about his progress in school. There are ten mistakes in the use of noun clauses. The first mistake is already corrected. Find and correct nine more.

MADISON
JUNIOR HIGH SCHOOL

March 27

Dear Mr. and Mrs. Chen,

    I'm writing to give you a progress report on your son James. In general, I would say
that
~~what~~ he is doing better than previously, though he still isn't performing up to his abilities.

That stands out to me is his tendency to daydream. It's clear what he is paying better

attention during class activities, and that is a good sign. At this point, his two weakest

subjects are math and science. This is quite surprising, given the fact what he scored highly

on the recent national achievement tests in both those subjects. Currently, he is failing math

and barely passing science. I am quite puzzled by that he is doing so poorly in these areas.

However is preventing him from achieving success needs to be identified. I recently asked

him what is his difficulty in math and science, but he did not seem to have a clear idea.

    On the positive side, James is doing very well in English. He is also performing

reasonably well in history and art. However, there is still the problem of missing

assignments. Up until recently, I thought the fact that he wasn't doing the work. But last

week I asked him did he do the work but simply forgot to submit it, and he said which was

the case.

    Thank you for your efforts to monitor James's study time in the evenings. Children

today have so many distractions. Your son is lucky to have parents who care about his

education. Please call me if you have any concerns.

Sincerely,
Paula Brand

Go to **MyEnglishLab** for more focused practice.

EXERCISE 6 LISTENING

▶20|02 **A** Listen to the conversation. Why are the husband and wife visiting the counselor?

_____

▶20|02 **B** Listen to the conversation again. For each statement, check (✓) _True_ or _False_.

		True	False
1.	Amanda is the couple's youngest child.	☐	✓
2.	Amanda is an unhappy child.	☐	☐
3.	Amanda believes her parents don't care about her.	☐	☐
4.	Tim and Anne can understand why Amanda feels that.	☐	☐
5.	Amanda has a great many interests.	☐	☐
6.	Tim and Anne's older son is successful in everything he does.	☐	☐
7.	Tim and Anne have been spending a lot of time with Amanda.	☐	☐
8.	The counselor feels she understands what the issue is.	☐	☐
9.	The counselor says Tim and Anne should suggest an interest for Amanda.	☐	☐
10.	The counselor believes that Amanda needs special attention.	☐	☐

C Work with a partner. Do you agree with the advice the counselor has given the parents? What do you think it is important that the parents do to solve Amanda's problems? Discuss.

EXERCISE 7   WHAT'S YOUR BIRTH ORDER?

A **QUESTIONNAIRE** Fill out this questionnaire. Of the three choices in each question, circle the one that you feel describes you most closely. Then check your answers on page 349. According to the questionnaire, are you a firstborn, middle born, or lastborn? What about in real life?

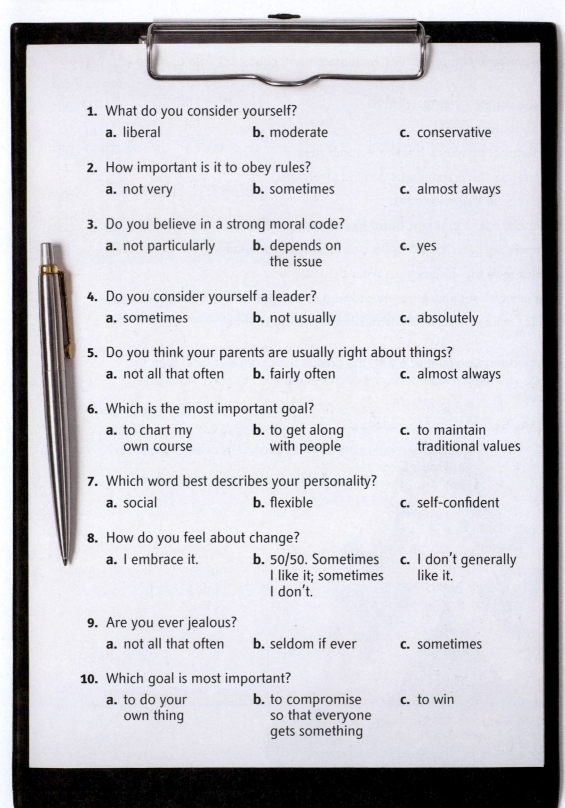

1. What do you consider yourself?
   a. liberal   b. moderate   c. conservative

2. How important is it to obey rules?
   a. not very   b. sometimes   c. almost always

3. Do you believe in a strong moral code?
   a. not particularly   b. depends on the issue   c. yes

4. Do you consider yourself a leader?
   a. sometimes   b. not usually   c. absolutely

5. Do you think your parents are usually right about things?
   a. not all that often   b. fairly often   c. almost always

6. Which is the most important goal?
   a. to chart my own course   b. to get along with people   c. to maintain traditional values

7. Which word best describes your personality?
   a. social   b. flexible   c. self-confident

8. How do you feel about change?
   a. I embrace it.   b. 50/50. Sometimes I like it; sometimes I don't.   c. I don't generally like it.

9. Are you ever jealous?
   a. not all that often   b. seldom if ever   c. sometimes

10. Which goal is most important?
    a. to do your own thing   b. to compromise so that everyone gets something   c. to win

B Work with a partner. Discuss your questionnaire results and your situation in real life.

EXAMPLE: **A:** I feel that I fit well into the birth-order theory. My questionnaire results show that I am a middle-born child, and I actually am a middle born.

B: Really? My questionnaire results were wrong. . . .

EXERCISE 8 WHAT'S THEIR BIRTH ORDER?

A GAME You are going to play a guessing game related to birth order. First, think about a person you know or a famous person you know about. How would you describe the person's background and personality? What is his or her birth order?

B Work in a group. Describe the person to the other members of your group. Talk about the person's background and personality, but do not reveal his or her birth order. Your group tries to guess the birth order of the person you have written about, giving reasons for their answers that are based on the birth-order theory.

EXAMPLE: **A:** My best friend, Samantha, is very outgoing and flexible, but she also has a rebellious streak. She does whatever she likes most of the time, and she doesn't seem to care about what other people think of her.

B: I think Samantha must be a lastborn. She's rebellious.

C: That Samantha isn't a firstborn is obvious, but I'm not sure she's a lastborn. She's flexible, and the theory says that middle borns are supposed to be flexible. . . .

C Report interesting examples to the class.

EXERCISE 9 PUTTING IT ALL TOGETHER

CRITICAL THINKING Work with a group. Use what you've learned in the readings and exercises in this unit to make determinations about the overall accuracy of the birth-order theory. Then report the conclusions of your group to the class.

EXAMPLE: **A:** I think it's hard to say if the birth-order theory is accurate or not. Some of the examples we've talked about fit into the theory, but some don't.

B: To me, it's obvious that the theory is wrong. None of the people that I talked to fit into it.

C: Whenever you have a theory that puts people into different categories, there are always exceptions. That doesn't mean the theory is completely wrong. . . .

Exercise 7 Questionnaire Answers

Count up the number of a., b., and c. answers. The category in which you have the greatest number of answers shows what your birth order is.

Mostly **a.** responses = You are a lastborn.
Mostly **b.** responses = You are a middle child.
Mostly **c.** responses = You are a firstborn.

Go to MyEnglishLab for more communication practice.

A BEFORE YOU WRITE You are going to write an essay about whether you feel you do or do not fit into the birth-order theory. Write a few sentences about each of the following points.

- Where you fit in a family structure
- What your personal characteristics are
- Why you believe you do or do not fit into the theory

B WRITE Using your ideas in A, write a five-paragraph essay about yourself or the person you have chosen. Remember to use noun clauses. Try to avoid the common mistakes shown in the chart. Use the example below to help you begin your essay.

EXAMPLE: I can't say whether the birth-order theory is true for everyone or not, but I think that I fit very well into it. In my family, there are three children, and all three of us have the characteristics of the firstborn, the middle child, and the lastborn. My older brother Roger is the firstborn; I'm the middle child; and my sister Nancy is the lastborn. That Roger is a typical firstborn person is clear. He's very conservative, and he agrees with whatever our parents say. . . .

Common Mistakes in Using Noun Clauses

Don't confuse *what* and *that*. **What** refers to something **specific**. *That* is a word that begins a clause but has **no concrete meaning**.	I'm not sure **what** she meant. **NOT** I'm not sure ~~that~~ she meant.
Be sure to use **statement word order** in embedded questions. Don't use question word order.	Do you know **who their daughter is**? **NOT** Do you know who ~~is their daughter~~?
Don't use *do*, *does*, or *did* in embedded questions.	Do you know **what "conscientious" means**? **NOT** Do you know what ~~does mean "conscientious"~~?
Don't use *if* to introduce a **subject noun clause**. Use **whether** (*or not*).	**Whether or not** they're going to be here isn't clear. **NOT** ~~If or not~~ they're going to be here isn't clear.

C CHECK YOUR WORK Look at your essay. Underline noun clauses. Use the Editing Checklist to check your work.

Editing Checklist

Did you . . . ?

☐ avoid confusing *what* and *that*

☐ use statement word order, not question word order, in embedded questions

☐ avoid using *do*, *does*, or *did* in embedded questions

☐ use *whether* (*or not*), not *if*, in subject noun clauses

D REVISE YOUR WORK Read your essay again. Can you improve your writing? Make changes if necessary.

Go to MyEnglishLab for more writing practice.

UNIT 20 REVIEW

Test yourself on the grammar of the unit.

A Circle the correct noun clause to complete each sentence.

1. I'm not sure what <u>the birth-order theory is</u> / <u>is the birth-order theory</u>.

2. I don't know why <u>does he always want</u> / <u>he always wants</u> to be in charge.

3. I'm not sure what time <u>does the meeting start</u> / <u>the meeting starts</u>.

4. I don't remember what <u>"configuration" means</u> / <u>means "configuration"</u>.

5. I don't know <u>whether Samira</u> / <u>Samira</u> enjoyed the party.

6. I have no idea <u>that</u> / <u>what</u> your daughter does for a living.

7. I'm not sure how long <u>she's been</u> / <u>has she been</u> a counselor.

8. We're not sure <u>if or not</u> / <u>whether or not</u> Danilo is really their son.

B Complete the sentences with the correct forms of the words in parentheses and the words in the box.

however	the fact that	what	whatever	whether or not	whomever

1. Did you have any idea _____ ?
   (Mary / mean)

2. We're not sure _____ .
   (Jama / be coming)

3. _____ to do is fine with me.
   (you / want)

4. _____ is obvious.
   (Allison / love / Kahlil)

5. Invite _____ to the dinner.
   (you / want)

6. _____ is acceptable to me.
   (you / want / proceed)

C Find and correct six mistakes.

A: Do you know who are our new neighbors?

B: Yes, I run into them whoever I go out in the yard.

A: Oh, yeah? What do you think are they like?

B: They seem really nice. I know what they both work.

A: Hmm. I wonder they have children.

B: They have three. I'm happy about that their daughter is the same age as Maria.

Now check your answers on page 432.

Go to MyEnglishLab to complete the review online.

Direct and Indirect Speech
COMMUNICATION AND MISUNDERSTANDING

OUTCOMES
- Report what someone said, using direct and indirect speech, making necessary changes
- Identify key concepts in a transcribed interview
- Identify details in an interview
- Discuss the topic of communication, expressing opinions and reporting on what others said
- Write an essay about a past conflict

STEP 1 | **GRAMMAR IN CONTEXT**

BEFORE YOU READ

Discuss the questions.

1. Do you sometimes have misunderstandings with other people? In your experience, what kinds of misunderstandings are the most difficult to deal with?

2. How can misunderstandings best be avoided?

READ

▶ 21|01 Read this interview with an expert on communication.

Understanding Misunderstandings

NESS: Hello, everyone. I'm Ann Ness. Please welcome today's guest—communication expert Ellen Sands.

SANDS: Thanks for having me. You know, Ann, I think we're seeing a lot more verbal conflict these days than in the past. There seems to be a lot more rancor and a lot less civility. Today I want to talk about ways to avoid verbal conflict, or at least minimize it.

NESS: Sounds good, Ellen. Tell us more.

SANDS: All right. First, people need to listen actively to each other. We hear things, but often we don't really listen. A couple of weeks ago, I was at a restaurant in Los Angeles, sitting near an Indian couple being served by an American waitress. The service was slow, and the couple seemed distressed. When the waitress brought the check, the man said, "The bill seems very high. Did you include the service in it? How much is the service?" The waitress said, "You have to pay the tax." The man said, "The service was very slow. We have never waited so long to be served. We will pay the bill, but we won't pay for service." Then they left angrily. The waitress just glared at them and didn't say anything. It wasn't a good situation, mainly because the waitress didn't listen actively.

NESS: Let me see if I understand. When the waitress brought the check, the man said the bill seemed very high. He asked how much the service was. The waitress said they had to pay the tax. The man said the service had been very slow and they had never waited so long to be served. He said they would pay the bill but they wouldn't pay for service. Now, what did the waitress do wrong?

SANDS: She didn't listen carefully. The man asked if she had included the service in the bill. Unfortunately, she never answered his question. That was the key thing he wanted to know.

NESS: Did she do anything else wrong?

SANDS: She didn't address his concern about the slow service. She could have said something like, "Yes, I'm really sorry about the service. We're short-handed[1] today."

NESS: Very interesting. Now, what's another way to avoid verbal conflict?

SANDS: Another really good strategy is to state things positively instead of negatively. Recently, I was sitting in as a consultant at a school board meeting. Right at the start, the chair gave instructions in an arbitrary way: "We're on a very tight schedule. Make your reports brief; no one will be allowed to take more than three minutes. And no one will be allowed to interrupt the person who's speaking. No one will ask any questions." It wasn't a good meeting. You could have cut the silence with a knife.

NESS: How could the chair have done better?

SANDS: He told them to make their reports brief, but he could have asked them to try to limit their reports to three minutes. He said no one would be allowed to interrupt the person who was speaking. He also said no one would ask any questions. He had a rigid manner, spoke with a self-righteous tone, and basically treated the attendees like schoolchildren instead of like adults. That's a good way to inhibit any kind of productive discussion. He could have asked them to hold their questions for the duration of the speeches. The bottom line is this: You don't have to sugarcoat[2] your statements, but people will respond much better if you put a positive spin[3] on things.

NESS: All right. Thanks, Ellen. We'll be back shortly, after this commercial break.

---

1 *short-handed:* without enough help
2 *sugarcoat:* make something appear or sound nicer than it really is
3 *spin:* interpretation

AFTER YOU READ

A VOCABULARY Match the words in **bold** with their meanings.

_____ **1.** You should treat people with civility, not with **rancor**.

_____ **2.** The couple seemed **distressed**.

_____ **3.** The waitress didn't **address** the couple's concern.

_____ **4.** The chair gave instructions in an **arbitrary** way.

_____ **5.** He spoke in a **rigid** manner.

_____ **6.** The chair's tone was **self-righteous**.

_____ **7.** That is a good way to **inhibit** a productive discussion.

_____ **8.** The audience had to hold their questions for the **duration**.

a. time something lasts

b. unreasonable

c. stiff, inflexible

d. discourage

e. angry feelings

f. properly deal with

g. upset

h. sure that one is right

B COMPREHENSION Complete the sentences based on the reading.

1. Ellen Sands is a(n) _____ expert.

2. Sands believes there is _____ rancor in communication today than in the past.

3. She also believes there is _____ civility today than previously.

4. Sands says that a key aspect of good communication is _____ listening.

5. In her first example, the couple from India thought the service was too _____.

6. In her second example, Sands talks of the need to state things in a(n) _____ manner.

7. The chair in her second example treated the attendees like _____.

8. Sands suggests that in a discussion, people should be treated like _____.

C DISCUSSION Work with a partner. Compare and justify your answers in B. Then discuss this question: Do you agree with Ellen Sands's advice on how to minimize verbal conflict? What strategies do you use to avoid conflict in your own life?

Go to MyEnglishLab for more grammar in context practice.

STEP 2   GRAMMAR PRESENTATION

DIRECT AND INDIRECT SPEECH

Statements: Direct Speech

Subject	Reporting Verb	Direct Statement
He	said,	"The food **is** delicious."
		"The bill **includes** service."
		"The service **was** ridiculously slow."

Statements: Indirect Speech

Subject	Reporting Verb	Noun/Pronoun	Indirect Statement	
He	said	Ø*	(**that**)	the food **was** delicious.
	told	Miriam/her		the bill **included** service.
				the service **had been** slow.

*Ø: not used.

Yes/No Questions: Direct Speech

Subject	Reporting Verb	Direct Question
The chair	asked,	"**Have you finished** your report?"
		"**Do you think we are going** to have time to finish?"

Yes/No Questions: Indirect Speech

Subject	Reporting Verb	Noun/Pronoun	Indirect Question	
The chair	asked	(Marta)	**if**	**she had finished** her report.
		(her)	**whether (or not)**	**she thought they were** going to have time to finish.

Wh- Questions: Direct Speech

Subject	Reporting Verb	Direct Question
The customer	asked,	"**What time does the manager arrive?**"
		"**Who is the manager?**"

Wh- Questions: Indirect Speech

Subject	Reporting Verb	Noun/Pronoun	Indirect Question	
The customer	asked	(the waitress)	**what time**	**the manager arrived.**
		(her)	**who**	**the manager was.**

Verb Changes in Indirect Speech

Direct Speech			
		Verb	
He said,	"I	report	the news."
		am reporting	
		reported	
		have reported	
		had reported	
		will report	
		can report	
		should report	

Indirect Speech			
		Verb	
He said	(that) he	reported	the news.
		was reporting	
		had reported	
		would report	
		could report	
		should report	

Other Changes in Indirect Speech

	Direct Speech	Indirect Speech
Pronouns	"Andy, are **you** listening?" Mary asked.	Mary asked Andy if **he** was listening.
Possessives	The boss said, "Sue, bring **your** camera."	The boss told Sue to bring **her** camera.
This	"Can I have **this** film?" Sam asked.	Sam asked if he could have **that** film.
Here	Mrs. Brown asked, "Will you be **here**?"	Mrs. Brown asked if I would be **there**.
Ago	"We came a year **ago**," Jim said.	Jim said (that) they had come a year **previously / before**.
Now	Bob asked, "Are you leaving **now**?"	Bob asked if I was leaving **then**.
Today	"I need to work **today**," Jack said.	Jack said (that) he needed to work **that day**.
Yesterday	The reporter asked, "Did you call **yesterday**?"	The reporter asked if I had called **the previous day / the day before**.
Tomorrow	"Are you arriving **tomorrow**?" Sarah asked.	Sarah asked if we were arriving **the next day**.

GRAMMAR NOTES

1 Direct vs. Indirect Speech

We can report speech in two ways: with **direct speech** and with **indirect speech**.

Direct speech (also called **quoted speech**) is the **exact words** (or thoughts) of someone speaking (or thinking). It is enclosed in quotation marks. Use a **reporting verb** such as *say*, *tell*, and *ask* to introduce direct speech.	Ellen Sands said, **"I want to talk about ways to avoid verbal conflict."** **"Asha is really angry at me,"** I thought.
To report direct speech, use a **comma** followed by **quotation marks** at the **beginning** of the quotation. Use a **question mark** or an **exclamation point** at the **end** of a question or exclamation, followed by quotation marks.	John said, **"Tell me what's really bothering you."** The man asked, **"Does the bill include service?"** He said, **"We won't pay for the service!"**
In direct speech, the quoted part of the sentence can come either at the **beginning** or at the **end** of the sentence.	**"Turn in your exams now,"** the teacher said. The teacher said, **"Turn in your exams now."**
If a quotation is interrupted by a reporting verb, do not capitalize the first word in the second part of the quotation.	**"Mr. Gomez,"** Kayoko asked, **"*may* I talk to you about my grades in this class?"**
Indirect speech (also called **reported speech**) is someone's **report** of direct speech. It does not contain the exact words of a speaker and is not enclosed in quotation marks. Indirect speech reports what a speaker said in a **noun clause** or **phrase** introduced by a reporting verb.	NOUN CLAUSE She said **(that) she wanted to talk about ways to avoid verbal conflict.**
To report a statement, you can use *that* to introduce the noun clause. The word *that* can also be omitted. To report a question, use *if*, *whether (or not)*, or a *wh-* question word to introduce the noun clause.	NOUN CLAUSE The man asked *if* **the bill included service.**
BE CAREFUL! Don't use quotation marks in indirect speech.	He said **(that) he would be there.** **NOT** John said ~~"he would be there."~~

2 Reporting Verbs

The verbs *say*, *tell*, and *ask* are the most common reporting verbs. Other reporting verbs include *claim*, *reply*, *state*, and *wonder*. We usually use the **simple past** forms of these verbs in both direct and indirect speech.	Hal **said**, "Martha, we have to leave." Hal **told** Martha they had to leave. Hal **asked** Martha if she was ready to leave.
USAGE NOTE *Say* and *tell* have similar meanings, but they are used differently. We *say something* but *tell someone something*. Normally, *tell* must be followed by an object.	Andy **told Freda** (that) she shouldn't worry. Andy **said** (that) Freda shouldn't worry.
USAGE NOTE We often use *tell* when the listener is mentioned. Use *say* if the listener is not mentioned.	The chair **told us** to pay attention. The chair **said** to pay attention.
BE CAREFUL! Don't use *tell* when the listener is *not* mentioned. Don't use *say* immediately before an object. Use *say* + *to* + **object**.	Ms. Tanaka **said** (that) she was going to the meeting. **NOT** Ms. Tanaka ~~told~~ (that) she was going to the meeting. Mr. Egiofor **told us** (that) he'd be lecturing. Mr. Egiofor **said to us** (that) he'd be lecturing. **NOT** Mr. Egiofor ~~said~~ us (that) he'd be lecturing.

3 Reporting *Yes/No* Questions

To **report indirect questions**, we normally use *ask* in its simple past form.	The director asked, "Do you want to talk about the issue?" The director *asked* if we wanted to talk about the issue.
Use **statement word order**, not question word order, to report *yes/no* questions.	I asked if **we would** know the answer soon. **NOT** I asked ~~would we~~ know the answer soon.
USAGE NOTE Use *if* or *whether (or not)*, not *that*, to introduce an **indirect yes/no question**. *If* and *whether (or not)* are similar in meaning and are often used interchangeably.	Bob asked, "Do you think she'll take the job?" Bob asked **if** I thought she would take the job.
We often use *whether (or not)* to emphasize alternatives or different possibilities.	Bob asked **whether (or not)** I thought she would take the job.
BE CAREFUL! Indirect questions end with a **period**, not a question mark.	Sue asked Helen **if she had talked with her boss.** **NOT** Sue asked Helen if she had talked with her boss~~?~~
BE CAREFUL! Don't use *do*, *does*, or *did* in an indirect question. Use the simple present, simple past, or past perfect.	Ahmed asked Mandy **if she got** along well with her boss. **NOT** Ahmed asked Mandy ~~did she get~~ along well with her boss.

4 Reporting Wh- Questions

Use **question words** to introduce **indirect wh- questions**.	The man asked, "**How much** is the service?" The man asked *how much* the service was. "**Which** entrée do you prefer?" the waiter asked. The waiter asked *which* entrée I preferred.
The **predicate** of a sentence is the part that makes a statement about the subject. Use **statement word order** to **report indirect questions** about a predicate.	My daughter asked, "Why **didn't he take** our order?" My daughter asked why **he hadn't taken** our order.
We also use **statement word order** to report indirect questions about the **subject**.	"Who **is going to do** the dishes?" Mom asked. Mom asked who **was going to do** the dishes.

5 Changes in Verbs

If the reporting verb is in the simple past, the **verb in the noun clause** often **changes**.

• imperative → infinitive	The teacher said, "**Open** your books." The teacher told us **to open** our books.
• simple present → simple past	Bill said, "I **invest** in the stock market." Bill said (that) he **invested** in the stock market.
• present progressive → past progressive	Mary asked, "John, **are** you **studying** math?" Mary asked John if he **was studying** math.
• simple past → past perfect	"Priscilla **made** a delicious meal," Mark said. Mark said (that) Priscilla **had made** a delicious meal.
• present perfect → past perfect	"Sam, **have** you ever **eaten** at that café?" Jack asked. Jack asked Sam if he **had** ever **eaten** at that café.

6 Verbs That Don't Change

In spoken English, we sometimes **do not change verbs** in indirect speech, especially if what we are reporting happened a **short time ago**.	Lu just said, "Jack **didn't come** to work." Lu just said Jack **didn't come** to work. **OR** Lu just said Jack **hadn't come** to work.
Even in more formal English, we often do not change verbs to past forms if **general truths** are reported.	"**Does** it **snow** here in the winter?" Kenny asked. Kenny asked if it **snows** here in the winter. **OR** Kenny asked if it **snowed** here in the winter.
When the reporting verb is in the **simple present**, **present progressive**, **present perfect**, or **future**, the verb in the noun clause does not change.	Betty says, "**I'm going to** buy a new car." Betty says she **'s going to** buy a new car.

Certain **modals change** in indirect speech. Other modals do not change.

• *can* → *could*	"Sam, **can** you come by at 6:00 p.m.?" Ann asked.
	Ann asked Sam if he **could** come by at 6:00 p.m.
• *may* → *might*	"I **may** be able to," Sam said.
	Sam said he **might** be able to.
• *must* → *had to*	"I absolutely **must** leave at 6:15," Ann said.
	Ann said she absolutely **had to** leave at 6:15.
• *shall* → *should*	"**Shall** I drive you to the airport?" Sam asked.
	Sam asked if he **should** drive her to the airport.
• *will* → *would*	"I **won't** need a ride," Ann replied.
	Ann replied that she **wouldn't** need a ride.

Could, had better, might, ought to, should, and *would* **do not change** in indirect speech.	I said, "Helen, I **might** attend the conference."
	I told Helen (that) I **might** attend the conference.
	"Sarah, you **should** be more careful," Dad said.
	Dad told Sarah (that) she **should** be more careful.

In addition to verbs, certain **other words change** in indirect speech.

• pronouns/possessive adjectives → other forms	Jeremy said, "**My** boss just promoted **me**."
	Jeremy said (that) **his** boss had just promoted **him**.
• *this* → *that* and *these* → *those*	Don asked, "Have you read **this** book?"
	Don asked if I had read **that** book.
• *here* → *there*	"Please be **here** for the meeting," Sally asked.
	Sally asked me to be **there** for the meeting.
• *now* → *then*	Mac said, "Alan's just arriving **now**."
	Mac said (that) Alan was just arriving **then**.
• *ago* → *before/previously*	Julie said, "I got the job three years **ago**."
	Julie said (that) she had gotten the job three years **previously**.
• *yesterday* → *the day before/the previous day*	Mickey said, "I called **yesterday**."
	Mickey said that he had called **the day before**.
• *today* → *that day*	"Hans, are you coming **today**?" Abdul asked.
	Abdul asked Hans if he was coming **that day**.
• *tomorrow* → *the next day/the following day*	"I can see you **tomorrow**," said Kayoko.
	Kayoko said (that) she could see me **the next day**.

REFERENCE NOTES

For information on **reporting statements and questions in conditional sentences**,
see Unit 22 on page 377.
For a list of **reporting verbs**, see Appendix 25 on page 421.

Go to MyEnglishLab to watch the grammar presentation.

EXERCISE 1   DISCOVER THE GRAMMAR

A GRAMMAR NOTES 1–8   Read the direct speech sentences based on the reading and the reports of those sentences in indirect speech. Is the change to indirect speech correct (*C*) or incorrect (*I*)?

_C_   **1.** She said, "I want to talk about ways to avoid verbal conflict."
       REPORT: She said she wanted to talk about ways to avoid verbal conflict.

_____   **2.** The man said, "The bill seems very high."
       REPORT: The man said the bill seems very high.

_____   **3.** The man asked the waitress, "Did you include the service in the bill?"
       REPORT: The man asked the waitress did she include the service in the bill.

_____   **4.** The waitress said, "You have to pay the tax."
       REPORT: The waitress said they had to pay the tax.

_____   **5.** The man told the waitress, "We won't pay for service."
       REPORT: The man told the waitress we wouldn't pay for service.

_____   **6.** The waitress could have said, "I'm really sorry about the service."
       REPORT: The waitress could have said she was really sorry about the service.

_____   **7.** The chair said, "We're on a very tight schedule.
       REPORT: The chair said they were on a very tight schedule.

_____   **8.** The chair said, "Make your reports brief."
       REPORT: The chair said them to make their reports brief.

_____   **9.** The chair said, "We might need to have another meeting tomorrow."
       REPORT: The chair said they might need to have another meeting the next day.

_____   **10.** The chair said, "No one will ask any questions."
        REPORT: The chair said no one will ask any questions.

B GRAMMAR NOTES 5, 7   Each of the following direct speech sentences has been changed to indirect speech. Identify how the verb has changed in each item.

1. The chair said, "Make your reports brief." ➔ The chair told them to make their reports brief.

     CHANGE: _imperative ➔ infinitive_____

2. The waitress said, "You have to pay the tax." ➔ The waitress told them they had to pay the tax.

     CHANGE: _____

3. The waitress could have said, "I'm really sorry about the service." ➔ The waitress could have said she was really sorry about the service.

     CHANGE: _____

4. The man asked the waitress, "Did you include the service in the bill?" ➔ The man asked the waitress if she had included the service in the bill.

     CHANGE: _____

5. The customer said, "I have never eaten such terrible food." → The customer said he had never eaten such terrible food.

CHANGE: _____

6. The chair said, "No one will ask any questions." → The chair said no one would ask any questions.

CHANGE: _____

7. The man from India asked his wife, "Shall we leave?" → The man from India asked his wife if they should leave.

CHANGE: _____

8. The man asked the waitress, "Can you explain the bill?" → The man asked the waitress if she could explain the bill.

CHANGE: _____

EXERCISE 2 DIRECT SPEECH TO INDIRECT SPEECH

GRAMMAR NOTES 5–7 Put the headlines into indirect speech. Add any necessary articles.

1 Divorced Man's Children Won't Speak to Him

2 Famous Actress Says She's Leaving Her Husband for the Third Time

3 Couple Is Going to Sue Restaurant Because of Rude Waiters

4 Congress Says President Vetoed Health Bill Because of Miscommunication

5 Woman's Sister Refuses to Invite Her to Her Wedding

6 Legislature Says Governor Lied about His Intentions to Sign Tax Bill

7 Rock Star and Band Are No Longer Performing Together

8 High School Students Will Soon Be Required to Take Communication Course to Graduate

1. The headline said *(that) a divorced man's children wouldn't speak to him.* _____

_____

2. A famous actress said _____

_____

3. The headline said _____

_____

4. Congress said _____

_____

5. The headline said _____

_____

6. The legislature said _____

_____

7. The headline said _____

_____

8. The headline said _____

_____

EXERCISE 3 INDIRECT SPEECH TO DIRECT SPEECH

GRAMMAR NOTES 3–4 A substitute teacher, Ms. Wong, had some communication difficulties with the students in her class. The students asked Ms. Wong questions. Read Ms. Wong's indirect speech answers to the questions. Then write the students' questions in direct speech.

1. One student, Mia, asked, *"Who are you?"* _____

Ms. Wong told the class she was Ms. Wong, their substitute teacher.

2. Mia asked, _____

She told the class their regular teacher was out of town.

3. Another student, Jordan, asked, _____

She said she would be with them for at least a month.

4. Jordan asked, _____

Ms. Wong told the class she was going to teach them how to do algebra.

5. Another student, Brianna, asked, _____

She answered that algebra is a type of math that uses letters and other signs to show numbers.

6. Brianna was still confused. She asked, _____

She told Brianna that yes, she could explain that again.

7. Another student, Caden, asked, _____

Ms. Wong told the class that yes, they would have to do homework.

8. Caden asked, _____

She said that they would have to do homework every week.

9. Caden said that that wasn't fair. He asked, _____

_____

Ms. Wong said that Caden had misunderstood. She wasn't going to make them do homework every night.

10. Another student, Lucas, asked, _____

The teacher said that yes, she really did have a teaching degree.

EXERCISE 4 PUNCTUATION OF DIRECT SPEECH

GRAMMAR NOTE 1 Read Linh's narrative about a time when she felt she was insulted. Punctuate the sentences that are direct speech.

"So what happened?" I asked.

Well Linh said we were all seated in the living room. There were about twelve people there. Several of them were high-society types.

What were you doing with a bunch of high-society people I asked.

Good question Linh answered. Actually, I was visiting my cousin, and I was her guest.

So what went wrong I asked.

Well, a woman asked me where I was going to school. I said I was attending a community college. Then the woman's husband asked me if I was going to a real college after that. That made me pretty mad, and I got red in the face Linh said. I guess I raised my voice.

Oh, wow I said. Then what?

Well, Linh said my cousin came to the rescue. She explained to the man that a community college education can be just as good as a university education, and it's cheaper. It turned out that the man and his wife were from a European country, and they didn't understand our system. He said he hadn't understood and was sorry.

How did you feel about the whole thing I asked.

Embarrassed at first Linh answered. But it all turned out OK because of my cousin. It's great when there's someone who can smooth things over.

EXERCISE 5 MULTIPLE CHANGES TO INDIRECT SPEECH

GRAMMAR NOTES 3–7 Read the conversation. Then complete the father's account of the conversation with indirect speech forms. The number in parentheses indicates how many words are needed in each case.

SALLY: Dad, can you help me with my homework?

DAD: Yes, I can. What do you need?

SALLY: I have to write a report for my communications class. It's on a quotation.

DAD: OK. What's the quotation?

SALLY: It's by William Mizner, and it says, "A good listener is not only popular everywhere, but after a while he gets to know something."

DAD: What do you think it means?

SALLY: Well, maybe it means that people will like you if you're a good listener.

DAD: Good. That's part of it. Do you think it means anything else?

SALLY: Well, maybe that you can learn something if you listen.

DAD: Very good! You understand the quotation really well.

My daughter Sally asked me _____*if I could help her with her*_____ homework. I told her
                                      1. (seven words)

_____ and asked her _____. She said
  2. (two words)   **3.** (three words)

_____ a report on a quotation for _____
         4. (four words)   **5.** (one word)

communications class. I asked her _____. She said
                                                    6. (four words)

_____ by William Mizner and went like this: "A good listener is not only
  7. (two words)

popular everywhere, but after a while he gets to know something." I asked her

_____. She said she thought maybe
                    8. (five words)

_____ that people _____ you if you were a good
  9. (two words)   **10.** (two words)

listener. I told her that _____ part of it and asked
                              11. (one word)

_____. anything else. She said she
                    12. (five words)

thought maybe it meant you _____ something if you listened. I told her
                                      13. (two words)

_____ the quotation really well.
  14. (two words)

EXERCISE 6 EDITING

GRAMMAR NOTES 1–8 Read the letter. It has nine mistakes in the use of direct and indirect speech. The first mistake is already corrected. Find and correct eight more.

To: EmilyL@yoohoo.com
Fr: CharlesM@yoohoo.com

Dear Emily,

I just wanted to fill you in on Tim's school adventures. About two months ago, Melanie

said she ~~feels~~ *felt* we should switch Tim to the public school. He'd been in a private school

for several months, as you know. I asked her why did she think that, and she said, "He's

miserable where he is, and I don't think the quality of education is good there. He tells he

doesn't feel like he can communicate with the teachers and that no one understands him.

He also doesn't think he has many friends." She said she thought we can move him to the

local high school, which has a good academic reputation. I told to her that I agreed with

her, but that we should ask Tim. The next morning, we asked Tim if he wanted to stay at

the private school. I was surprised at how strong his response was. He said me that he

hated the private school and didn't want to go there any longer. So we moved him. He's

been at the new school for a month now, and he's doing well. Whenever I ask him does

he have his homework done, he says, "Dad, I've already finished it." He's made several new

friends. Every now and then, he asks us why didn't we let him change schools sooner. He

says people are treating him as an individual now. I'm just glad we moved him when we did.

Not much else is new. Oh, yes—I do need to ask are you coming for the holidays. Email

soon and let us know. Or call.

Love,
Charles

Go to MyEnglishLab for more focused practice.

EXERCISE 7 LISTENING

▶ 21|02 **A** Listen to the next part of the interview with Ellen Sands about communication and misunderstanding. What method of minimizing verbal conflict does Sands discuss here?

_____

▶ 21|02 **B** Listen again. Then answer each question in a complete sentence.

1. What did Sands say that speaking about yourself instead of the other person involves?
   She said that it involves focusing on how the other person's statements are affecting you.

2. What did she say about how people should respond to anger?

_____

3. What did the host ask Sands to give?

_____

4. What did Sands say the two women were arguing about?

_____

5. What did Rosa say about Alicia?

_____

6. What did Alicia say in response to Rosa?

_____

7. What is the first thing Alicia could have said?

_____

8. What is the second thing Alicia could have said?

_____

C Work with a partner. Discuss this question: Do you agree with what the communication expert said about not returning anger for anger? Why or why not? Give personal examples.

EXERCISE 8 WHAT REALLY HAPPENED?

A **ROLE PLAY** You are going to perform a role play. First, work in a group of five students. Look at the picture. Discuss what happened to cause the accident. Who is most likely to give the most objective report of what happened, and why?

EXAMPLE: I think that neither driver is likely to give an objective report. The bystander is likely to give an objective report because . . .

B Invent conversations for the two police officers, the two drivers, and the bystander. Then perform them as a role play.

EXAMPLE: **POLICEMAN 1:** What happened here?
              DRIVER 1: Well, the accident wasn't my fault. The other driver was speeding. I wasn't . . .

C Perform your role-play conversation for the class.

EXERCISE 9 A TIME OF MISUNDERSTANDING

A DISCUSSION You are going to have a discussion about a misunderstanding. First, think of an example of a time when you experienced a conflict or a misunderstanding in your life. For example, think of a time when you were hurt or insulted by what someone said to you. How did you react? Did you resolve the situation satisfactorily, or not?

B Work in a group. Tell the members of your group about your experience. Did you and the other person return anger for anger? Did you listen actively? Did you state things positively or negatively?

EXAMPLE: **A:** Once someone I thought was my friend told me I was stupid.
B: What did you do?
A: Well, I was furious at first. I got really angry. After a while, though, I calmed down, and I told the friend that . . .

EXERCISE 10 GET WHAT THEY SAID RIGHT

A GAME You are going to play a reporting game. First, work with a partner. Work together to write a short dialogue in direct speech about communication and misunderstanding. The dialogue should be no longer than six sentences.

JOMO: My girlfriend isn't speaking to me.
MARIA: Why isn't she speaking to you?
JOMO: She thinks that I . . .

B Work with another pair. Take turns reporting each line of your dialogue to the other pair, using indirect speech. The other pair tries to guess what the original line of the dialogue was in direct speech. Make corrections if necessary.

EXAMPLE: **A:** First, Jomo said that his girlfriend wasn't speaking to him.
B: This is what Jomo said: "My girlfriend wasn't speaking to me."
C: No! I said, "My girlfriend *isn't* speaking to me."

Go to MyEnglishLab for more communication practice.

FROM GRAMMAR TO WRITING

A BEFORE YOU WRITE You are going to write an essay about a recent misunderstanding or conflict that you witnessed or took part in, and how it was resolved. Write a few paragraphs about the incident.

B WRITE Using your ideas in A, write a five-paragraph essay about the incident. Remember to use both direct and indirect speech. Try to avoid the common mistakes shown in the chart. Use the example below to help you begin your essay.

EXAMPLE: Recently, I was involved in a situation that shows how easy it is to misunderstand someone. I was at a party, and there was a major political discussion going on. Before I knew it, I was heavily involved in the discussion. Someone asked me which party I supported, and I gave him my answer. He said, "Well, you should switch parties because your party can't possibly win." This made me really angry. I thought I was being attacked, and I got angrier and angrier. . . .

Common Mistakes in Direct and Indirect Speech

Don't use **quotation marks** in indirect speech. Use them in **direct speech**.	I said, "Jay, you need to tell me what's wrong." I told Jay **he needed to tell me what was wrong**. **NOT** I told Jay ˣhe needed to tell me what was wrong.ˣ
Don't use question word order in **indirect speech**. Use **statement word order**.	I asked Hassan **what time it was**. **NOT** I asked Hassan what time ~~was it~~.
In indirect speech, don't use *say* if the listener is mentioned. Use *tell*.	Mia **told** me I should call Ted. **NOT** Mia ~~said~~ me I should call Ted.
In indirect speech, use *say* if the listener is *not* mentioned.	Cherie **said** she would be coming to the party. **NOT** Cherie ~~told~~ she would be coming to the party.

C CHECK YOUR WORK Look at your essay. Underline direct and indirect speech. Use the Editing Checklist to check your work.

Editing Checklist

Did you . . . ?

☐ use quotation marks in direct speech but not in indirect speech

☐ use statement word order in indirect speech

☐ use *tell* if the listener is mentioned and *say* if the listener is not mentioned

D REVISE YOUR WORK Read your essay again. Can you improve your writing? Make changes if necessary.

Go to MyEnglishLab for more writing practice.

UNIT 21 REVIEW

Test yourself on the grammar of the unit.

A Complete the sentences. Circle the correct answers.

1. Min-Ji told Ho-Jin <u>it's / it was</u> time to get up.

2. Mom told Mary she hoped she <u>had finished / have finished</u> her homework.

3. Rob asked Marisol <u>are you / if she was</u> ready to leave.

4. Dad told Tadao <u>to be sure / be sure</u> to feed the pets.

5. Juan told Maria <u>don't / not to</u> forget to turn off the TV.

6. John asked Dad <u>would he / if he would</u> pick him up.

7. Sally said that <u>"she would come by" / she would come by</u>.

8. She assured us she <u>could / can</u> be there by 8:00.

B Complete the sentences with the words in parentheses.

1. Marta asked José _____ late for dinner.
   (he / will / be)

2. José told Marta he _____ late.
   (not / will / be)

3. Emiko told her father, _____
   ("I / not / feel / well.")

4. Emiko's father told her _____ her medicine.
   (she / need / take)

5. Ali asked Jihan _____
   (she / ever / see / snow)

6. She said, _____
   ("I / see / snow / many times.")

7. The teacher told the students _____ in ink.
   (not / write)

C Find and correct five mistakes in the conversation.

Carlos said, "Ho-Jin, why you haven't called me lately?"

Ho-Jin said, "I just haven't had time. I have to study a lot right now."

Carlos said, "You said me you were going to try to relax more."

Ho-Jin said, "No, I didn't. I told I was going to relax as much as possible."

Carlos said, "Well, OK, but are we still friends."

Ho-Jin said, "Of course we are!"

Now check your answers on page 432.

Go to MyEnglishLab to complete the review online.

Direct and Indirect Speech　**371**

Conditionals and the Subjunctive

PART 9

OUTCOMES

- Describe hypothetical results of a present or past situation, using present and past conditionals
- Express wishes, sadness, or regret with *wish*, *hope*, and *if only*
- Identify key information in an article and academic discussion
- Discuss hypothetical situations in the present and past
- Write an essay about the impact of a technological development or invention

OUTCOMES

- Express hypothetical situations and their results with implied and inverted conditions and the subjunctive
- Identify key details from an advice column and a conversation
- Participate in group discussions, giving advice and responding to suggestions
- Write an essay about a time when you took good or bad advice

UNIT 22

Conditionals; Other Ways to Express Unreality

ACHIEVEMENTS AND INVENTIONS

OUTCOMES
- Describe hypothetical results of a present or past situation, using present and past conditionals
- Express wishes, sadness, or regret with *wish*, *hope*, and *if only*
- Identify key information in an article and academic discussion
- Discuss hypothetical situations in the present and past
- Write an essay about the impact of a technological development or invention

---

STEP 1   GRAMMAR IN CONTEXT

BEFORE YOU READ

Discuss the questions.

1. What do you think is one of the greatest scientific achievements of all time?

2. What do you consider the most significant invention of the last 150 years?

READ

▶ 22|01   Read this article about famous achievements and inventions.

How Would Our World Be Different?

What causes people to make remarkable discoveries or invent remarkable devices? How would our world be different if certain remarkable discoveries or inventions hadn't been made? The experiences of Isaac Newton and Henry Ford, both of whom showed great determination, can shed some light on these questions.

Sometimes chance plays a role in scientific and technological advancement. In 1666, according to legend, young scientist Isaac Newton was sitting under an apple tree in his orchard. He looked up and saw an apple fall to the ground. This was a major historical moment: We could say that if Newton hadn't seen the apple fall, he wouldn't really have understood the force of gravity, and he probably wouldn't have formulated his famous theories. The apple did fall, though, and Newton did see it. Determined to understand this force, he theorized that two objects attract and mutually influence each other. If an apple, for example, falls from a tree, the much greater mass of the earth will attract and pull the apple to the ground.

Isaac Newton's theory of gravitation was first sparked by a chance occurrence, but it was realized through his strong dedication and determination. After the scientist's death, his French author friend Voltaire said that Newton had never had any deep relationships with other people. Newton never married, perhaps feeling that if he started a family, he wouldn't be able to devote his life to achieving his real passion: the advancement of science. Newton may even have died for science before his time. Upon his death, toxic levels of mercury were found in his body. If he hadn't exposed himself to mercury in chemical experiments, he might have lived much longer than he did. It seems clear that if Newton hadn't made such sacrifices, he might not have had such a powerful impact on the development of mathematics, optics, and physics during the next centuries. If it hadn't been for Newton, we might not have many of the inventions that characterize our time— e.g., high-powered telescopes, airplanes, rockets, or the space station.

Fast forward to 1908, when Henry Ford introduced his Model T Ford in Detroit, an action which was to change the world. Ford didn't invent the car; that accomplishment is generally attributed to German inventor Karl Benz. However, Ford was instrumental in bringing the automobile to the masses.[1] Before 1908, cars were complicated machines, difficult to operate and repair, and expensive to own. Ford utilized the assembly line in his factories to efficiently produce an automobile that the average person could afford to buy and maintain. In his own way, Ford was as determined as Newton. Before he succeeded as an automaker, Ford had persuaded wealthy businessmen to finance two other businesses to produce "horseless carriages"—i.e., cars. Both businesses failed, but Ford was undeterred.[2] In 1903, he started a new business, once again gaining the support of wealthy financiers. This time, his business was wildly successful. If Ford hadn't persisted, the revolutionary Model T might never have been produced.

Today, the car is ubiquitous, but what would our world be like if Ford hadn't been so determined to make it available to the common person? There would probably be fewer cars on the roads and fewer, if any, traffic jams. Car ownership might still be restricted to the wealthy. We probably wouldn't have as many suburbs as we presently do because the car makes it possible to live outside central cities. We can argue that if Ford hadn't marketed his Model T and made it widely available, someone else would have. But the result would have been vastly different. Ford was in the right place at the right time, and his efforts have changed the world. There are those today who wish that Ford had never popularized the gasoline-burning auto. There are even those who wish gasoline-powered cars would just disappear. "If only all cars were electric-powered," they might say. The car is here to stay, though, and it will continue to evolve.

Inventor Thomas Edison said that genius is one percent inspiration and ninety-nine percent perspiration. This seems an oversimplification. We might restate Edison's idea in this way: Genius is thirty-three percent inspiration, thirty-three percent perspiration, and thirty-four percent motivation. If Newton, Ford, and countless others hadn't been determined to forge ahead[3] with their enterprises, today's world would undoubtedly be quite different. Will the efforts of future innovators will be as far-reaching? That remains to be seen.

---

1 *the masses:* the working class, the common people
2 *undeterred:* not discouraged or stopped from taking action
3 *forge ahead:* move forward in a strong and powerful way

AFTER YOU READ

Ⓐ VOCABULARY Choose the answer that is closest in meaning to the word in **bold**.

1. If he hadn't seen the apple fall, Newton probably wouldn't have **formulated** his theory.
   a. announced   b. changed   c. developed

2. Newton theorized that objects attract and **mutually** influence each other.
   a. both   b. partially   c. strongly

3. The invention of the car is generally **attributed to** Karl Benz.
   a. praised by   b. credited to   c. sent to

4. Ford **utilized** the assembly line in his factories.
   a. bought   b. replaced   c. used

5. Today the car is **ubiquitous**.
   a. limited   b. everywhere   c. expensive

6. Ford started a project to produce horseless carriages—**i.e.**, automobiles.
   a. for example   b. whereas   c. that is

7. If it hadn't been for Newton, we might not have many of the inventions that characterize our time—**e.g.**, rockets and the space station.
   a. for example   b. in other words   c. above all

8. The car is here to stay, and it will continue to **evolve**.
   a. increase in size   b. change gradually   c. be important

Ⓑ COMPREHENSION Read the statements. Check (✓) *True* or *False*.

	True	False
1. Sometimes technological advances happen partly by chance.	☐	☐
2. Isaac Newton understood gravity before he saw the apple fall in 1666.	☐	☐
3. Newton had a minimal impact on the development of the sciences.	☐	☐
4. Henry Ford invented the automobile.	☐	☐
5. The automobile has influenced the growth of suburbs.	☐	☐
6. Cars were quite cheap before Ford introduced the Model T.	☐	☐
7. Ford had two successful businesses before 1903.	☐	☐
8. The article concludes that motivation is at least as important as perspiration in scientific or technological achievement.	☐	☐

Ⓒ DISCUSSION Work with a partner. What do you think genius consists of? Do you agree more with Edison's statement or with the conclusions of the article? Discuss.

Go to MyEnglishLab for more grammar in context practice.

CONDITIONALS; OTHER WAYS TO EXPRESS UNREALITY

Present and Future Real Conditionals

Present Conditionals	
If Clause	Result Clause
If scientists **are** motivated,	they often **achieve** great things.
If an object **falls**,	gravity **pulls** it to the earth.

Future Conditionals	
If Clause	Result Clause
If you **show** determination,	you **will be** successful.
If a scientist **perfects** a new invention,	the world **will** probably change.

Present Unreal Conditionals

Actual Situations
It **is** rarely easy to invent something new.
Inventors **are** often frustrated at first.
A new invention rarely **works** perfectly at first.
It usually **takes** a long time to perfect an invention.

Conditionals	
If Clause	Result Clause
If it **were** easy,	it **would be** unusual.
If they **weren't** frustrated,	
If it **worked** perfectly at first,	
If it **didn't take** a long time,	

Past Unreal Conditionals

Actual Situations
He **stopped** working on his invention, so he **lost** his funding.
He **didn't stop** working on his invention, so he **didn't lose** his funding.
His colleague **encouraged** him, so he **was able** to start again.
His colleague **didn't help** him, so he **wasn't able** to start again.

Conditionals	
If Clause	Result Clause
If he **hadn't stopped**,	he **wouldn't have lost** his funding.
If he **had stopped**,	he **would have lost** his funding.
If his colleague **hadn't encouraged** him,	he **wouldn't have been able** to start again.
If his colleague **had helped him**,	he **would have been able** to start again.

"Mixed" Conditionals

Actual Situations
Most cars **have been** gasoline-powered from the beginning.
Even today, many people **are not committed** to reducing pollution.

Conditionals	
If Clause	**Result Clause**
PAST If cars **had been** electric-powered from the beginning,	PRESENT there **wouldn't be** as much pollution today.
PRESENT If people **were** really **committed** to reducing pollution,	PAST we **might have done** something to address the problem sooner.

Other Ways to Express Unreality

Actual Situations
Cars are essential, but they cause pollution.
Some people can barely afford to buy gasoline.
Cars were gasoline-powered from the beginning.

Wish/If only Statement
Some people **wish** (that) all cars **were** electric-powered.   **If only** they **were** all electric-powered.
I **wish** (that) I **could afford** gasoline.   **If only** I **could afford** gasoline.
Some people **wish** (that) cars **had never been invented**.   **If only** they **had never been invented**.

GRAMMAR NOTES

1 Definition of Conditionals

Conditional sentences describe situations that occur (or do not occur) because of certain **conditions**.

Conditional sentences consist of two clauses, a **dependent condition clause** (also called the *if*-clause) and an **independent result clause**.

CONDITION	RESULT
DEPENDENT CLAUSE	INDEPENDENT CLAUSE
If people **work** hard,	they **are** often successful.

CONDITION	RESULT
DEPENDENT CLAUSE	INDEPENDENT CLAUSE
If I **were** a scientist,	I **would try** to help the world.

There are two types of conditional sentences, **real** and **unreal**.

Real (also called **factual**) **conditionals** are sentences that describe situations that:

• occur **regularly**

If people use cars, the air **becomes** polluted.
(present)

• are **likely or possible** in the present and the future

If it **snows** today, we**'ll close** the lab.
(present and future)

CONTINUED ▶

Unreal conditionals are sentences that describe situations that are:	
• **untrue** in the present or past	If Maryam **worked** here, she **could help** us.
• **unlikely** in the present or past	If I **could afford** a new cell phone, I **could stay** in touch with people.
• **impossible** in the present or past	I **wouldn't have done** that **if I'd been** in your situation.

In conditional sentences, the clauses can come in either order, and the meaning is the same. We place a **comma** after the *if-clause* if it comes **first**. We don't generally place a comma after the result clause if it comes first.	**If I had** a computer**, I could get** my homework done. I **could get** my homework done **if I had** a computer.
Either or both clauses can be **negative**.	I **wouldn't buy** that computer if I **were** you. I **wouldn't have bought** that car if I **hadn't gotten** a good deal.
Form conditional **questions** in the usual way.	A: **Would** you **have become** a scientist if you**'d known** how difficult it would be? B: Yes, I certainly **would**.

2 Present Real Conditionals

Use **present real conditionals** to talk about general truths, scientific facts, or habits and repeated events.	
Use **present-time verbs** in both the *if-clause* and the **result clause**. Most commonly, the present-time verbs are in the simple present.	Plants **die** if they **don't get** enough water. People with diabetes **can control** their disease if they **take** insulin regularly.
You can also use the present progressive in the *if*-clause.	If I**'m flying**, I always **feel** nervous.
In **future-time situations**, use the simple present or the present progressive in the *if*-clause and the **future** with *will* or *be going to, may, might, can, could,* or *should* in the **result clause**.	If Barry **passes** the final exam, he **might pass** his calculus course.
In addition to *if*, you can also use other subordinating conjunctions in the *if*-clause. These include *unless* and *in case*.	*Unless* he **studies** hard, however, he **won't pass** the final exam. We**'ll repeat** the experiment *in case* it **fails**.
BE CAREFUL! Use the **simple present** in the *if-clause* even if the time referred to is future.	I'll contact you as soon I **get** the lab results. **NOT** I'll contact you as soon as ~~I'll get~~ the lab results.

3 Present Unreal Conditionals

Use the **present unreal conditional** to talk about present unreal, untrue, imagined, or impossible conditions and their results.

Use the simple past form of the verb in the *if*-clause. If the verb is *be*, use *were* for all persons. Use *could, might,* or *would* + the base form of the verb in the result clause.	If he **were** really motivated, he **would be working** on his invention. We **wouldn't stay up** so late if we **weren't doing** these experiments. If I **were** you, I **wouldn't accept** the offer. I **might clean** up my lab if I **had** the day off.
USAGE NOTE The simple past verb in the *if*-clause is past in form only. It is **not past in meaning**.	If I **had** a million dollars, I**'d give** it to scientific research. *(I don't have a million.)*
USAGE NOTE Use *were* for all forms of the past of *be* in conditional sentences to describe situations that are **impossible** or **improbable**. In other conditional sentences, *was* is correct in the singular.	If I **were** you, I'd buy a new computer. *(an impossible situation; I'm not you.)* If my computer **wasn't** working properly, I would get it fixed. *(not impossible or improbable)*
BE CAREFUL! Don't use *would* in the *if*-clause in present unreal conditional sentences.	I would build a new lab if I **had** the money. **NOT** I would build a new lab if I ~~would have~~ the money.

4 Past Unreal Conditionals

Use the **past unreal conditional** to talk about past unreal, untrue, imagined, or impossible situations and their results.

Use the **past perfect** in the *if*-clause. Use *would, might,* or *could* + *have* + past participle in the result clause.	If I **had listened** to you, I **wouldn't have made** that mistake. Ali **might have accepted** your offer if you**'d asked** him in time.
We often use the past unreal conditional to express **regret** about a situation that actually happened in the past.	I **would have lent** you money if I **had known** you wanted to go to college.
BE CAREFUL! Don't use *would have* in the *if*-clause in past unreal conditional sentences. Use *would have* only in the **result** clause.	I would have lent you money if I **had known** you wanted to go to college. **NOT** I would have lent you money if I ~~would have known~~ you wanted to go to college.

5 Mixed Conditionals

The times of the *if*-clause and the result clause are sometimes different. Present unreal and past unreal conditional forms can be **"mixed"** in the same sentence. The time in the *if*-clause can be past, while the time in the result clause is present.

Similarly, the time in the *if*-clause may be present, while the time in the result clause is past.

PAST ACTION	PRESENT RESULT

If I **hadn't gone** to college, **I'd** be unemployed now.

PRESENT ACTION	PAST RESULT

If Sam **were coming**, he **would have arrived** by now.

6 *Wish* and *Hope* + Noun Clause

We often use unreal conditionals to express regret or sadness. In a similar way, we use *wish* + **noun clause** to express **sadness** or a **desire** for a **different situation**.

Use:

* *wish* + *could/would* + base form to express a wish about the future

    I **wish** (that) you **would** change your mind about working for us.

* *wish* + **simple past** to express a wish about the present

    My wife **wishes** (that) I **didn't work** such long hours.

* *wish* + **past perfect** to express a wish about the past

    My son **wishes** (that) he **hadn't taken** that job.

USAGE NOTE Don't confuse *wish* with *hope*. Use *wish* to express regrets about things that are **unlikely** or are **impossible to change**. Use *hope* + simple present/future to express a desire about **events** that are **possible** or **probable**.

I **wish** (that) she **would join** our team.
  (*I don't think she will.*)
I **hope** (that) she **accepts** our job offer.
  (*It's possible or probable that she will.*)

7 *If Only* + Noun Clause

If only has a meaning similar to that of *wish*. *If only* is followed by a noun clause **without** *that*.

Use the **simple past** after *if only* to express a wish about something that is contrary to fact at the **present** time.

I **wish** (that) I **had** a car.
If only I **had** a car.
If only cars **were** cheaper.

Use the **past perfect** after *if only* to express a wish that something had happened differently in the **past**.

If only I **hadn't said** that!

BE CAREFUL! Don't confuse *if only* with *only if*.

If only Jerry **studied** more.
  (*I wish he studied more.*)
Only if Jerry **studied** more **would** he **have** a chance of passing.
  (*This would be the only way for him to pass.*)

Go to MyEnglishLab to watch the grammar presentation.

EXERCISE 1   DISCOVER THE GRAMMAR

A   GRAMMAR NOTES 1–4   Look at the sentences based on the reading. Identify each sentence as a *real* (*R*) or *unreal* (*U*) conditional.

_R_   **1.** If an apple falls from a tree, gravity will pull it to the ground.

_____   **2.** If Newton hadn't seen the apple fall, he probably wouldn't have formulated his theories.

_____   **3.** Chance can play a role in technological development if people understand how to use new ideas.

_____   **4.** If Newton hadn't exposed himself to mercury, he might have lived longer.

_____   **5.** There would be far fewer cars on the road if Ford hadn't brought the car to the masses.

_____   **6.** Would today's society be recognizable if there were no cars?

_____   **7.** Pollution will decrease if we promote the use of electric cars.

_____   **8.** People can achieve great things if they show determination.

B   GRAMMAR NOTES 2–6   Look at the sentences based on the reading. Identify each sentence as a *past*, *present*, *future*, or *mixed* (present and past) conditional.

past   **1.** If Newton hadn't been in his orchard, he wouldn't have seen the apple fall.

_____   **2.** If the wind blows strongly, the apples will fall from that tree.

_____   **3.** Newton might not have become a scientist if the orchard experience hadn't happened.

_____   **4.** What would our world be like today if Ford hadn't produced the Model T?

_____   **5.** Some people wish gasoline-powered cars would just disappear.

_____   **6.** If only all cars were electric-powered.

_____   **7.** If driverless cars become widespread, we won't have to drive anymore.

_____   **8.** Innovators often have success if they believe in themselves.

EXERCISE 2   PRESENT AND FUTURE REAL CONDITIONALS

GRAMMAR NOTES 1–2   Unscramble the sentences. Write the words in the correct order to create present real conditional sentences. Use correct punctuation.

1. (decrease / we / Pollution / popularize electric cars / if / will)

Pollution will decrease if we popularize electric cars.

2. (We / develop efficient space travel / if / colonize Mars / might / engineers)

_____

3. (run out of energy / don't develop alternative fuel sources / if / will / We / researchers)

_____

4. (stop climate change / If / the polar ice caps / melt / could / we / don't)

_____

5. (drive hybrid cars / If / people / the environment / they / help)

_____

6. (current population trends continue / the world / will / If / nine billion people by 2060 / have)

_____

EXERCISE 3 PRESENT AND FUTURE REAL AND UNREAL CONDITIONALS

GRAMMAR NOTES 2–3 Complete the conversation. Circle the correct answers.

MARISA: Hi, Fabio. Come on in.

FABIO: Hi, Marisa. Got a couple of minutes? I need to ask you about something.

MARISA: Always. What's up?

FABIO: (If I ask) / If I will ask you a question, will you give / do you give me an honest answer?
        1.   2.

MARISA: Of course I do / I will. Shoot.
                      3.

FABIO: What would you be doing / would you do if someone you liked and respected
                      4.

        takes / took credit for your work and presented it to the CEO?
        5.

MARISA: I'd report / I report it to the CEO. Why?
                 6.

FABIO: Well, I wrote a new computer program that zaps most of the bugs in our programs. I

        told Stanley about it. He asked if he could study it for a while. I said yes. Later, I was

        in the CEO's office, and he showed me the program I'd written and said he was really

        impressed with Stanley for writing it. I was pretty shocked, and I didn't know what to do.

        If I go / I'd go to the CEO, I feel / I'll feel like a tattletale.
        7.   8.

MARISA: What is it with Stanley these days, anyway? It seems like he's been acting really weird lately.

FABIO: The thing is, Stanley is my brother-in-law. He and my sister are on the verge of a divorce.

        I'm afraid that if I exposed / expose him, it had / it would push him over the edge.
                         9.   10.

MARISA: Fabio, you wrote this great new program. You deserve credit. I guess if I was / were you,
                                                                                    11.

        I'd talk / I'll talk to Stanley first. Just tell him that if he won't / wouldn't go to the CEO
        12.   13.

        soon, you'll have to / you had to do it yourself.
                    14.

FABIO: OK. Thanks a lot, Marisa. You gave me an honest answer and not what you thought I

        wanted to hear.

EXERCISE 4 *WISH* AND *IF ONLY*

A GRAMMAR NOTES 6–7 Look at the photos. Using the words in parentheses, write a sentence with *wish* for each. Photos 1 and 2 go together; 3 and 4 go together; 5 and 6 go together. Make the sentences negative if necessary.

1. (drivers / be / stuck in traffic)

The drivers wish they weren't stuck in traffic.

2. (they / take / the subway instead)

_____

_____

3. (he / have / a better computer)

_____

_____

4. (he / can afford / a new computer)

_____

_____

5. (people / their cell phones / work / in this area)

_____

_____

6. (they / have / good cell phone service)

_____

_____

B GRAMMAR NOTE 7 Look at the photos in A again. Write a statement about each photo with *if only* and the words in parentheses.

1. (someone / invent / a flying car)

   If only someone would invent a flying car.

2. (subways / not / be / noisy and crowded)

   _____

3. (researchers / invent / a computer / that would never break down)

   _____

4. (all computers / be / affordable for everyone)

   _____

5. (someone / invent / a cell phone / that could work everywhere)

   _____

6. (cell phones / not / need / cell phone towers)

   _____

EXERCISE 5 MIXED AND PAST UNREAL CONDITIONALS

GRAMMAR NOTES 4–5 Complete the story with mixed or past unreal conditional sentences. Use the correct forms of the words in parentheses. Use contractions where possible.

A year ago, I took a train from Montreal to Toronto. If I _____ *hadn't missed* _____
1. (not / miss)
the bus to the train station, I _____ the particular train I took, and
2. (not / take)
I _____ Professor Lozano. My life
3. (never / meet)
_____ very different today. Professor Lozano was rather elderly,
4. (be)
and he was having trouble putting his suitcase on the luggage rack. If I
_____ to help him, we _____
5. (not / offer)   **6.** (never / start)
talking. Professor Lozano told me that he had invented a robotic arm that is now used in the space

program. I told the professor I was a science major, and it turned out that the professor taught at

the same university I was attending. He told me there was an unfilled lab position in his department

and that I could apply for it. If I _____ that I was a science major,
7. (not / mention)
the professor _____ me about the unfilled lab position, and I
8. (never / tell)
_____ for it. I _____ for my
9. (never / apply)   **10.** (not / be studying)
doctorate in nuclear physics right now. Let's see . . . I guess it all happened because I missed that bus.

I'll always be glad that I did.

GRAMMAR NOTES 1–7   Read the email. There are ten mistakes in the use of conditionals and related forms. The first mistake is already corrected. Find and correct nine more.

Hi, Bruce,

This has been one of those days when I wish I ~~would have~~ *had* stayed in bed. When I turned on my computer this morning, it crashed immediately. It's not like this has never happened before . . . but I certainly wish the computer didn't choose this day, of all days, to crash. My scholarship application was due this afternoon by 3:00 p.m., and I had almost everything ready for it. I just needed half an hour or so to put some finishing touches on it. So I was pretty desperate. As soon as my computer crashed, I took it straight to a repair shop, but it took me two hours to get there. If I got it there by 11 a.m., they probably could fix it in time for me to make the three o'clock deadline. But I didn't get there until 12.

Everything would have worked out if there wouldn't have been a major traffic jam on the freeway. I was stuck in traffic for an hour and a half. I wish I had the sense to take another highway and not the freeway. I'm also mad at myself for another reason. If I sent in the application a week ago, they would already receive it, and everything would be fine right now.

Anyway, the computer will be fixed by tomorrow. If I'll get the application emailed by the end of the day, I might still be eligible for the scholarship. If only someone invented a computer that would never crash!

Send me a text on my cell phone, which is working fine. I need some cheering up.

Elena

Go to **My**EnglishLab for more focused practice.

EXERCISE 7
LISTENING

▶ 22|02 **A** Listen to the classroom discussion. When and why did people start using the word "bug" to indicate a computer problem?

_____

_____

_____

▶ 22|02 **B** Read the statements. Listen again to the class discussion. For each statement, check (✓) *True* or *False*.

	True	False
1. The teacher asks the students what actions they would take if their computers had problems.	✓	☐
2. Most students in the class would take their computers to a shop if they weren't working properly.	☐	☐
3. Andrea says that a computer probably has a bug or a virus if it isn't working.	☐	☐
4. There is probably a real insect inside a computer if it isn't working properly.	☐	☐
5. Grace Harper used the term "bug" in 1947 because it hadn't been invented yet.	☐	☐
6. Before 1947, researchers would have used the term "bug" to refer to insects causing problems in machines.	☐	☐
7. If Harvard hadn't been working closely with the Navy, Grace Harper would not have written a report about the "bug."	☐	☐
8. If Grace Harper and others hadn't started using the term "bug," it might not have become the accepted term for a computer problem.	☐	☐

C Work with a partner. What problems with computer bugs have you experienced? How do you react if you discover that your computer is not working on a particular day? Are you upset? Angry? Discuss.

EXERCISE 8 WHO WOULD YOU BE IF . . . ?

GAME Form two teams. With your team, use the prompts to construct eight conditional questions, four in the present and four in the past. Then create two questions of your own. Ask the other team each question. They guess what person or thing is being referred to, choosing from the words in the box. Take turns. To check answers, see page 436.

EXAMPLE: **Prompt:** Who / been / if / formulated / the theory of gravity

TEAM A: Who would you have been if you had formulated the theory of gravity?

TEAM B: If I had formulated the theory of gravity, I would have been Sir Isaac Newton.

a blue whale	Alexander Graham Bell	Grace Harper	one of the Wright Brothers
a dinosaur	between eighty and eighty-nine	Italy	thirty years old
a mammoth	between ninety and ninety-nine	Karl Benz	thirty-five years old
Abraham Lincoln	Bill Gates	Mount Everest	Thomas Edison

Team A's Prompts:

1. Who / been / if / invent / the electric light

2. How old / have to / be / if / be / the president of the United States

3. What creature / been / if / be / an ancestor of the elephant

4. How old / be / if / be / a nonagenarian

5. Who / been / if / made / the first successful airplane flight in 1903

6. Who / been / if / invented / the car

7. What country / been from / if / been / Marco Polo

8. What mountain / climbed / if / been / with Edmund Hillary and Tenzing Norgay in 1953

9. _____

10. _____

Team B's Prompts:

1. How old / be / if / an octogenarian

2. Who / be / if / be / the founder of Microsoft

3. What / be / if / be / the largest mammal

4. How old / have to be / if / be / a United States senator

5. Who / been / if / been / the inventor of the telephone

6. What kind of creature / been / if / been / a stegosaurus

7. Who / been / if / popularized / the term *bug*

8. Who / been / if / been / president of the United States during the Civil War

9. _____

10. _____

EXERCISE 9 HENRY FORD'S ASSEMBLY LINE

INFORMATION GAP Work with a partner. Student A will follow the instructions below.
Student B will follow the instructions on page 442.

STUDENT A

- The article below is missing some information. Your partner has the same article that contains your missing information. Ask your partner questions to find the missing information.

    EXAMPLE: **A:** What would Ford never have done if he hadn't changed the makeup
    of his original assembly line?
    B: He would never have achieved success with the Model T.

- Your partner's article is missing different information. Answer your partner's questions so that he or she can fill in the missing information.

    EXAMPLE: **B:** When did Ford introduce his Model T to the world?
    A: He introduced his Model T to the world in 1908.

The First Moving Assembly Line

HENRY FORD introduced his Model T to the world in 1908. However, he never would have

_____ if he hadn't changed the makeup of his original assembly

line. Ford knew that ordinary people wouldn't buy his cars if they were expensive. If Ford could

make Model Ts cheaper than other cars, he knew that _____. So

Ford introduced a new, more efficient method of auto production that involved division of labor.

On Ford's original assembly line, auto workers had to do several separate tasks to put each car

together. If workers have to move around a lot and do many different tasks, they can't

_____. If you divide a big job into many different smaller tasks,

however, everyone can do his or her task faster. So, Ford and his staff divided the assembly process

into eighty-four different steps. In this way, they minimized the motion of each worker as much as

possible. There was another advantage: If each worker was responsible for only one task, he or she

would also be easier to train.

In 1913, Ford introduced the moving chassis assembly line and a mechanized belt, which sped

up the car assembly process a great deal. If a business makes many products quickly, it can

_____. So, Ford's plan to make Model Ts cheaper than other

cars succeeded.

If Ford hadn't figured out a way to build his cars more efficiently, it's possible that cars

_____. However, might the world be a better place now if there

were fewer cars in it? And what about the workers themselves? _____

if these changes hadn't been made? Could they have felt like machines who had to perform the same

repetitive actions endlessly? It's difficult to say. The bottom line is that Ford achieved his goal.

Go to **MyEnglishLab** for more communication practice.

FROM GRAMMAR TO WRITING

A BEFORE YOU WRITE You are going to write an essay about a technological advance or invention that has changed the world. Write a few sentences about one of these inventions or another invention or advance of your choice.

- television
- the telephone
- the airplane

B WRITE Using your ideas from A, write a five-paragraph essay about the technological advance or invention you have chosen. Remember to use real and unreal conditionals in present and past time. Try to avoid the common mistakes shown in the chart. Use the example below to help you begin your essay.

EXAMPLE: On December 17, 1903, in Kitty Hawk, North Carolina, Wilbur and Orville Wright successfully completed a flight in an airplane. They weren't the first ones to build and fly aircraft, but their successful flight set in motion the development of air travel. How would our world be different today if the Wright Brothers had never existed?

First, travel would be very different. It would take us a month to travel across the Atlantic Ocean. We'd still be traveling by ship. . . .

Second, the airline industry would never have gotten started. . . .

Common Mistakes in Using Real and Unreal Conditionals

When using the verb *be*, don't use *was* in **present unreal situations** that are contrary to fact. Use *were* in all persons.	I wouldn't buy that computer if I **were** you. **NOT** I wouldn't buy that computer if I ~~was~~ you.
Don't use *had* in the **result** clause in **past unreal conditional** constructions. Use *would + have +* **past participle**.	People wouldn't **have** bought Ford's Model T if it had been expensive. **NOT** People wouldn't ~~had~~ bought Ford's Model T if it had been expensive.
Don't use *would have* + past participle in the *if-*clause in **past unreal conditional** constructions. Use *had* + **past participle**.	If I **had finished** college, I would be working in a scientific laboratory now. **NOT** If I ~~would have~~ finished college, I would be working in a scientific laboratory now.

C CHECK YOUR WORK Look at your essay. Underline the conditional sentences. Use the Editing Checklist to check your work.

Editing Checklist

Did you . . . ?

- ☐ use *were* in the verb *be* in present unreal situations that are contrary to fact
- ☐ use *would have* + past participle in the result clause in past unreal conditionals
- ☐ avoid using *would have* + past participle in the *if*-clause in past unreal conditionals

D REVISE YOUR WORK Read your essay again. Can you improve your writing? Make changes if necessary.

Go to MyEnglishLab for more writing practice.

UNIT 22 REVIEW

Test yourself on the grammar of the unit.

Ⓐ Complete the sentences. Circle the correct answers.

1. Our world would be a lot different if the Wright Brothers didn't build / hadn't built the world's first successful airplane.

2. If it hadn't been / wouldn't have been for the Wright Brothers, the major airline companies wouldn't have arisen.

3. We won't have / wouldn't have the airline industry today.

4. It would take / will take weeks to cross the Atlantic Ocean.

5. A lot more people will be / would be traveling by ship.

6. We hadn't had / wouldn't have had the terrible plane crashes that we have had.

7. We hadn't been able / wouldn't be able to get fresh food delivered overnight.

8. If it weren't / hadn't been for the Wright brothers, the space program might not exist.

Ⓑ Complete the sentences with the correct forms of the verbs in parentheses.

1. Bao _____ to change the oil in his car.
   (wish / he / not / forget)

2. If he had changed the oil, the engine _____ working.
   (not / stop)

3. If the engine _____ working, the car wouldn't have broken down.
   (not / stop)

4. If that hadn't happened, he _____ pay a towing bill.
   (not / have to)

5. He also _____ replace the engine.
   (not / have to)

6. He _____ a lot more money in the bank right now.
   (have)

7. If his car had still been working, he _____ it to the job interview.
   (could / make)

8. In fact, he probably _____ unemployed now.
   (not / be)

Ⓒ Find and correct four mistakes.

A: Jim wants to market his new invention. Would you buy it if you have the money?

B: If I was Jim, I won't market it.

A: Why not?

B: Who wants a robot that drives your car? People will laugh at him.

A: You're just jealous. I'll bet you wish you would have invented it yourself.

Check your answers on page 432.

Go to MyEnglishLab to complete the review online.

UNIT
23

**More Conditions;
The Subjunctive**

ADVICE

OUTCOMES
- Express hypothetical situations and their results with implied and inverted conditions and the subjunctive
- Identify key details from an advice column and a conversation
- Participate in group discussions, giving advice and responding to suggestions
- Write an essay about a time when you took good or bad advice

STEP 1 GRAMMAR IN CONTEXT

BEFORE YOU READ

Discuss the questions.

1. Do you ever read advice columns? Do you think they contain useful information?

2. What is a problem that you might potentially ask a columnist about?

READ

 23|01 Read these letters to an advice columnist and her responses.

Ask Rosa

Dear Rosa,

Hank and I were best friends in high school, so when he suggested we room together in college, I thought it was a great idea. Wrong! Had I known what a slob Hank really is, I never would have agreed to room with him. We have a small suite that has become a pigsty[1] because Hank thinks it's beneath him to wash a dish and is convinced the floor is the place to keep clothes. Whenever I talk to Hank about it, he just says, "Hey, Jason, you need to lighten up. You're too tense." I'm no neat freak, but I do prefer a semblance of order. I still like Hank and want to stay friends, but I'm feeling more like a doormat[2] every day. What would you recommend I do?

Jason

---

1 *pigsty:* a very dirty room or house
2 *doormat:* someone who is treated badly by other people

Dear Jason,

No one should have to feel like a doormat. Unfortunately, there's no easy solution to your problem. I can suggest three potential remedies: First, Hank may be unaware there's actually a problem. If so, ask him if he really likes having dirty dishes and bugs all over the place. If he doesn't, he might lend his muscles and help with the cleaning. There's a chance this approach will work, but if not, remedy two is teaching him how to clean up—he just may not be used to it. You might suggest he do the dishes one day and you the next. Should that not work, remedy three is to remind him you both have a right to a reasonably clean and orderly living space, and you feel your rights are being violated. Sometimes an appeal to a person's sense of fairness can do the trick. Whatever you do, it's important that Hank not feel criticized. Otherwise, he'll probably become resistant, so be moderate in your suggestions. Good luck.

Rosa

Dear Rosa,

Jim and I have been married for over four years now, and our marriage would be ideal were it not for the overbearing personalities of some of the people in his family. I love Jim dearly, but there are times when I feel like I'm married to his family members as well. They often drop in without letting me know they're coming, and at this point I'm spending more time with them than with Jim. Besides that, his sister Hannah constantly bombards me with requests that I do favors for her. For example, she insists I take her grocery shopping every week, even though she has her own car and is perfectly capable of doing this on her own. Even worse, his cousin Helen often requests I lend her money. At this point, Helen owes me about $750, but if I mention it she just says, "Carla, you know I'm good for it. I just need to get some bills paid off, and then I can pay you back." Rosa, I feel like I'm being manipulated by his family members. I know how important Jim's family is to him, but I'm at the end of my rope.[3] What would you suggest that I do?

Carla

Dear Carla,

You're experiencing lack of privacy, one of the most common problems faced by young married people, so don't feel you're alone. The problem sounds quite fixable. My guess is that your husband probably doesn't know what's going on and doesn't realize the depth of your frustration. Here's my advice: Have a heart-to-heart talk with Jim. First, tell him you appreciate his family but also feel you and he need more time alone together, and that without that time together, your relationship won't be able to develop as it should. Suggest these people call before they come over. Also tell him

---

3 *at the end of my rope:* in an almost desperate situation

you want to be helpful, but you feel his sister and cousin are asking too much of you. I'll bet he'll be willing to speak to them privately or at least mediate between you and Helen. When you're telling Jim about this, of course, it's essential that you not criticize his family members. That would probably cause resentment. Just give an honest statement of your feelings. With a little bit of extra communication with Jim, you can right the ship⁴ and make your marriage stronger. Good luck, and hang in there!

Rosa

---

4 *right the ship:* fix the situation

AFTER YOU READ

A **VOCABULARY** Match the words in **bold** with their meanings.

_____ **1.** Hank is really a **slob**.

_____ **2.** I do prefer a **semblance** of order.

_____ **3.** You feel your rights are being **violated**.

_____ **4.** Otherwise, he'll probably become **resistant**.

_____ **5.** His family members are **overbearing**.

_____ **6.** She is perfectly **capable** of doing that on her own.

_____ **7.** I feel like I'm being **manipulated** by his family members.

_____ **8.** He might even **mediate** between you and Hannah.

a. stubborn

b. having the ability

c. act as a peacemaker

d. outward appearance

e. controlled and influenced

f. messy or lazy person

g. disrespected

h. trying to make others obey

B **COMPREHENSION** Complete the sentences based on the reading.

1. It was Hank's suggestion that he and Jason _____ together in college.

2. Jason is not a compulsively neat person, but he likes a certain amount of _____.

3. Jason is feeling more like a _____ every day.

4. Rosa says Hank may just not be _____ cleaning up.

5. Rosa suggests that appealing to Hank's sense of _____ may help the situation.

6. Carla is bothered by the fact that some of her husband's family _____ without letting her know they're coming.

7. Rosa says lack of privacy is a common problem faced by young _____.

8. Rosa says Carla should suggest to Jim that his family members _____ before they come over.

C **DISCUSSION** Work with a partner. Compare and justify your answers in B. Then discuss: Do you agree with the advice columnist's suggestions for Jason and Carla? Why or why not?

Go to MyEnglishLab for more grammar in context practice.

MORE CONDITIONS; THE SUBJUNCTIVE

Implied Conditions

Implied Condition (= Standard Condition)	Result Clause
With a bit of luck, (If we have a bit of luck,)	we can fix the problem.
Without your help, (If you hadn't helped,)	I wouldn't have succeeded.
But for his investments, (If he didn't have investments,)	he'd have no income.
She might be lucky; **if so,** (If she is lucky,)	she'll meet some new friends.
He might get the chance; **if not,** (If he doesn't get the chance,)	he won't take the job.
She is lonely; **otherwise,** (If she weren't lonely,)	she wouldn't need company.

Inverted Conditions

Inverted Condition (= Standard Condition)	Result Clause
Were he in love, (If he **were** in love,)	he would get married.
Were he **not** in love, (If he **weren't** in love,)	he wouldn't get married.
Had I **seen** her, (If I **had seen** her,)	I would have called you.
Should we **do** it, (If we **should do** it,)	we will celebrate.

The Subjunctive in Noun Clauses

Verbs of Advice, Necessity, and Urgency + Subjunctive	
Main Clause	Noun Clause
Frank's teacher **suggested**	(that) he **take** an additional class.
The boss **demanded**	(that) Rosa **arrive** at work by 9:00.
The fireman **insisted**	(that) she **leave** the burning building immediately.

Adjectives of Advice, Necessity, and Urgency + Subjunctive

Main Clause	Noun Clause
It is **advisable**	(that) he **arrive** one-half hour before the appointment.
It is **mandatory**	(that) no one **enter** the building without a permit.
It is **urgent**	(that) she **call** home at once.

GRAMMAR NOTES

1 Implied Conditions

Conditions in conditional sentences are sometimes **implied** rather than stated directly in an *if*-clause.

Use these phrases to imply conditions:
 	
but for   *otherwise*
if not   *with*
if so   *without*
	Your brother may be lonely. **If so**, he should join a singles group.
	   (If he is lonely . . .)
	Safiya may not want your advice right now. **If not**, just let her solve her own problems.
	   (If she doesn't want your advice . . .)

In a sentence with an implied condition, there is **no change** in the **result** clause.	Mary needs to be part of the decision. **Otherwise**, she'll never be happy. *(If she isn't part of the decision, she'll never be happy.)*
As with other conditional sentences, the conditional phrase may **precede** or **follow** the result clause.	**With a little extra communication**, you can fix the problem. You can fix the problem **with a little extra communication**.
IN WRITING The implied conditional *but for* is formal and generally used only in writing and formal speech.	Mei-Ling just moved here. **But for** her co-workers, she wouldn't have any friends. *(If she didn't have her co-workers . . .)*

2 Inverted Conditions

We can express unreal conditions by **deleting** *if* and **inverting** the subject and the verb.

We often use the following forms in inverted conditions: *had* (past perfect), *were*, and *should*.	**If I had known** he was lazy, I wouldn't have roomed with him. *(past unreal conditional)* ***Had* I known** he was lazy, I wouldn't have roomed with him. *(inverted condition)*
If there is an inverted condition, there is **no change** in the **result** clause.	If I were to accept the job, **I would insist on benefits**. **Were I** to accept the job, **I would insist on benefits**.
As with other conditional sentences, the inverted condition clause can **precede** or **follow** the result clause.	**Were I to move**, I'd have to get a new roommate. I'd have to get a new roommate **were I to move**.

CONTINUED ▶

Sentences with inverted condition clauses have the **same meaning** as conditionals with *if*, but they are somewhat more **formal**.	**If I were** to accept the job offer, I would ask for a salary increase. **Were I** to accept the job offer, I would ask for a salary increase.
USAGE NOTE In both the normal conditional and the inverted condition with *should*, the meaning of *should* is quite different from its normal meaning of advice or expectation. Both sentences mean that the action is relatively **unlikely to occur**.	**If you should return** before I do, start the newspaper delivery. **Should you return** before I do, start the newspaper delivery. **Should something go wrong**, we need to have a backup plan. *(It is relatively unlikely that something will go wrong, but we need to be prepared.)*
BE CAREFUL! To form negative inversion, add *not* after the inverted verb and the subject. Don't contract *not* and the verb.	**Had I *not* received** the phone call, I wouldn't have been able to help. **NOT** ~~Hadn't I~~ received the phone call, I wouldn't have been able to help.

3 Form and Function of the Subjunctive

The **subjunctive** is a verb form that expresses **unreal conditions**, **wishes**, and **possibilities**.	
We often use *were* for all persons of the verb *be* in the subjunctive.	If I ***were*** you, I'd visit my parents more often. *(I'm not you, but this is what I would do.)* We could go on a picnic if it ***weren't*** raining. *(I wish it weren't raining, but it is.)*
Another form of the subjunctive occurs in **noun clauses** and uses the **base form** of the verb. In noun clauses with subjunctive constructions, we can usually omit the word *that*.	**MAIN CLAUSE** **NOUN CLAUSE** We recommend **(that) he *see* a lawyer**. They insist **(that) she *visit* her doctor**.
The verb in a main clause can be past, present, or future. However, the **subjunctive verb** is always the **base form**.	We **recommended** that he *see* a lawyer. We**'re going to recommend** that she *sell* her house.
To form the **negative** of a subjunctive verb, place *not* before the base form.	My aunt and uncle insisted (that) we ***not* come** to visit them today.
To form a **passive subjunctive**, use *be* + the past participle.	The doctor recommends (that) Uncle John **be hospitalized**.
BE CAREFUL! Use *were* in a subjunctive construction only in present unreal conditions. **Do not use** it for **past situations**.	If I **were** there, I would help her. **NOT** ~~If I were there~~, I would have helped her.

4 The Subjunctive with Verbs of Advice, Necessity, and Urgency

Use the subjunctive with the base form of the verb in noun clauses following **verbs of advice**, **necessity**, and **urgency**.

The five principal verbs of advice, necessity, and urgency are *demand*, *insist*, *propose*, *recommend*, and *suggest*.	I *propose* (that) we **ask** Mom and Dad about their wishes. My parents *insisted* (that) I **come** to visit them more often.
USAGE NOTE The verbs *ask*, *order*, *require*, *urge*, etc., can be followed by subjunctive constructions. When they occur with subjunctive constructions, the word *that* is usually not omitted. These verbs can also occur in the more usual pattern **verb + object + infinitive**. For a list of verbs that can be used in both patterns, see Appendix 26 on page 422.	I **asked that** my brothers and sisters **be** present. **OR** I **asked** my brothers and sisters **to be** present.
USAGE NOTE The verbs *insist (on)*, *propose*, *recommend*, and *suggest* can also be followed by a **gerund** phrase. The meaning of this structure is essentially the same as that of a sentence with a subjunctive in a noun clause.	We **suggest** *getting* another bid for the job. They **recommended** *getting* a second opinion from another doctor.
BE CAREFUL! Don't use infinitives after *demand*, *insist*, *propose*, *recommend*, and *suggest*.	Bi-Yun suggested **(that) we talk**. **NOT** Bi-Yun suggested ~~us to talk~~.

5 The Subjunctive with Adjectives of Advice, Necessity, and Urgency

Use the subjunctive with the base form of the verb in noun clauses after **adjectives** of **advice**, **necessity**, and **urgency**.

Common adjectives of advice, necessity, and urgency are: *advisable* *important* *urgent* *crucial* *mandatory* *desirable* *necessary* These adjectives + subjunctive occur in the pattern *It + be + adjective + that-clause*.	**It is** *essential* that elderly people **be treated** with dignity. **It is** *important* that she **understand** her options. **It was** *necessary* that my brother **see** a lawyer.
USAGE NOTE We can replace the *that*-clause with *for* + noun or object pronoun + infinitive. These are more informal constructions.	It's **important for her to understand** her options. It was **necessary for my brother to see** a lawyer.

REFERENCE NOTE

For a list of **verbs and expressions followed by the subjunctive**, see Appendix 26 on page 422.

Go to MyEnglishLab to watch the grammar presentation.

EXERCISE 1 DISCOVER THE GRAMMAR

GRAMMAR NOTES 1–5 Read the sentences based on the reading. Look at the underlined words. Are they *implied conditionals* (*IM*), *inverted conditionals* (*IV*), or *subjunctive verb constructions* (*SV*)? Write the correct answers.

__SV__ **1.** Hank <u>suggested we room</u> together in college.

_____ **2.** <u>Had I known</u> what a slob Hank really is, I never would have agreed.

_____ **3.** What would you <u>recommend I do</u>?

_____ **4.** This may work, but <u>if not</u>, try teaching him how to clean up.

_____ **5.** <u>Should that not work</u>, remedy three is to appeal to his sense of fairness.

_____ **6.** Our marriage would be ideal <u>were it not</u> for the overbearing personalities of his family members.

_____ **7.** Be moderate in your suggestions; <u>otherwise</u>, he may become resistant.

_____ **8.** It's essential <u>that you not criticize</u> his family.

_____ **9.** <u>With</u> a little bit of extra communication, you can right the ship.

EXERCISE 2 INVERTED CONDITIONS AND THE SUBJUNCTIVE

GRAMMAR NOTES 2–5 Read the pairs of sentences. Is the second sentence a correct rewriting of the first? Check (✓) *Yes* or *No*.

		Yes	No
1.	I would have recommended she sell it a long time ago. I would have recommended her selling it a long time ago.	✓	☐
2.	She's always said it's important for her to keep her independence. She's always said it's important that she keep her independence.	☐	☐
3.	I propose you make a new offer on the house. I propose you to make a new offer on the house.	☐	☐
4.	I'd recommend you look into joining a singles group. I'd recommend you to join a singles group.	☐	☐
5.	It's essential that you understand what your job responsibilities would be. It's essential for you to understand what your job responsibilities would be.	☐	☐
6.	I would like my roommate were it not for his terrible taste in music. If it weren't for my roommate's terrible taste in music, I would like him.	☐	☐

EXERCISE 3 IMPLIED CONDITIONS

GRAMMAR NOTE 1 Read the conversation between a man and his doctor. Rewrite the six underlined conditional sentences. Replace the *if*-clauses with these phrases: *if so*, *if not*, *otherwise*, *with*, or *without*.

DOCTOR: Bob, there are heavy circles under your eyes. You've got to get more sleep. <u>If you don't, you'll get sick.</u>

BOB: It's crunch time at work. The boss is insisting I work twelve hours a day right now. <u>If I work a lot of overtime, I'll keep my job.</u>

DOCTOR: Maybe your boss will let you cut your hours to ten a day. <u>If he will, that would help solve your problem.</u>

BOB: <u>And if he won't, what can I do?</u> He's a task master.

DOCTOR: Try to work in a nap during your lunch hour. But now, here's another thing. You told me you're drinking ten or more cups of coffee a day. You've got to cut down on it. <u>If you don't, it might damage your kidneys.</u>

BOB: Impossible. <u>If I don't have coffee, I can't make it through the day.</u>

DOCTOR: There must be a way. You can do it. Just find a buddy who's willing to monitor your coffee consumption. You have friends at work, don't you?

BOB: I sure do.

DOCTOR: Good. So, promise me you'll try to cut down.

BOB: OK. I can promise to try.

1. If you don't, you'll get sick.

   Otherwise, you'll get sick.

2. If I work a lot of overtime, I'll keep my job.

   _____

3. If he will, that would help solve your problem.

   _____

4. And if he won't, what can I do?

   _____

5. If you don't, it might damage your kidneys.

   _____

6. If I don't have coffee, I can't make it through the day.

   _____

EXERCISE 4 INVERTED AND IMPLIED CONDITIONS

A GRAMMAR NOTES 1–2 Complete the story with words from the box.

had Daria	if not	if so	otherwise	~~were she~~	with

Daria Allen wanted to move to St. Louis from Russellville, the small city where she had grown up and attended college. For some time, Daria had felt it was necessary for her to leave Russellville. _____Were she_____ to stay there, she felt, she would just fall into a rut she would
1.
never escape from. She decided to go to the big city and start a new life. However, she needed to work. She asked her friend Hei-Rim for advice on finding a job because Hei-Rim had recently lived in a big city and knew something about job-hunting. Hei-Rim gave her two pieces of advice: first, to avoid employment agencies; and second, to regularly check online for job opportunities.

_____ known how difficult it would be to find employment, she might have
2.
stayed in her hometown. She tried to find a job for weeks but without any success. After a month had gone by, she had checked for available jobs online many times, but nothing had materialized. She needed to find employment fairly soon; _____, she wouldn't be
3.
able to afford her apartment.

One morning, Daria decided it wouldn't hurt just to walk around downtown and see if she saw any "help wanted" signs posted in store windows. She thought that _____ a bit of luck
4.
she might find something. A few moments later, she walked by a florist shop and saw a "help wanted" sign in the window. She didn't know how long the sign had been in the window. Maybe they were still hiring; _____, she might
5.
get a job. _____, she wouldn't lose
6.
anything by going in and asking. She walked right in and said, "I'm Daria Allen, and I saw your notice in the window. I was a botany major in college, and I have a lot of experience with flowers and gardening. Is the job still available?"

The manager said, "Amazing. I just put that notice up a couple of hours ago. I haven't put the ad online yet. We're expanding and need someone to work part-time. The position could become full-time eventually. Tell me more about your experience."

Daria got the job.

B Rewrite each word or phrase from A with an *if*-clause that restates the condition.

1. _____ If she were _____ to stay there, she felt, she would just fall into a rut she would never escape from.

2. _____ known how difficult it would be to find employment, she might have stayed in her hometown.

3. She need to find employment fairly soon; _____ , she wouldn't be able to afford her apartment.

4. She felt that _____ a bit of luck she might find something.

5. Maybe they were still hiring; _____ , she might get a job.

6. _____ , she wouldn't lose anything by going in and asking.

EXERCISE 5 VERBS WITH THE SUBJUNCTIVE

GRAMMAR NOTES 3–4 Describe what is happening in each picture by completing each sentence. Use subjunctive verb forms and appropriate subjects.

1. The police officer is suggesting _(that) the woman call a towing company_____.

2. The workers are demanding _____.

3. The wife is insisting _____.

4. The woman is proposing _____.

5. The real estate agent is recommending _____.

6. The travel agent is suggesting _____.

EXERCISE 6   ADJECTIVES WITH THE SUBJUNCTIVE

A GRAMMAR NOTE 5   **What do young people need to make a good start to adult life?**
Complete each sentence with the adjective in parentheses + *that* + the correct form of a
verb from the box.

communicate	find	~~have~~	make	stay	take

1. It is _____desirable that they have_____ good self-esteem.
   (desirable)

2. It is _____ responsibility for their own actions.
   (necessary)

3. It is _____ good jobs.
   (important)

4. It is _____ most of their own decisions.
   (essential)

5. If they are in a relationship, it is _____ with each other.
   (crucial)

6. It is _____ in touch with family and close friends.
   (advisable)

B Write six sentences in which you give your own advice for young people. Use the
structure adjective + *for* + noun or object pronoun + infinitive.

It's important for young people to find the right kind of friends.
It's essential for them to work . . .

EXERCISE 7 EDITING

GRAMMAR NOTES 1–5 Daria (see Exercise 3) has recently moved to St. Louis. Read her email to her friend Hei-Rim. It has eleven mistakes in conditions and the subjunctive. The first mistake is already corrected. Find and correct ten more.

December 10

Dear Hei-Rim,

It's time I wrote and filled you in on what's been happening since I left Russellville. I finally got

a job! Remember when you suggested I ~~checked~~ *check* online for job offers? It was a good suggestion,

but for some reason there were no available jobs being advertised. A couple of weeks ago, I

was getting worried since I had spent almost all my savings. I had gotten to the point where it

was absolutely essential that I found something. If so, I would have to go back to Russellville. I

had known how difficult this would be, I would probably have stayed in Russellville! Anyway, I

decided to just walk around downtown and see what turned up. That's when I saw a beautiful

little florist's shop with a "help wanted" sign in the window. I walked right in and asked if the job

was still open. Can you believe that it was? The owner said that he hadn't had time to post the

job online yet. So your advice would have worked the timing had been different. The bottom line

is that I'm employed!

I was really happy in my job until my boss hired a new assistant manager who has been making

my life miserable. Among other things, he demands me to make coffee for him. He also insists

that I'm doing other things that aren't in my job description. I took this job to work with plants,

not to serve him coffee. I think it's crucial tell him where I stand. It's important that he stops

treating me as his personal assistant.

I have a few days off for the holidays. Do you have some time off? If not, how about coming

down here for a visit? Wouldn't that be fun? I have a spare bedroom in my apartment. If you can

come, I suggest you to drive, since it isn't far. Please email or text and let me know.

Love,
Daria

Go to MyEnglishLab for more focused practice.

EXERCISE 8   LISTENING

▶ 23|02   **A**   Listen to the conversation. Why does Nancy need advice?

_____

▶ 23|02   **B**   Read the questions. Listen again to the telephone conversation and answer the questions in complete sentences.

1. What did Nancy's daughter ask her to do?

   Nancy's daughter asked her mother to babysit for her kids.

2. What did the daughter almost do when Nancy said no at first?

   _____

3. Had Nancy known what her daughter was calling about, what would she have done?

   _____

4. What did Nancy have to do the last time this happened?

   _____

5. Why is the daughter asking that her mother babysit so much?

   _____

6. According to Nancy, what is it important that her daughter do?

   _____

7. What does Marge suggest Nancy do?

   _____

8. According to Marge, what can Nancy accomplish with a little firmness?

   _____

C   Work with a partner. Which person in the listening do you identify with more: the mother or the daughter? Why? How much responsibility should grandparents have to assume for their grandchildren? Discuss.

EXERCISE 9 HERE'S OUR ADVICE

A **CRITICAL THINKING** Work in a group. Think about this problem: A young woman was awarded a scholarship, but she wants to take time off before she goes to college. If she takes time off, she may lose the scholarship. What would you advise? In small groups, work together to suggest advice for the woman. Each group member proposes a piece of advice.

EXAMPLE: **A:** I would suggest she give up the scholarship and take time off. She needs to be ready for college. Otherwise, she won't do well . . .

B: I recommend that she . . .

B What is the best advice? Vote on the different pieces of advice your group has proposed and justify your opinions. Count the votes and discuss the results further. Then share your results with the class.

EXERCISE 10 TRAVEL ADVICE

A **PRESENTATION** You are going to give a presentation in which you offer advice to someone who is going on a trip. First, look at the postcards below and on the next page. Choose one of the locations and do research on the Internet about places to visit there. Then write sentences offering travel advice. Use subjunctive verb constructions with *suggest*, *recommend*, and *it is essential that*.

B Work in a group. Give your presentation. Do the other members of your group agree with your advice?

EXAMPLE: If the person is visiting China, I suggest he or she visit the Great Wall and the Forbidden City. . . .

EXERCISE 11 CAN YOU GIVE ME SOME ADVICE?

A ROLE PLAY You are going to role-play a conversation about a problem. First, think of a problem that needs to be solved. Write a few sentences about it.

My roommate, Elena, is always borrowing money from me. She did it again yesterday. Without a loan, she said, she won't be able to pay the rent. . . .

B Work with a partner. Present your problem to your partner and ask for his or her advice. Have a conversation with your partner about the problem. Then switch roles.

EXAMPLE: **A:** Sergei, I'm having a problem with my roommate, Elena.

B: Oh. What's the problem?

A: Well, Elena is a great friend, but she's always short of money. I've had to lend her money to help pay our rent. I don't have much money myself. What would you recommend I do?

B: Hmm. Let's see. Well, I guess I'd recommend that, first, you sit down and explain your feelings and say why this bothers you. Then . . .

C Present your role plays to another group. Ask for their advice on what to do about the problems.

BEAUTIFUL BRAZIL

EGYPT

Go to MyEnglishLab for more communication practice.

FROM GRAMMAR TO WRITING

A BEFORE YOU WRITE You are going to write an essay about a time when you followed either some good advice or some bad advice. Decide on the situation and write a few sentences about it.

B WRITE Using your ideas in A, write a five-paragraph essay about the good or bad advice you took. Remember to use subjunctive constructions, inverted conditions, and implied conditions. Try to avoid the common mistakes shown in the chart. Use the example below to help you begin your essay.

EXAMPLE: One of the worst pieces of advice I've ever followed was to try out for the football team in high school. My friend Mark had suggested I try to make the team. He had assured me I would be chosen for the team if I did try out. I've never been very good at football, and I knew that in the back of my mind, but because of my desire for popularity, I took Mark's suggestion. Had I known how badly the situation would turn out, I never would have done it. Here's what happened. . . .

Common Mistakes in Using Conditionals and Subjunctives

Don't use *were* in past-time unreal situations. Use it only in **present** time situations.	If she **were** in love with Dennis, she **would** marry him. **OR** If she **had been** in love with Dennis, she **would have married** him. **NOT** If she ~~were~~ in love with Dennis, she would have married him.
Don't use past or future time verbs in **subjunctive** constructions. Use the **base form**.	I suggest that Mary **listen** more carefully to what people say. **NOT** I suggest that Mary ~~listens~~ more carefully to what people say.
Don't contract *had*, *were*, or *should* + *not* in **inverted** conditionals.	**Had I not** put in the extra work, I wouldn't have passed the course. **NOT** ~~Hadn't I~~ put in the extra work, I wouldn't have passed the course.

C CHECK YOUR WORK Look at your essay. Underline the subjunctive constructions, inverted conditions, and implied conditions. Use the Editing Checklist to check your work.

Editing Checklist

Did you . . . ?

☐ avoid using *were* in past-time unreal situations

☐ use the base form of the verbs in subjunctive constructions

☐ avoid contracting *not* with *had*, *were*, and *should* in inverted conditions

D REVISE YOUR WORK Read your essay again. Can you improve your writing? Make changes if necessary.

Go to MyEnglishLab for more writing practice.

UNIT 23 REVIEW

Test yourself on the grammar of the unit.

(A) Complete the sentences. Circle the correct answers.

1. You need to get some job retraining. With / Without it, you risk being laid off.

2. Juan may or may not go to college. If so / If not, he will have to get a full-time job.

3. I think something is wrong with the car. If so / If not, we'd better have it fixed.

4. You have to take notes; if not / otherwise, you'll forget what you learned.

5. We want to buy a house. If so / With a loan from the bank, we'll be able to.

6. I may not pass the class; if not / if so, I'll have to take it over.

7. Ana has a daughter; without / if not her daughter, she'd be all alone.

8. The traffic is heavy, but with / if a bit of luck, we'll be on time.

(B) Complete the sentences with words from the box.

but for	call	had I	if so	otherwise	should that	understand

1. Give me a call; _____, I may forget the meeting.

2. _____ not reminded Jiro of the party, he would have forgotten.

3. Hana suggested that I _____ the airline, but I didn't.

4. I might be late. _____ happen, go without me.

5. _____ her pension, she would never be able to survive financially.

6. It's crucial that Linh _____ the gravity of his situation.

7. Jae-Yong may be coming; _____, you can ride back with him.

(C) Find and correct five mistakes.

A: I'm glad you suggested we hired Bob Burnham. He's done a great job.

B: Yes. I had known how good he is, I'd have recommended him sooner.

A: Do you recommend Jen Valdez for the sales position? If not, let's interview her.

B: I do, yes. However, I suggest we offered a higher salary for that position.

A: Really? Why?

B: With a salary increase, we'll never be able to hire Jen.

Check your answers on page 433.

Go to MyEnglishLab to complete the review online.

Appendices

1 Irregular Verbs

When two or more forms are given, the first form is considered the more common.

BASE FORM	SIMPLE PAST	PAST PARTICIPLE	BASE FORM	SIMPLE PAST	PAST PARTICIPLE
arise	arose	arisen	fly	flew	flown
awake	awoke/awaked	awaked/awoken	forbid	forbade/forbad	forbidden/forbid
be	was/were	been	forecast	forecast/forecasted	forecast/forecasted
bear	bore	borne/born	forget	forgot	forgotten
beat	beat	beaten/beat	forgive	forgave	forgiven
become	became	become	forsake	forsook	forsaken
begin	began	begun	freeze	froze	frozen
bend	bent	bent	get	got	gotten/got
bet	bet	bet	give	gave	given
bind	bound	bound	go	went	gone
bite	bit	bitten	grind	ground	ground
bleed	bled	bled	grow	grew	grown
blow	blew	blown	hang	hung/hanged*	hung/hanged
break	broke	broken	have	had	had
breed	bred	bred	hear	heard	heard
bring	brought	brought	hide	hid	hidden/hid
broadcast	broadcast/broadcasted	broadcast/broadcasted	hit	hit	hit
build	built	built	hold	held	held
burn	burned/burnt	burned/burnt	hurt	hurt	hurt
burst	burst	burst	keep	kept	kept
buy	bought	bought	kneel	knelt/kneeled	knelt/kneeled
cast	cast	cast	knit	knit/knitted	knit/knitted
catch	caught	caught	know	knew	known
choose	chose	chosen	lay	laid	laid
cling	clung	clung	lead	led	led
come	came	come	leap	leaped/leapt	leaped/leapt
cost	cost	cost	learn	learned/learnt	learned/learnt
creep	crept	crept	leave	left	left
cut	cut	cut	lend	lent	lent
deal	dealt	dealt	let	let	let
dig	dug	dug	lie (down)	lay	lain
dive	dived/dove	dived	light	lit/lighted	lit/lighted
do	did	done	lose	lost	lost
draw	drew	drawn	make	made	made
dream	dreamed/dreamt	dreamed/dreamt	mean	meant	meant
drink	drank	drunk	meet	met	met
drive	drove	driven	mislead**	misled	misled
dwell	dwelt/dwelled	dwelt/dwelled	pay	paid	paid
eat	ate	eaten	plead	pleaded/pled	pleaded/pled
fall	fell	fallen	prove	proved	proved/proven
feed	fed	fed	put	put	put
feel	felt	felt	quit	quit	quit
fight	fought	fought	read	read	read
find	found	found	rid	rid/ridded	rid/ridded
fit	fitted/fit	fitted/fit	ride	rode	ridden
flee	fled	fled	ring	rang	rung

* *hung*: put an object up on a hook   (**EXAMPLE:** We hung the picture carefully.)
  hanged: executed by hanging   (**EXAMPLE:** I wouldn't want to be hanged.)

** Note that verbs with prefixes have the same past forms as the base verb without prefixes
  (**EXAMPLE:** *mislead misled misled* follows the same pattern as *lead led led*.)

BASE FORM	SIMPLE PAST	PAST PARTICIPLE	BASE FORM	SIMPLE PAST	PAST PARTICIPLE
rise	rose	risen	spread	spread	spread
run	ran	run	spring	sprang/sprung	sprung
saw	sawed	sawed/sawn	stand	stood	stood
say	said	said	steal	stole	stolen
see	saw	seen	stick	stuck	stuck
seek	sought	sought	sting	stung	stung
sell	sold	sold	stink	stank/stunk	stunk
send	sent	sent	strike	struck	struck/stricken
set	set	set	strive	strove	striven/strived
sew	sewed	sewn/sewed	swear	swore	sworn
shake	shook	shaken	sweat	sweated/sweat	sweated/sweat
shave	shaved	shaved/shaven	sweep	swept	swept
shear	sheared	sheared/shorn	swell	swelled	swelled/swollen
shed	shed	shed	swim	swam	swum
shine	shone/shined*	shone/shined	swing	swung	swung
shoot	shot	shot	take	took	taken
show	showed	shown/showed	teach	taught	taught
shrink	shrank/shrunk	shrunk/shrunken	tear	tore	torn
shut	shut	shut	tell	told	told
sing	sang	sung	think	thought	thought
sink	sank/sunk	sunk	thrive	thrived/throve	thrived/thriven
sit	sat	sat	throw	threw	thrown
slay	slew/slayed	slain/slayed	thrust	thrust	thrust
sleep	slept	slept	tread	trod	trodden/trod
slide	slid	slid	upset	upset	upset
slit	slit	slit	wake	woke/waked	waked/woken
smell	smelled/smelt	smelled/smelt	wear	wore	worn
sneak	sneaked/snuck	sneaked/snuck	weave	wove/weaved**	woven/weaved
sow	sowed	sown/sowed	wed	wedded/wed	wedded/wed
speak	spoke	spoken	weep	wept	wept
speed	sped/speeded	sped/speeded	wet	wetted/wet	wetted/wet
spell	spelled/spelt	spelled/spelt	win	won	won
spend	spent	spent	wind	wound	wound
spill	spilled/spilt	spilled/spilt	withdraw	withdrew	withdrawn
spin	spun	spun	withhold	withheld	withheld
spit	spat/spit	spat/spit	wring	wrung	wrung
split	split	split	write	wrote	written

* *shone*: intransitive   (**EXAMPLE**: The sun shone brightly.)
   shined: transitive   (**EXAMPLE**: He shined his shoes.)

** *wove/woven*: created a fabric   (**EXAMPLE**: She wove a rug.)
   weaved: moved in and out or side to side   (**EXAMPLE**: The driver weaved from one lane to another on the freeway.)

2 Non-Action Verbs

EXAMPLES: She **seems** happy in her new job.
I **have** a terrible headache.
The food **smells** good.
Mary **owes** me money.

APPEARANCE	EMOTIONS	MENTAL STATES		SENSES AND PERCEPTION	POSSESSION	OTHER
appear	abhor	agree	hesitate	ache	belong	cost
be	admire	amaze	hope	feel	have	include
concern	adore	amuse	imagine	hear	own	lack
indicate	appreciate	annoy	imply	hurt	pertain	matter
look	care	assume	impress	notice	possess	owe
mean *(signify)*	desire	astonish	infer	observe		refuse
parallel	detest	believe	know	perceive	WANTS AND PREFERENCES	suffice
represent	dislike	bore	mean	see		weigh
resemble	doubt	care	mind	sense	desire	
seem	empathize	consider	presume	smart	need	
signify *(mean)*	envy	deem	realize	smell	prefer	
	fear	deny	recognize	sound	want	
	hate	disagree	recollect	taste	wish	
	hope	disbelieve	remember			
	like	entertain *(amuse)*	revere			
	love	estimate	see *(understand)*			
	regret	expect	suit			
	respect	fancy	suppose			
	sympathize	favor	suspect			
	trust	feel *(believe)*	think *(believe)*			
		figure *(assume)*	tire			
		find *(believe)*	understand			
		guess	wonder			

3 Non-Action Verbs Sometimes Used in the Progressive

EXAMPLES: The students **are being** silly today.
We**'re having** dinner right now. Can I call you back?
Mary **is smelling** the roses.

ache	bore	expect	hear	include	perceive	sense
admire	consider	favor	hesitate	indicate	presume	smell
agree	deny	feel	hope	lack	realize	sympathize
amuse	disagree	figure	hurt	look	refuse	taste
annoy	doubt	find	imagine	notice	represent	think
assume	empathize	guess	imply	observe	see	wonder
be	entertain	have	impress			

4 Irregular Noun Plurals

SINGULAR FORM	PLURAL FORM	SINGULAR FORM	PLURAL FORM	SINGULAR FORM	PLURAL FORM
alumna	alumnae	elk	elk	paramecium	paramecia
alumnus	alumni	fish	fish	people**	peoples
amoeba	amoebae	foot	feet	person	people
analysis	analyses	genus	genera	phenomenon	phenomena
antenna	antennae/antennas*	goose	geese	—	police
appendix	appendices	half	halves	policeman	policemen
axis	axes	index	indices	policewoman	policewomen
basis	bases	knife	knives	protozoan	protozoa
businessman	businessmen	leaf	leaves	radius	radii
businesswoman	businesswomen	life	lives	series	series
cactus	cacti	loaf	loaves	sheaf	sheaves
calf	calves	louse	lice	sheep	sheep
—	cattle	man	men	shelf	shelves
child	children	millennium	millennia	species	species
crisis	crises	money	monies	thesis	theses
criterion	criteria	moose	moose	tooth	teeth
datum	data	mouse	mice	vertebra	vertebrae
deer	deer	octopus	octopi	wife	wives
dwarf	dwarves	ox	oxen	woman	women
elf	elves				

* *antennae*: insects' feelers
  antennas: devices to receive radio or television signals

** *a people*: an ethnic group

5 Non-Count Nouns

ABSTRACTIONS		ACTIVITIES		DISEASES	FOODS	GASES
advice	inertia	badminton	judo	AIDS	barley	carbon dioxide
anarchy	integrity	baseball	karate	appendicitis	beef	helium
behavior	intelligence	basketball	reading	bronchitis	bread	hydrogen
capitalism	love	biking	rowing	cancer	broccoli	neon
chance	luck	billiards	sailing	chicken pox	cake	nitrogen
consent	momentum	bowling	singing	cholera	candy	oxygen
decay	motivation	boxing	skating	diabetes	cereal	
democracy	oppression	canoeing	skiing	diphtheria	chicken	
determination	peace	cards	soccer	flu (influenza)	corn	
energy	pollution	conversation	surfing	heart disease	dessert	
entertainment	responsibility	cycling	tae kwon do	malaria	fish	
evil	sadness	dancing	talking	measles	meat	
falsehood	slavery	football	tennis	mumps	oats	
freedom	socialism	golf	volleyball	pneumonia	pasta	
fun	spontaneity	hiking	wrestling	polio	pie	
good	stupidity	hockey		smallpox	rice	
grief	time			strep throat	salad	
happiness	totalitarianism			tuberculosis (TB)	wheat	
hate	truth					
hatred	violence					
honesty						

LIQUIDS	NATURAL PHENOMENA	OCCUPATIONS	PARTICLES	SOLID ELEMENTS	SUBJECTS	OTHER
coffee	air	banking	dust	aluminum	accounting	clothing
gasoline	cold	computer technology	gravel	calcium	Arabic	equipment
juice	electricity	construction	pepper	carbon	art	film
milk	fog	dentistry	salt	copper	astronomy	furniture
oil	hail	engineering	sand	gold	biology	news
soda	heat	farming	spice	iron	business	play
tea	ice	fishing	sugar	lead	chemistry	work
water	lightning	law		magnesium	civics	
	mist	manufacturing		platinum	computer science	
	rain	medicine		plutonium	economics	
	sleet	nursing		radium	English	
	slush	retail		silver	geography	
	smog	sales		sodium	history	
	smoke	teaching		tin	linguistics	
	snow	therapy		titanium	literature	
	steam	writing		uranium	mathematics	
	thunder			zinc	music	
	warmth				physics	
	wind				psychology	
					science	
					sociology	
					Spanish	
					speech	
					writing	

6 Ways of Making Non-Count Nouns Countable

ABSTRACTIONS
a matter of choice
a piece of advice
a piece/bit of luck
a type/form of entertainment
a unit of energy

ACTIVITIES
a badminton game/a baseball game, etc.
a game of badminton/baseball/basketball/
    cards/football/golf/soccer/tennis, etc.

FOODS
a cut/piece/slice of beef
a grain of barley
a grain of rice
a loaf of bread
a piece of cake
a piece/wedge of pie
a portion/serving of ...

LIQUIDS
a can of oil
a can/glass of soda
a cup of coffee, tea, cocoa
a gallon/liter of gasoline
a glass of milk, water, juice

NATURAL PHENOMENA
a bolt/current of electricity
a bolt/flash of lightning
a clap of thunder
a drop of rain
a ray of sun/sunshine

PARTICLES
a grain of pepper, salt, sand, sugar
a speck of dust

SUBJECTS
a branch of accounting/art/astronomy/
    biology/chemistry/economics/geography/
    linguistics/literature/mathematics/music/
    physics/psychology/sociology, etc.

OTHER
an article of clothing/jewelry
a news item/an item of news/a piece of news
a period of time
a piece of equipment/luggage
a piece/article of furniture/machinery

7 Non-Count Nouns Not Usually Made Countable

anger	courage	happiness	intelligence	patience	safety	violence
baldness	feedback	hospitality	knowledge	peace	shopping	warmth
chaos	foliage	humidity	leisure	precision	softness	weather
cholesterol	fun	importance	melancholy	progress	traffic	wildlife
conduct	gravity					

8 Nouns with Non-Count and Count Meanings

NON-COUNT MEANING

Cancer is a dread disease.
Cheese is a healthy food.
We eat **chicken** at least once a week.
Coffee helps me wake up.
Exercise is essential for good health.
Experience is a good teacher.
Film is my favorite art form.
We always eat **fish** on Fridays.
Maria has just gotten her **hair** curled.
History has always been my favorite subject.
Light is essential for plants to grow.
Pasta is a popular food.
People need times of work and times of **play**.
Elena doesn't drink much **soda**.
Space is sometimes called the final frontier.
There's **talk** of building a skyscraper on that lot.
We drink **tea** every evening.
I never have enough **time** to finish things.
Work should be fulfilling.

COUNT MEANING

There is **a cancer** on the presidency.
Brie is **a** soft **cheese** produced in France.
I saw **a chicken** running down the road.
Please bring us two **coffees**.
Alice did some **exercises** in her grammar book.
We had **a** fascinating **experience** at the game.
Steven has directed a great many **films**.
My son caught **a** big **fish** yesterday.
There's **a hair** in my soup!
Stephanie is writing **a history** of World War I.
Do you see **a light** in the distance?
Lasagna is **an** Italian **pasta**.
We're going to see the new **play** tonight.
Please bring us three **sodas**.
There's **an** empty **space** in that row.
Indira and I had **a** good **talk** last night.
Earl Gray is **a** well-known **tea**.
I've told you that three **times**.
Asha's painting is truly **a work** of art.

9 Nouns Often Used with the Definite Article

the air
the Arab League
the atmosphere
the authorities
the Bhagavad Gita
the Bible
the cosmos
the Creator
the earth
the economy
the Empire State Building
the environment
the European Union
the flu

the gross national product (the GNP)
the Internet
the King
the Koran
the measles
the Milky Way (galaxy)
the moon
the movies
the mumps
the ocean
the police
the President
the Prime Minister
the Queen

the radio
the sky
the Solar System
the stock market
the stratosphere
the sun
the Taj Mahal
the theater
the *Titanic*, etc.
the tropics
the United Nations
the universe
the Vatican
the world

10 Countries Whose Names Contain the Definite Article

the Bahamas
the Cayman Islands
the Central African Republic
the Channel Islands
the Comoros
the Czech Republic
the Dominican Republic
the Falkland Islands

the Gambia
the Isle of Man
the Ivory Coast
the Leeward Islands
the Maldives (the Maldive Islands)
the Marshall Islands
the Netherlands
the Netherlands Antilles

the Philippines
the Solomon Islands
the Turks and Caicos Islands
the United Arab Emirates
the United Kingdom (of Great Britain and Northern Ireland)
the United States (of America)
the Virgin Islands

11 Geographical Features with the Definite Article

GULFS, OCEANS, SEAS, AND STRAITS

the Adriatic Sea	the Indian Ocean
the Aegean Sea	the Mediterranean (Sea)
the Arabian Sea	the North Sea
the Arctic Ocean	the Pacific (Ocean)
the Atlantic (Ocean)	the Persian Gulf
the Baltic (Sea)	the Philippine Sea
the Black Sea	the Red Sea
the Caribbean (Sea)	the Sea of Japan
the Caspian (Sea)	the South China Sea
the Coral Sea	the Strait of Gibraltar
the Gulf of Aden	the Strait of Magellan
the Gulf of Mexico	the Yellow Sea
the Gulf of Oman	

MOUNTAIN RANGES

the Alps	the Himalayas
the Andes	the Pyrenees
the Appalachians	the Rockies (the Rocky Mountains)
the Atlas Mountains	
the Caucasus	the Urals

RIVERS

All of the following can contain the word *River*.

the Amazon	the Ob
the Colorado	the Ohio
the Columbia	the Orange
the Congo	the Orinoco
the Danube	the Po
the Don	the Potomac
the Ebro	the Rhine
the Euphrates	the Rhone
the Ganges	the Rio Grande
the Huang	the Seine
the Hudson	the St. Lawrence
the Indus	the Tagus
the Jordan	the Thames
the Lena	the Tiber
the Mackenzie	the Tigris
the Mekong	the Ural
the Mississippi	the Uruguay
the Missouri	the Volga
the Niger	the Yangtze
the Nile	the Zambezi

OTHER FEATURES

the Arctic Circle
the Antarctic Circle
the Atacama (Desert)
the equator
the Far East
the Gobi (Desert)
the Kalahari (Desert)
the Middle East
the Near East
the North Pole
the Occident
the Orient
the Panama Canal
the Sahara (Desert)
the Sonoran (Desert)
the South Pole
the Suez Canal
the tropic of Cancer
the tropic of Capricorn

12 Passive Verbs Followed by a *That*-Clause

EXAMPLE: It **is alleged that** he committed the crime.

allege	believe	fear	hold	predict	theorize
assume	claim	feel	postulate	say	think

13 Stative Passive Verbs + Prepositions

EXAMPLE: The island of Hispaniola **is divided into** two separate nations.

be bordered by	be covered by/with	be intended	be located in/on, etc.	be placed near/in
be composed of	be divided into/by	be joined to	be made (out) of	be positioned near/in
be comprised of	be filled with	be known as	be made (up) of	be related to
be connected to/with/by	be found in/on, etc.	be listed in/as	be measured by	be surrounded by

14 Verbs + Gerunds

EXAMPLE: Jane **enjoys playing** tennis.

abhor	celebrate	dislike	fear	mention	prevent	risk
acknowledge	confess	dispute	feel like	mind (object to)	put off	shirk
admit	consider	dread	feign	miss	recall	shun
advise	defend	endure	finish	necessitate	recollect	suggest
allow	delay	enjoy	forgive	omit	recommend	support
anticipate	deny	escape	give up (stop)	permit	report	tolerate
appreciate	detest	evade	imagine	picture	resent	understand
avoid	discontinue	explain	keep (continue)	postpone	resist	urge
be worth	discuss	fancy	keep on	practice	resume	warrant
can't help						

15 Verbs + Infinitives

EXAMPLE: The Baxters **decided to sell** their house.

afford	claim	endeavor	incline	plan	resolve	threaten
agree	come	expect	intend	prepare	say	turn out
appear	consent	fail	learn	pretend	seek	venture
arrange	dare	get	manage	profess	seem	volunteer
ask	decide	grow (up)	mean	promise	shudder	wait
attempt	demand	guarantee	need	prove	strive	want
beg	deserve	hesitate	neglect	refuse	struggle	wish
care	determine	hope	offer	remain	swear	would like
chance	elect	hurry	pay	request	tend	yearn
choose						

16 Verbs + Gerunds OR Infinitives; No Change in Meaning

EXAMPLES: Martha **hates to go** to bed early.
Martha **hates going** to bed early.

begin	can't stand	hate	love	propose
can't bear	continue	like	prefer	start

17 Verbs + Gerunds OR Infinitives; Change in Meaning

forget
I'd almost **forgotten meeting** him. *(I was hardly able to remember meeting him.)*
I almost **forgot to meet** him. *(I almost didn't remember to meet him.)*

go on
Jack **went on writing** novels. *(Jack continued to write novels.)*
Carrie **went on to write** novels. *(Carrie ended some other activity and began to write novels.)*

quit
Ella **quit working** at Sloan's. *(She isn't working at Sloan's anymore.)*
Frank **quit to work** at Sloan's. *(He quit another job in order to work at Sloan's.)*

regret
I **regret telling** you I'm taking the job. *(I'm sorry that I said I would take the job.)*
I **regret to tell** you I'm taking the job. *(I'm sorry to tell you that I'm taking the job.)*

remember
Velma **remembered writing** to Bill. *(Velma remembered the previous activity of writing to Bill.)*
Melissa **remembered to write** to Bill. *(Melissa didn't forget to write to Bill. She wrote to him.)*

stop
Hank **stopped eating**. *(He stopped the activity of eating.)*
Bruce **stopped to eat**. *(He stopped doing something else in order to eat.)*

try
Martin **tried skiing**. *(Martin sampled the activity of skiing.)*
Helen **tried to ski**. *(Helen attempted to ski but didn't succeed.)*

18 Adjective + Preposition Combinations

These phrases are followed by nouns, pronouns, or gerunds.

EXAMPLES: I'm not **familiar with** that writer.
I'm **amazed at** her.
We're **excited about** going.

accustomed to	concerned with/by	furious with/at	nervous about	sick of
afraid of	content with	glad about	obsessed with/about	slow at
amazed at/by	curious about	good at	opposed to	sorry for/about
angry at/with	different from	good with	pleased about/with	suited to
ashamed of	excellent at	guilty of	poor at	surprised at/about
astonished at/by	excited about	happy about	ready for	terrible at
aware of	familiar with	incapable of	responsible for	tired from
awful at	famous for	intent on	sad about	tired of
bad at	fascinated with/by	interested in	safe from	used to
bored with/by	fed up with	intrigued by/at	satisfied with	weary of
capable of	fond of	mad at *(angry at/with)*	shocked at/by	worried about
careful of				

19 Verbs Followed by Noun or Pronoun + Infinitive

EXAMPLE: I **asked Sally to lend** me her car.

advise	choose*	forbid	invite	permit	teach	want*
allow	convince	force	need*	persuade	tell	warn
ask*	encourage	get*	order	remind	urge	would like*
cause	expect*	hire	pay*	require		

*These verbs can also be followed by the infinitive without an object.

EXAMPLES: I **want** Jerry **to go**.
I **want to go**.

20 Adjectives Followed by the Infinitive

EXAMPLE: I was **glad to hear** about that.

advisable*	curious	eager	frightened	interested	possible	shocked
afraid	delighted	easy	furious	intrigued	prepared	sorry
alarmed	depressed	ecstatic	glad	likely	proud	surprised
amazed	desirable*	embarrassed	good	lucky	ready	touched
angry	determined*	encouraged	happy	mandatory*	relieved	unlikely
anxious	difficult	essential*	hard	necessary*	reluctant	unnecessary*
ashamed	disappointed	excited	hesitant	nice	right	upset
astonished	distressed	fascinated	important*	obligatory*	sad	willing
careful	disturbed	fortunate	impossible	pleased	scared	wrong
crucial*						

*These adjectives can also be followed with a noun clause containing a subjunctive verb form.

EXAMPLES: It's **essential to communicate**.
It's **essential** that she **communicate** with her parents.

21 Sentence Adverbs

EXAMPLES: **Clearly**, this is the best course of action.
This is **clearly** the best course of action.
This is the best course of action, **clearly**.

absolutely	certainly	fortunately	hopefully	mercifully	possibly	surprisingly
actually	clearly	frankly	importantly	obviously	probably	thankfully
amazingly	definitely	generally	mainly	overall	significantly	understandably
apparently	essentially	happily	maybe	perhaps	surely	unfortunately
basically	evidently	honestly				

22 Words and Phrases That Begin Dependent Clauses

SUBORDINATING CONJUNCTIONS
(To Introduce Adverb Clauses)

after	no matter if
although	no matter whether
anywhere	now that
as	on account of the fact that
as if	once
as long as	only if
as many as	plus the fact that
as much as	provided (that)
as soon as	providing (that)
as though	since
because	so ...that (in order to)
because of the fact that	so that
before	such ...that
despite the fact that	though
due to the fact that	till
even if	unless
even though	until
even when	when
everywhere	whenever
if	where
if only	whereas
in case	wherever
in spite of the fact that	whether (or not)
inasmuch as	while

PRONOUNS
(To Introduce Adjective Clauses)

that
when
where
which
who
whom
whose

OTHERS
(To Introduce Noun Clauses)

how
how far
how long
how many
how much
however (the way in which)
if
that
the fact that
what
what color
whatever
what time
when
where
whether (or not)
whichever (one)
whoever
whomever
why

23 | Transitions to Connect Sentences

TO SHOW ADDITION	TO SHOW A CONTRAST	TO SHOW AN EFFECT/RESULT	TO SHOW TIME AND SEQUENCE
additionally	actually	accordingly	after this/that
along with this/that	anyhow	as a result	afterwards
also	anyway	because of this/that	an hour later (several hours later, etc.)
alternatively	as a matter of fact	consequently	at last
as a matter of fact	at any rate	for this/that reason	at this moment
besides	despite this/that	hence	before this/that
furthermore	even so	in consequence	from now on
in addition	however	on account of this/that	henceforth
indeed	in any case	otherwise	hitherto
in fact	in contrast	then	in the meantime
in other words	in either case	therefore	just then
in the same way	in fact	this/that being so	meanwhile
likewise	in spite of this/that	thus	next
moreover	instead (of this/that)	to this end	on another occasion
plus (the fact that)	nevertheless		previously
	nonetheless		then
	on the contrary		under the circumstances
	on the other hand		until then
	rather		up to now
	still		
	though		

24 | Transitions to Connect Blocks of Text

all in all	in short	most importantly	to conclude
another reason/point, etc.	in sum	second(ly)	to resume
finally	in summary	the most important reason/factor, etc.	to return to the point
first(ly)	last(ly)	third(ly), fourth(ly), etc.	to summarize
in conclusion			

25 | Reporting Verbs

EXAMPLES: "This is the best course of action," Jack **added**.
Rhonda **said**, "I don't agree with your proposal."

add	ask	confess	murmur	point out	respond	tell
allege	claim	exclaim	note	query	say	wonder
allow	comment	maintain	observe	report	shout	yell

26 Verbs and Expressions Followed by the Subjunctive

EXAMPLES: We **demand** (that) he **do** it.
It is **essential** (that) he **do** it.
The professor **suggested** (that) we **buy** his book.

AFTER SINGLE VERBS		AFTER *IT* + ADJECTIVE + NOUN CLAUSE	
ask*	recommend	it is advisable that	it is necessary that
demand	request*	it is crucial that	it is obligatory that
insist	require*	it is desirable that	it is reasonable that
order*	suggest	it is essential that	it is required that
prefer*	urge*	it is important that	it is unnecessary that
propose		it is mandatory that	it is unreasonable that

*These verbs also take the form verb + object pronoun + infinitive.

EXAMPLES: We **asked** that she **be** present.
We **asked her to be** present.

27 Pronunciation Table

▶ A|01   These are the pronunciation symbols used in this text. Listen to the pronunciation of the key words.

VOWELS

SYMBOL	KEY WORD	SYMBOL	KEY WORD
i	**bea**t, **fee**d	ə	ban**a**na, **a**mong
ɪ	b**i**t, d**i**d	ɚ	sh**ir**t, m**ur**der
eɪ	d**a**te, p**ai**d	aɪ	b**i**te, cr**y**, b**uy**, **eye**
ɛ	b**e**t, b**e**d	aʊ	ab**ou**t, h**ow**
æ	b**a**t, b**a**d	ɔɪ	v**oi**ce, b**oy**
ɑ	b**o**x, **o**dd, f**a**ther	ɪr	b**eer**
ɔ	b**ou**ght, d**o**g	ɛr	b**are**
oʊ	b**oa**t, r**oa**d	ɑr	b**ar**
ʊ	b**oo**k, g**oo**d	ɔr	d**oor**
u	b**oo**t, f**oo**d, st**u**dent	ʊr	t**our**
ʌ	b**u**t, m**u**d, m**o**ther		

CONSONANTS

SYMBOL	KEY WORD	SYMBOL	KEY WORD
p	**p**ack, ha**pp**y	z	**z**ip, plea**s**e, goe**s**
b	**b**ack, ru**bb**er	ʃ	**sh**ip, ma**ch**ine, sta**ti**on,
t	**t**ie		spe**ci**al, discu**ssi**on
d	**d**ie	ʒ	mea**s**ure, vi**s**ion
k	**c**ame, **k**ey, **qu**ick	h	**h**ot, **wh**o
g	**g**ame, **g**uest	m	**m**en
tʃ	**ch**urch, na**t**ure, wa**tch**	n	su**n**, **kn**ow, **pn**eumonia
ʤ	**j**udge, **g**eneral, ma**j**or	ŋ	su**ng**, ri**ng**ing
f	**f**an, **ph**otogra**ph**	w	**w**et, **wh**ite
v	**v**an	l	**l**ight, **l**ong
θ	**th**ing, brea**th**	r	**r**ight, **wr**ong
ð	**th**en, brea**the**	y	**y**es, **u**se, m**u**sic
s	**s**ip, **c**ity, **ps**ychology	t̬	bu**tt**er, bo**tt**le

Glossary of Grammar Terms

action verb A verb that describes an action.

> James **exercises** three days a week.

active sentence A sentence in which the subject acts upon the object.

> **William Shakespeare** wrote **Hamlet**.

adjective A part of speech modifying a noun or pronoun.

> The **blue** sofa is **beautiful**, but it's also **expensive**.

adjective clause A clause that identifies or gives additional information about a noun.

> The man **who directed the film** won an Oscar.

adjective phrase A phrase that identifies or gives additional information about a noun.

> In that movie, the actress **playing the heroine** is Penélope Cruz.

adverb A part of speech modifying a verb, an adjective, another adverb, or an entire sentence.

> Ben drives his **incredibly** valuable car **very carefully**.

adverb clause A dependent clause that indicates how, when, where, why, or under what conditions things happen; or which establishes a contrast. An adverb clause begins with a subordinating conjunction and modifies an independent clause.

> We're going to leave for the airport **as soon as Jack gets home**.

adverb / adverbial phrase A phrase that indicates how, when, where, why, or under what conditions things happen. An adverb phrase modifies an independent clause.

> We learned a great deal of Spanish **while traveling in Mexico**.

An adverbial phrase performs the same functions as an adverb phrase but does not contain a subordinating conjunction.

> **Having had the professor for a previous class**, I knew what to expect.

auxiliary (helping) verb A verb that occurs with and "helps" a main verb.

> **Did** Mary contact you? She **should have** called at least.

base form The form of a verb listed in a dictionary. It has no endings (-s, -ed, etc.).

> It is mandatory that Sally **be** there and **participate** in the discussion.

causative A verb construction showing that someone arranges for or causes something to happen. *Get* and *have* are the two most common causative verbs.

> We **got** Martha to help us when we **had** the house remodeled.

clause A group of words with a subject and a verb that shows time. An **independent clause** can stand by itself. A **dependent clause** needs to be attached to an independent clause to be understood fully.

> | INDEPENDENT | DEPENDENT |
> | --- | --- |
> | We'll go out for dinner | when Mom gets back from the bank. |

comma splice An error resulting from joining two independent clauses with only a comma.

> I understand the point he made; however, I don't agree with it.
>
> **NOT** I understand the point he made, however, I don't agree with it. *(comma splice)*

common noun A noun that does not name a particular thing or individual.

> We bought a **turkey**, cranberry **sauce**, mashed **potatoes**, and **rolls** for the special **dinner**.

complement A noun or adjective (phrase) that describes or explains a subject or direct object.

> Hal is **a man with unusual tastes**. He painted his house **orange**.

compound modifier A modifier of a noun that is composed of more than one word. A compound modifier is usually hyphenated when it precedes a noun.

> My **five-year-old** daughter can already read.

conditional sentence A sentence containing a dependent clause showing a condition and an independent clause showing a result. The condition may or may not be fulfilled.

> | CONDITION | RESULT |
> | --- | --- |
> | If I had enough time, | I would visit Morocco. |

coordinating conjunction A word connecting independent clauses or items in a series. The seven coordinating conjunctions are *and*, *but*, *for*, *nor*, *or*, *so*, and *yet*.

> Mom had forgotten to buy groceries, **so** we had a supper of cold pizza, salad, **and** water.

count noun A noun that can be counted in its basic sense. Count nouns have plural forms.

> The **students** in my **class** all have at least one **sibling**.

definite article The article *the*; it indicates that the person or thing being talked about is unique or is known or identified to the speaker and listener.

> China is **the** most populous nation in **the** world.

definite past The simple past form; it shows an action, state, or event at a particular time or period in the past.

> I **lived** in Spain in the '90s and **visited** there again last year.

dependent clause A dependent clause is a group of words that cannot stand alone as a sentence. It requires a main (independent) clause for its meaning.

> MAIN CLAUSE DEPENDENT CLAUSE
> They saw the movie star, who was wearing sunglasses.

direct object A noun or pronoun that receives the action of a verb.

> Martin discovered a large **dog** in his yard.

direct (quoted) speech The exact words (or thoughts) of a speaker, which are enclosed in quotation marks.

> **"Barry,"** Phyllis said, **"I want you to tell me the truth."**

embedded question A question that is inside another sentence.

> He didn't know **what he should buy for his mother**.

focus adverb An adverb that focuses attention on a word or phrase. Focus adverbs come before the word or phrase they focus on.

> **Even** I don't support that idea. It's too radical.

fragment A group of words that is not a complete sentence. It is often considered an error.

> He's asking for our help because he doesn't know what to do about the situation.
> NOT ~~Because he doesn't know what to do about the situation.~~ *(fragment)*

future in the past A verb construction showing a state, action, or event now past but future from some point of time in the past.

> We **were going to help** Tim move but couldn't. Sam said he **would help** instead.

generic Referred to in general; including all the members of the class to which something belongs.

> **The computer** has become essential in today's world.
> **Whales** are endangered.
> **An orangutan** is a primate living in Borneo and Sumatra.

gerund A verbal noun made by adding *-ing* to a verb.

> Dad loves **cooking**, and we love **eating** what he cooks.

identifying (essential) clauses and phrases Clauses and phrases that distinguish one person or thing from others. They are not enclosed in commas.

> The student **who is sitting at the end of the second row** is my niece.
> The film **starring Johnny Depp** is the one I want to see.

***if* clause** The clause in a conditional sentence that states the condition.

> **If it rains**, they will cancel the picnic.

implied condition A condition that is suggested or implied but not stated fully. Implied conditional sentences use expressions such as *if so*, *if not*, *otherwise*, *with*, and *without*.

> You may be able to get the item for half price. **If so**, please buy one for me as well. *(if you are able to get the item for half price)*

indefinite article The articles *a* and *an*; they occur with count nouns and indicate that what is referred to is not a particular or identified person or thing.

> In the last year I have bought **an** old **house** and **a** new **car**.

indefinite past The present perfect; it shows a past action, event, or state not occurring at any particular or identified time.

We **have seen** that movie several times.

indirect object A noun or pronoun that shows the person or thing that receives something as a result of the action of the verb.

Martin gave **Priscilla** an autographed copy of his new novel. He also gave **her** a DVD.

indirect (reported) speech A report of the words of a speaker. Indirect speech does not include all of a speaker's exact words and is not enclosed in quotation marks.

Phyllis told Barry **that she wanted him to tell her the truth**.

infinitive *To* + the base form of a verb.

Frank Jones is said **to be** the author of that article.

inverted condition The condition of a conditional sentence, stated without the word *if*. Inverted conditions occur with the verbs *had*, *were*, and *should*, which come first in the sentence and are followed by the subject.

Had I known that would happen, I never would have agreed.

main (independent) clause A clause that can stand alone as a sentence.

MAIN CLAUSE · · · · · · · · · · DEPENDENT CLAUSE
They saw the movie star, · who was wearing
 · · · · · · · · · · · · · · · · · sunglasses.

mixed conditional A conditional sentence that shows the hypothetical present result of a past unreal situation or the hypothetical past result of a present unreal situation.

If I had taken that job, I **would be living** in Bucharest now.

Sam **would have arrived** by now **if he were planning** to come.

modal (auxiliary) A type of helping verb. *Can*, *could*, *had better*, *may*, *might*, *must*, *ought to*, *shall*, *should*, *will*, and *would* are modals. They each have one form and no endings.

You certainly **can** do that; the question is whether you **should** do it.

modal-like expression An expression with a meaning similar to that of a modal. Modal-like expressions have endings and show time.

Russell **has to** find a new job.

non-action (stative) verb A verb that in its basic sense does not show action.

It **seems** to me that Joe **has** a problem.

non-count noun A noun that in its basic sense cannot be counted.

Smoke from the **fire** filled the **air**.

nonidentifying (nonessential) clauses and phrases Clauses and phrases that add extra information but do not distinguish one person or thing from others. They are enclosed in commas.

Henry**, who is a member of the hockey team,** is also a star basketball player.

noun clause A dependent clause that performs the same function as a noun. Noun clauses function as subjects, objects, objects of prepositions, and complements.

What I want to do is spend a week relaxing on the beach.

noun modifier A noun that modifies another noun.

What did you buy, **milk** chocolate or **chocolate** milk?

parallelism (parallel structure) The placing of items in a series in the same grammatical form.

Marie loves **hiking**, **riding** horses, and **collecting** artifacts.

participial adjective An adjective formed from present and past participial forms of verbs.

The **bored** students were not paying attention to the **boring** speaker.

passive causative A verb structure formed with *have* or *get* + **object** + **past participle**. It is used to talk about services that you arrange for someone to do for you.

I usually **have my dresses made** by Chantal.

passive sentence A sentence that shows the subject being acted upon by the object.

Hamlet was written by **William Shakespeare**.

perfect forms Verb constructions formed with the auxiliary verbs *had*, *has*, and *have* and a past participle. They include the **past perfect**, **present perfect**, and **future perfect**.

> I **had** never **been** to Brazil before 1990. Since then **I've been** there eight times. By this time next year, **I'll have been** there ten times.

phrase A group of related words without a subject or a verb showing time.

> **Relaxing in the hammock**, I pondered my future.

proper noun The name of a particular individual or thing. Proper nouns are capitalized.

> **Stella** and I both think that **Rio de Janeiro** and **Paris** are the world's two most beautiful cities.

quantifier A word or phrase showing the amount or number of something.

> Ken earned **a lot of** money selling books. I bought **a few of** them myself.

relative pronoun A pronoun used to form adjective clauses. *That*, *when*, *where*, *which*, *who*, *whom*, and *whose* are relative pronouns.

> The fairy tale **that** always scared me when I was a child was "Rumpelstiltskin."

reporting verb A verb such as *said*, *told*, or *asked*, which introduces both direct and indirect speech. It can also come after the quotation in direct speech.

> The mayor **said**, "I've read the report." **or** "I've read the report," the mayor **said**.

result clause The clause in a conditional sentence that indicates what happens if the condition occurs.

> If it rains, **they'll cancel the picnic**.

run-on sentence An error resulting from the joining of two independent clauses with no punctuation.

> She is a good student. Her grades are always excellent.
>
> **NOT** She is a good student, ~~her grades are always excellent~~. *(run-on sentence)*

sentence adverb An adverb that modifies an entire sentence. It can occur at the beginning, in the middle, or at the end of a sentence.

> **Fortunately,** Sarah was not hurt badly in the accident.

stative passive A passive form used to describe situations or states.

> North and South America **are connected by** the Isthmus of Panama.

subjunctive A verb form using the base form of a verb and normally following a verb or expression showing advice, necessity, or urgency. The verb *be* has the special subjunctive form *were*, which is used for all persons.

> We always **insist** that our daughter **do** her homework before watching TV.
>
> If I **were** you, I would pay off my mortgage as soon as possible.

subordinating conjunction A connecting word used to begin an adverb clause.

> We were relieved **when** Jack finally called at 1 a.m.

tag question A statement + tag. The **tag** is a short question that follows the statement. Tag questions are used to check information or comment on a situation.

> She's an actor, **isn't she?**

topic sentence A general sentence that indicates the content of a paragraph.

> There are several things to keep in mind when you visit a Japanese home.

transition A word or phrase showing a connection between sentences or between larger blocks of text.

> Climate change is a serious problem. **However,** it is not as serious as the problem of poverty.

unreal conditional sentence A sentence that talks about untrue, imagined, or impossible conditions and their results.

> If I were you, I would study a lot harder.

zero article The absence of a definite or indefinite article. The zero article occurs before unidentified plurals or non-count nouns.

> **Whales** are endangered.
> **Water** is necessary for survival.

Unit Review Answer Key

UNIT 1

A
1. we're doing
2. loves
3. he takes
4. I'm getting
5. They seem
6. attends
7. she's making
8. she texts

B
1. have been living
2. has directed
3. has been working
4. have owned
5. have been remodeling
6. has been running

C

My neighbor Jeff is a teacher. His job is going ~~good~~ *well*

in general, and he likes it. But sometimes he sounds

~~angrily~~ *angry* when he talks about it. He feels ~~frustratedly~~ *frustrated*

because a few students in his class behave ~~bad~~ *badly*. They

pretend to listen to him, and they look ~~quietly~~ *quiet* and

innocent in class. But they don't take their studies

~~serious~~ *seriously*. Instead, they surf the Internet and text each

other during class.

UNIT 2

A
1. got
2. have done **or** 've done
3. have been **or** 've been
4. have visited **or** 've visited
5. was
6. went
7. wanted
8. have never known **or** 've never known

B
1. came
2. met
3. didn't know
4. didn't speak
5. had lived
6. had learned
7. was

C

Solange grew up in Brazil, and she misses it. When

she was a teenager, she ~~didn't used to~~ *didn't use to* study very hard

at school. Instead, she ~~will~~ *would* go to the beach every day

and have fun with her friends. Solange has ~~been being~~ *been*

married to Ty, who is American, for ten years. Solange

and Ty have two children, Ava and Jacob. Solange

wants to show her homeland to her family. They

~~would~~ *were going to* go to Brazil last year, but unfortunately, they

had to call off the trip, though they *had* been planning

it for months. Solange hopes that they can go next

year instead.

UNIT 3

A
1. have to
2. 'll be **or** 'm going to be **or** will be **or** am going to be
3. 'll call **or** will call
4. lets
5. 'll stop by **or** will stop by
6. come

B
1. Sam and I are taking
2. Our flight leaves
3. we get
4. we'll have been flying
5. We'll be
6. We're spending **or** We'll be spending **or** We're going to be spending
7. We'll send
8. we're

C

A: Hey, Cheryl! How are you doing?

B: Good! I've been traveling all over the country for

work. By the time the summer is over, I'll have

~~visiting~~ *visited* ten cities, and I'll have been ~~traveled~~ *traveling* for

three months straight!

A: Wow! That's a lot! ~~Do you come~~ *Are you coming* **or** *Will you be coming* to New York, too?

B: Yes! Actually, ~~I'll come~~ *I'm coming* **or** *I'm going to come* to New York next week!

Can we get together?

A: Sure! Call me when ~~you're getting~~ *you get* to town. It'll be

great to see you!

B: ~~I~~ *I'll* call you as soon as I arrive at my hotel!

UNIT 4

A
1. weren't supposed to
2. didn't have to
3. shouldn't have
4. could
5. We'd better not
6. must have
7. Chie's got to
8. aren't allowed to
9. could have
10. Hadn't we better

B 1. must
2. should
3. may not **or** cannot **or** can't
4. must
5. Should (you)

C A: Did you see the email? All employees ~~is~~ *are* to attend

the good-bye party for our CEO, Brent Chang.

B: Yes, I did see it. His wife was invited too, but she
had to
~~must~~ decline because she is going on a trip.

A: Since it's a good-bye party, we ~~don't have to~~ *mustn't* **or** *must not* forget

to buy him a present. We had better ~~to~~ get him

something nice. We ought *to* buy him something

useful, too.

B: I agree.

A 1. must
2. might
3. might
4. couldn't
5. should
6. ought not to
7. had to
8. has got to be
9. must have been
10. must

B 1. Jeremy might have **or** Jeremy may have **or** Jeremy could have
2. Mari must have
3. They couldn't have **or** They can't have
4. We should **or** We ought to
5. You could have gotten

C A: Hi, Jack. I'm glad you finally made it to the party!

But where's Gina? Do you think she might have
have
forgotten about the party, or could she had to

work late?

B: I think Gina ~~must to~~ *must* be sick. She didn't look good

earlier today.

A: That's too bad. What about Al and Lisa?

B: Al told me to tell you that he couldn't get here by
should
7:00, but he ~~should to~~ make it by 8:00. I don't know
working
about Lisa. I suppose she could be ~~work~~ late, but

she didn't say anything to me about it.
be
A: I guess she might ~~been~~ on her way here right now.

I hope so!

A 1. is being constructed
2. had his car serviced
3. were caught
4. died
5. has been
6. being
7. been
8. by noon

B 1. is reported
2. is being reported
3. has been reported
4. was reported
5. was being reported
6. had been reported
7. will be reported
8. will have been reported

C The Turkish city of Trabzon has just ~~being~~ *been* hit by
was
a tsunami. The tsunami ~~got~~ caused by an earthquake

centered in the Black Sea. At this time last year,
being
international talks were ~~been~~ held on how to protect

countries from tsunamis, but no significant decisions

were agreed upon. U.N. officials said, "We must get
started
these talks ~~start~~ again."

A 1. is bordered by
2. as
3. is claimed
4. is believed to be
5. by
6. is located in
7. is thought
8. are alleged

B 1. are thought to have come
2. It is said
3. is claimed by witnesses
4. is assumed by experts to date
5. is believed to have been

C Hawaii is regarded ~~by~~ *as* one of the most beautiful
of
places in the world. It is composed ~~from~~ a number

of islands, some large and some small. An island is
is surrounded
an area of land that ~~surrounds~~ on all sides by water,
by
so Hawaii is not bordered ~~of~~ any other country. It
claimed
is ~~claiming~~ by some that mythical creatures live in
are said
Hawaii. For example, the Menehune ~~say~~ to be very

small people who live deep in the forests there. They
alleged
are ~~allege~~ to have lived in Hawaii since before the

Polynesians arrived from Tahiti many centuries ago.

UNIT 8

A
1. not smoking
2. making
3. Emiko's
4. giving
5. having
6. seeing
7. being awakened
8. not having been invited

B
1. Mary's inviting
2. Being invited
3. not having called
4. children's not having
5. have trouble understanding
6. used to being assigned

C
A: Going to that movie was a good idea; it's definitely

worth ~~to see~~ *seeing*.

B: I agree! It was great. So, how's it going at work

these days? Are you excited about having ~~hiring~~ *hired*

your friend Jack to work with you?

A: Well…no! I thought I'd enjoy ~~to work~~ *working* with him,

but I'm kind of upset with him right now. First

of all, he has trouble ~~finish~~ *finishing* his work on time. And

sometimes he's rude. At a meeting yesterday, I

was bothered by ~~he~~ *his* coming in without asking

permission. Also, he seems to hate ^*being* told what to do;

he prefers making his own decisions.

UNIT 9

A
1. to do
2. to accept
3. to give up
4. smoking
5. to lock
6. locking
7. to confront
8. to be criticized

B
1. not to put off
2. allowed to choose
3. not to have happened
4. to have been hit
5. tired to finish
6. to have forgotten

C
I decided ^*to* buy an apartment last year. My friends

warned ^*me* not to procrastinate. They told me ~~buying~~ *to buy*

the apartment as soon as possible before prices went

up. But there are occasionally good reasons ^*to* postpone

things. I found an apartment I liked on the beach, but

it wasn't ~~enough cheap~~ *cheap enough* to buy. So I procrastinated…

and the prices went down! I'm lucky to ^*have* gotten my

apartment for a very low price.

UNIT 10

A
1. C
2. NC
3. NC
4. C
5. NC
6. C
7. NC

B
1. a. exercise
   b. exercises
2. a. pieces of advice
   b. advice
3. a. grain of rice
   b. Rice
4. a. Cheese
   b. a cheese

C
Many people ~~needs~~ *need* to lose weight these days. I

do too. My doctor gave me ~~an advice~~ *advice* **or** *some advice* **or** *a piece of advice* to help me lose

weight. He said I should improve my diet. But it takes

~~a work~~ *work* to prepare a nutritious meal. Also, I dislike

cauliflower, carrots, beans, and most other ~~vegetable~~ *vegetables*.

And I like to drink a can of ~~sodas~~ *soda* with every meal.

What can I do?

UNIT 11

A
1. G
2. N
3. D
4. G
5. G
6. D
7. N
8. N

B
1. the
2. a
3. the
4. an
5. the
6. Ø
7. Ø

C
One of the most famous animals in the history of

Earth is ~~a~~ *the* dinosaur. The extinction of the dinosaurs

is still a matter of debate in ^*the* scientific community.

Why did they die out? Many scientists now believe

that ^*a* giant meteorite flew through ~~the space~~ *space* and hit

our planet very hard. This changed ~~an~~ *the* earth's climate,

making it too cold for dinosaurs to survive.

UNIT 12

A
1. Most
2. amount
3. any
4. a lot of
5. a couple of
6. number
7. many
8. little
9. plenty of
10. no

B
1. many **or** a great many
2. much **or** a great deal of **or** lots of
3. a lot of **or** lots of
4. a number of
5. a lot of **or** lots of **or** a great many
6. Every

C   On the whole, I have *a* lot of fun at my new job.

I earn less money than I used to, but I have a lot
less
~~fewer~~ stress. Most of my co-workers are responsible
little
and work hard, but a few of them do ~~a little~~ if any

work. The majority of my colleagues have a lot of

experience, so I can ask them for advice and help.

The only real negative about my new position is
amount
the ~~number~~ of traffic on the roads in the morning

and afternoon.

UNIT 13

A 1. sweltering, humid summer
2. challenging five-hour job
3. new striped cotton
4. handsome young Asian
5. last World Cup soccer
6. dirty, little old

B 1. an eleven-year-old son
2. an unexpected pleasure
3. a surprising new experience
4. six fifty-five-minute periods
5. a voter-initiated proposal
6. a forty-five-story building
7. a Chinese ivory statue
8. a heavy gray cat

C   Over the weekend, I attended a
wonderful film
~~film wonderful~~

festival. As I expected, the films were excellent in

general, with one major exception. This one exception
terrible horror   *silly special*
was a ~~horror terrible~~ movie with a lot of ~~special silly~~
strange-looking
effects and ~~strange looking~~ creatures. The best film

overall, surprisingly, was a digitally remastered version

of *Gone with the Wind*. I'd seen it previously and wasn't

all that excited about seeing it again. I was pleasantly
four-hour-long
surprised. Even though it's a nearly ~~four hours long~~

movie, it never gets boring. Everyone should see this

awesome,exciting movie at least once.
         ^

UNIT 14

A 1. who   5. which
2. where   6. when
3. whom   7. likes
4. whose   8. who

B 1. no commas
2. no commas
3. Mrs. Ching, whose dog is always barking, is very
   wealthy.
4. no commas
5. no commas
6. Ms. Voicu, who is a student, is from Romania.
7. Tumba, whose children are very energetic, is
   always exhausted.

C   Last week in my psychology class, we took
                              that **or** *which*
a personality test ~~who~~ is designed to determine
                                   which
what kind of person you are. The test, ~~that~~ I found

interesting, took a couple of hours to complete.
                                   which
Today I got my results, ~~whose~~ were pretty much what
                              who **or** *that*
I expected. I have many friends ~~whom~~ mean a lot

to me, so it's not surprising that I'm classified as an
                              who **or** *that*
extrovert. I would recommend that everyone wants to
                                                ^
find out more about himself or herself should take a

test like this.

UNIT 15

A 1. whom   5. who
2. whose   6. interested
3. whom   7. born
4. which   8. including

B 1. whom   5. whose
2. which   6. who **or** that
3. whom   7. that **or** which
4. which

C   *who* **or** *that*
     Newcomers to a country begin to suffer from
                                    ^
culture shock often develop communication problems.

They may be acquainted with many people, most of
whom
~~which~~ they were previously able to talk with easily.

Now they find it difficult to talk to these people.
                                               which
Moreover, aspects of the new culture, most of ~~whom~~

used to seem interesting and exciting, now begin to

seem boring and unappealing. These newcomers
                                             including
may begin to experience negative emotions, ~~included~~

anger, hostility, and depression. Fortunately, this
                    that **or** *which*
is only a temporary attitude is soon replaced by
                             ^
gradual acceptance.

A 1. just don't
2. had we
3. he even thinks
4. only members can
5. don't just
6. even he can
7. does Eva
8. comes the train

B 1. are kangaroos found
2. Clearly, something has to change. **or** Something clearly has to change. **or** Something has to change, clearly.
3. Not only should education be available to everyone
4. Seldom does our team lose.
5. Only citizens can vote;
6. Here is the money
7. There goes the plane.

C   Ben is my partner on our debate team, and he's one of my best friends, but sometimes he irritates me. Not only ~~he is~~ *is he* often late for debates, but I never know if he's going to be prepared. Rarely ~~he will~~ *will he* accept criticism, and at times ~~even he won't~~ *he won't even* listen. I ~~never just~~ *just never* know what kind of mood he's going to be in. He's an excellent debater, fortunately. So, if his heart is in the debate, we usually win it.

A 1. unless
2. Even though
3. in case
4. As
5. Once
6. now that
7. wherever
8. when

B 1. whenever
2. As soon as
3. Unless
4. Because
5. Only if
6. Although **or** While
7. While **or** Although

C A: As soon as Mom ~~will get~~ *gets* here, we can leave for the game.

B: You mean Mom is coming with us to the game? She won't understand what's going on even *if* we give her a long explanation.

A: ~~Unless~~ *If* we explain it slowly and carefully, she'll get the basic idea.

B: I'm not so sure. Only if we can take an hour or so to explain it ~~she'll~~ *will she* get the overall picture.

A: Even though she might not understand everything, she'll enjoy being with us.

A 1. Not knowing
2. Caught cheating
3. Having gotten the tickets
4. before leaving
5. On realizing
6. Relaxing
7. Having visited
8. being given

B 1. Hearing
2. while doing
3. Having eaten
4. Upon finishing
5. Having been
6. after being taken
7. Given

C   *On* **or** *Upon*
~~When~~ arriving at the Cairo airport, I was certain I had plenty of time to make the connection for my next flight. Not ~~eating~~ *having eaten* on the plane and ~~feel~~ *feeling* very hungry, I stopped at a restaurant to get some food. ~~Lost~~ *Losing* track of time, I enjoyed my meal. Then I glanced at my boarding pass and saw I had fifteen minutes to make it to my flight gate. I had a lot of heavy bags, so I grabbed them and started running toward the gate, ~~known~~ *knowing* I'd never make it on time. Just then, out of the blue, a man I'd never met took a couple of my suitcases and got me to the gate with five minutes to spare. I wish I could have returned the favor.

A 1. however
2. though
3. Because
4. therefore
5. besides
6. and
7. or
8. otherwise

B 1. I was exhausted, so I went to bed at 8:00 p.m.
2. I've visited many exotic places; for instance, I've been to Bali, Marrakesh, and Tasmania.
3. We need to remember to get tickets; otherwise, we won't get seats.
4. Nora forgot her passport; as a result, she missed her flight.
5. Even though Bao has a degree, he has a low-paying job.
6. As soon as I got off the train, I took a taxi to the hotel.
7. You're too young to have a car; besides, cars are very expensive.

C A: I heard you're taking a memory improvement
course; how's **or** *course. How's*
~~course, how's~~ it coming along?
However,
B: The course itself is fine. ~~Although~~ it's pretty
though
expensive. It's worth it, ~~but~~.
too; however, **or** *too. However,*
A: I've been thinking about taking one, ~~too, however~~

I wonder if I would really learn anything. Would

you recommend your course?
so
B: Yes, I would, ~~for~~ why don't you sign up?

UNIT 20

A 1. the birth order theory is
2. he always wants
3. the meeting starts
4. "configuration" means
5. whether Samira
6. what
7. she's been
8. whether or not

B 1. what Mary meant
2. whether (or not) Jama is coming **or** whether Jama
is coming (or not)
3. Whatever you want
4. The fact that Allison loves Kahlil
5. whomever you want
6. However you want to proceed

C
who our new neighbors are
A: Do you know ~~who are our new neighbors~~?
whenever
B: Yes, I run into them ~~whoever~~ I go out in the yard.
they are **or** *they're*
A: Oh, yeah? What do you think ~~are they~~ like?
that they **or** *they*
B: They seem really nice. I know ~~what they~~

both work.
if
A: Hmm. I wonder ^ they have children.
about the fact that **or** *that*
B: They have three. I'm happy ~~about that~~ their older

daughter is the same age as Maria.

UNIT 21

A 1. it was
2. had finished
3. if she was
4. to be sure
5. not to
6. if he would
7. she would come by
8. could

B 1. if he would be
2. would not be
3. "I don't feel well."
4. she needed to take
5. if she had ever seen snow
6. "I've seen snow many times."
7. not to write

C Carlos said, "Ho-Jin, why
haven't you
~~you haven't~~ called me

lately?"

Ho-Jin said, "I just haven't had time. I have to study a

lot right now."
^
told **or** *said to*
Carlos said, "You ~~said~~ me you were going to try to

relax more."
told you **or** *said*
Ho-Jin said, "No, I didn't. I ~~told~~ I was going to relax as

much as possible."
friends?
Carlos said, "Well, OK, but are we still ~~friends.~~"

Ho-Jin said, "Of course we are!"

UNIT 22

A 1. hadn't built
2. hadn't been
3. wouldn't have
4. would take
5. would be traveling
6. wouldn't have had
7. wouldn't be able
8. hadn't been

B 1. wishes he hadn't forgotten
2. wouldn't have stopped
3. hadn't stopped
4. wouldn't have had to
5. wouldn't have had to
6. would have had **or** 'd have had
7. could have made
8. wouldn't be

C A: What do you think of Jim's new invention? He's

thinking of marketing it. Would you buy it if you
had
~~have~~ the money?
were *wouldn't*
B: If I ~~was~~ Jim, I ~~won't~~ market it.

A: Why not?

B: Who wants a robot that drives your car? People

will laugh at him.

A: You're just jealous. I'll bet you wish you
had
~~would have~~ invented it yourself.

UNIT 23

A
1. Without
2. If not
3. If so
4. otherwise

5. With
6. if not
7. without
8. with

B
1. otherwise
2. Had I
3. call
4. Should that

5. But for
6. understand
7. if so

C
A: I'm glad you suggested we ~~hired~~ *hire* Bob Burnham. He's done a great job.

B: Yes, he has. ~~I had~~ *Had I* known how good he is, I'd have recommended him sooner.

A: Do you recommend Jen Valdez for the sales position? If ~~not~~ *so*, let's interview her.

B: I do, yes. However, I suggest we ~~offered~~ *offer* a higher salary for that position.

A: Really? Why?

B: ~~With~~ *Without* a salary increase, we'll never be able to hire Jen.

Games and Pronunciation Answer Key

UNIT 3

EXERCISE 8

Team A's prompts and the answers:

1. We'll be landing in the capital of Egypt in half an hour. (Cairo)
2. We're going to arrive in the largest country in South America in three hours. (Brazil)
3. We're arriving in the largest city in Canada in an hour. (Toronto)
4. We're going to cross the longest river in Europe in two hours. (the Volga)
5. We leave for **or** We're leaving for the largest city in the United States at 8 p.m. tonight. (New York)
6. We'll be in the world's most populous country tomorrow. (China)
7. We'll see Africa's highest mountain when we land. (Mount Kilimanjaro)
8. We're arriving **or** We'll be arriving in the Eternal City in forty-five minutes. (Rome)

Team B's prompts and the answers:

1. We'll be landing in the capital of Iran in forty-five minutes. (Tehran)
2. We're going to arrive in the largest country in North America in an hour and twenty minutes. (Canada)
3. We're arriving **or** We'll be arriving in the largest city in India in an hour and a half. (Mumbai)
4. We're going to cross the longest river in Africa in four hours. (the Nile)
5. We leave for **or** We're leaving for the largest city in South Africa tomorrow night. (Johannesburg)
6. We'll be **or** We'll be in the world's smallest continent tomorrow morning. (Australia)
7. We'll see **or** We're going to see the highest waterfall in the world when we land. (Angel Falls)
8. We're arriving **or** We'll be arriving in the City of Love in ninety minutes. (Paris)

UNIT 7

EXERCISE 8

Team A's prompts and the answers:

1. Which island is composed of the nations of Haiti and the Dominican Republic? (Hispaniola)
2. Which Central American country is bordered by Panama and Nicaragua? (Costa Rica)
3. Which people are considered by some to be the descendants of Atlanteans? (the Basque people)
4. Which legendary creature is thought to live in the Himalayas? (the yeti)
5. Which man is claimed to have been the greatest playwright ever? (William Shakespeare)
6. Which individuals are regarded as great humanitarians? (Albert Schweitzer and Mother Teresa)

Team B's prompts and the answers:

1. Which Caribbean nation is composed of many islands? (the Bahamas)
2. Which Caribbean nation is located about 90 miles south of Florida? (Cuba)
3. Which forest creature is said to live in the Pacific Northwest? (Bigfoot)
4. Which lost continent is thought to have been located in the Atlantic Ocean? (Atlantis)
5. Which planet was thought to be the center of the universe before Copernicus? (Earth)
6. Which two presidents are regarded as the greatest American presidents? (George Washington and Abraham Lincoln)

UNIT 10

EXERCISE 9

A

a. film
b. advice
c. talk
d. baldness
e. a work
f. a tan
g. traffic
h. cancer
i. a space
j. a criterion
k. sunblock
l. cholesterol
m. criteria
n. fast food
o. news
p. lightning
q. the police
r. rice
s. work
t. people
u. a film
v. thunder
w. a people
x. space
y. a talk

UNIT 11

EXERCISE 8

2. What is a bank?
3. Who are the poor?
4. What is poaching?
5. What is plastic?
6. What are wolves?
7. What is a humpback whale?
8. What is the brain?
9. Who are the rich?
10. What is the telephone?

11. What is a species?
12. What is an elk?
13. What is a silverback?
14. What is the sun?
15. What is water?
16. What is the post office?

UNIT 13

EXERCISE 5

1. She's going to wear her new red silk dress.
2. Everyone expected that ugly, strange, old building to be torn down.
3. The trip we took was an expensive, silly, miserable waste of time.
4. She was upset by her disappointing, terrible test scores.
5. My intelligent, gracious twenty-five-year-old sister just got engaged.
6. My parents just bought an attractive old condo.

UNIT 22

EXERCISE 8

Team A's prompts and the answers:

1. Who would you have been if you had invented the electric light? (Thomas Edison)
2. How old would you have to be if you were the president of the United States? (thirty-five years old)
3. What creature would you have been if you were an ancestor of the elephant? (a mammoth)

4. How old would you be if you were a nonagenarian? (between ninety and ninety-nine)
5. Who would you have been if you had made the first successful airplane flight in 1903? (one of the Wright brothers)
6. Who would you have been if you had invented the car? (Karl Benz)
7. What country would you have been from if you had been Marco Polo? (Italy)
8. What mountain would you have climbed if you had been with Edmund Hillary and Tenzing Norgay in 1953? (Mount Everest)

Team B's prompts and the answers:

1. How old would you be if you were an octogenarian? (between eighty and eighty-nine)
2. Who would you be if you were the founder of Microsoft? (Bill Gates)
3. What would you be if you were the largest mammal? (a blue whale)
4. How old would you have to be if you were a United States senator? (thirty years old)
5. Who would you have been if you had been the inventor of the telephone? (Alexander Graham Bell)
6. What kind of creature would you have been if you had been a stegosaurus? (a dinosaur)
7. Who would you have been if you had popularized the term *bug*? (Grace Harper)
8. Who would you have been if you had been president of the United States during the Civil War? (Abraham Lincoln)

Information Gaps, Student B

EXERCISE 9 WHAT'S THE STORY?

A **INFORMATION GAP** Work with a partner. Student B will follow the instructions below.
Student A will follow the instructions on page 31.

STUDENT B

- The story below is missing some information. Your partner has the same story that contains your missing information. Ask your partner questions to find the missing information.

  EXAMPLE: **B:** How long would he stay on the road?
  A: He would stay on the road for . . .

- Your partner's story is missing some information. Answer your partner's questions so that your partner can fill in his or her missing information.

  EXAMPLE: **A:** What kind of company did he use to work for?
  B: He used to work for a company that . . .

Jack Strait's life is quite different now from the way it used to be. He used to work for a company that sold carpets and flooring. His job required him to do a lot of traveling. He would stay on the road for _____. It was always the same: As soon as he pulled into a town, he would look for a cheap motel to stay in.

The next morning, he'd _____ at a lot of different establishments, hoping that someone would agree to see him. If he'd been lucky enough to arrange an appointment in advance, he'd show them his samples. Occasionally they would order _____; most often they wouldn't.

Jack's marriage began to suffer. His wife had come to the United States from Russia to marry him. She didn't know anyone in their town, and her family was back in Russia. She was lonely. He missed his wife a lot, but there wasn't much he could do about the situation. And when he was on the road, he hardly ever saw his children. He would try to call them in the evenings if he had a spare moment. Usually, however, it was so late that they had already gone to bed. The children were growing up without him.

Finally, Ivana laid down the law, saying, "Why should we even be married if we're never going to see each other? I didn't come to this country to be a job widow." Jack decided she was right. He took a risk. He quit his job and started his own business. Things were difficult at first, but at least the family was together.

That was five years ago. Things have changed a lot since then. Jack and his family used to live _____. Now they own a house. Life is good.

EXERCISE 8 THE KINDNESS OF STRANGERS

INFORMATION GAP Work with a partner. Student B will follow the instructions below. Student A will follow the instructions on page 65.

Student A will follow the instructions on page 65.

STUDENT B

- The story below is missing some information. Your partner has the same story that contains your missing information. Ask your partner questions to find the missing information.

  EXAMPLE: **B:** What should the couple have gotten?
  A: They should have gotten...

- Your partner's story is missing different information. Answer your partner's questions so that he or she can fill in the missing information.

  EXAMPLE: **A:** Where were the married couple supposed to stay?
  B: They were supposed to stay at...

A married couple was traveling in Europe and had just entered a new country. They had been having a wonderful time, but now everything was going wrong. The first problem was finding accommodations. They were supposed to stay at the Grand State Hotel, but when they got to the hotel, there was no record of their reservation. The wife said they should have gotten _____. They hadn't, unfortunately, so they had to spend the night at the train station. The next day, they finally found a room at a hotel far from the center of town. There were two rooms available: a large one and a tiny one. Since they were on a tight budget, they decided they had better _____.

The second problem was communication. They were starving after spending hours looking for accommodations, so they went into a restaurant. A waiter brought them a menu, but they couldn't understand it. The husband said they should have brought along a phrasebook. They hadn't done that, though, so they didn't know what to order.

Time passed. Other people were being served, but they weren't. Frustrated, they decided _____. But what? They noticed that a boy about eleven years old seemed to be listening to their conversation. Soon the boy came over to their table. "Excuse me," he said. "You have to pay for your meal first. Then they'll take your order." The husband and wife were both astonished but grateful. The wife said, "You speak our language very well. Did you study it somewhere?" The boy said, "I lived in Australia for three years. I learned English there." He asked, "_____? I can translate the menu."

When the couple got back home, their friends asked them what they had liked best about the trip. The wife said, "Well, the best part was visiting that country where everything went wrong, and that boy helped us. He could have _____, but he didn't. It's wonderful when strangers help you. It made me realize that we should all be ready to help others when the need arises."

EXERCISE 9 WHO STOLE THE PAINTING?

INFORMATION GAP Work with a partner. Student B will follow the instructions below. Student A will follow the instructions on page 101.

STUDENT B

- The story below is missing some information. Your partner has the same story that contains your missing information. Ask your partner questions to find the missing information.

  EXAMPLE: **B:** When was the *Mona Lisa* stolen from the Louvre Museum in Paris?
  A: It was stolen from the Louvre Museum on August 21, 1911.

- Your partner's story is missing different information. Answer your partner's questions so that he or she can fill in the missing information.

  EXAMPLE: **A:** What has been called the world's most famous painting?
  B: The *Mona Lisa* has been called the world's most famous painting.

The *Mona Lisa*, which has been called the world's most famous painting, was stolen from the Louvre Museum in Paris on _____. Amazingly, the theft was not even noticed until the day after the theft. _____ was eventually discovered to be the thief. Peruggia had been hired by the museum to build glass cases. How did he manage to steal the painting? He first hid in a closet overnight. After the museum had been closed for the day, Peruggia _____. He then hid it under his coat and walked out of the building. No one stopped him because at this time, security was not given much attention by museum authorities. Also, the actions of the police investigating the crime were unimpressive, to say the least. Peruggia was named a suspect and was questioned _____ before it became clear that he had perpetrated the crime. Famous painter Pablo Picasso was even treated as a suspect for a time. Two years later, after he tried to sell the *Mona Lisa*, Peruggia _____ in a successful police operation. He was finally arrested and was sentenced to _____ of jail time, and the painting was returned to the Louvre.

EXERCISE 7 THE MOUNTAIN GORILLA

INFORMATION GAP Work with a partner. Student B will follow the instructions below. Student A will follow the instructions on page 189.

STUDENT B

- The article below is missing some information. Your partner has the same article that contains your missing information. Ask your partner questions to find the missing information.

  EXAMPLE: **B:** What kind of ape is the mountain gorilla?
  A: It is the largest of the great apes.

- Your partner's story is missing different information. Answer your partner's questions so that he or she can fill in the missing information.

  EXAMPLE: **A:** What is the mountain gorilla?
  B: The mountain gorilla is a great ape.

THE MOUNTAIN GORILLA is a great ape; in fact, it is _____ apes. Mountain gorillas inhabit national parks in three countries in central Africa: Uganda, Rwanda, and the Democratic Republic of the Congo.

Mountain gorillas have thick fur, a characteristic that enables them to live in cold, mountainous areas. An adult male is called _____ and can grow as tall as 6 feet 3 inches, or 1.9 meters. Adult males can weigh up to 430 pounds or 195 kilograms. Mountain gorillas live together in social groups dominated by an adult silverback. A group is composed mainly of _____ and several females and young gorillas. The mountain gorilla is _____; silverbacks can often remove the traps left by poachers. Since these animals are _____, they need a good deal of food daily in order to support their great bulk.

The mountain gorilla is a critically endangered species. There are two principal causes of its endangerment: poaching and loss of habitat. Mountain gorillas are sometimes hunted for food, and they are pursued by poachers for their fur and for sale to zoos. It is clear that _____ and encroachment on locales where mountain gorillas have traditionally lived has split their habitat into widely separated areas. There were only 254 mountain gorillas in 1981, and there are now about 880. This sounds positive, but since particular groups of mountain gorillas are not able to interact with other gorilla groups, the result is lack of genetic diversity within the species. This is _____.

EXERCISE 10 STUDY SKILLS

INFORMATION GAP Work with a partner. Student B will follow the instructions below.
Student A will follow the instructions on page 208.

 STUDENT B

- The article below is missing some information. Your partner has the same article that contains your missing information. Ask your partner questions to find the missing information.

  EXAMPLE: **B:** Who is at their best late at night?
  A: A few people are at their best late at night.

- Your partner's article is missing different information. Answer your partner's questions so that he or she can fill in the missing information.

  EXAMPLE: **A:** Who feels most alert early in the morning?
  B: Many people feel most alert early in the morning.

Want to be the best student you can be? Here are several suggestions.

■ Do your studying when you are the most awake and alert. Many people feel most alert early in the morning. _____, however, are at their best late at night. Identify your own particular characteristics.

■ Take plenty of good notes in class. _____ prefer just to listen to a lecture, believing that note-taking distracts them from what the professor is saying. Relatively few people, however, learn effectively by following this strategy. You interact with the course material when you take notes about it, and that kind of active learning is highly beneficial.

■ Review your notes regularly. Do this _____ if possible. You don't have to spend a lot of time doing this. Going over your notes for _____ daily can really help you to learn and retain information.

■ Examine your lifestyle and make improvements in it if necessary. According to a well-known English proverb, "All work and no play makes Jack a dull boy." You need to work hard, but your life will be dull indeed if you never have _____. Build in time for entertainment and socializing. And while you're at it, make sure you eat healthy food and get enough sleep. You'll have _____ if you do.

■ Finish whatever you start. Once you start something, keep working at it until you've made a visible _____. Then stay with the project until it's done. If you don't do this, you'll simply waste a great deal of time. Don't worry if this takes a long time. Rome wasn't built in a day, but it did get built.

EXERCISE 9 HENRY FORD'S ASSEMBLY LINE

INFORMATION GAP Work with a partner. Student B will follow the instructions below. Student A will follow the instructions on page 389.

STUDENT B

- The article below is missing some information. Your partner has the same article that contains your missing information. Ask your partner questions to find the missing information.

  EXAMPLE: **B:** When did Ford introduce his Model T to the world?
  A: He introduced his Model T to the world in 1908.

- Your partner's article is missing different information. Answer your partner's questions so that he or she can fill in the missing information.

  EXAMPLE: **A:** What would Ford never have done if he hadn't changed the makeup of his original assembly line?
  B: He never would have achieved success with the Model T.

The First Moving Assembly Line

HENRY FORD introduced his Model T to the world in _____. However, he never would have achieved success with the Model T if he hadn't changed the makeup of his original assembly line. Ford knew that ordinary people wouldn't buy his cars if they _____. If Ford could make Model Ts cheaper than other cars, he knew that people would buy them. So Ford introduced a new, more efficient method of auto production that involved division of labor.

On Ford's original assembly line, auto workers had to do several separate tasks to put each car together. If workers have to move around a lot and do many different tasks, they can't produce as much. If you divide a big job into many different smaller tasks, however, everyone can _____. So, Ford and his staff divided the assembly process into eighty-four different steps. In this way, they minimized the motion of each worker as much as possible. There was another advantage: If each worker was responsible for only one task, he or she _____.

In 1913, Ford introduced the moving chassis assembly line and a mechanized belt, which sped up the car assembly process a great deal. If a business makes many products quickly, it can charge less for each one. So, Ford's plan to make Model Ts cheaper than other cars succeeded.

If Ford hadn't figured out a way to build his cars more efficiently and cheaply, it's possible that cars would never have become popular with the masses. However, might the world be a better place now if _____? And what about the workers themselves? Might they not have been happier if these changes hadn't been made? Could they have _____ who had to perform the same repetitive actions endlessly? It's difficult to say. The bottom line is that Ford achieved his goal.

Index

This index is for the full and split editions. All entries are in the full book. Entries for Volume A of the split edition are in black. Entries for Volume B are in blue.

Text Sources

The following sources were consulted during the writing of *Focus on Grammar 5*, Fifth Edition.

15: "Distracted Driving in the United States and Europe," Centers for Disease Control and Prevention: www.cdc.gov/features/distracteddriving, October 20, 2014.

69–70: "Who the Heck Did Discover the New World?" by Donald Dale Jackson, *Smithsonian*, September 1991, pp. 76–85; additional source: "St. Brendan's Isle," www.castletownpress.net/brendan.htm.

78: "Why We Itch," by David Feldman, *Imponderables: The Solutions to the Mysteries of Everyday Life*, New York: William Morrow, 1986–87.

80: *Almanac of the Gross, Disgusting, and Totally Repulsive*, by Eric Elfman, New York: Random House, 1994, for puzzle 1; additional source: *The Quiz Kids, Questions and Answers*, by Louis G. Cowan, Akron, OH: Saalfield Publishing, 1941, for puzzles 2 and 3; additional source: *The Macmillan Book of Fascinating Facts*, by Ann Elwood and Carol Orsag Madigan, New York: Macmillan, 1989, for puzzle 4.

86–87: "D. B. Cooper: Perfect Crime or Perfect Folly?" by Richard Severn, *Seattle Times*, November 17, 1996; additional source: "15 Minutes of Fame," by Mark McGwire, *Biography Magazine*, September 1998.

99: "The Legend of Judge Crater," by E. Randall Floyd, *Great American Mysteries*, Little Rock, AR: August House Publishers, 1990.

105–106, 118: "Body Ritual Among the Nacirema," by Horace Miner, *American Anthropologist*, Vol 58, Vol 1 156, pp. 18–21, June 1956.

115: "Yeti," by Kenneth B. Platnick, *Great Mysteries of History*, New York: Dorset Press, 1971.

211: "Maze Amazes As She Wins Slovenia's First Gold" by Rosa Khutor, www.reuters.com, February 12, 2014.

228–230: *Morphing into the Real World: The Handbook for Entering the Work Force*, by Tim Bryce, Palm Harbor, FL: MBA Press, 2007.

298–299: "Journey: A Brave Family Changes Horror into Healing After a Child Dies," by Brad Darrach, *Life*, October 1, 1995, pp. 42+.

306: "Animal Instincts: Not What You Think They Are," by Tim Bekoff: greatergood.berkeley.edu/article/item/animal_instincts. March 8, 2011.

315–316: "How Quickly We Forget," by Emily Yoffe, *U. S. News and World Report*, October 13, 1997, p. 52.